JANE ELLEN HARRISON

Portrait of Jane Ellen Harrison by Augustus John, Newnham College. Reproduced by permission of the Principal and Fellows of Newnham College, Cambridge.

Jane Ellen Harrison

THE MASK AND THE SELF

Sandra J. Peacock

YALE UNIVERSITY PRESS

NEW HAVEN AND LONDON

The author wishes to thank the following for permission to quote from unpublished sources: Christopher F. Cornford, for permission to quote from the Cornford-Darwin Family Papers, British Library, London; the Principal and Fellows of Newnham College, Cambridge, for permission to quote from the Jane Ellen Harrison Papers, Newnham College Archive; Mrs. Jean Pace, for permission to quote from the Jessie Stewart Papers, Newnham College, Cambridge; Mrs. T. S. Eliot, John Saunders, and Margaret N. Ellis, literary executors for Hope Mirrlees, for permission to quote from the Hope Mirrlees Papers, Newnham College, Cambridge; and the Brotherton Library, University of Leeds.

Designed by JoAerne and set in Trump type by Huron Valley Graphics, Inc., Ann Arbor, Michigan. Printed in the United States of America by Halliday Lithograph Corporation, West Hanover, Massachusetts.

Library of Congress Cataloging-in-Publication Data
Peacock, Sandra J., 1955–
Jane Ellen Harrison: the mask and the self / Sandra J. Peacock. p. cm.
Bibliography: p.
Includes index.
ISBN 0–300–04128–4 (alk. paper)
1. Harrison, Jane Ellen, 1850–1928. 2. Classicists—Great Britain—Biography. 3. Archaeologists—Great Britain—Biography. 4. Newnham College—Biography. 5. Civilization, Ancient—Historiography. 6. Ritual—Historiography. 7. Mythology— Historiography. I. Title.
PA85.H33P43 1988
292'.08'0924—dc19
[B] 88–109 CIP

The paper in this book meets the guidelines for permanence and durability of the Committee on Production Guidelines for Book Longevity of the Council on Library Resources.

10 9 8 7 6 5 4 3 2 1

For Thomas W. Africa,
with affection and gratitude

. . . what other dungeon is so dark as one's own heart!
What jailer so inexorable as one's self!

—Nathaniel Hawthorne,
The House of the Seven Gables

Contents

Illustrations viii

Preface ix

Abbreviations xv

Prologue 1

1 A Yorkshire Childhood and the Education of a Young Lady 6

2 The First Circle: Newnham College 31

3 From Art to Mythology: London, 1880–1897 55

4 Scholar and Teacher: Newnham College, 1898–1922 91

5 The Second Circle. The Cambridge Ritualists: Gilbert Murray 124

6 The Second Circle. The Cambridge Ritualists: Francis Cornford 151

7 The *Prolegomena, Themis,* and the Furies at Bay 179

8 The Circle Completed: World War I, Paris, and the Return to London 223

Appendix Reconstructing a Life: Hope Mirrlees, Jessie Stewart, and the Problem of Biography 245

Notes 249

Index 279

Illustrations

Jane Ellen Harrison by Augustus John — *frontispiece*

Jane Harrison as Alcestis, 1877 — 42

Jessie Stewart, 1902 — 103

Jane Harrison and Hope Mirrlees in Paris, 1915 — 110

Gilbert Murray — 125

H. F. Stewart, Gilbert Murray, Francis Cornford, and Jane Harrison in Malting House Garden, Cambridge — 152

Drawing by Frances Darwin, presented as Christmas gift to Francis Cornford, 1908 — 161

Jane Harrison at Newnham College, ca. 1905–10 — 180

PREFACE

IN AN ERA in which social history dominates historical scholarship, writing a biography may seem hubristic. Social history's emphasis on the living conditions of the masses seems incompatible with a study of the life of a highly educated, upper-middle-class academic who aspired to membership in Edwardian Britain's intelligentsia. Yet one of the dangers contemporary historical study faces is that of losing sight of its most valuable source: the individual whose actions, for better or worse, make up history. The recent burgeoning interest in biographies of women, moreover, promises a new understanding of women's lives by encouraging us to look beyond a limited gallery of prominent figures.[1]

Jane Ellen Harrison—daughter, teacher, scholar—was in some ways an ordinary woman leading an ordinary life. But in many other ways, she was an extraordinary woman leading a fascinating life. Her journey from Yorkshire's merchant class to the Cambridge intelligentsia illuminates many trends in British culture of both the Victorian and the Edwardian eras, and her scholarly work provides insight into some complex issues, such as the character of the female experience in a male-dominated world, the influence of gender on scholarship, and the course of women's intellectual history.

In the first half of this biography, chapters 1–4, I offer a chronological account of Jane Harrison's life from her childhood to her decision to leave Cambridge in 1922. Chapters 5 and 6 examine her relations with her closest colleagues: Gilbert Murray and Francis Cornford. Chapter 7 weaves together the personal and intellectual strands by focusing on how her relationships influenced her major scholarly works. The final chapter deals with the last years of her life, notable mainly for a four-year sojourn in Paris and the writing of her autobiography.

One of the thorniest problems in biography centers upon how to address the subject. During the four years I spent researching and writing on Jane Harrison's life, I grew to believe that to refer to her by her last name would impose an artificial and unwarranted distance. Moreover, it seemed pointless to create this distance out of scholarly "objectivity" on the one hand while revealing painful, intimate evidence on the other. I decided to refer to her as "Jane" throughout most of the text. I made one exception by referring to her as "Harrison" when discussing her work in chapter 7. Because that is conventional practice when referring to a published author, it seemed fitting in that case. I do not by any means intend to appear disrespectful, overly familiar, or casual. To the contrary, I take Jane and her work very seriously. Part of her appeal as a scholar, though, is her intensity and engagement with her work. I have tried to present a portrait of a flesh-and-blood human being, and calling her "Jane" seemed the best way to do so.

I then decided to refer to the other principal players by their first names as well, reserving the formal use of last names for those characters who play small parts in the drama of Jane's life and for secondary references. Thus, I refer to Francis Cornford, Gilbert Murray, Mary Murray, Jessie Stewart, Hope Mirrlees, and Frances Darwin by first names. D. S. MacColl also played a central role in Jane's life. She called him "Sutherland," his middle name, in the few letters to him that survive, and I followed her example. Jane herself recognized the importance of the magical. She created names for her friends that captured their essence and gave her a primitive feeling of control over them. These names were playful in part, but also represented a means of bestowing or withdrawing approval.

Much of this book is based on the personal correspondence of Jane Harrison as well as revelatory passages in her printed works. Unfortunately, about 1922 Jane destroyed a good deal of the correspondence that she had received over the years. What remains of this primary material is largely in the archives of Newnham College. Her correspondence overflows with eccentric spelling and punctuation, which I have chosen not to correct or to burden with a cumbersome *sic.* Her grammatical idiosyncrasies usually do not interfere with the meaning of what she said; furthermore, they convey the sense of familiarity that permeated her relationships with her closest friends.

So far, little has been written about Jane's life. Two of her students tried to write about her: one succeeded, but the other did not. Jessie Stewart, who had been one of Jane's first archaeology students at Newnham, edited and published a collection of some of Jane's letters to Gilbert Murray interspersed with personal commentary. This brief sketch, *Jane Ellen Harrison: A Portrait from Letters,* appeared in 1959.[2] Jane and Jessie were close friends for nearly thirty years, and although their relationship lacked the same intensity as that between Jane and her other favorite pupil, Hope Mirrlees, it seems to have been in many ways equally satisfying.

Hope Mirrlees arrived at Newnham in 1909, studied Greek with Jane, and remained her faithful companion until Jane's death in 1928. Hope then began to gather materials for a life, but put the notion aside, feeling disqualified as a biographer by her admiration for her subject. Her extensive notes reveal both her bias against most of Jane's friends and her reluctance to face the full implications of Jane's personal history, but they survive to provide a great deal of information.

More recently, Robert Allen Ackerman has written on the Ritualist circle's theory of the ritual origin of myth and religion, but without exploring Jane's life in depth.[3] Harry Payne has recognized the intellectual importance of the Ritualist circle in relation to fin-de-siècle aestheticism and discussed the circle's contributions to the study of ancient drama.[4] The Swiss classicist Walter Burkert has led the revival of interest in Ritualist theory by reconsidering their work in the light of structuralist method.[5] Feminist scholars such as Martha Vicinus have lately taken an interest in Jane, whose independent and intellectually exciting life makes her a fine subject for such an approach.[6]

My quarrel with the scholarship on Jane to date lies in its refusal to explore her personality and work in depth. Scholars have largely ignored her early years. Yet the events of her childhood decisively shaped her unique vision of the past, and to ignore them is to ignore compelling evidence. Feminist scholars particularly, wishing to see in her a model of a successful female intellectual, have failed to understand how much her scholarly success cost her. By taking her words literally, they have subscribed to Jane's own view that she lived a happy, satisfying, fulfilled life. In many ways she did, but in some critical ways she did not. She lived a life too marginal and beset by conflict to be entirely carefree. Her periodic bouts with illness and depression and the complexity of her work attest to a fundamental sense of unhappiness about the world. Rather than being defeated, however, she held her own against this great sadness by using her inner anger to fuel a lively, vital creativity. She was most emphatically not a victim, but one can live a reasonably satisfying day-to-day life while still sensing the terror and tragedy of the human experience. I contend that this is exactly what Jane did and, furthermore, that this duality determined the nature of her work.

Jane once told Gilbert Murray that all her life she had wanted to be a Buddhist and that, when she found out what Buddhism was, she discovered she had been one all along without knowing it.[7] I always wanted to be a disciple of Freud, and when I discovered his work I reacted as Jane had. I felt as if I had finally arrived home. I found Freudian theory personally satisfying, but felt reluctant to rely on it as a guide in writing a biography.[8] Once I started to examine Jane's life closely, however, I saw that Freudian theory worked perfectly: not only because it appealed to my own thought, but also because Jane shared an intuitive kinship with it herself. Critics attacked her for allowing emotion into her scholarship. They complained about the nature of her theories, but one suspects that it was her emotions, rather than her theories, that made them uneasy. Most Victorian classicists strove to equate their age with the serenity of classical Greece. Jane refused to accept that interpretation and insisted on exposing the darker side of both eras. Like Freud, she sensed the turbulent emotion constantly threatening to break through the veneer of civilization. Contemporary male scholars often rejected her work because she refused to play by their rules. She did not pore over tragedies or pay homage to the Olympians and the triumph of reason. But neither did she set out to glorify her own age. She wrote, like one of J. H. Plumb's "true creators, to ease the ache within."[9] Because she trusted her intuition, she often saw with extraordinarily clear vision.

In a delightful and compelling examination of modern German classical scholarship, *The Tyranny of Greece over Germany,* Eliza M. Butler compares the Continental classicists to children at play on an imaginary island. Her characterization of the German romantics captures the essential difference between traditional scholarship and genius. When the Germans plunged into the sea of classical study, "they dug deeper, but built less securely; they swam faster, but not so far; they made larger boats which capsized sooner; they grew angry and created confusion and uproar; they either could not or would not assimilate the rules of the various games. And yet they knew something the others did not, something about the nature of the sea."[10] Jane also refused to play by traditional rules. Her passion for and intuitive understanding of the past enabled her to see very clearly. Present-day scholars may reject her theories, but that is irrelevant. The best history teaches us more than something about the past; it teaches us something about ourselves. Jane reminded her readers that we run grave risks by ignoring the emotional life, and the world of scholarship has been enriched by her efforts.

ACKNOWLEDGMENTS

A WORK SUCH as this has an extended family, not just one parent. I may have been primary caretaker, but the book would not have flourished without the help of its large family and stimulating environment. It gives me great pleasure to thank everyone who helped me write it, for working on Jane Harrison's life brought me into contact with many wonderful people. It is not often that one has the chance to honor one's family publicly, for reunions are all too rare; so I want to take full advantage of the opportunity to thank all who have played critical roles in the last five years.

Even before I began to write, some of them were rehearsing the supporting roles they would play in this production. From its earliest days, my friends Teresa Jenkins Butchko, John Butchko, Sharie Harless, and Naomi Lockwood Barletta helped me struggle with my ideas, cheered me up when I despaired, and made several different parts of the Northeast feel like home.

Ann Phillips, reference librarian at Newnham College Library, Cambridge, and her assistants, Julia Rowe Chadd and Tricia Lacey, made my three months of research there in 1983 and 1987 a richly rewarding and enjoyable experience. They provided not only superb research assistance but also genuine kindness and hospitality in the days when I was a student thousands of miles from home. I also thank the Inter-Library Loan staff at the Glenn G. Bartle Library, State University of New York at Binghamton, especially Diane Geraci and Carol Clemente, who cheerfully deciphered my scribbled requests and tracked down obscure texts.

During the years in which this work grew from a doctoral dissertation to a book, my friend Tracy Mitrano read every page of every draft and offered boundless intellectual and emotional support. Her keen insights into Jane Harrison's life and her critical comments on my interpretation of it clarified my thinking and kept me from intellectual fuzziness. For her generosity, friendship, and encouragement, I owe a debt that can never be repaid.

I found a new group of supportive friends when I moved to Newcomb College of Tulane University, and they helped see me through the final stages of turning a dissertation into a full-fledged book. Nancy Anderson of Loyola University in New Orleans, a fellow British historian who also shares my interest in psychohistory, gave me much valuable advice, especially on the theoretical framework. Karen Kingsley, Tulane University School of Architecture, took an interest in Jane Harrison's life and encouraged me to explore other aspects of it, especially her travels to Greece, that I had not had time to focus on in the dissertation. Beth Willinger, director of the Newcomb College Center for Research on Women, gave encouragement and assistance, and understood when my distraction over the work made me a less than congenial colleague. Sylvia Collins typed the manuscript and introduced me to the wonders of word processing. The support I received from this group of friends has been invaluable, and I could not have asked for better company.

Peter Green read the manuscript and made many excellent suggestions, based on a lifetime spent brooding about ancient Greek culture. His tolerance for diverse interpretations of the past made him a delightful critic. I am especially grateful to him for gently reminding me that Jane Harrison was disappointed with Greece when she visited there. Frank Turner also read the manuscript and offered both generous encouragement and several constructive ideas for improvcment. Both of these men gave me a great deal of excellent advice; that I did not follow all of it attests more to my own stubbornness than to the validity of their insights.

Ellen Graham, my editor at Yale University Press, offered valuable advice and assistance throughout the publication process. My research was funded in part by a National Endowment for the Humanities Travel to Collections grant, which enabled me to study the Cornford-Darwin family papers housed in the British Library in London.

Finally, I must acknowledge two people above all others: Elizabeth Fox-Genovese and Thomas Africa. Elizabeth Fox-Genovese took me on as a graduate student at SUNY-Binghamton and directed my dissertation with grace and good humor, believing in its value from the very start. Years ago, when I felt too unprepared and ill equipped even to complete my graduate course work, she encouraged me to continue. She gave freely of her vast knowledge of and insight into the female character, the nature of female experience, and intellectual history. She strengthened my ideas by constantly challenging me to be more precise and improved my work by editing my entire dissertation. For these reasons, and many more, I am in her debt.

Thomas Africa introduced me to Jane Harrison in a research seminar in 1980, somehow sensing that she and I would be compatible. Such perceptive matchmaking is rare. He followed my progress eagerly, reading chapters as they appeared and patiently pointing out their indiscretions. Jane Harrison has long been a special favorite of his, and I dedicate her story to him with gratitude for sharing her with me and entrusting me with a subject so close to his heart. I suspect there were times when he questioned the wisdom of his decision, but if there were, he kept his doubts to himself. His passion for history has opened up new worlds for me, and for that I am more grateful than I can say.

I could not have written this book without the help of the people named above, and their existence serves constantly to remind me how important friendship is in an academic world that often creates more chasms than bridges. In a sense, all my teachers have had a hand in shaping me and thus in shaping the book. I offer it to all of them as a gift of thanks for their efforts to make a good historian of me. They did their best with an often stubborn and recalcitrant pupil. What I have done with their fine training in the following pages is, of course, my responsibility.

ABBREVIATIONS

Titles given are of works by Jane Ellen Harrison. Abbreviations occur both throughout the text and in the notes.

A&O *Alpha and Omega: Essays from Experience* (London: Sidgwick & Jackson, 1915; reprint. New York: AMS Press, 1973).

CDP Francis Cornford–Frances Darwin Family Papers, British Library, London.

ISGA *Introductory Studies in Greek Art* (New York: Macmillan & Co., 1892).

JEH Jane Ellen Harrison Papers, Newnham College Archive, Newnham College, Cambridge University.

PSGR *Prolegomena to the Study of Greek Religion* (Cambridge: Cambridge University Press, 1903).

RSL "Reminiscences of a Student's Life" (*Arion* 4 [Summer 1965]; originally published London: Hogarth Press, 1925).

TH *Themis: A Study of the Social Origins of Greek Religion*, 1st Amer. ed. (New Hyde Park, N.Y.: University Books, 1962; reprint of 2d ed. rev. Cambridge: Cambridge University Press, 1927; originally published Cambridge: Cambridge University Press, 1912).

JANE ELLEN HARRISON

PROLOGUE

IN OCTOBER 1928, Virginia Woolf traveled to Cambridge to deliver the two lectures that later became *A Room of One's Own.* She spoke at Newnham and Girton, the two women's colleges at Cambridge. One of the lectures included a description of a ghostly scene glimpsed at Newnham, to which she gave—for the purposes of her talk—the mythical name of Fernham. Woolf painted an eerie portrait, for Fernham, it appeared, was haunted.

> Somebody was in a hammock, somebody, but in this light they were phantoms only, half guessed, half seen, raced across the grass—would no one stop her?—and then on the terrace, as if popping out to breathe the air, to glance at the garden, came a bent figure, formidable yet humble, with her great forehead and her shabby dress—could it be J—— H—— herself?[1]

The ghostly scholar was Jane Ellen Harrison, a Newnham teacher whose life had been entwined with Newnham's for the first quarter of the twentieth century. She had died the previous April, but Woolf still sensed her presence. One might wonder about a personality that could so interest Woolf, a rather formidable personality herself. Who was Jane Ellen Harrison, and why did her presence infuse both Newnham's atmosphere and Woolf's memory?

Jane Harrison was a British classical scholar whose life spanned both the Victorian and Edwardian eras—she was born in Yorkshire in 1850 and died in 1928. She was one of the earliest students at Newnham College, which had been founded at Cambridge in 1872. She studied classics there, against the advice of most of her teachers, who encouraged women to study the more genteel and suitable field of moral science. After receiving a second in the classical tripos in 1879, she spent nearly twenty years in London, first studying archaeology under Sir Charles Newton and then lecturing at the British Museum. During these years, she published works on *Myths of the Odyssey in Art and Literature* (1882), *Introductory Studies in Greek Art* (1885), and *Mythology and Monuments of Ancient Athens* (1890). These early works showed the influence of the aesthetic movement and reflected her close engagement with London intellectual culture in the 1880s. Had she remained in London, perhaps her vision of the ancient world would have continued in the same vein. She wanted to return to academic life, however, and finally got her chance in 1898 when she was awarded Newnham College's first research fellowship.

Jane Harrison's return to Newnham set the stage for her greatest scholarly achievements by nurturing her increasing fascination with ancient Greek religion. Two years after her return to Newnham, she met the two figures who most influenced the course of her subsequent career: the Oxford classicist Gilbert Murray and the Trinity College philosopher Francis Cornford. Together, these three formed a remarkable scholarly circle known as the Cambridge Ritualists. Their collaboration brought an entirely new perspective to classical scholarship. Following the lead of Sir James George Frazer, William Robertson Smith, and Edward Burnett Tylor, they incorporated the new evidence of anthropology and its theoretical framework into the study of the ancient world. To varying degrees, their work rejected traditional Victorian interpretations of ancient Greek culture. They challenged old ideas by extending the scope of scholarly inquiry beyond the classical age of Greece, back to the archaic period. Although Gilbert Murray's and Francis Cornford's studies have traditionally been cited as the important work of the Ritualists, Jane Harrison actually stood at the center of the circle. Her major works, the *Prolegomena to the Study of Greek Religion* (1903) and *Themis: A Study of the Social Origins of Greek Religion* (1912), constitute the most detailed and passionate defense of Ritualist theory. In them, she argued for the ritual origin of mythology, religion, theology, and drama.

Her work, as well as that of her Ritualist colleagues, places her in the vanguard of what H. Stuart Hughes has called "the revolt against positivism."[2] For many complex reasons explored in the following pages, she objected to the triumph of cold rationality in scholarship and used her work to create a more emotionally satisfying historical past. To some degree, she and the Ritualist circle were influenced by Frazer's monumental work, *The Golden Bough.* The Ritualists' vision of the past reflects a debt to Frazer's radical break with previous scholarship. But Jane Harrison, at least, argued that Frazer did not go far enough. As Robert Ackerman has pointed out, despite Frazer's important role in popularizing a kind of ritual theory, he can be identified as a Ritualist for only a short time in his distinguished career.[3] Like many other Victorian scholars, Frazer preferred to maintain distance between himself and the past; he also preferred the tragic but orderly death and rebirth embodied in fertility rites to the sheer terror in the face of a hostile universe that inspired it. Jane Harrison disagreed with Frazer on fundamental principles, writing to Gilbert Murray, for instance, that "Frazer was somehow all wrong when he would keep on saying that magic was the beginning of science—magic never proceeds by experiment but by imagined relations."[4] Although Frazer spent his career at Trinity College, not far from Jane Harrison at Newnham, they seem not to have crossed paths often.[5] Ultimately, Frazer rejected the work of the Ritualist circle, so he himself does not receive much attention in this book. Nevertheless, Jane Harrison acknowledged his achievements and influence, and any discussion of the Ritualist circle must acknowledge them as well.

Jane took Frazer's work several steps farther and tried to get at the core of human emotional experience, finding in the religious impulse and its expression in ritual the center of that experience. Rather than internalizing Victorian scholarly views of classical Greece as the model for nineteenth-century Britain, she explored the archaic period in order to understand the intense emotional experience that underlay both cultures. She looked not to classical Greece to glorify the achievements of Victorian Britain but to the archaic period to explain its failures.

Most Victorian classicists generally agreed that the glory of Victorian Britain's political accomplishments had been equaled only by the classical period in Greece.[6] They based their perceptions of the ancient world on that premise, thereby enhancing the image of both eras. Historians such as George Grote created a past, allegedly grounded in indisputable proof, that made their own era look remarkably—and equally—enlightened. So long as Victorian classical scholarship remained mired in studies of political and military exploits, it had no room for innovation and speculation. As the traditional intellectual playground of upper-class male scholars, the field of classics neither tolerated nor encouraged diversity of opinion. It required a revolution in classical scholarship—the integration of new anthropological theory—to break down the intellectual walls. This biography explores Jane Harrison's part in that revolution.

As scholarly debate over Ritualist theory grew more heated, Jane found herself in a position not shared by many women of her generation: at the center of an academic controversy. Women had earned the right to a university education in the mid-nineteenth century but with the general cultural expectation that they would use this education to become better wives and mothers, not academics who challenged their (male) elders. Jane Harrison's experience as a female intellectual alone would make her an interesting figure, but her impressive scholarly achievements and the controversy surrounding them make her even more fascinating.

Jane Harrison's experience provides a different perspective on one of the liveliest and most exciting periods of intellectual achievement. She shared her Cambridge years with some of the most interesting figures in its long and distinguished history. At Trinity College, Bertrand Russell, Alfred North Whitehead, and George E. Moore broke new ground in philosophy as she struggled with the development of Ritualist theory. She traveled to Sweden with Lytton Strachey and Pernel Strachey in search of an efficacious rest cure.

On a more personal level, she shared an enduring friendship with the art historian Dugald Sutherland MacColl, whose role in her life has not received much attention to date. Jessie Stewart and Hope Mirrlees, two of Jane's favorite students and her closest young female friends, played siblings locked in a rivalry for their surrogate mother's affections. Frances Darwin, granddaughter of Charles Darwin and daughter of Jane's closest friend, found herself in the pivotal role of ingenue.

Virginia Woolf, who spoke so eloquently for a generation of female intellectuals, knew Jane Harrison because of her own Cambridge connections. One can imagine that she would have responded enthusiastically to a woman whose experience clearly embodied some of the issues with which Woolf herself wrestled. How do women perceive the world? How do they create? Why is their work valued less highly than men's? All these questions, which so vexed Woolf, might be asked with regard to Jane Harrison's life. She might have mulled them over as she walked, "formidable yet humble," through Newnham's garden at twilight. In her case, she dealt with them by turning her attention to the ancient world.

My goal here is to flesh out Woolf's ghostly figure. The self that Jane Harrison tried to conceal shines through her scholarship, illuminating a particular episode in women's intellectual history. This self, however, also illuminates the process by which the creative imagination transforms personal experience into scholarship. As Frank Turner noted in *The Greek Heritage in Victorian Britain,* "writing about Greece was in part a way for the Victorians to write about themselves."[7] His observation holds true for Jane Harrison as well, who was certainly a Victorian by temperament if not strictly by chronology. The most important difference between her and her contemporaries is that she wrote about an entirely different kind of self than they did. She experienced her culture far differently from her colleagues for many reasons, not the least of which was that she was female. Her achievements alone are noteworthy, but deciphering the story behind them enriches our understanding of both their significance and the construction of the female self.

Any biographer faces many dangers. The worst of these is to make the subject seem larger than life. When viewed as a totality, Jane's experiences read more like a Victorian novel than a real life. But the challenge of biography lies in its reliance on the actions of people who once existed. The characters are all real people and, as such, often unruly and recalcitrant. Their unpredictability makes them fascinating, for real life is always more absorbing than fantasy. Jane literally acted out her life rather than merely live it, and her penchant for conducting her life as if it were a Greek tragedy may well be the most interesting thing about her. Her friends complained of this tendency. She skillfully, albeit unconsciously, designed a persona with which to protect herself from the world. She was a mass of contradictions: a woman who craved affection yet feared intimacy; a passionate woman who cultivated rigid self-control; a conservative provincial who donned the trappings of eccentricity to hide her uneasiness among the intellectual elite; a student of the past who denied its importance and power in her own life. But both sides are equally compelling and revealing—the mask as well as the self it conceals.

1

A Yorkshire Childhood and the Education of a Young Lady

To know people well is to know their tragedy: it is usually the central thing about which their lives are built.
—Bertrand Russell to G. Lowes Dickinson, July 19, 1903

JANE HARRISON'S entry into the world was not exactly the stuff of tragedy. Born on September 9, 1850, in Cottingham, near Hull, she was the third daughter of Charles Harrison and Elizabeth Hawksley Nelson Harrison. Her father was a Hull timber merchant and her mother a member of the gentry, the daughter of Thomas Nelson of Timber Grange, Lincolnshire.[1] A month after Jane's birth, however, her mother died. In many respects Jane built her subsequent life around this decisive event, which in her eyes was indeed the stuff of tragedy.

It is difficult to piece together a coherent picture of Jane's family because she rarely mentioned them directly. Her general denial of her past consigns them, like so much else about her, to obscurity. Yet they inevitably shaped the woman she became. The class differences between her parents' families and the influence of those differences on her played an important role in determining the course of her life. Moreover, her immediate family's ideas about woman's role, education, and work set the standard against which she finally rebelled.

When Hope Mirrlees began to collect information on Jane's background in preparation for her attempt at a biography, she received some details about the family from Jane's cousin, Marion Harrison. Marion's reminiscences depict the Harrisons as a fairly typical mid-Victorian middle-class merchant family, which included its share of eccentrics. The Harrisons descended "from seventeenth century farmers near Rudstone," near Bridlington. Jane's grandmother, a "very low-church" woman, bore twelve children, and "she and the sons rode rough-shod over the daughters." She may have controlled some of her daughters, but she provoked rebellion in others. She kept two of Jane's aunts, Kitty and Harriet, on a small allowance until they were over forty years old. Kitty and Harriet both married late in life, Harriet a warden of the family's church. Another, unnamed daughter ran away with a blind poet named Lambert. Yet another, Charlotte, married a "clergyman near Cheltenham." The youngest, Jessie, an adventurous woman who enjoyed hunting and amateur photography, nevertheless always "had breakfast in bed" because of "a bad heart" and died at only thirty-four years of age. According to Hope, Jessie, "Jane's first passion," "seemed to her a very romantic figure," although she never summoned enough courage to reveal her feelings to Jessie.[2]

The timber business prospered in mid-nineteenth-century Hull, and so did the Harrisons. Jane's uncles believed that their sisters had married "rascals" who were interested only in their money. These uncles were an intriguing group themselves. Crowther, the eldest, worked in the family business and also owned racehorses. He dabbled in the classics and in languages, and had "lived several months with the Gypsies to study Romany"—hardly the typical undertaking of a Victorian businessman. He lived in Melton, Yorkshire, and was educated, like his brothers after him, at Kingston College, Hull. His first wife died in a carriage accident that occurred when he was driving. Thereafter he became "temporarily insane" and had to be institutionalized for a short period. Joseph, the next in line, became a doctor, but abandoned his practice immediately after losing his first patient. Jane considered her uncle Edward, a classical scholar and aspiring architect, a "clever & cultivated man." Hope Mirrlees also mentioned an uncle named Arthur, but revealed nothing about the remaining two siblings.[3]

Charles Harrison made enough money in the timber business to retire early. Both Jessie Stewart and Hope Mirrlees described him uncharitably. In her *Portrait from Letters,* Stewart characterized him as "a silent serious man with deep prejudices: against Rome, against noise, against all things modern."[4] Hope Mirrlees wrote still more unkindly of him, describing him as "handsome & timid like a deer, entirely without intellect & yet w/a certain sensibility of his own . . . silent, with more than his share of the Harrison obstinacy & this tendency to brood over imaginary grievances." Jane's cousin Tetenka redeemed him by admitting "there was something about him one couldn't help liking." Significantly, Jane herself had little to say about her father, but her feelings about him colored every aspect of her life.[5]

Although the Harrisons engaged in respectable business and attempted to raise sons and daughters who would fulfill their expectations, evidence shows that the family comprised many unusual characters. The domineering grandmother, the rebellious daughters, and the neurotic sons sharpen the differences between the Harrisons and the more refined Nelsons.

Hope Mirrlees described the Nelsons as "people of property but not armiger." She related an incident Jane described to her that demonstrated an early awareness of class distinctions and family pride. A playmate taunted Jane with her own father's being a lord while Jane's was not. When Jane confronted her father and demanded the truth, he "solemnly produced the pedigree of her maternal grandmother Hawksley, in which there is a royal strain, & told her never to forget that she had as good blood in her veins as anyone in England."[6] His tracing of Jane's lineage back two generations on her mother's side is significant: the Nelson side had better blood, and the marriage, like so many others in the nineteenth century, probably allied money and status. In her "Reminiscences of a Student's Life," Jane ignored the schoolmate incident, but she recalled wanting very much to be "Lady Jane." Her governess dashed this hope by informing her that she could never be Lady Jane "unless they made my father an earl, which seemed somehow unlikely" (RSL, 315). Jane considered her mother's family superior to her father's, and perhaps Charles Harrison encouraged her by identifying more with the Nelsons than with his own family.

The Harrisons liked Elizabeth Nelson, although they, as good merchants, considered her love of poetry "odd."[7] Jane worshiped her dead mother's memory and suffered terribly from the knowledge that her birth had caused her mother's death from puerperal fever. When her Russian friend Prince D. S. Mirsky lost his mother in 1926, Jane wrote to console him. She urged him to be thankful that "thro' those last troublous years" he had been "her mainstay and comfort." She added, "I have always wondered what it was like to have a mother for I sent mine out of the world—but one has to pay the price in losing her." The pain of having grown up motherless was compounded by guilt over having been the cause of her death.[8]

Jane had good reason to construct such a loving memory of her mother. Her death had allowed her daughter to have her father to herself, and guilt over such an effortless Oedipal victory drove her to create an image of a mother good enough not to punish Jane for having won. Jane's recognition of her role in her mother's death represents more than simple adjustment to a horrifying fact; it also represents a tenuous reconciliation of her culpability with her satisfaction in achieving an Oedipal victory. She used her family's memories of her mother to create an all-forgiving figure and to relieve herself of a very heavy responsibility.

Elizabeth Harrison's death marked all three of her daughters. Lucy Harrison, the middle daughter, remembered her mother's suffering with puerperal fever and her own "horror on one day finding a basin of blood in the lavatory," left from when "mother had been 'bled.' " She also recalled that her father could not stand pain, for "it always made him faint." Hope Mirrlees recounted Lucy's "feeling that her father had a 'complex' about deaths" and her belief that "it must have been more than a coincidence that each time a member of his family died in a place, he left it shortly afterwards." The family left for Wales soon after Elizabeth's death and then moved to Filey in Yorkshire in 1855. They remained there for only one year, however, and spent 1856–58 in Barmouth, Wales. They returned to Filey in 1858 and then moved to Scalby in Yorkshire, where they remained until 1875, except for another year in Wales in 1870–71.[9]

Despite the pain of Elizabeth's death, Jane's early years passed happily. She exercised selective memory in her "Reminiscences," saying little about her early childhood, but Lucy Harrison spoke more freely about it. As they grew older, the girls enjoyed freedom to roam around the Welsh countryside. They had a series of nurses and governesses who, if not very intelligent, were at least amicable.[10] Lucy remembered and recorded the happier times, whereas Jane remembered the bad times and wrote about them in unlikely places. Nonetheless, both concur that Elizabeth's death created enormous changes. For Jane, the subsequent course of events etched the unhappy memories more indelibly in her mind than the happy ones.

In many middle-class families, an aunt often assumed the role of nurturer in the event of a mother's death. In the Harrisons' case, Charles's unmarried sister Harriet, or "Auntie" as she was known to the children, came to care for the house and the three young girls. Lucy remembered that "during 'Auntie's' reign Jane used to sit on her lap with her head on her shoulder—she called this 'dudding' (loving)." In those days, Charles Harrison "used to help them with their little garden-plots, & their Sunday treat was to walk over to their Uncle Crowther's with him to see the horses." Auntie treated the girls as their mother had done, dressing them, for instance, "exquisitely" in their mother's style. Interestingly, Jane never mentioned this apparently tranquil period. Yet these years, by providing her with a fine model, allowed her to construct an ideal mother. Harriet set the standard for a good and loving mother while, like Elizabeth Nelson, not threatening Jane's ties to her father. Despite this advantage, Jane's first memories seem to coincide with the arrival of the Welsh governess who completely changed the little girls' lives.[11]

This upheaval occurred when Auntie Harriet decided, late in life, to marry. Jane was five years old at the time. Psychologically, Harriet's departure proved to be a more significant event than Elizabeth Nelson's death. On one hand, Harriet's marriage heralded another easy victory in Jane's battle for her father's affections at a critical time in her development. Just as Jane's interest in her father became more proprietary, Harriet left the scene. On the other hand, the change came at a time when Jane was extraordinarily vulnerable. An Oedipal victory could not quite compensate for the sense of abandonment she felt when her aunt left to create a home of her own. A brief excerpt from the 1914 essay "Crabbed Age and Youth" reveals how deeply Jane suffered at the disintegration of the circle in which she had felt so secure.

This being the centre of your own . . . universe is best seen in the extreme case of the megalomania of young children, as yet untaught by life. . . . I had as a child—I was about seven—a very kind and much-adored aunt, aged about forty. At forty-one she quite unexpectedly married. I can never forget the shock her marriage gave me. My whole universe was deranged. . . . I had been at the centre of my own universe, my aunt gently and protectively hovering over that centre. Suddenly she had made a centre of her own, and I was at the circumference, with no tendency at all to hover sympathetically round her. . . . At seven years old one cannot analyze, so one must agonize. That is why it is so terrible to be a child, or even a young thing at all. One sees things, feels them, whole. There is no such devastating, desolating experience as to have been at the centre, warm and sheltered, and suddenly to be at the outmost circumference, and be asked to revolve as spectator and sympathizer round a newly-formed centre.[12]

There is a discrepancy in ages here, but clearly Jane referred to her aunt Harriet's marriage. To be "untaught by life" meant to expect events to conform to one's wishes; experience taught one, however, to expect nothing and to live a more orderly life by gaining control over one's emotions. This passage exposes the roots of some central themes in Jane's life: the image of the circle, with her at the center, as emblem of security; the hatred of marriage as an institution that destroys more personal bonds than it creates; and the apparent indifference she evinced toward other people's children resulting from her own knowledge, gained through bitter experience, of what they faced in their lives. These themes coalesced to become the central thesis of her scholarly work and directly influenced how she lived her life.

Before leaving to start her new circle, Auntie engaged a young Welsh woman, Miss Gemimi Meredith, as governess through the recommendation of a friend. She herself never met Miss Meredith until her arrival at the family home, when the new governess turned out to be a lovely young woman. A school friend of Jane's, Caroline Dutton Mitchell, later described Miss Meredith as "very odd-looking—just like a Gypsy, with jet black corkscrew curls."[13] Beauty notwithstanding, "the narrowness of her provincialism was only equalled by that of her Evangelicalism." She had been brought up near Barmouth in Wales and educated at a Birmingham boarding school. "Jane adored her at first," Hope stated, but Jane's cousin Tetenka, daughter of the classical scholar Arthur, said "she was always nicer to the children when their father was there." The beautiful Miss Meredith angered Charles Harrison by attracting many suitors, but within six months he himself proposed marriage. Five years after Jane lost her mother, and only months after Auntie's abandonment, she lost her father to a second wife.[14]

Scholars have been reluctant to discuss Jane's relationship with her parents. Enough evidence exists, however, to conclude that Jane adored her father and felt the perceived loss of his love to his second wife very keenly. She related his less serious foibles with genuine understanding and love, and hinted at a deep attachment between them that survived even his betrayal. Jane described him as "the shyest man I ever knew, and terribly absentminded" (RSL, 325). The family remembered with amusement the day two years after his first marriage when he "rode up to Timber Grange, my maternal grandfather's house, and asked to see Miss Elizabeth Nelson [his wife]" (RSL, 325). Jane could testify that the presence of "unexpected visitors in the drawing-room" might prompt him to "give a frightened look round, shake hands courteously with his embarrassed wife and daughters, and disappear like a shot deer" (RSL, 325). She spoke more charitably than Hope Mirrlees and Jessie Stewart of her father's distrust of all things modern. Granted, she remembered that he "left Yorkshire because of the threatened approach within a mile of our house of a small branch railway connecting Scarbro' and Whitby" and his fear that "it would bring with it tourists, char-a-bancs, gas lighting, and all the pollution of villadom." But she commented only "I think he was unduly anxious" (RSL, 326).

Two poignant remembrances of her father stand out in Jane's autobiography. She fell in love with Russia at an early age because of her father's extensive business dealings with Russian timber merchants, and one of her fondest memories was of a Russian sledge in which he sometimes took her for drives. Describing these outings, Jane remarked, "thank God it held only one, so I could dream undisturbed of steppes and Siberia and bears and wolves" (RSL, 312). Thank God too, no doubt, that it allowed her time with her father by herself. Much later in her life, she tried to share her work with him.

> I always sent a copy of every book I wrote to my father, and he always acknowledged them in the same set words: "Thank you for the book you have sent me, your mother and sisters are well. Your affectionate father." I am sure he never read them, and I suspect his feeling towards them was what the Freudians call *ambivalent*—half shame, half pride. Years after his death I learnt, and it touched me deeply, that, on the rare occasions when he left home, he took with him a portmanteau full of my books. Why? Well, after all, he was a Yorkshireman, it may have been he wanted a "bit o' coompany." (RSL, 325)

This passage evokes a marvelous image of the young Jane trying to please her father, who was, however, a taciturn man unable to show his approval directly.

Despite their shared pain, Jane stood in a special relationship to her father. As the youngest daughter of his first wife, her birth intimately connected to her mother's death, she remained his last link to that part of his life. Understandably, then, father and daughter felt conflicting emotions toward each other. For his part, Charles Harrison must have often experienced a twinge of sadness when he glanced at the daughter whose birth had cost him his first wife. For her part, Jane could not have helped resenting what she perceived as his rejection of her in favor of a stepmother. The other side of such pain, however, was closeness and fierce attachment based on a common regret over Elizabeth Harrison's death and their attempts to atone for having inflicted such pain on each other.

As the figure who turned Jane's tiny circle into a triangle, Miss Meredith played a decisive role in Jane's life. Religious, class, and temperamental differences between the two created conflict in the home and shaped Jane's intellectual and personal life. Miss Meredith's background and her treatment of her stepdaughter also contributed to Jane's lifelong abhorrence of and flight from provincialism.

Deborah Gorham asserts in *The Victorian Girl and the Feminine Ideal* that "only a limited number of families ever employed" a governess and that "presumably they were upper-middle-class and upper-class families." The expense of paying and supporting another member of a household could be prohibitive, so the Harrisons must have been at least upper middle class in status. Governesses tended to be genteel women whose families' inability to support them in leisure forced them into service. Normally this arrangement might work out to each party's benefit and provide a proper middle-class home for a young woman turned out on her own. Such, initially, may have been the case in the Harrison household. But the children of an upper-middle-class family would have found it very difficult to accept a former employee as stepmother, a figure of authority and superiority. Thus, many conflicts arose between the former governess and her charges in the Harrison family.[15]

First, Elizabeth Nelson and Gemimi Meredith differed in temperament. Although Jane could not remember her mother, she idealized her as "a silent woman of singular gentleness and serenity" (RSL, 320). Regardless of Elizabeth's true nature, Jane needed an idealized image of her to compensate for her anger at her mother's abandonment. The garrulous Miss Meredith, in contrast, could (as her own son remembered) "talk the hind leg off a donkey" (RSL, 320). She treated the girls decently while serving as their governess, but "as soon as she was married, a great change came over her attitude to the three little sisters." Hope Mirrlees recorded that Jane was raised "*entirely* without love [after the second marriage], though, as she often told me, she was, by nature, an unusually affectionate child." Aunt Harriet concurred; she told one of her great-nieces, Hilda Lane, that Jane had been called "the Professor of Dodoism because she had such loving caressing ways & as a little girl seems to have used the word dodo as a term of affection."[16]

The second Mrs. Harrison was strict, perhaps at times unduly so, with the girls. Even as governess she had been "severe on Jane," who had trouble with her consonants, "for her babyish way of talking & soon got her out of it." After her marriage, she also refused to allow the girls their Sunday walks with their father to visit Uncle Crowther's horses. She objected to these excursions as a breach of the Sabbath, although Lucy later saw it as an attempt at "keeping them away from their father." These rules probably reflected Mrs. Harrison's adherence to Evangelical precepts more than a dislike of her stepdaughters. Nevertheless, the girls interpreted her actions as a deliberate attempt to deny them their father's attention.[17]

The status difference between the Harrisons and Gemimi Meredith exacerbated their temperamental difference. Theoretically, it must have been difficult for the daughters to accept a woman who had formerly worked for a wage as their equal in status. Not even Jane's eccentric aunts were so unconventional as to hold a job. They married men who could support them and presumably lived middle-class lives. Jane's mother, with her roots in the gentry and her love for poetry, could not have differed more radically from her provincial, Evangelical stepmother. Since the Harrisons exhibited some upper-class pretensions, the gulf between mother and stepmother must have seemed enormous. But economic issues also struck home at the practical level, as Charles Harrison and his new wife began a second family.

The size of the new family, which eventually numbered seven daughters and two sons, exacerbated financial worries. But concerns left over from the first marriage plagued Charles Harrison as well. He brooded for many years over the terms of his first father-in-law's will, "which he considered a reflection on himself." Thomas Nelson had arranged for his daughters to hold the money he left them independently of their husbands. To make matters worse, Elizabeth Harrison in turn left this money solely to her daughters, once again allowing it to slip from Charles's hands.[18] He held a grudge against "the Law for granting his children the right to their own money."[19] In fact, the prospect of his daughters' gaining financial independence so disturbed him that when Jane's eldest halfsister, Gemma, inherited some money separately and decided to use it to train as a nurse, Charles "forbade her the house for years."[20] At age twenty-three, Jane composed a tract for the Religious Tract Society to earn money to contribute to a Cheltenham fund. She received three guineas for her effort, but "dared not tell" her father about it. "He held old-fashioned views as to women earning money. To do so was to bring disgrace on the men of the family" (RSL, 324–25). But his disapproval would seem ironic, since he could not afford to support his numerous children anyway.

Hope Mirrlees provided a more sinister account of the financial woes caused by the second marriage. From Lucy's memories, Hope concluded that Miss Meredith "evidently was working towards her final triumph—the disinheriting of the first family." Hope implied that the Harrisons lived comfortably before Miss Meredith appeared on the scene. The rapid succession of children depleted Charles's resources, though, and the girls were fortunate to have inherited from their mother approximately a hundred pounds apiece that Charles could not touch. Hope cited one example of the second Miss Harrison's profligacy. She owned a piece of land in Wales whose value Charles increased from three hundred pounds to eight thousand pounds, but at his death she used profits from its sale to pay off her oldest son's debts. How she came to own the land or what Charles did to increase its value so enormously remains unclear, but it provides the most tangible accusation against her. The incident also hints that at least one of Jane's half brothers was not as financially responsible as the parents would have liked.[21]

Hope asserted that Gemimi Harrison was not "actively unkind" to the daughters, "but they were neglected, & she evidently grudged every penny their father spent on them."[22] Charles Harrison left virtually all his money to the second family, even some he had inherited from his sister Harriet on the condition that it would go to Elizabeth's daughters.[23] Eventually, Gemimi's behavior forced the daughters either to marry or to support themselves. Lucy, the middle daughter, chose the first path in order to get away from home, but Jane took the harder road of an independent life.[24] For a woman of the upper middle class this was not a common choice, but the need to work for a living directly influenced Jane's decision to attend Newnham College and study the classics. She determined that if such a pursuit was acceptable labor for upper-middle-class men, it would suit her equally well. And, too, pursuing an academic career would restore, albeit through the back door, the status of which her stepmother had deprived her. The experience with a stepfamily also influenced Jane's perceptions of family in general, and she projected her ideas about family life back into the ancient world through her scholarly work.

Religious differences also plagued Gemimi's relationship with the Harrisons. Jane believed her Nonconformist father "incapable of formulating a conviction," but felt "he really would have sympathised with the eminent statesman who 'had a great respect for religion as long as it did not interfere with a gentleman's private life' " (RSL, 316). She recalled that he "attended church with fair regularity," although the family "noticed that on what used to be called 'Sacrament Sundays' he was apt to have a slight attack of lumbago" (RSL, 316).[25] But Gemimi Harrison "was made of quite other metal. She was a Celt and her religion was of the fervant semi-revivalist type" (RSL, 316). When the family visited London in 1861, she showed her true colors. On this trip, Jane's only visit to London until she moved there in 1880, the Harrisons made just one purchase: a copy of a German Bible.[26] The clash of Charles Harrison's tepid Nonconformism with his wife's passionate Evangelicalism only emphasized their differences in status and temperament, as well as in religious conviction.

Little evidence exists to illuminate Gemimi's life, but enough survives to suggest that her family and religious background aroused both attraction and repulsion in her youngest stepdaughter. A wave of Evangelical revivals had swept Wales throughout the first half of the nineteenth century, culminating in 1840 and 1849 with powerful movements fueled by a visit by American evangelical Charles Finney and the threat of a cholera epidemic, respectively. Welsh Evangelicalism combined rational, Calvinist nonconformity with a passionate, emotional sense of mystery and superstition. Gemimi Harrison seems to have exhibited both traits. In everyday life, her compulsive propriety clashed with Jane's high spirits, but intellectually, her "fervent semi-revivalist" faith stimulated her stepdaughter's imagination. Its effect became apparent decades later, when Jane turned her attention to the wild emotion of the Greek chthonic cults, Gemimi's religious fervor having contributed to her passion for the emotional element of religion.

Evangelical attitudes toward the family also influenced Jane's thought, although in a more negative way. Evangelicals took seriously their responsibilities to their families, which accounts for their somewhat rigid views on proper behavior. Parents stood in relation to their children as God to mortals and exercised (or attempted to exercise) comparable control over them. They exalted the family as the ideal unit since it mirrored this relation. Above all, they rejected celibacy as verging on popery.[27] Jane rebelled against the established order by rejecting the family as an ideal and remaining celibate. Although she would undoubtedly have justified this rebellion on grounds of intellectual incompatibility with Evangelical precepts, its real root must have lay in her fury at her father and stepmother for creating a circle that she felt excluded her.

However dubious the reliability of personal recollections, the vituperation of Jane and other members of her family on the subject of Gemimi Harrison merits attention. Despite their class and religious differences, the daughters' greatest complaint against her was simply that she was their stepmother. They resented her for seducing their father, drawing his attention from them, and consolidating her position by bearing so many children. At best, Jane grudgingly admitted that she was "a conscientious woman and tried to do her duty . . . to the three rather dour little girls who had been her charges and were later presented to her as step daughters" (RSL, 316).

Helene Deutsch's *Psychology of Women* offers some insight into the problem of stepmothers in general and Jane's case in particular.[28] After cautioning readers that the image of the wicked stepmother found in fairy tales is much more damning than flesh-and-blood stepmothers deserve, Deutsch examines why children and stepmothers so often clash. She perceptively points out that women who take over a mother's role as nurturer and homemaker, such as governesses and housekeepers, are more acceptable to children, for they are perceived to be more interested in the children than in their father and therefore do not compete for his attention. If a woman assumes the role of stepmother, however, their response changes, "for it is the sexual character of the relationship that principally stirs up the infantile protest and the hate impulses of the children of both sexes against the stepmother" (439). A good stepmother tries to restore the family unity "broken by the mother's departure" (447), whether through death or divorce. "But as long as the stepmother is merely the father's wife, or even worse, the father's sexual object, the woman who sleeps with him, she must remain the wicked stepmother" (447). Extrapolating from Deutsch's theory, one could surmise that the worst possible case would be one in which a female figure originally brought into the house to care for the children suddenly becomes the father's sexual object: a case perfectly illustrated by Jane's childhood experience.

Deutsch focuses on another obstacle, potentially more damaging because of its effects on a little girl's later life. "It is harder to overcome the infantile Oedipus complex with regard to a stepmother than with regard to the natural mother," she claims (444). "The little girl can more easily tolerate the renunciation of intimacy with her father when the presence of the mother as a rival no longer spurs her fantasy activity. When she has a new rival in her stepmother, she feels betrayed and deserted by her father" (445–45). Whatever disadvantages the young girl suffers through the loss of her mother, she can substitute for the mother-daughter bond the rich closeness of a father-daughter bond, unencumbered by the negative aspects of a rivalry with her mother. Certainly the father-daughter bond is illusory since it is grounded in unrealistic although unspoken expectations, but the little girl can reconcile herself equally well to her father's inaccessibility if her mother is present or absent. Problems arise when an intruder threatens the little girl's security.

Deutsch also recognizes and sympathizes with the stepmother's hardships. Such a woman suffers especially if the child has lost its mother by death; for unlike the case of divorce, where the mother can be openly perceived as having abandoned the child, a child whose mother has died "must often remain loyal to her out of his own guilt feelings, and hates the stepmother who woos him, because she thus exposes him to the danger of disloyalty" (444). Deutsch's study illuminates Jane's tenacious clinging to her mother's memory and her steadfast refusal to accept her stepmother. Gemimi Harrison's character clearly hurt her efforts to court the children's approval: Deutsch emphasizes that the least successful stepmothers are "women whose personalities are rigid, congealed under a definite formula, aplastic, unintuitive" (447). By all accounts, these characteristics describe Gemimi Harrison perfectly. At age five, Jane was too old to accept any proffered benevolence gratefully and without qualification, and in any case she had already been indulged by an aunt whose sole responsibility had been caring for her and her sisters. Deutsch's observation that "orphaned children are often pampered by friends and relatives and their narcissistic demands are reinforced" (444) applies here, as does its inevitable corollary. The children's "emotional attitude toward a reality that must gradually limit their demands is full of disappointment and hatred. Since the stepmother often personifies this limitation, she comes to be regarded as invidious" (444). For better or worse, Jane exemplified this phenomenon.

She perceived her father's remarriage as yet another abandonment. In 1914, sixty years after the fact, she discussed his betrayal of her in an essay. "Homo Sum" purports to address the suffrage question, but it is in fact a thinly disguised criticism of her father. It attacks the "sex egotism" that makes lovers useless to society as a whole because their interest in each other blinds them to the needs of those around them. She uses her father and stepmother, in hypothetical terms, of course, to show how completely lovers are lost to the world. Her discourse on the subject, although lengthy, is absorbing enough to quote in full.

> Take a simple instance, constantly occurring, almost always misunderstood. A man loses his wife early in life; his daughter grows up; they live in constant companionship, in close sympathy. She helps him with his work. They are "all-in-all" to each other. In middle life the father falls in love and marries again. Father and daughter still love each other, but the daughter wakes up to find herself wounded, inwardly desolate. The father is too intensely happy to mind anything very acutely, but in a dim way he is irritated with his daughter for her obvious uncontrollable misery, and conscious that, if she, who used to be his only earthly joy, were out of the way, things would be for him more comfortable.
>
> What has happened, and what does the father say?
>
> If he is an early Victorian father, now is the time for him to revel in a perfect orgy of self-deception. "My love," he will begin, "at your age you need a woman's guidance. Putting aside my own inclinations, I have formed new ties, I have sought and found for you a new mother. Welcome her, love her, and obey her, as your own." Nowadays, however, public opinion is barely tolerant of self-delusion so besotted. The father is more likely to feel uncomfortable than complacent, and he will take refuge by gliding into the nearest and safest moralizing rut. "My dear, be reasonable. The love I feel for my new wife has nothing to do

> with my affection for you, my daughter, and cannot conflict with it. It is impossible that I should take from you what was never yours." Perhaps even, warming to his subject, he will add: "My love for my new wife makes me a better and a nobler man. Instead of loving you less, I love you more. Some loss there may be, but much gain. We should both of us be thankful to her who—" etc., etc.
>
> The father is, of course, with the best intentions, talking rubbish, and rather insulting rubbish at that. In the daughter's heart anger at his stupidity is added to desolation. She knows him to be the prey of his own strong, blinding sex delusion. His life *is* richer and happier, so he demands that hers should follow suit. His horizon *is* enlarged and brightened, so he fondly expects that hers, too, will glow with a new light. She, unexcited—nay, depressed with the sense of imminent loss—knows quite well the source of his delusion, the impossibility already pointed out, of a strong double emotional focus. What one gains, the other loses. If the father is a man who cares for truth, he will know, and—if he has also the keen instinct of the surgeon's knife—he will perhaps say, "Everything *is* different. In the old days, when life left *me* cold and desolate, *you* were the focus, the fire at which I warmed my frozen hands. On my hearth a new fire is lit now, by the side of which your flame is pale and cold. By it you cannot stand. Face facts. You are young. Go out into the cold and rain, make for yourself no false shelter; for my sake and yours, flinch as little as may be." And the girl, if she is wise and brave, accepts the inevitable. She will stretch out no appealing hand; she will silence the reproach upon her lips. How should she blame her father? He cannot help himself or her.[29]

Since Jane was only five years old when her father remarried, she clearly did not recognize these feelings as events unraveled. Equally clearly, she brooded over her father's betrayal for more than half a century.

Before "Homo Sum" was published, Jane sent a copy to Mary Murray, wife of fellow Ritualist Gilbert Murray and one of Jane's closest correspondents, for comment. Mary Murray objected to her inclusion of such sensitive material, and Jane agreed in her response. She was "sure" that she was right and claimed that she "accepted" Mary's criticisms. She admitted that the "Father and Daughter" section "was autobiographical" and agreed to eliminate it, for "one should not put one's Father's sins into a tract. . . . I felt, when I read it after your letter, that it was splenetic and personal." She asserted that "someday I believe I shall write a treatise on step-mothers and second marriages, but *that* wasn't the place." Finally, she revealed that she "always felt that it was not the second marriage but the early Victorian *lies* that poisoned my life—nothing is poisonous except lies." She sensed how deeply her father's betrayal had hurt her, but she could never consciously admit it to herself. She did indeed excise this passage from the pamphlet version. But when "Homo Sum" appeared in *Alpha and Omega,* the passage had crept back into the text.[30]

Jane's anger at her father expressed itself in various ways. It surfaced most clearly in her attitude toward sexuality, both his and her own. The above passage indicts her father's, and indirectly all men's, sexuality. The hypothetical father's statements get closer and closer to the truth until at the end of the passage he scornfully rejects his daughter's pitiful offerings in favor of his new wife's "fire." The little girl can never fulfill her father's needs, and his rejection is (in her eyes) complete. Thus, sexuality must be avoided since it is the force that separates her from her father, the force that cast her out of his circle. As she wrote to Mary Murray, "I think [sex] *the* wonder and beauty of the world—only apt to go all wrong and ugly." To blame the father totally, however, is dangerous. She relies on him for love and approval, so despite his rejection of her, she cannot place the blame squarely on his shoulders. The only psychologically acceptable solution is to focus her anger on the stepmother who has exposed her inadequacies. Jane certainly deflected a great deal of her anger onto Miss Meredith. She never recovered from the trauma of the second marriage, and she revealed her sympathy with other stepdaughters in a letter dating from 1912. While on a holiday in Arundel with Alys Russell, Bertrand Russell's first wife, Jane noticed Alys's fondness for Julia Strachey. Julia also had a stepmother, and Jane felt a kinship with her, which prompted her to write, "how my heart goes out to a step-child however kind the step-mother."[31]

Jane's fear of sexuality offers a striking contrast to some of the current scholarship on Victorian sexuality. For example, Peter Gay has marshaled an impressive array of evidence suggesting that the Victorian bourgeoisie was much more enlightened about sex and love than twentieth-century scholars have believed. His work has provided a necessary counter to contemporary snobbishness toward the Victorians. In general, the nineteenth century may well have approached sex and love openly, but Jane's case offers compelling evidence that, for some Victorians at least, sexuality remained a frightening and unfathomable force. Her attitude was, of course, overdetermined, but the experiences that nurtured it were not so uncommon as to make her ambivalence unique. Whatever the upper levels of the bourgeoisie thought about sex, their influence did not reach the Harrison household.[32]

The passage from "Homo Sum" also demonstrates Jane's successful internalization of the Victorian obsession with self-control. Her own prevented her from directly attacking her father, and she veiled all her criticism of him, although often very poorly. Her self-control stemmed from both personal experience and cultural conditioning. Deborah Gorham, for example, after surveying Victorian prescriptive literature on child rearing, has concluded that conventional wisdom encouraged mothers to inculcate habits important to bourgeois culture. "Cleanliness, plenty of exposure to fresh air, and simplicity of diet" possessed both "health-giving properties" and "moral significance." Victorian child-rearing advice emphasized "the need for a strict routine in handling children, from the time of their birth, and . . . the need to teach habits of order, cleanliness and self-control." Experts generally agreed that "if children were treated in an orderly manner, they would come to expect and prefer it, and in this way they would be well on the way to becoming orderly, self-controlled adults."[33] These practices produced both family and social harmony, but they allowed no outlet for anger, especially in little girls. Another childhood incident from Jane's "Reminiscences" reveals how well she learned to "silence the reproach upon her lips."

> I learnt to ride . . . on an adorable donkey with long furry ears and soft kind eyes, and a small furry donkey slept in my bed every night for years. One night the nurse took it away, saying it was time I learnt not to be a baby. I said not a word, *I had long learnt to keep silence.* But I was found at midnight with swollen eyes, staring wide awake. The nurse, being a sensible woman, put back my donkey, and I slept soft and warm. (RSL, 315; italics mine).

This passage and the longer excerpt from "Homo Sum," both emphasizing repression of anger and misery, clearly demonstrate how well Jane internalized the denial of all improper emotion. Instead of fussing over the removal of her donkey, she suffered in silence until the nurse took pity on her sleeplessness. Instead of reacting overtly angrily to her father's remarriage, she brooded silently over his betrayal and finally wrote about it sixty years later. The little girl who had "long learnt to keep silence" grew up to have, in Hope Mirrlees's words, "such splendid self-control."[34] But anger, an irrepressible emotion, will manifest itself in subtle ways, and Jane, as a young woman, expressed hers through rebellion.

Her discontent at home increased as the second family grew. Hope blamed Jane's unhappiness on the communal life necessarily led by such a large family. "Don't blame Jane for not getting on with her step-family," Hope admonished, for "it was quite natural to find that almost communal life trying—& is an evidence of the beautiful temper of Jane's own mother. Jane's equanimity & perfectly just mind were partly an inheritance from her mother & partly a lesson learned from the chaos produced by the opposite." After years of hearing Jane's stories, Hope had come to share her almost morbid reverence toward Elizabeth Harrison. They had the ideal mother at hand—a mother who died before she could disillusion her child. Hope would have been prey to this same delusion because of her problematic relationship with her own mother, who lived more than long enough to prove herself, unfortunately, only too human. At any rate, Jane's unhappiness more likely resulted from her being supplanted in her father's attention by his growing brood. She had no inherent predilection for solitude; she preferred a group so long as she shone at its center. But the large family eclipsed her by sheer strength of numbers. Faced with a stepmother of lower status and vastly different background who had nonetheless managed to alienate her from her father, Jane rebelled against her rule. But overt rebellion would antagonize her father, so she settled for looking disdainfully upon her half brothers and half sisters. Unable to be the center of the circle that revolved so stubbornly around the second family, Jane had to beat a retreat. Ever resourceful, though, she found many ways to show her displeasure. To ensure that she made herself clear, she chose two actions guaranteed to upset her Evangelical stepmother most thoroughly.[35]

Her first, relatively minor infraction was to start smoking. Jane named her brother-in-law, Elizabeth's husband William Lane, as the culprit who taught her to smoke "in her girlhood." "It always tickled her," Hope recalled, "to think that she had learned this sinful habit from an Evangelical clergyman." There is no evidence of a row over the smoking issue, so perhaps Jane's parents never learned of her habit.

A more serious escapade in 1867 resulted in Jane's literal expulsion from the family circle.[36] She and her stepmother finally came to figurative blows over Jane's adolescent romance with a Scalby curate named Houseman. Jane's humorous account of the incident in her "Reminiscences" revealed that the curate, "fresh from Oxford and not . . . averse to showing off" caught her attention by pointing out a mistranslation from the Greek Testament during one of his sermons. This revelation filled Jane "with excitement and alarm," as she could see "that the whole question of the 'verbal inspiration of the Bible' was at issue." She later "waylaid the hapless curate," whose knowledge of Greek turned out to be "more slender" than her own. She related that even "if embarrassed, he was friendly" and could not "confine his attentions to the Greek text" (RSL, 320). Jane could not understand how a purely intellectual interest, so innocently expressed, could evoke a romantic response.

Lucy Harrison, however, related a far different version of the episode, and comparing the two accounts reveals Jane's shameless editing of her memories. According to Lucy, "Jane fell madly in love with him [Mr. Houseman] & he within the limits of his nature . . . with her." They flirted during choir practice, at which Jane played the organ, and met surreptitiously between the Harrison house and the church. Unfortunately, Mrs. Fox, the gossipy wife of the curate in charge, revealed the truth to her good friend Mrs. Harrison. A "terrible scene" ensued, with Mr. Houseman "forbidden the house" (much forbidding of the house occurred in this family) and Jane sent off to visit an aunt and uncle in Normanton while her parents pondered her future. Her scandalous behavior prompted Mrs. Harrison to accuse her of "behaving 'like a kitchen-maid.' " But "considering the subject" of her discussion with the curate, Jane wrote maliciously, she failed "to see the analogy" (RSL, 320). Although Jane shrugged off the incident, Lucy recalled that she threw herself to the floor "in a paroxysm of grief" when she heard, a year after the incident occurred, that Mr. Houseman was engaged.[37]

If Jane wished to anger her stepmother, she certainly succeeded. But her father's reaction astonished her. As she put it, "my father, as usual, said nothing. He scarcely ever did say anything" (RSL, 320). These two terse sentences hide an enormous sense of anger and betrayal. Jane could not believe that he would side with her stepmother. Although she minimized the curate episode in her "Reminiscences," she also stressed her father's "great natural silence." She described hearing her stepmother once "passionately haranguing my father. From him not a sound. But when we met for dinner, we saw with some embarrassment that a portrait of my mother, long consigned to an attic, was hanging on the wall opposite my father's seat. Such was his dumb reprisal" (RSL, 320). Jane and her father shared two characteristics: an inability to articulate anger and a tendency to wield the image of Elizabeth Harrison, either figuratively or literally, as a weapon against the second Mrs. Harrison.

Jane's description of the whole curate incident is revealing, and remarkable both for the style in which it is told and the editing of its content. The event proved more significant than it might appear at first glance. Rather than fading away as a youthful indiscretion, it escalated into a battle of wills: Jane pitting her quiet, calm natural parents against her stepmother's "Celtic volubility" (RSL, 320). The ostensible Harrison calmness connected her to her father. She faced the terrible dilemma of watching her father, who by nature and blood should take her part, side with her stepmother, the Welsh intruder so strangely different in temperament, religion, and status. In light of the punishment she suffered as a result of her romance with Mr. Houseman, she considered herself betrayed once again. But this time she was not only excluded from the center of the circle; she was literally cast out of the circle altogether. Because of her indiscretion, Jane was "summarily dispatched in dire disgrace to Cheltenham [College]" (RSL, 320).

Both Jessie Stewart and Robert Ackerman insist that Charles Harrison recognized Jane's talent and that this recognition motivated him to send her to Cheltenham.[38] But given his views on woman's role, such clear vision seems unlikely. Morever, Jane knew better than anyone that the running battle for her father's affection could not be effectively fought from a hundred miles away. She blamed her father for banishing her to Cheltenham, thus making clear that her interests came second to Mrs.

Harrison's. But protest proved useless, and off she went. For a young girl with such a craving for attention, it was a bitter punishment. Despite this inauspicious beginning, though, Jane achieved great success at Cheltenham. She triumphed over her traditional and inadequate at-home education because of her natural ability and benefited from Cheltenham's more stimulating atmosphere.

Like most proper Victorian middle-class young ladies, Jane's education had begun at home under a series of governesses. Her stepmother engaged "a rather rapid succession of governesses," all of whom were "grossly ignorant," albeit "good women, steadily kind to me" (RSL, 317–18). Jane recalled that "they taught me deportment, how to come into a room, how to get into a carriage, also that 'little girls should be seen and not heard,' and that I was there (in the schoolroom) 'to learn, not to ask questions' " (RSL, 318). Although she perceived Victorian education as "ingeniously useless" and believed that she had "learnt certainly a great deal of miscellaneous rubbish," she conceded that "odd scraps of information are stimulating to a child's imagination" (RSL, 318). Her favorite governess was "a woman of real intelligence, ignorant but willing and eager to learn anything and everything I wanted." They attempted languages such as German and Latin, but "alas! my kind governess was shortly removed to a lunatic asylum" (RSL, 319–20). About Jane's contribution to her breakdown she "did not care to inquire" (RSL, 320).

Many women raised in the Victorian era shared Jane's unhappiness with their useless education. Mary Paley, one of the earliest students at Newnham College and later a lecturer in economics there, spent the years between the ages of nine and thirteen being taught by a series of governesses. Languages and literature were taken most seriously, but she had similar feelings about her experience. Ironically, the next step in her education appeared to be a step back. Mary and her sister went "once a week to a select school for young ladies in our nearest town, kept by two maiden ladies, where we were taught 'Magnall's Questions,' the 'use of globes' and deportment."[39] Two related factors contributed to the appalling quality of girls' education, both at home and in school: Victorian ideas of what women should learn and the incompetent governesses and teachers the system produced.

Recent scholarly attention to women's education has fostered great debate and achieved virtually no agreement on the relationship between education and the ideal of womanhood.[40] Few nineteenth-century educators, either male or female, viewed girls' education as a vehicle for making concrete changes in women's status. Elizabeth Sewell's *Principles of Education* (1865) represented the typical conservative view of women's education and their place in the world. She favored home instruction and thought "gregarious" education, as she called it, "injurious" to young girls and detrimental to preparing them for their roles. "Girls are to dwell in quiet homes, amongst a few friends; to exercise a noiseless influence; to be submissive and retiring. There is no connexion between the bustling mill-wheel life of a large school, and that for which they are supposed to be preparing." One reviewer of Sewell's book lashed out at the opening of local examinations for university entrance to girls, citing a statement by Miss F. Martin, head of the Bedford College School in London, that "the Local Examinations for girls and women 'foster vanity.' " Women had no power to choose their lot, Sewell believed, and education could at most prepare them to cope with whatever might befall them. Overtraining only threatened to make women discontented.[41]

Even the founders of the best girls' schools certainly believed that, although women were capable of different levels of learning, the provision only of some form of vocational training for women who might not marry justified education. They envisioned single life as a last resort. Ideally, women should marry, but education enabled a woman to earn her own living if her father could not support her or, given an unfavorable ratio of men to women, she never had the opportunity to marry. Women such as Dorothea Beale and Frances Mary Buss, headmistresses of two influential girls' schools, opted for a single life, but they stressed their commitment to a noble cause.[42] Whatever their unconscious motives for remaining unmarried, they did not believe that many women would share their dedication.

Nineteenth-century England produced many women educational theorists. Some addressed the questions of primary education, some those of secondary education; they also varied according to their interests in different social classes. A host of conservative writers opposed them out of fear of the inevitable changes that would occur if women were educated. All these theorists contributed to dominant attitudes toward women's education in this period, but Dorothea Beale, headmistress of Cheltenham College for nearly fifty years, played an even more direct role in Jane's life.[43]

Dorothea Beale based her convictions on a religious view of womanhood. She was born in 1831, the daughter of a London physician who dominated the Beale family. He also exerted "a strong and formative influence on her life."[44] Her family held firm religious beliefs, which echo in her writing and ideas about woman's education. She viewed religion as "an integral part of family life . . . not mere observance but a potent, vigorous element."[45] After a succession of daily governesses had provided her with a "disjointed and incomplete education," Beale attended a boarding school. Ill health forced her to return home at age thirteen, whereupon she began a course of self-education. "She was given every encouragement to study," sharing her brothers' lessons in the classics and having "access to two libraries, at the London Institution and Crosby Hall."

When she was sixteen, she and her sisters attended a "fashionable finishing-school in Paris." In 1848 Beale entered Queen's College, originally founded to improve teacher training. After completing her studies, she taught for seven years at the preparatory school attached to Queen's College. She resigned over a difference of opinion on the issues of the limited power given to women tutors and a lowering of admission standards.[46] She then taught for one year at the Clergy Daughters' School at Casterton (the model for Lowood School in *Jane Eyre*) before becoming principal at Cheltenham Ladies College in 1858.[47]

Founded in 1853, Cheltenham had already become a "favourite abode of the strictest sect of the Evangelicals,"[48] which explains why Jane's stepmother sent her there. The college had been designed as an institution for upper-middle-class daughters. In testimony before the Taunton Commission investigating the state of women's education in 1866, Beale stated that "none are admitted but the daughters of independent gentlemen or professional men."[49] Cheltenham's founders were concerned "primarily for the larger class of girls who were not likely to teach or to follow any particular calling, but whose influence as they grew to womanhood was wide and pervasive." For a fee ranging from six to twenty guineas per year, girls studied " 'Holy Scripture and the Liturgy of the Church of England' . . . 'the Principles of Grammar' and . . . 'the Elements of Latin;' . . . Arithmetic; and . . . Callisthenic Exercises." They also learned "Drawing, French, Geography, History, Music and Needlework." Initially, townspeople and parents applauded this curriculum. But in the 1850s, feelings turned against the college. Critics complained "of 'imperfect knowledge in serving and cutting out': that the children had not enough use of the garden: that there was not enough conversational French." In short, they complained of too much emphasis on real education and insufficient training in accomplishments.[50]

One of the most interesting aspects of college life, however, was its silence rule. Students were not allowed to speak to each other during school hours, except for a twenty-minute period in the morning. Beale enforced this rule, begun by Cheltenham's first vice-principal, Anne Proctor, to "inculcate habits of self-control," to avoid "the making of undesirable friendships," and to discourage "gossip and the betrayal of confidences." Furthermore, Beale asked parents' help at home in "carrying out the spirits of these regulations [in such a way as to prevent all] indiscriminate conversation." In the school's boardinghouses, where Jane lived during her student days, "talking was not allowed in the bedrooms," for Beale believed that silence was " 'a great boon to those who find the value of quiet at the beginning and end of the day.' " The same rule applied at Frances Buss's North London Collegiate School for Girls, and the Girls' Public Day School Trust adopted it for its own schools. In the late 1970s, the silence rule still held during the change of classes at Cheltenham, although it had disappeared from the North London Collegiate School. Josephine Kamm, biographer of Buss and Beale, states that at least at Cheltenham the girls did not mind the silence rule, but it is difficult to believe that they never resisted or even overtly rebelled against such a strict practice.[51]

Some parents and staff opposed Beale's appointment as principal, finding her "too intellectual, not genial enough in manner, too 'High Church.' " Nonetheless, her long reign over Cheltenham indicates that parents and colleagues eventually accepted her ability and personality. Certainly her view of education encouraged such acceptance. She defined an educator's job as provision of "an environment where light with its life-giving power could flow in freely and energize the whole personality: the special field of service was then decided by vocation."[52] She envisioned a community of women scholars, "an order of teachers, a dedicated sisterhood vowed to a life of austerity and self-denial."[53] This unmistakably religious image of educated women as a sort of cloistered sect reverberated in some of Jane's later writings, and she found herself cast into just such a milieu in 1868.

At this point, Jane's story and Cheltenham's converge, and her experiences there give some insight into a girl's life at school. Little material remains, but reminiscences from Jane's sister and from a school friend, Caroline Dutton Mitchell, offer a glimpse into those early days.

Charles Harrison agreed only reluctantly to send Jane away to school. Lucy Harrison told Hope that "Mr. Harrison had promised his first wife that none of her girls should ever go to school."[54] He must have found breaking his word on this important question painful, and that he did so at all testifies to the second Mrs. Harrison's power in the household. No wonder Jane felt betrayed by his refusal to take her part. But Cheltenham, a haven for Evangelicals, would certainly have appealed to Mrs. Harrison, and the gossipy Mrs. Fox sent her daughter there, so the Harrisons decided it was the place for Jane.

Some of the themes that recur in Jane's life originated, or at least first came to light, in this period, notably her ill health. Lucy Harrison told Hope that Jane had started to menstruate at age thirteen, but that she stopped for six months while at Cheltenham.[55] Hope blamed this cessation on the climate; Jane herself, although not mentioning this condition, told Hope that she "was missing Yorkshire." Hope also recorded that Jane suffered from severe headaches while a student at Cheltenham, and that "Mrs. M [Caroline Dutton Mitchell] used to soothe them by stroking her broad head & said that not only was it so beautiful to look at but the feel of it was so wonderful."[56] Jane also had a troublesome cough that she eased by wearing a respirator. She later saw Sir James Paget, a noted Cambridge physician, about the same problem, and "he diagnosed it as purely nervous."[57]

Although a physiological root to these problems cannot be dismissed out of hand, all of them could have been psychosomatically induced by stress, repressed anger, and unresolved conflict. The incidence of respiratory problems is particularly revealing. Difficulty in breathing may testify to the internalization of anger, the manifestation of stress that results from repressing emotion. A young girl caught between anger at her father for his actions and a need to retain what love he offers her will not allow herself to feel anger: it is too dangerous. Yet she must acknowledge its existence, if only unconsciously. Respiratory difficulties can offer both a symbol of the valiant attempt to keep emotions contained and a punishment for harboring such destructive feelings. Illness of any sort may be, paradoxically, a means of indirectly admitting defeat while reminding those around one that there is still something amiss. The Victorians, who valued order and self-control above all else, considered anger a terribly upsetting emotion. Jane had already learned to keep silent when in distress, but her body allowed expression of the emotions her mind would not admit.

Jane arrived at Cheltenham during a difficult period in her life, and the circumstances surrounding her arrival there hardly facilitated a peaceful transition from sheltered daughter to student. It is impossible to determine if Jane knew of her mother's wishes regarding her education, but if, as is likely, she had sensed her father's conflicting feelings, she must have been angry at him for reneging on his word.

Another theme that crystallized during this period concerns Jane's conduct in her friendships. F. Cecily Steadman, writing about Jane's arrival, stated that "her mind was far in advance of her companions, who were considerably in awe of her at first, though, as one of them says, she became much more human in her intercourse with them after a time."[58] The separateness of the highly intelligent girl figured prominently in Jane's life at Newnham, but even Hope admitted that "there is no doubt that a great many of Jane's old friends are rather bitter when they talk about her. There seems to be an almost universal sense of Jane's having been ruthless & fickle in her friendships." She remembered hearing D. S. MacColl say to Jane soon after World War I that "the reason why *you* keep young is that you are always making new friends & forgetting your old ones!"[59]

Jane's friendship with Dorothea Beale best illustrates her penchant for throwing people over during the Cheltenham period. Caroline Dutton Mitchell revealed that Jane had a passion for Beale that Beale reciprocated. Hope reported on Jane's reaction when her parents decided that she should return home for good at the end of her second year. Hope recalled "Jane's telling me herself that her G.P. [grand passion] was so violent that when Miss B. told her that her people wanted to take her away, Jane fainted dead away."[60] Since Beale viewed fainting as "a major crime, indicating a quite unnecessary and most reprehensible loss of concentration and control," one wonders how she reacted to Jane's fainting at the thought of leaving Cheltenham.[61] Nevertheless, fainting as a response to crisis became almost a habit with Jane, and fainting episodes figure at various points in her life. This is the first recorded one. In response to the threat of Jane's departure, Beale offered to keep her on as a student for free, as "she was such a credit to the school." Her fainting had worked, and the Harrisons allowed Jane to remain for one more year.[62]

Beale had good reason to want Jane to remain, if only to enhance her school's reputation in the long run. Hilda Lane, Jane's niece, recalled Beale's astonishment at Jane's intellectual abilities.

> My grandmother once told me that when she wrote to Miss Beale sketching a course of the things she wished Aunt Jane to study (Aunt Jane was always interested in everything) she had a very severe snub as Miss Beale intimated no girl could manage such an extended course— But after Aunt Jane had been a little time at Cheltenham Granny had a letter saying she had no way exaggerated her abilities but even understated them.[63]

Beale's appreciation of Jane's intelligence is not surprising, but Mrs. Harrison's interest in Jane's course of study is.

Jane in the end rejected Dorothea Beale after experiencing a drastic change in religious belief. Until her early twenties, Jane seems to have held conventional beliefs, her later unorthodoxy notwithstanding. She kept up a secret correspondence with her old governess, Miss Cook (the unfortunate woman who was later consigned to an asylum), and included comments on Miss Beale's Scripture lessons. Miss Cook, who was apparently even more conventional in belief than Jane, "began to suspect Miss Beale's orthodoxy" because she was "tending toward Ritualism" and threatened to tell the Harrisons of the apostasy being taught at the college. Instead, she turned first to the Reverend William Lane, Jane's brother-in-law, who put her mind at ease.[64] But before leaving school, Jane's convictions wavered. She began to sympathize, through some very schoolgirlish poetry, with those German writers who claimed that "Nature . . . is God."[65] D. F. Strauss's *Life of Jesus,* which had appeared in English in the 1840s, apparently shook Jane's faith completely. His interpretation of Christ as a mythical representation did more than challenge her religious faith, however. Her interest in his theory also illustrates how early she turned to ritual and mythology.[66] Dorothea Beale, who tried to coax Jane back to the straight and narrow path, paid for her efforts by being rather brutally dropped. Hope stated emphatically that "Jane detested Miss Beale after she left school,"[67] and Jane's remembrances of Cheltenham in her "Reminiscences" support that assertion.

Jane "carried away from Cheltenham College a dislike for history which has lasted all my life," and criticized her lessons as nothing more than "moralisings on the doings and misdoings of kings and nobles." Besides finding the method unsatisfactory, the fact that "Miss Beale was Cromwellian and I, like all children, a passionate Royalist," kept her in a "constant state of irritation" as they studied the Stuart period "in tedious detail" (RSL, 323). She also claimed that "there was an odd rule throughout the College that no girl might buy a book," stemming from "Miss Beale's horror of what she called 'undigested knowledge.' " Of course, Jane triumphantly "broke the rule and bought a small life of Archbishop Laud" (RSL, 323). Interestingly, though, Steadman, in her biography of Dorothea Beale, found no evidence to corroborate the existence of this rule.[68] Nevertheless, while relating an incident centering on receipt of a postcard, Jane spoke most contemptuously of Beale. Peveril Turnbull, a childhood friend of Jane's, promised to send her a postcard just before she sat for the London matriculation exam. Her own words best describe the subsequent uproar.

> No letter reached me, but one morning I was summoned before Miss Beale's throne where she sat in state before the Lower School came into prayers. She had in front of her a post-card (post-cards had only just been invented) written in a schoolboy scrawl and signed "Peveril." "That," she said, pointing a disgusted finger at the signature, "is a boy's name." "Yes," I said, "it's Peveril; he promised to write to me before the examination," and I put out my hand for the post-card. "No, this must go to your parents," and then came a long harangue. It ended with these words which intrigued me so that I remember them exactly: "You are too young, and I hope too innocent, to realize the gross vulgarity of such a letter or the terrible results to which it might lead." I was indeed, and still am, for what do you think was the offense? After his signature "Peveril" had written *"Give my love to the Examiners!"* The story may stand to mark the abyss of fatuous prudery in to which the girls' schools of the middle Victorian period—even the very best—had fallen. (RSL, 320–21)

Partly Jane's indignation reflected changes in standards over the years; partly, though, her words also constituted an attack on Beale herself. Beale's intrusiveness and her religious bias became intolerable to Jane the more both came to resemble those qualities in her stepmother, inevitably leading to a complete break.

In addition to their religious differences, however, Jane rejected Beale's power over her. Beale might have served as a good model because of her belief in women's right to an education, but her vision of an educated woman's future differed considerably from Jane's. Jane had not yet fully articulated or even formulated her own ambitions, but she did not plan to use her innate intelligence to fulfill Beale's vision. Ultimately, she found Beale's association of education with personal responsibility stifling. Whereas Beale viewed the life of the mind as a way of serving others, Jane explicitly rejected that model.

Another memory of Lucy Harrison's provides a final look at the state of stepmother-stepdaughter relations. Lucy described the rather dowdy fashion in which Mrs. Harrison dressed the girls and remarked that Jane traveled to Cheltenham with an unimaginative wardrobe and a piece of gray stuff to be made into a Sunday dress. Upon her arrival, Miss Caines, the boardinghouse mistress, took Jane to a dressmaker in Cheltenham's best shop and had the fabric made up into a stylish frock that cost two pounds. Mrs. Harrison, accustomed to paying the Hull seamstresses five shillings, created a scene when Jane presented her with the bill at the end of the term. "As Lucy says, it was a strange greeting for a girl who had so brilliantly distinguished herself. And not a word of praise did she ever get from her parents for all her triumphs at Cheltenham."[69]

Little evidence survives concerning events of the years between Jane's departure from Cheltenham and entry at Newnham. Charles Harrison offered to have her teach her younger siblings at home, and she spent a good part of her time between 1870 and 1874 at this task. Hope says this was also the period during which Jane read Strauss's *Life of Jesus*, which set her permanently at odds with Dorothea Beale. It was now, too, that Jane developed an overwhelming desire to see something of the world, and Hope says her family thought her very selfish for acting on her desire. No doubt the stifling provincial atmosphere and the fact of being closeted with so many younger siblings took their toll on her. Jane paid for her trips abroad with the money she had inherited from her mother, however, so there was little the family could do to stop her. She visited Holland in 1871, accompanied by a chaperone, and traveled in 1872 and 1873 with the Duttons. Her fortunes changed in 1874, when she took and passed the Cambridge University examination and received a scholarship to Newnham.[70]

Poised for flight to Cambridge, Jane presented the image of a frustrated and angry young woman. It is a sad portrait: an extraordinarily bright woman trapped in a provincial home and surrounded by a family unwilling and perhaps unable to recognize and cultivate her talents. Faced with opposition at every turn, it is no wonder that Jane found happiness and relief when she finally escaped to Newnham. Once arrived there, she created a new family—a new circle—and firmly established herself at its center.

2

The First Circle: Newnham College

The one thing men do not like is the man-woman, and they will never believe the College or University woman is not of that type. Sensible men will always like sensible and cultivated women; but they will always prefer that their good sense and cultivation should have come through channels which they recognise as suitable for the womanly character.

—*"Female Education,"* Quarterly Review, *April 1869*

I sometimes fancy I shall do great things, but will it not all come to nothing? Yet I should like never to be forgotten, to do something great for my country which would make my name live for ever. But I am only a woman.

—*Anne Clough's diary*

IN THE SECOND half of the nineteenth century, English women who sought an education inevitably confronted doubt or hostility. Jane Harrison's experience at Newnham illuminates several critical aspects of the debate over women's education. On a personal level, her college experience freed her from her stultifying provincial and Evangelical upbringing. On a broader level, it illustrates the quandary that confronted women who aspired to an intellectual life rather than a traditional family life. Finally, the women's colleges generally reflected an emerging social trend: the difficulties northern provincials faced in assimilating into the English intelligentsia.

To date, scholars have primarily described and analyzed the campaign for reform in women's education. The opening of women's colleges, although unquestionably important, is perceived as having been an end in itself. But, in addition, women students' experience at college profoundly affected their lives. The opening of women's colleges, far from closing the debate over women's social role, raised it to a new level by creating both new problems and new opportunities for women. Reformers and students viewed education differently, and they inevitably clashed over their differences. The reformers saw it as a political issue, whereas the students saw it as a personal one.

Critics of women's education presented their arguments in both ideological and economic terms. Conservatives dreaded the inevitable changes in gender relations. "We have to consider," a representative critic, the Oxford historian Montagu Burrows, wrote in the *Quarterly Review*, "the whole complex phenomena of life, the relations between the sexes, the formation of the *whole* character of woman, the difference between men and women." Occasionally, however, supporters of women's higher education advocated learning for learning's sake. Joshua Fitch, an examiner for the Taunton Commission, based his belief in women's right to higher education on the ideas "that human beings, whether male or female, come into the world not only to 'get a living' but to live; that the life they live depends largely on what they know and care about, upon the breadth of their intellectual sympathy, upon their love of truth, upon their power of influencing and inspiring other minds; and that for these reasons mental culture stands in just as close relation to the needs of a woman's career in the world as to that of a man." Both sides believed that women had a responsibility to fulfill social expectations but disagreed on how to define their duty and how best to prepare them for it. Some believed the status quo offered the best for society, whereas others pressed for substantive changes in gender relations.[1]

Women educational reformers, however, often believed even more firmly than men in the traditional ideal of womanhood, and their writings frequently invoked the educated motherhood argument. Aside from Emily Davies, founder of Girton College, few educational reformers favored education for self-improvement alone. Women reformers also utilized the economic arguments for women's education. Even critics of higher education approved of better teacher training in order to provide jobs for the increasing number of "redundant" women. In response to Emily Davies's plan for Girton College, Montagu Burrows advised her to abandon the idea of equal education in favor of a college that would simply train good women teachers. In pragmatic terms, he claimed that parents would not pay "for this University education which is to lead to nothing tangible, if it does not lead away from much that is tangible." Offering "a word of friendly advice," he exhorted Davies to make Girton "a *true College for women*. Let its promoters give up the ambitious notion of an institution on the same footing as a man's College." As a course of study, he suggested that "simplicity of living, the strictest economy, so as to suit governesses; training in housekeeping, regular needlework, and, if possible, actual schoolteaching should be parts of a system to which all should, with very slight exceptions, conform." He then invoked medical arguments against strenuous education, citing the dangers of "evening reading" and advocating strict rules. He posed this solution for women of the middle classes and above; for lower-class women, "there is nothing effectual on a large scale but emigration." His article advanced nearly all popular arguments against women's education.[2]

As much of the recent secondary literature on women's higher education points out, leaders of the movement generally supported traditional Victorian ideas of womanhood and did not initially challenge them.[3] Economic realities dictated some action to relieve the dire poverty even middle-class women could slip into if forced to support themselves with inadequate training. But the educated motherhood argument at least allowed that education did not necessarily have to be vocational training in order to gain acceptance. All these theories paid lip service to upper-class ideas of womanhood.

The women who founded or governed the earliest colleges, such as Emily Davies at Girton and Eleanor Balfour (later Sidgwick) and Anne Clough at Newnham, guarded their charges carefully to keep their behavior above reproach. Yet their students—only one generation younger—developed their own, different ideas about the purposes of education. Many students arrived at college fully convinced that they were preparing for educated motherhood or making themselves better companions for the educated men they anticipated marrying. Some of them wanted to break from these projected futures and found comfort in the colleges in which they no longer felt themselves anomalies. Still others arrived with traditional expectations but found that their needs and desires changed during the course of their stay. Regardless of their individual circumstances, finding themselves surrounded by other intelligent and often ambitious women encouraged them to create a female culture based on intellectual kinship. The women's schools, at both the secondary and the college levels, proved to be radical simply because they offered young women the chance to form strong extradomestic bonds. This different focus put students in conflict with society in general and their college guardians in particular. But escaping from an often dreary home life and associating with like-minded women eased the transition from traditional home life to the predominantly masculine world of academia.

Such a shift in focus, however, still left unresolved the question of women's role. The first two women's colleges at Cambridge themselves embodied this conflict, in which Emily Davies at Girton and Henry Sidgwick at Newnham took opposite positions. Davies used her plan for Girton's structure to make a point about women's equality, while Sidgwick tackled the larger question of university reform and seized the issue of women's education in order to strike a blow in this larger context.[4]

Davies's tactics in her passionate crusade for women's equality often provoked resentment among critics of women's education. She believed that women were capable of performing intellectually under the same conditions as men, and she founded her college (originally at Hitchin, a few miles from Girton) to prove this point. Critics reacted strongly to her single-mindedness. "They [the founders of Girton College] believed that it would be of great service to the cause of women's education generally if they could prove conclusively that women were capable of the same intellectual work as men, and it seemed to them that any difference in the conditions observed would weaken their case in the judgment both of the University and of the world outside."[5] To that end, women students had to complete their requirements for the degree (which they could not receive) in the same amount of time as men, with the same residency requirements, and with no special treatment when they took their exams. Girton paved the way for women students to take the tripos examination by having examiners first test them independently. Cambridge formally opened the tripos to women in 1881, although until 1948 they received only certificates, not degrees.[6]

Although Davies expected resentment from people outside the college, she probably did not expect it from her students. Louisa Lumsden, an early Girton student, pointed out a disadvantage of the Girton experiment that Newnham students escaped. Lumsden asserted that Davies's blind determination to prove her students' abilities closed her eyes to their needs. The student was "a mere cog in the wheel of her great scheme. There was a fine element in this, a total indifference to popularity, but . . . it was plain that we counted for little or nothing, except as we furthered her plans." In addition, despite Davies's ideological radicalism, she feared the potential harm from perceived irregularities in personal behavior. She coupled her zealousness to prove women's equality with a strong streak of conventionality. She aimed to show the world that her charges could remain true women. Barbara Stephen, Davies's biographer, states that she had "what seemed to some of the students an excessive regard for the proprieties which caused resentment against what they thought unnecessary restrictions."[7]

Louisa Lumsden again provided one example of the students' fomenting a small rebellion. In the dining hall during the first year at Hitchin, "it was expected that we should sit in a formal row down one side of our table, lest we be guilty of the discourtesy of turning our backs upon the 'High.' But this was too much, and we rebelled." The students eventually won the right to face each other at table so that they could talk. "So academically formal . . . was the order imposed from the first at Hitchin—we might have been fifty undergraduates instead of five harmless young women."[8]

Notwithstanding Davies's contradictory attitudes toward public opinion, she understood what female students needed to succeed. She recognized the importance of privacy to students who had generally spent their lives in a family setting and included provisions for solitude in her original outline drawn up in 1868.

Each student will have a small sitting room to herself, where she will be free to study undisturbed, and to enjoy at her discretion the companionship of friends of her own choice. Of all the attractions offered by the College life, probably the opportunity for a certain amount of solitude, so necessary an agent in the formation of character, will be the one most welcomed by the real student.[9]

Davies directed her efforts toward providing women with as rigorous and rewarding an education as men received. She believed that women should seek self-improvement, not vocational training, through education.

Newnham's founders followed different principles. Henry Sidgwick, the noted Trinity College philosopher and the driving force behind the plan for Newnham, first broached the subject of organizing lectures for women at Cambridge in 1869. Since 1867, women had attended the Cambridge local lectures given in other cities, but they followed no structured program. Now Sidgwick enlisted the aid of Millicent Garrett Fawcett and several Cambridge dons in forming a General Committee to study this question. The lectures scheme began in 1870, and nearly eighty women attended in the first term.[10]

Sigdwick married Eleanor Balfour in 1876, and together they built Newnham into a strong women's college. But Sidgwick had other concerns in mind when he agitated for the admission of women to Cambridge. He envisioned a larger plan of university reform and saw the women's college as a means of accomplishing his goal. Sidgwick especially castigated the traditional approach to classical education, which required students to perform such tasks as composing poetry in Greek and Latin. "An artificial education," he claimed, "is one which, in order that a man may ultimately know one thing, teaches him another, which gives the rudiments of some learning or accomplishment, that the man in the maturity of his culture will be content to forget." He despised this education for show and campaigned tirelessly for reform. In fact, he opposed compulsory classical study for both men and women. He believed that "a liberal education has for its object to impart the highest culture, to lead youths to the most full, rigorous, and harmonious exercise, according to the best ideal attainable, of their active, cognitive, and aesthetic faculties." He believed this "natural" education far superior to the "artificial" education Cambridge then offered. Part of the liberal reform of higher education allowed—even required—the admission of women to the universities. He envisioned Newnham as part of a more all-encompassing plan for change. Thus, in a sense, Davies at Girton forced women to strive for an ideal that other reformers considered obsolete.[11]

Sidgwick's scheme permitted women to take different exams to reflect variations in their preparation. It also allowed them more time before taking the exams to compensate for inadequate training. He believed that

> while the more elementary lectures should prepare students for the Higher Local Examination, more advanced teaching, supplementing the professional lectures opened to women, should enable those who had passed through this preliminary trial, and wished to go further, to go through a complete course of academic education in one or other of the departments into which academic study is divided at Cambridge, and which form the subjects of the Honours Degree Examinations.

In her description of Sidgwick's efforts, Blanche Clough, niece of Newnham's first principal, Anne Clough, points out that few women desired to prepare for the honours degree. The group's size and the need to educate its members separately made their education particularly expensive. "The Lectures Association [governing Newnham College] . . . required all students who wished to enter for a Tripos Examination to give evidence of general education, and expected them, as a rule, to prove this by passing the Higher Local Examination; but it did not require or, indeed, encourage them to take the Previous Examination, and it did not insist upon exact adherence to the rules as to terms." Women received preferential treatment because they were often ill prepared for study. Moreover, Sidgwick and some of the other founders, "while they were anxious that the classical curriculum should be fully opened to women as any other of the Honours Courses," believed that "the education of girls would not be benefited by the imposition of Greek and Latin, required for passing the Little-go [Previous Examination], as a necessary preliminary to all higher branches of academic study."[12]

Sidgwick's experiment finally started when the lectures began in 1870. Sympathetic Cambridge professors helped by donating money or offering their services either free of charge or for a nominal payment. Several dons, including Cayley (algebra), Seeley (modern history), Jebb (history), and Sidgwick himself, taught women students in separate lectures. The women attended in small groups, always accompanied by chaperones even though they did not mix with the male undergraduates. Despite the inconvenience, the women students enjoyed the same high-quality education as the men. In 1873, twenty-two of thirty-four professors formally granted women permission to attend their lectures; within a few years, the number had increased to twenty-nine. Christ's College was the first men's college to admit women to lectures alongside men.[13]

Meanwhile, however, the earliest students in residence needed housing and proper guidance. Regardless of Davies's and Sidgwick's disagreement over the structure of women's education, both recognized the necessity of maintaining appearances. Therefore, both Girton and Newnham adhered to strict notions of propriety. Much depended on choosing the right woman to govern the young ladies who would be the first students. Sidgwick felt so strongly about his cause that he hand-picked his staff and even paid for the housing out of his own pocket. In the spring of 1871, Sidgwick took a house in Newnham for the use of students and asked Anne Clough, an educator from Liverpool with connections to such reformers as Emily Davies, Barbara Leigh-Smith Bodichon, and Frances Mary Buss, to preside over it.[14]

Anne Clough, the daughter of a Welsh cotton merchant, was a conservative Evangelical who became active in women's education reform after the death of her father in the 1840s and her mother and brother in the 1860s. Clough was one of the founders of the North of England Council for the Higher Education of Women in 1867, and through this organization she met such active reformers as Josephine Butler and Emily Davies. Blanche Clough rightly claims that Clough facilitated the women students' acceptance in the Cambridge community because "it was impossible to associate her with anything unfeminine, and her character gave an assurance to all who came in contact with her, that any movement with which she was concerned would be conducted with moderation and with scrupulous consideration for the feelings of others." Her impeccable character assuaged Sidgwick's fears but alienated her students.[15]

The term began in October 1871 with 5 students in residence. By the end of the academic year, 3 more had arrived. In its first ten years, Newnham served 215 students. Ironically, many of them were teachers who came for only a term or two in order to enhance their skills and improve their marketability. Only 20 of the first 215 students read for the tripos.[16] The founders extended opportunities for higher education to greater numbers of women by keeping costs low and encouraging those interested in teaching.[17] The teachers who attended Newnham only briefly paid less for their courses, however, and often received special treatment, but the most interesting aspect of their association with Newnham is their conspicuous absence from most descriptions of college life. They usually lived in lodgings, not in college, and remained only for a term or two. Although they composed the majority of the first 215 students, few accounts mention them. No doubt their experience of college life bore no resemblance to that of the residential students, but their story needs to be told elsewhere. For privileged upper-middle-class daughters, living communally among intellectual equals proved important to their intellectual development.

At both Newnham and Girton, the students resented their guardians' watchfulness. Sidgwick chose Anne Clough not only for her teaching background but also for her character; he thought her sufficiently upright and disciplined to keep the students in line. Despite assistance and support from many Cambridge dons, "many people in the University disapproved strongly of the presence of women students in Cambridge, and probably most people looked upon them with some suspicion. . . . There was, of course, also a widely diffused prejudice against all women who desired opportunities of obtaining higher learning." Sidgwick believed Anne Clough the perfect choice to allay these suspicions and fears. Clough felt that "education should be kept quite apart from other questions and causes, and she meant to show that a desire for education, and even the possession of it, did not involve any departure from recognised customs and conventions."[18] H. M. Kempthorne (Peile), a daughter of one of Newnham's founders, remembered Anne Clough's relating "with amusement how Professor Henry Sidgwick came to her lamenting the 'unfortunate personal appearance' of the first students," who "were all remarkably good-looking women" and whose attractiveness disturbed the founders.[19] The early reformers insisted on the compatibility of education and true womanhood, genuinely believing that education would not alter women's characters or aspirations. Some of the young women arrived at Newnham harboring the same conviction. Experience proved them all wrong.

Although the students had been raised as young ladies, their status allowed them a certain amount of freedom. They brought this past experience, along with intelligence and youthful spirit, with them to Newnham. Henry Sidgwick noted their independence of mind. "There is such a strong impulse towards liberty among the young women attracted by the movement," he wrote, "that they will not submit to maternal government." Blanche Clough described Anne Clough as "always nervous lest the students should attract attention and criticism by any eccentricity in dress or conduct, for her great desire was to be unnoticed, and to make it clear that this little colony of women was harmless and inoffensive."[20]

This insistence on the college woman's harmlessness demonstrates that both students and guardians recognized the experimental nature of their undertaking. At the outset, most did not want to appear unique and conformed to established norms of female behavior. Members of the college community believed that if they maintained outward appearances, education would not drastically affect women's perceptions of their roles. Many women students undoubtedly felt that they only desired to learn, but the guardians, in their almost pathological fear of public opinion, may have had a better understanding of what dangers lay ahead. In any case, despite the students' initial docility, clashes soon occurred. They resulted largely from the closeness of communal life, combined with the intellectual freedom that the college experience afforded.

In 1870, Emily Davies, writing to Anna Richardson, described Louisa Lumsden's experience as a young woman. Lumsden had told her that "before she came [to Girton], she used to feel fearfully solitary. She was always having said to her, 'Oh, but you're so exceptional.' Now, she feels herself belonging to a body and has lost the sense of loneliness." Mary

Kennedy and Mary Paley Marshall, two members of Newnham's first class, shared Lumsden's feelings. They recalled how deeply their intellectual aspirations and their attendance at college distressed their families. Mary Kennedy's "brother who was up at Corpus was so annoyed with my venture that he wouldn't speak to me!" Mary Paley's father, an Evangelical minister, although "proud and pleased" that she earned a scholarship, agreed to the "outrageous proceeding" of sending her to Cambridge only because "his admiration for Miss Clough overcame his objections." Public opinion militated against women's presence at Cambridge, and often the students faced family objections as well. Once they arrived, however, they no longer felt out of place. They finally belonged to a group.[21]

The most compelling evidence for an unacknowledged ambition lies in the women students' frequent identification with their fathers. Whereas the women often mention their fathers' support, mothers are curiously and conspicuously absent.[22] If women students accepted their future roles, they were reluctant to talk about it. Opposition from siblings and mothers counted for little. If a father supported his daughter's educational desires, she satisfied them. Furthermore, the students barely concealed their hostility toward their conventional female guardians. If women like Anne Clough symbolized their mothers, then the young women clearly had difficulties with them. Consciously or unconsciously, some women recognized that acquiescence to social expectations led to a dead end. Although many women married after college, their educational experience brought them irrevocably into the larger world. Helping an academic husband, which many of the women students eventually did, represented a vastly different way of life than presiding over teas and supervising children and servants. The earliest generation of women students therefore took a greater leap than has been previously recognized.

The early students suffered other discomforts. In October 1871, Anne Clough and the first Newnham class moved into a house at 74 Regent Street in Newnham. As Mary Paley described it,

> We lived very much the life of a family; we studied together, we had our meals at one table, and in the evening we usually sat with Miss Clough in her sitting-room. . . . During that first year at Regent Street there were certain discomforts to be put up with. We went twice a week to the town gymnasium, but otherwise walks were our only form of exercise . . . and no doubt we made up for want of outdoor exercise by being rather noisy in the house, especially at meals.

Behind the fond memories, she conveyed a sense of the oppressive atmosphere. Constant isolation in such a small group without exercise or freedom would have been a difficult adjustment for young women accustomed to a certain degree of liberty. When the group moved in the fall term of 1872 to a larger residence in Merton Hall, the situation improved somewhat. Mary Paley stated that "everything went better. . . . [Anne Clough] had her own sitting room; when we were together, it was from choice, not from necessity." But Anne Clough's journal made clear that the new house also had its disadvantages: "The new house was old and picturesque, with a lovely garden, but the students' rooms were very poor. . . . The garden seemed to make up for all, and the quiet. We were shut in from Cambridge in a corner among trees and shrubs and creeping plants, which bowered us all round." Although this passage conveys a sense of claustrophobia, Clough clearly preferred the closed-in atmosphere, probably because it kept her charges out of the public eye. The real enclosure reflected a symbolic separation from the life of the university. All the same, "their life was a joy to them, but they did work." For the students, the greatest benefit lay in the distance their new residence allowed between them and Clough. The constant separation from the rest of the university and the enforced closeness among students offered an opportunity for the women to create their own culture that nurtured their newly discovered intellectual freedom.[23]

Newnham was still in its precarious infancy when Jane arrived there in October 1874 after her high score on that year's Cambridge higher local examination won her a scholarship. She spent her first year in one of the two houses in Bateman Street taken as an interim measure while the college constructed its first building. When Newnham Hall opened in 1875, Anne Clough and her students

> had now a good dining-hall, a library and other sitting-rooms for the students, and the students' own rooms were nearly all of them pleasant and convenient. Each student had a room to herself, which was furnished so as to serve both as study and bedroom, and the common sitting-rooms were always available. They had fires in their rooms when they liked . . . and they could and did see one another and give tea-parties and cocoa-parties among themselves freely.

College life now began to resemble more closely that of the male undergraduate. Yet a brief comparison of their environments immediately makes clear the modesty of the aspirations of the women's colleges. The men's colleges clustered in the bustling center of Cambridge, very much engaged in the public world while simultaneously enclosing a haven of manicured lawns and immaculately kept gardens. Even today the lawns are off limits to all but fellows of the colleges and their guests to protect them from the hordes of tourists who flock to view the majestic Gothic and baroque buildings. Newnham Hall, far less imposing even now, despite its additions, is set in the middle of a pasture and boasts small patches of garden scattered around well-traveled lawns. Although the buildings are handsome enough, Newnham's founders expended neither money nor effort to create an imposing facade with which to face the world. No hordes of tourists here; yet here Jane flourished.[24]

Jane settled on Newnham after a visit with her old acquaintance, Mary Paley, in Yorkshire. Mary "admired her exceedingly" and recalled that "she was graceful and her figure reminded me of one of the Sistine Sybils, and her eyes were most beautiful." She had "known her as a girl and even then she was called 'the cleverest woman in England.' " Jane undoubtedly felt even more keenly the sense of being exceptional that troubled Louisa Lumsden. Like Lumsden, she discovered a place for herself in the college setting. She quickly became one of the central figures among the Newnham students and the scourge of Miss Clough's days as principal.[25]

Some remarks Jane's friends made about her conduct at Newnham echoed sentiments voiced by her Cheltenham schoolmates. Elinor Ritchie, a contemporary Newnham student and friend of Jane's recalled that Jane would be alternately friendly and nasty to the younger students—"rabbits" as they were called—and could reduce them to tears simply by her "way of flickering her eyelids." Margaret Merrifield first mentioned Jane in a letter of October 1876. "Miss Harrison," she stated, "is much more amiable generally, this term; I do not think the new girls have any reason to complain of her, for though she does not go out of her way to be friendly, she has none of that very stand-offish manner." Apparently Jane grew more congenial after she had been at Newnham for a time. Students certainly sought her out. Alice Dew-Smith reminisced about Jane's flamboyance at the dining-hall table.

> I can see her now, her tall willowy figure clad in a tight-fitting olive-green serge such as used to be supplied to Newnham students by Messrs. Boyd Burnett in the days of the aesthetic craze; her long neck and well-set head, with brown hair in a Greek coil at the back; her fine, deeply fringed eyes—all made an ineffaceable picture. . . . I can think of no one else who could pour forth such a continuous stream of delightful nonsense as Jane entertained us with evening after evening.

Jane's wit and intellect drew people to her even then, but her friends generally agreed that she was, as Hope wrote, "fickle in her passions, but very faithful in her loves." Perhaps her behavior is not so very hard to understand. Having been cast out of her family circle and hurt by her father's second marriage, Jane had difficulties maintaining close relationships with others. She needed to be the center of the circle, and at Newnham she found a group willing to revolve around her. The young women, drawn together by the common bond of a desire to learn, recognized Jane's fine intellect and offered her a chance to shine.[26]

Yet if Jane could be fickle and superficial in her attachments, she could also be passionate and irresistibly drawn to some people. She told

Jane Ellen Harrison as Alcestis, Oxford University Dramatic Society, Oxford 1877. Reproduced by permission of the Principal and Fellows of Newnham College, Cambridge.

Hope Mirrlees that as soon as she saw Ellen Crofts, a fellow Newnhamite, she wanted to be her friend. She came to admire Ellen's "extreme delicacy & sensitiveness of her moral sense." For her part, Ellen immediately noticed that Jane had "the most extraordinary eyes I ever saw." Jane's immediate and lasting fondness for Ellen Crofts confirms that she could as easily be attracted to some people as she shrank from others. And she could drop acquaintances abruptly. Alice Dew-Smith remembered that "Jane never chucked people for conduct; but invariably chucked them if they grew boring." She continued, "and she was so easily bored: people bored her if they talked too much, or if they had a vivacious manner; or if they were egoists. And if they put their faces too close to hers they completely alienated her." In other words, Jane "chucked" people if they threatened her supremacy. She was actually more easily threatened than "bored." A person who talked too much threatened a young woman who relied on her delightful conversation for popularity and acceptance. A vivacious manner threatened to eclipse her own. An egoist threatened her position at the center of the circle, for such a person might break off some of Jane's circle and induce it to revolve around her. Jane invested much more than a desire for education in her Newnham career. No longer encumbered by a provincial family and an antagonistic stepmother, she set out to prove that she belonged in this cultured world that represented the pinnacle of the English intelligentsia. Jane had found a surrogate family, and she feared losing her privileged place in it.[27]

Martha Vicinus points out the importance of class distinctions among college women and the pervasiveness of "patronizing condescension."[28] Although economic status and intellect largely defined cliques, place of origin quickly became an even more insidious criterion. Jane could hold her own on the first two counts, but she faced a serious struggle to overcome the handicap of her Yorkshire background. To the sophisticated southerners who filled Newnham, Yorkshire represented the depth of provincialism.

Vicinus cites a story written by "An Old Newnham Student" for a girls' magazine in 1903. The story conveys the cultural differences between North and South and southern perceptions of northern gaucherie. The author encountered a "North Country 'fresher' " at breakfast one day, and described their exchange.

> At first I am rather stiff and bored with her (Miss Brown is not quite, quite—you understand), and we converse very stupidly about the weather and the thickness of the bacon; but by-and-by, I let myself go, and become quite witty and brilliant on the subject of Miss Hill's new blouse. The next stage is that Miss Brown becomes confiding and asks me how it is some people get invitations to parties in the town. I say I

presume that most of us have had a cousin or brother or friend at Cambridge, and through them we have one or two introductions to dons.

Miss Brown says she supposed it was that way, but just wondered if it would be any good putting your name down anywhere!

I shake my head emphatically at this.[29]

The glaring contrast between the two women and the author's perverse delight in cutting down the other woman illustrate the difficulties that northerners faced in trying to assimilate. Presumably the author represented a common southern perception of northerners, since the article appeared in a popular magazine; she obviously expected sympathy from her readers. She unwittingly conveyed the loneliness northerners experienced at Newnham since they were so far removed from their own element. With their fewer contacts and less sophistication, northerners found it difficult to mesh with their southern classmates. The presence of many northerners in Jane's Newnham days indicates that they were beginning to filter down to the South, but they faced a very difficult journey. Vicinus's story makes Jane's behavior toward the younger students more comprehensible. Despite her intellect, she felt ashamed of her provincial background and reacted defensively. She renounced her provincial roots and identified wholly with the dominant culture, and could assure her own status only by repeatedly proving to herself that she had left her past behind. Her incessant battle to suppress her heritage indicates that it continually threatened to intrude on the present.

Both northerners and southerners, however, shared impatience with many aspects of college life. During the early years, the women students chafed at the regulations that governed their conduct. So ingrained were the rules that Mary Agnes Hamilton, a Newnham student forty years later, remembered the same restrictive atmosphere from her tenure there. Public opinion still dictated "total separation from the masculine undergraduate population" and "timid restrictions that irked and offended students." A "certain limitation in the variety of the student body" proved even more stifling; "too many were going, and knew they were going, to be teachers." But in Jane's day, contact with the future teachers remained, rightly or wrongly, limited. Her contemporaries in the college experienced a new freedom that often led to the formation of strong extradomestic bonds and a varying degree of alienation from their families. The students could not thank their guardians, however, for consciously fostering these changes. The measures designed to protect them from the public eye only inadvertently encouraged a sense of community that proved a boon to serious students.[30]

Jane herself did not mention any details of her Newnham days beyond listing the notables who journeyed to Cambridge for a look at the college, but others remembered her from their own experiences and can provide a brief description of both college life in general and Jane's antics in particular. Mary Paley recalled that during the early 1870s, just before Jane arrived at Newnham, all teaching was done "by weekly or fortnightly papers, without coaching or supervision." Among the faculty, Henry Sidgwick and Alfred Marshall had most to do with the women students. Professors Birks and Fawcett also played a significant role. Mary Paley remembered Sidgwick's reducing some of his students to tears by reading them the scene in *The Mill on the Floss* that portrays Maggie Tulliver's reunion with her brother, Tom. The most interesting recorded conflict over policy occurred in 1877, when the students clamored to stage Euripides' *Electra.* Anne Clough naturally vetoed the idea, fearing the reaction of "the Cambridge ladies." Although the students' desire to stage a play about matricide raises intriguing questions, they chose Euripides partly to defy convention, for Victorian classicists associated Euripides with chaos and irrationality. Yet the students may also have been tempted to revolt against their surrogate mother, Anne Clough, when they still could not rebel against their own mothers. After all, Clough was not such an essential figure, and her compulsive propriety infuriated the young women. She represented traditional womanhood, despite her position as principal. The male teachers both served as surrogate fathers and represented the life of the mind. Women students thus reconstituted family relations in a complex manner: the male teachers represented good fathers, and the female administrators bad mothers. This split infused college life with conflicting emotions. The women found communal support invaluable, but tensions permeated their relations with male faculty and female guardians.[31]

On the positive side, seclusion from the Cambridge community offered an idyllic existence. After completing work in moral sciences and lecturing near her home in Stamford, Mary Paley returned to Newnham to become resident lecturer in Newnham Hall. The hall opened in 1875 with twenty students. "Among these early students were Katherine Bradley . . . Alice Gardner, Mary Martin . . . Ellen Crofts, Miss Merrifield . . ., and Jane Harrison." She described the atmosphere in the hall:

> This was the Pre-Raphaelite period, and we papered our rooms with Morris, bought Burne Jones photographs and dressed accordingly. We played lawn tennis and JH designed the embroidery for our tennis dresses. Hers was of pomegranates and mine of virginia creeper and we sat together in the evenings and worked at them and talked.

Mary claimed that Alfred Marshall, her future husband, almost persuaded Jane to read for the moral science tripos rather than classics. Jane "always afterwards called him 'the camel' for she said that she trembled at the sight of him as a horse does at the sight of a camel." Perhaps Marshall, who later become a steadfast opponent of degrees for women, already showed evidence of his prejudice. Jane also took credit for bringing about the engagement, said Mary, by "stitching clean, white ruffles into my dress on that day," which must have made Mary look more attractive to him.[32]

Mary Paley mentioned Sunday evening parties for students and their teachers in the hall as a favorite entertainment. Elinor Ritchie described these to Hope Mirrlees as "very innocent and provincial affairs," with refreshments and music.[33] Jane often sang at these gatherings, her repertoire ranging from German songs to favorites such as "Adelaide" and "In the Gloaming." Such Cambridge figures as Henry and Eleanor Sidgwick and Professors Seeley, Cayley, R. C. Jebb, Alfred Marshall, and R. D. Archer-Hind attended.[34] Before her marriage, Eleanor Sidgwick hosted "sittings" for the Cambridge group interested in psychic research.[35] Students, however, most fondly remembered the cocoa party. They would finish their daily studies late in the evening and take turns inviting each other for cocoa and treats. Oddly enough, the cocoa party tradition originated in a grant from a benefactor. Originally, the donor had intended to provide a lady's maid for every five students, a provision that clearly reflected the benefactor's mind-set. The students claimed that they did not know what they would do with a maid, so Newnham's administrators altered the terms of the grant to provide half a pint of milk for each student when she had finished studying.[36]

Cambridge men viewed the Newnham students with "curiosity mingled with hostility." Hope Mirrlees mentioned "a particularly brilliant group of young M.A.'s either actually in residence, or often in Cambridge on visits, who used to come and play tennis with the Newnham students. This group included F. W. Maitland, A. W. Verrall, H. S. Butcher . . . Harry Cust, and the present Lord Balfour [Eleanor Sidgwick's brother, Arthur Balfour]." Clough's regimen, then, allowed for some carefully supervised mingling with the men.[37]

The novel experiment attracted many other visitors as well, both male and female. Turgenev came, and Jane was "sent off to show him round," only to be disappointed to find that "he spoke fluent English," depriving her of a chance to hear him speak Russian (RSL, 327). Ruskin visited, and Jane showed him the college's library. He gravely informed her that "each book . . . that a young girl touches should be bound in white vellum" (RSL, 327). Jane, a "rigid Tory," refused to "join the mob of students in cheering and clapping" for Gladstone's visit, and when her "friendly enemy" and fellow student, Gladstone's daughter, Helen, playfully brought him to Jane's room, she shocked him by citing Euripides as her favorite Greek playwright (RSL, 327). Jane may have been a Tory because of her northern roots, but it is interesting to note that she remained one while repudiating her background in so many other ways. She never completely rejected Yorkshire, and her politics were as much a subtle rebellion as a genuine conviction. She might don the trappings of Cambridge culture, but her anger at being forced to deny her past found other ways to emerge. Helen Gladstone represented everything Jane aspired to, but Jane felt ambivalent about those aspirations. Apparently she used Helen as a scapegoat and projected her mixed emotions onto both Helen and her father. She could rebel safely on political grounds, since politics never interested her. Disagreement on such issues posed no serious threat.

Among the visitors, "last, but oh, so utterly first, came George Eliot," who visited Jane's room, making her "almost senseless with excitement. I had just repapered my room with the newest thing in dolorous Morris papers. Some one must have called her attention to it, for I remember that she said in her shy, impressive way, 'Your paper makes a beautiful background for your face.' The ecstasy was too much, and I knew no more" (RSL, 327).

Contact with such distinguished visitors and the aura of Cambridge seemed heavenly to Jane. She had "quickly become the centre of a very select little coterie that included all the most sophisticated of the Newnham students."[38] This group accepted her partly because of her intellect and character, but primarily because of the persona she had created. She was able to preserve the Yorkshire elements she admired and look disdainfully at her companions while simultaneously embracing the ideal of a higher status. Cambridge signified a great step up for Jane, since she gained admission to a circle of upper-class families and exposure to important literary and scholarly figures. But the past proved inescapable. After outwardly casting off the taints of business, of provincialism, and of her stepmother's strict Evangelicalism, she now confronted the power of yet another stern Welsh woman, Anne Clough.

Hope Mirrlees perceptively pointed out that Jane disliked Clough because she shared Mrs. Harrison's Welsh background. The two older women differed greatly in temperament, but they also shared two characteristics: a pathological concern for public opinion and a certain power over Jane's behavior. Once again, Jane defied the attempt to curb her independence. Clough's "main work was . . . the management of the hall of residence, and it was in the internal life there that her influence was chiefly felt." That life entailed virtually constant interaction, in which Jane and Clough regularly clashed. Blanche Athena Clough, writing about the tension between Anne Clough and her students, might have had Jane specifically in mind when she described it. She wrote that although most early Newnham students accepted Clough's leadership,

> they were most of them old enough to have already tasted some amount of liberty, and there were some among them who, not unnaturally, thought that they could judge for themselves what it was or was not

> well for them to do, and who consequently saw no necessity for Miss Clough's supervision of their doings, and were not disposed to submit to her authority. Nor was Miss Clough possessed of precisely those qualities which were likely to make an immediate impression on girls in this stage of development. She was not learned, and her way of talking was rather confused, and she seemed to them to be fussy and nervous and inclined to interfere unnecessarily with what they chose to do.

Jane, whose career at Newnham spanned her twenty-fourth to twenty-ninth years, had successfully escaped her home only to fall under the supervision of another version of her stepmother.[39]

Elinor Ritchie and Alice Dew-Smith remembered Jane's clashes with Clough over her appearance. All accounts concur that Jane's unique style made her a striking woman, but Ritchie claimed that many, Jane included, considered Jane's face very plain, despite her aesthetic dress.[40] Violet Hunt, who met Jane after she had turned thirty, "says that her mouth & chin were always those of an elderly man. She herself [Jane] used to say that whenever artists painted her the portrait was sure to turn into that of a very distinguished gentleman." But Hunt also admitted that Jane had "the most beautiful figure she [Hunt] has ever seen." Jane's height and her often garish clothing particularly disturbed Anne Clough, and Ritchie recalled her pleading plaintively with her and Jane, " 'my dears, don't you think you could try to look a little less *tall*!' " Jane's ulster, "a frightful object, very loud yellow checques," offended Clough, who once offered to loan Jane a shawl to wear in its place.[41] She offered a shawl on another occasion "when she considered Jane's dress too *outré*," observing that "you can go in something, then you can take it off."[42] These offers infuriated Jane, who balked at the idea of pandering to convention. Clough also objected to the women's tennis clothes, "narrow flannel skirts and white shirts." Elinor Ritchie believed that Clough did not like the closeness that developed between her and Jane, and that she was "terrified" of Jane.[43]

Some of the few accounts of these years that survive indicate that her behavior as a student resembled her behavior as a young woman at home. She continued to rebel, and she attempted to set her own stamp on her life by wearing outrageous clothing and smoking. Had she been faced with another principal her response might have been less extreme. But Miss Clough, with her religious beliefs, Welsh heritage, and fear of public opinion which so closely resembled the same traits in Jane's stepmother, stirred her anger. Clough's role turned out to be that of a standard against which Jane rebelled.

Ostensibly, Jane rejected Clough's control because she felt that the movement for women's education needed no special protection or fostering.[44] In Jane's eyes, woman's desire for education did not directly challenge her place in society. In fact, the students generally went out of their way to assert their harmlessness. In many ways, they remained genuinely unselfconscious about their role. Although they perceived the portentousness of their experience, they were not politically minded enough to foresee its ramifications. Being on their own and enjoying the company of equals was a heady experience, but at first they were satisfied to study and were thankful for the opportunity. Their joy at having rooms of their own, sharing ideas over hot cocoa, and being away from home seemed harmless enough. Newnham students, at the start, did not aim to change the world; they merely wanted to fulfill their female roles as best they could. Their families, who had recognized their talents, allowed them an education, but they too expected no radical changes in behavior or ethos. Some of the students did indeed pass through the college relatively unscathed, but others, like Jane, sought something much more revolutionary than access to the public sphere. They discovered the power and attraction of the life of the mind and determined to use it to carve out a new place for themselves. Yet to a woman like Jane, becoming a part of the public world soon took second place to the other advantages of education: it became a means to regain lost status, to reject her provincialism once and for all, and to find a circle of which she could be the center.

College life, then, often alienated women students from their families by exposing them to new ideas. In her autobiography, Mary Paley offered a poignant glimpse of the breakdown of family ties. Her father, an Evangelical minister, "cared little for the outward forms of religion and had a horror of all tendencies towards laying stress on those rather than on its spirit." This was the religious atmosphere Paley grew up in, but her experience at Newnham confirmed society's fears about women's education. "Mill's Inductive Logic and *Ecce Homo* and Herbert Spencer and the general tone of thought gradually undermined my old beliefs. I never talked on these subjects with my father but we both knew that the old harmony between us had melted away." Jane described her alienation even more dramatically. Rather than to Mill or Spencer, she attributed her revelation to Aristotle. "It happened," she recorded,

> that the *Ethics* was among the set books for my year at Cambridge. To realise the release that Aristotle brought, you must have been reared as I was in a narrow school of Evangelicalism—reared with sin always present, with death and judgment before you, Hell and Heaven to either hand. It was like coming out of a madhouse into a quiet college quadrangle where all was liberty and sanity, and you became a law to yourself. The doctrine of virtue as the Mean—What an uplift and revelation to one born in sin! The notion of the *summum bonum* as an 'energy,' as an exercise of personal faculty, to one who had been taught that God

claimed all, and the notion of the "perfect life" that was to include as a matter of course friendship. I remember walking up and down in the College garden, thinking could it possibly be true, were the chains really broken and the prison doors open. (RSL, 342)

This passage made clear the stifling provincial atmosphere in which she had grown up. Aristotle's work alone could not account for the sense of liberation she experienced. Exposure to new ideas in general freed her from old constraints. No wonder that Janet Hogarth Courtney, daughter of a Lincolnshire Anglican clergyman, was sent to Oxford's Anglican Lady Margaret Hall in the 1880s rather than to one of Cambridge's women's colleges, which were thought to be centers of " 'advanced,' and therefore 'dangerous' notions."[45]

Carol Dyhouse points out that many women reconciled their ambitions with ideals of womanhood ingrained since childhood by marrying men far above them in ability and public stature.[46] Many Newnham students followed this path: Mary Paley married the Cambridge economist Alfred Marshall; Margaret Merrifield married the Cambridge classicist and subsequent colleague of Jane's, A. W. Verrall; Ellen Crofts, Jane's closest friend, married the Cambridge botanist Sir Francis Darwin. Having come to terms with their places in society, these women could marry and, in some cases, still teach (as did Mary Paley) without feeling deprived. They both internalized Victorian ideals of womanhood and utilized their knowledge in the new lives they led as members—if only by marriage—of the academic community. They rejected many values inherited from their families, but retained much of the old ideology of women's place and function in society. Jane, however, chose a different path. She could never reconcile that ideology with her own ambitions and spent most of her life using her intellectual work to make sense of her personal experience. The perpetuation of this tension, which her close contemporaries resolved fairly easily, accounts in large part for her extraordinary creativity and intellectual achievements.

Since education brought alienation from the family, it threw the women into even greater reliance upon each other for encouragement and companionship. College life as well as study fostered such intimacy. Thus the cocoa parties, tennis playing, and amateur theatricals assumed an even greater meaning. For the family was the center of Victorian life, especially among the upper classes. To reject it, if only to a small degree, meant leaving oneself unprotected from the rest of the world. The college provided a surrogate family based on common goals, and the intimacy fostered by shared living space and interests brought the women closer together.[47] Tension between students and principal further strengthened the relationships among students. For the first time, these women possessed power; power of the intellect and power to govern their own thoughts. Even if they never entered political life (Jane barely noticed the suffrage movement), their experience and contribution differed radically from their mothers'. These women took a giant step away from the security of traditional family life and began, albeit tentatively, to form a sort of female intellectual elite.

This intelligentsia became much more than a group of educated women, however. Besides absorbing new ideas, the students used their newfound intellectual freedom and mutual support to redefine their place in the world. Once they arrived at college and discovered mutual interests with other bright young women, they created a community in which they fit. At first fragile and tentative, their community grew and flourished as it reinforced their needs and desires. Having loosened the bonds that tied them to traditional ideas of womanhood, the women students set about filtering their acquired knowledge through their own experience and questioning old interpretations of women's role.[48]

Despite taking the radical step of forming their own fledgling intelligentsia, the women students remained conservative in motivation. They had not yet developed the self-consciousness to formulate a distinctly feminist ethos. Instead, they acted out of a desire to appropriate male experience. They identified with the concept of an intelligentsia because they wanted what their brothers—literal or figurative—had. Common intellectual experience seemed to set men apart and confer advantages that women lacked. Unconsciously, women students strove to create a separate but equal institution for themselves. They had no female models to follow. If they wanted to achieve, they could look only to their fathers or brothers for guidance. Nevertheless, identifying with males brought them firmly into the public world. Once they established themselves in academia, however, they used their knowledge to reflect on their own experience.

Jane turned her attention to the past by studying classics, and she offers a fine example of the influence of female experience on scholarship. She brought her own past to bear on the ancient past. By studying ancient Greece, she wrestled indirectly with the problems that troubled her. In turn, studying the ancient world helped her come to grips with her own world. Her gender influenced her work, and her years in the female community at Newnham helped reinforce this influence. The female community helped cushion the landing when she leaped from the stifling security of family life.

Like Dorothea Beale, Jane recognized the importance of communal life to the scholar. "If I had been rich," she wrote in her "Reminiscences," "I should have founded a learned community for women, with vows of consecration and a beautiful rule and habit; as it is, I am content to have lived many years of my life in a college. I think, as civilisation advances, family life will become, if not extinct, at least much modified and curtailed" (RSL, 345). The college thus took on the air of a convent, for it excluded men. College life could not completely eliminate hierarchy or personal responsibility, but it could free women from their most burdensome duties: their obligations to families and, especially, to men. In the traditional family, women's needs were subordinated to men's, whether they played the role of wife, mother, or daughter. Jane recognized, as had Christine de Pisan and Mary Astell, that so long as society tied women primarily to family interests, they could not carve out an independent existence.[49] The college offered intimacy and companionship without the necessity of family obligations. It vanquished, by replacing, the family, that center of conflict and barrier to independence. Jane sought not so much public participation as an end in itself as intellectual freedom and the chance eventually to understand her own experience through authorship. The act of writing conferred power—power to interpret and therefore control her own experience.[50]

Although college life may have seemed idyllic to those women who succeeded in forming new bonds, it could not protect them from all unhappiness or totally erase family ties. Two events shadowed Jane's years at Newnham: the death of her favorite half sister, Jessie, and a mysterious unhappy love affair, both of which occurred in 1876.

Jane rarely mentioned any of her stepfamily in either her correspondence or her memoirs, but Hope Mirrlees asserted that Jane thought Jessie very bright and urged her to come to Newnham. But in 1876, Jessie died of complications from appendicitis, a subsequent abcess, and scarlet fever. Jane so loved Jessie that she had missed a term at Newnham to nurse her at home.[51] But a subsequent event eclipsed even the tragedy of Jessie's death.

The event was an unhappy love affair with a Trinity College lecturer that Jane's friends, especially Hope Mirrlees, tried—even decades later—to cover up. When Hope referred to it in her papers, she wrote in the man's name and then scribbled over it, as she did with the name of the woman he eventually married. But she referred to him as Jane's "coach," which indicates that it was Henry Butcher. He came from Trinity to tutor Jane in Latin and Greek and often played tennis with the Newnham women. Two of his sisters, Augusta and especially Eleanor, became close friends of Jane's. All accounts describe him as a brilliant scholar, even as a young man, and his work in classics won him many honors throughout his career. He became a lecturer in classics in Trinity in the fall of 1874 and during the next year became engaged to Rose Trench. Since he could not marry and remain at Cambridge, he accepted a tutorship at Oxford in 1876. He was "the centre of a brilliant group of friends" as an undergraduate at Trinity and sounds the ideal match for Jane; but for his engagement to Rose Trench, he might have been.[52]

Hope gathered some of her information by writing down questions asked of and answers received from her correspondents, and she asked Elinor Ritchie if Jane knew of the man's engagement. Elinor replied, "We knew vaguely that there was a sort of engagement but I don't know why we didn't think it was final & it certainly came as a terrible shock when he told her it was irreparable—he broke it to her." Jane and her friends hoped he would change his mind about marrying Rose Trench, but he did not. Elinor wrote years later that "the tragedy of the wedding day is still as poignant with me as if it had been yesterday—but in spite of all she suffered I believe she would rather have gone through it than not." In her outline of Jane's life, Hope wrote melodramatically that "the great overshadowing event of her Newnham years was her tragic passion for [Henry Butcher]. He was her coach, & his beauty & charm were that of some Fairy Prince. He was already engaged to Miss [Trench] to whom he was devoted. This, however, did not prevent his falling in love (I gather) also with Jane. He seems to have been in love simultaneously with both young ladies. Everything else during her student years shrink into significance [*sic*]. The passion lasted for a good many years." Hope's description certainly made the affair appear tragic. But her caveat, the "(I gather)," gives reason to pause and examine this incident further. The estimable Mr. Butcher may well have been a cad, but Jane may also have misinterpreted his intentions. Proper Victorians took engagements seriously. The evidence suggests that Jane loved Henry Butcher, but that he did not love her.[53]

Jane herself connected the fate of her love affair and Jessie's death. Hope recorded that "Jane told me (but without a trace of bitterness) that it was partly owing to [Jessie's illness and death] that she only got a Second in her Tripos [in 1879]. It meant also leaving the man she was in love with at a very critical moment. And Lucy told me that she ascribed the calamity to her absence."[54] Hope makes yet another revealing parenthetical statement here. If she felt compelled to emphasize Jane's lack of bitterness over the tripos standing and the failed romance, odds are that Jane actually felt very bitter about them. Hope tended to protest too much when she feared Jane might appear human.

It is also interesting that Jane attributed her second to events that had occurred three years earlier. Either the affair truly devastated her or she needed a scapegoat on which to cast the blame for her academic performance and the unhappy love affair. Jessie, safely dead, could be held responsible for these failings. By playing a truly female nurturing role with her, Jane had fulfilled her responsibility and could not be held accountable for subsequent events. Above all, although references to Jane's love for Henry Butcher exist, no concrete proof that he ever made advances toward her survives. He broke the news of his engagement and presented it as final, but he may have done so only to discourage Jane from becoming interested in him. His engagement preceded his meeting

Jane, and that fact effectively made him unavailable. Hope commented acerbically in her notes, "mercy they didn't marry, as his mind remained stationary." In any case, he married Rose Trench in June 1876 and moved to Oxford, leaving Jane to pick up the pieces and continue her study of classics.[55]

In March 1879 Jane sat for the classical tripos. While waiting for the list to come out, a fellow student, Mabel Malleson, remembered, "Miss Harrison stayed in bed to hide her excitement." When the list appeared, she discovered she had received a second. She scored the highest of anyone in philosophy and the examiners were divided over giving her a first or second, but finally agreed on the latter. Jane mentioned the second only once, to Jessie Stewart. Her standing upset her, but it never stood in her way.[56]

No record remains to tell where Jane spent the remainder of 1879 or early 1880, but she probably returned home for a rest. In 1880, she took a job teaching Latin at Notting Hill High School, an Oxford girls' school, for one term. Notting Hill, only the second girls' public day school, had opened in 1874. Hope corresponded with a certain Mrs. Hogg, who had been a student of Jane's that term and remembered her as an uninspiring teacher. In a rare fit of generosity, Hope declined to blame this perception on Mrs. Hogg's inadequacies as a student. Instead, she attributed Jane's ineffectiveness to the belief that "both her heart & her brain were too full that year" for her to be a good teacher. No wonder: she had ended up right in the town where Henry Butcher was living, presumably in wedded bliss. Her students liked her, though, despite her distracted air. Hope wrote that they would "rush up after her lesson & ask if they might engage her for walking round the playground during the recess—'Miss Harrison, will you walk with me next Thursday?' 'With me next Friday?' etc.," to which she would reply " 'by all means, as long as you don't expect me to remember.' "[57]

Teaching did not satisfy Jane, however, and she remained in Oxford for only one term. Certainly, proximity to the man who aroused such painful memories must have made her uncomfortable. Still determined to escape her provincial background, Jane decided to go to London. She had heard Sir Sidney Colvin lecture in 1878 on his archaeological excavations at the Temple of Zeus at Olympia, and this lecture had stimulated her interest in archaeology. She left Oxford for London in 1880 to study Greek art and archaeology at the British Museum under Sir Charles Newton, keeper of Greek and Roman antiquities and a distinguished scholar who had excavated the Olympia site with Colvin in 1875. Jane felt she was leaving her past behind her and gazed hopefully toward the future, arriving in London on the heels of the aesthetic movement and embarking on a new plan of study.[58]

3

FROM ART TO MYTHOLOGY: LONDON, 1880–1897

"Comparatively few people care for art at all, and most of them care for it because they mistake it for something else," which in a way is true, but not necessarily unwise on the part of the majority, for art, as the Nineties were beginning to learn, was less important than life.

—*Holbrook Jackson,* The Eighteen-Nineties

Happily . . . bit by bit, art and archaeology led to mythology, mythology merged in religion; there I was at home.

—*Jane Ellen Harrison, "Reminiscences of a Student's Life"*

FIN-DE-SIÈCLE London's artistic and literary culture formed the backdrop for the eighteen-year sojourn between Jane Harrison's departure from and return to Cambridge. In addition to studying art and archaeology with Sir Charles Newton, she began to lecture and lead tours at the British Museum. Her published works dating from this period reflect the influence of her training at the museum: these years saw the appearance of her *Myths of the Odyssey in Art and Literature* (1882), her *Introductory Studies in Greek Art* (1885), and her collaborative effort with the art historian, D. S. MacColl, *Greek Vase Paintings* (1896). But although she finally attained the status she desired through education and a life in the city, her success left her dissatisfied. Her struggle to reconcile autonomy and dependence, love and work, exhausted her. Nevertheless, a new intellectual direction emerged from her experience and set a different course for both her intellectual and her personal lives.

Of all the swirling ideas and images of London in this period, Jane embraced aestheticism most enthusiastically. Besides drawing new attention to art, aestheticism also challenged conventional Victorian notions of propriety, gender relations, and sexual stereotypes. The debate over whether aestheticism's popularity justified its being referred to as a "movement" or an "ism" or whether it even existed at all matters less than its appeal to Jane. She embraced aesthetic tenets warmly enough to hope that readers of her *Introductory Studies in Greek Art* could "nurture their souls on the fair sights and pure visions of Ideal art."[1] Moreover, her enthusiasm for ideality in art led directly to a personal and intellectual crisis that steered her away from the study of art and down the road to mythology and, eventually, religion. She needed the Cambridge experience to find her home in the study of religion, but the London period marked the transition from art to mythology.

London life heightened the tension between Jane's background and her aspirations. Success in the city freed her from the stigma of provincial philistinism but challenged some of her most deeply rooted illusions about the superiority of high culture. She tried to leave her Yorkshire past behind, but she could not easily disregard the fundamental characteristics and beliefs formed by her Yorkshire childhood. Her presence in London, to say nothing of her conduct there or the people with whom she associated, itself constituted a repudiation of her past. Yet Jane rebelled more against the way in which her family imposed its Yorkshire ethos on her than against the ethos itself. Her excursion into high culture assumed an intensity of purpose because it freed her from the narrow vision of her family as well as providing scope for her many and genuine talents.

Judging by much of the company she kept in London, Jane was only one participant in a sizable migration of provincials to London. Sir Charles Newton, Jane's mentor at the British Museum, grew up in the county of Shropshire on the Welsh border, and D. S. MacColl came from a Scottish family. Jane gravitated toward fellow provincials who shared her cultural background. Ultimately, however, they assimilated far more successfully than she did. A man's university career provided him with contacts in the city that could be easily exploited. In addition, the desire to reject one's past and aim for a higher status seemed more appropriate in men than in women. Many of her acquaintances shared another important advantage. They came from clerical, rather than merchant, families. Jane knew many fellow northerners, but few of them faced similar class barriers. Finally, some obstacles remained insurmountable to women, as Jane learned during her London years. Despite her fine education and obvious capabilities, not all doors opened for her.

These London years also highlighted the larger social issue of the increasing number of women who chose to remain single. This trend created social upheaval, especially in London. For one thing, the presence of several thousand unmarried bourgeois women in London raised the issue of appropriate housing. Working-class women had obviously faced this dilemma for decades, but the influx of middle-class professional women brought a heightened awareness of the need for adequate housing. In addition, the growing number of single women created a demand for women's clubs. Initially, the clubs answered a need for good meals and companionship for busy women, but increasingly they created intellectually satisfying surroundings as well. Most important, though, the trend toward the single life (always assumed, in the public mind, to be celibate) made social critics and the general public reconsider its meaning. Most saw it as an alarming trend, but some looked beyond the immediate issue to examine why women might choose not to marry. At bottom, the debate centered upon the issue of choice. Did women consciously choose to remain single, or were they simply not asked to marry? The most perceptive writers on the question recognized that bright, educated women had to choose between an interesting career and a traditional marriage. All these issues played a part in Jane's London experience.

In later life, Jane looked back on this period as "mentally demoralising and very exhausting," and admitted, "I regret those lecturing years" (RSL, 335). She felt then, as at Cambridge later, nervous in front of audiences. Although "almost fatally fluent," she "could never face a big audience without a sinking in the pit of what is now called the solar plexus" (RSL, 335). Because she was a member of a large family, her "fortune was slender," while "social life [was] costly" (RSL, 335). Nonetheless, she still traveled extensively, making three journeys to Greece and then lecturing to varied audiences in London and the provinces. Her circle widened at this time, and she formed some of her lasting, if not most intimate, relationships. And, in spite of the difficulties of the period, she achieved great success.

Hope Mirrlees described Jane in her London days as a "passionate excited creature always in love & always emballée with someone fresh, rushing down to Cambridge to pour it all out to Mrs. V. [Margaret Merrifield Verrall]—who evidently took it all with a certain cool cynicism." Hope stated that "Jane suffered very much by what were purely Platonic attachments on her side not being understood & their object suddenly flinging his arms round her neck."[2] Jane's suffering, like the number of such attachments gone awry, should be taken with a grain of salt, although clearly she experienced intense emotions during this period. She worked hard in the mornings but was "socially at the disposition of her friends in the afternoon and evening" in her "rather austere sitting-room . . . which was furnished chiefly with books, a large writing-table, and a few comfortable armchairs."[3]

In 1880, Jane began studying at the British Museum, started on her *Myths of the Odyssey in Art and Literature,* and successfully applied to the Albemarle Club. She met Sir Charles Newton through a Newnham friend, Mabel Malleson. Jane was the "country cousin" in London, and the Mallesons' introduction to Newton "enabled her to get her foot upon the first rung of the ladder." Jane told Hope that Newton tried to "teach her worldly wisdom & the art of cultivating people who would be useful," but gave it up as a "hopeless task" because she was "too North-country." Jane cast off as many provincial traits as possible, but she never lost her contempt for mere social climbers. Eugenie Sellers, an acquaintance who later became an expert on Roman art, angered Jane by the "unscrupulous way she used people just to get on."[4] In that regard, then, Jane never fully assimilated into London circles. Newton helped Jane gain entrée to London cultural circles despite her social shortcomings. Although Elinor Ritchie characterized him as "very cold & inhuman," Jane enshrined him as "the original of one of her favourite comic characters, 'the old gent'—a dealer in what she called 'polished jests,' & quotations from Horace." As a fellow provincial, she probably better understood his character. Her own fear of appearing provincial may have accounted for her "very formal manner" with strangers, but Newton's exasperation with her, finally, proves that she never completely overcame her background.[5]

The Malleson family played a central role in Jane's early London career. Besides introducing her to Newton, Mrs. Malleson served as a personal confidante. Jane felt closer to her than to the daughter, Mabel, with whom she had been up at Newnham. Alice Dew-Smith described Hope Malleson paradoxically as "a chronic invalid with amazing vitality & an eager humorous delightful mind." Jane once "pleased her very much by telling her that her crest should be 'an express train rampant,' " which seems a decidedly odd insignia for an invalid. Late in 1881, Jane and Mabel Malleson set out on a trip to the Continent. They traveled to Hamburg, Berlin, and Munich, where they met the archaeologist Heinrich Brunn. They also visited Rome, Naples, and Athens, which they toured with Jane's old friend Henry Butcher and his wife, Rose Trench. Jane wrote to Mrs. Malleson that, with Jane's "Oxford friends" (the Butchers) for company, "Mabel's theology is likely to be well seen to," as "the husband is the son of a bishop and the wife the daughter of an archbishop." Not a hint of the old unhappiness over Henry Butcher's marriage appeared in the letter.[6]

Myths of the Odyssey was published while Jane was away on this trip. She wrote to Mrs. Malleson expressing pleasure over its publication. "I was delighted to see that my poor little book is not to perish unprinted," she wrote. "I began to tremble for it—but I am very cross with Mr. Rivington for exposing the fact that I belong to the frail gender. I specially desired to stand or fall irrespective of that." She had good reason to wish her sex kept secret. First, men dominated classical scholarship and would undoubtedly deride a woman's attempt to enter their field, which had long been an integral part of upper-middle-class male identity. Men who aspired to gentlemanly status built their self-image around a classical education.[7]

Even more important, *Myths of the Odyssey* constituted Jane's first scholarly endeavor. Both insecurity about the strength of her claim to a place in the world of classical scholarship and fear of what the initial reaction could mean for subsequent works fed her anger. So much was at stake, and she feared that disparaging critics would sabotage her first venture. Moreover, she recognized male society's devaluation of women's abilities. If she had used only initials instead of her full name, readers and critics would have assumed her to be a man, an assumption that would have made them more favorably disposed toward what she had to say.

The great contradiction of Jane's life, however, was that she combined an intense desire to succeed in a male field with an insistence on using a distinctly female voice. Such a voice remained tremulous in her first book, for she lacked conviction and faith in its validity. Writing about art under the influence of the aesthetic movement did not allow her to speak freely. She was, after all, still an outsider in London, and in *Myths of the Odyssey,* she tried to mimic the voices around her rather than train her own. Perhaps unconsciously she sensed this dissonance and worried that it marred the book. By the time of her great works on Greek religion two and three decades later, Jane had discovered her own voice and was no longer concerned about her gender. She later challenged traditional scholarly perceptions of Greek culture partly because she had learned from the new trends in anthropology and archaeology, but mostly because she refused to accept the preeminent theories of male scholars. During the London period, she was still internalizing a sense of control over her own experience and rejecting male society's attempts to interpret it for her. This rebellion against male authority joined forces with her rebellion against her family's authority, enabling her finally to control the interpretation of her experience and the creation of her sense of self.

Through her connections with the Mallesons and Charles Newton, Jane had the opportunity to lecture at the British Museum and at schools in the provinces. Although she found her life exhausting, her memoirs indicate she also benefited from her experience. If nothing else, she learned to look more realistically at the haute bourgeoisie to whose ranks she aspired. She observed women of London's upper class firsthand and criticized the emptiness and futility of their lives. In an 1891 interview in the *Pall Mall Gazette,* Jane came closest to addressing women's issues directly until her publication of two essays on women's questions between 1912 and 1914. Commenting on the popular revival of interest in Greece, Jane asserted that "what people want who attend lectures on Greek subjects is not a deep insight into these subjects," but rather "something, not very much, of the life and manners of a highly-cultured and intellectual race of older times." She accused her audiences of being driven by "curiosity rather than a desire for thorough knowledge." Women constituted a majority of her audience, and she divided them into two camps. The "mothers of young children are the most eager attendants" because they "want to share the interests of their children" and "to be able to talk to their boys . . . about these things, or they want to assist them in their studies." A few attend "so that they themselves may teach their children at home." But

> another large section of the audience is formed by the well-to-do women who have a good deal of leisure. They have nothing to do in the afternoon; their lives are somewhat dull and empty; they want some outside interest, and have not the energy to create one. To them the lectures come as a new amusement. They do not require very much, and the lecturer has to make the subject as light and varied as possible. Also he or she must be prepared to generalize a good deal, which is apt to result in much personal demoralization—the hunger for generalization in half-educated women is a fact that I have observed without quite understanding.

This passage contains a mixture of contempt and envy: contempt for the perceived frivolity of these women's lives, yet envy of their leisure. Throughout her London years, Jane had to worry about money and clearly resented her audiences which, with all their privileges, lacked the self-discipline to pursue a strenuous course of study and exhibited a high degree of philistinism. Moreover, had it not been for her stepmother's intervention, Jane might have aspired to the status of leisured lady herself. Instead, economic hardship had forced her to support herself by working.[8]

Aside from the economic motive, Jane also projected her own drive for intellectual growth and achievement onto her audiences. She realized that, as attractive as it might appear on the surface, the life of the leisured lady could also be stultifying. Her lectures drew the ladies out of themselves.

> I believe the great good is that lectures on Greek art create for these ladies an interest that is *non-personal.* You want to be a woman to know what the rest of that is. People talk of the good that lectures do by bringing people and classes together. I should like to talk of the good they do—for women, at least—by sending them away from each other into a decent place, to think where you only can think—alone; and the more remote the subject, the more averse from modern association—as Greek art is—the better.[9]

She recognized that conflicting demands on women created a fragmented life and prohibited female achievement. Even more significant, she emphasized education as discipline of the mind rather than vocational training. She accorded the greatest value to individual thought. Tellingly, she also believed that the ancient world made better food for thought than the modern. Its romance captured students' attention, but its paramount virtue for Jane lay in its potential for deflecting attention from the muddled present.

In her "Reminiscences," Jane spoke more maliciously about her London audiences. She referred to them as "British Lions and Lionesses" (RSL, 330). The Lionesses made an indelible impression on her. They were

> all spinsters, well-born, well-bred, well-educated, and well off. They attended my lectures on Greek Art. Greek Art was at that time booming and was eminently respectable. At home they gardened a great deal; they, most of them, had country houses. Their gardens were a terror to me, for I never could remember the names of the plants with slips attached to them, and to blunder over a plant's name was as bad to a Lioness as a false quantity. They kept diaries in which they entered accurately the state of the weather on each day. If they lived in London they promoted Friendly Girls and Workhouse Nursing. Above all, they kept a vigilant eye on the shortcomings of local officials. . . . In the spring and early summer they went to Italy, accompanied by a "young relative," whose expenses they paid; they voyaged mainly to Rome and Florence, but the more adventurous went to Assisi. Attired in mushroom hats, veils, and dust cloaks, they sketched a great deal. . . . The ordinary man was to them negligible, but they spoke of their own male relatives with respect and frequently quoted the opinions of "my uncle, the Dean," or "my cousin, the Archdeacon." They were a fine upstanding breed, and I miss them. They had no unsatisfied longings, had never heard of "suppressed complexes," and lived happily their vigorous, if somewhat angular, lives. (RSL, 330)

Jane sketched only a brief description of the Lions, noting that she had to watch them "from afar" as "real intimacy between the two genders was not in those days usual" (RSL, 330). From her experience with them at prize-givings during her tenure on the Girls' Public Day School Company, she observed that no Lion could give an address on such occasions "without telling you that it was the writing of Latin Prose that had made him what he was!" (RSL, 330). She concluded with an anecdote from a yachting trip she took with an unnamed British Lion: "He was oldish and had a deck-cabin. I happened to look in in passing. On the table lay a Bible, on the Bible a toothbrush. Cleanliness was 'next to Godliness' " (RSL, 331). These are mischievous portraits—loving, yet with an edge of contempt.

In addition to her work at the British Museum, Jane also lectured on Greek art at prestigious boys' schools. Both her style and her sex created a stir in these schools, which epitomized male privilege. Clifton's Archbishop Wilson, who arranged for Jane's visit there, later admitted that "he had not dared to tell his Council that the lecturer was a woman till all was over." In her audience, she later learned, had been Roger Fry and J. M. McTaggart, who "had deigned to discuss my lecture" (RSL, 331). She spoke at Eton and Winchester as well. At the latter, "one of the masters asked a very small Winchester 'man' if he had liked the lecture. 'Not the lecture,' he said candidly, 'but I liked the lady; she was like a beautiful green beetle.' In those days one's evening gowns were apt to be covered with spangles, and mine of blue-green satin had caught the light of the magic-lantern" (RSL, 331). Needless to say, neither blue-green satin nor the magic-lantern were standard equipment for most lecturers, and Jane undoubtedly appeared very dramatic. Her youngest half brother attended Harrow at this time and "wrote to say he had heard I was lecturing at Eton. It didn't matter, apparently, what I did at that benighted place, but he 'did hope I wasn't coming lecturing at Harrow as it would make it very awkward for him with the other fellows." Jane "saw his position and respected it" (RSL, 331). She had good reasons for avoiding professional contact with her family. At a Hull lecture she gave on Greek funereal monuments, her uncle Edward whispered, after viewing a slide depicting a mourning dog, "I don't think much of the Greek breed of dog!"[10] Spoken like a true Yorkshireman.

Jane succeeded as a lecturer not only because of her fluency but also because of her distinctive style. Besides her aesthetic dress, she used the technique (never quite abandoned) of incorporating dramatic bursts of light and sound in order to stir up her audience. Alice Dew-Smith recalled that she "lectured in a high strained voice, quite different to the voice her friends were accustomed to in her less formal moments, and had numerous affectations of speech about which we, her none the less devoted and admiring pupils, did not fail to chaff her afterwards." Alice also told Hope Mirrlees that one of Jane's favorite phrases was " 'this beautiful figure which I will now place before you,' " after which "would appear some very archaic figure . . . with arms pinned to its sides."[11] Frederick Myres, a Cambridge don but a prefect at Winchester when Jane lectured there, described her as a "splendid creature . . . with her splendid head of hair & bright eyes." Hope wrote that at the Winchester lecture, Jane spoke and showed her slides, and then finally, "throwing back her head, she burst into a chorus of Euripides in Greek. . . . The school jumped onto the chairs & cheered themselves hoarse—& for a week she was the talk of the school."[12] No wonder the Winchester man preferred the lady to her lecture.

Jane's work brought her into contact with some of the period's leading artistic and literary figures, and she described some of them briefly in her "Reminiscences." Robert Browning was "a cheerful, amusing gossip"; Tennyson, a "vain old thing" who was "very kind . . . according to his fierce lights. . . . He was intensely English and therefore not at his best as a conscious thinker; but he felt soundly, and his mastery of language was superb." Walter Pater and his sisters "opened their home" to her; she characterized Pater as "a soft, kind cat" who "purred so persuasively that I lost the sense of what he was saying." Henry James was an "ingenious spider" whom she liked to watch "weaving his webs," but to her "he had no appeal." Edward Burne-Jones "used often to come and sit with me, turning over drawings of Greek vases with eager, delighted fingers." She sometimes "sat with him as he drew strange visions" and regretted destroying the "many letters with whimsical illustrative drawings" that he sent her. She became close friends with Walter Raleigh and his sisters, especially Katherine (Kate). But the two figures she "most longed after, Christina Rossetti and Swinburne, were not diners-out," so she never met them (RSL, 328–39).

Other friends shared their memories of this period with Hope Mirrlees. Alice Dew-Smith and Henry Butcher's sister, Augusta, made slides for her lectures.[13] Elinore Ritchie Paul acted with Jane in a series of Homeric theatricals and tableaux staged in the 1880s. Jane appeared in some performances to benefit the London University Fund. These performances boasted "everybody of note—except Bernard Shaw" as participants, according to one source.[14] A professor of Greek at London University staged other theatrical performances at a Mrs. Peke's house. Hope Mirrlees dismissed the artistic Mrs. Peke as "a very rich vulgar woman." In one performance of *The Tale of Troy*, Jane appeared as Penelope, Elinor Ritchie Paul as Andromache, and Lionel Tennyson (the poet's son) as Odysseus. Jane's performance "caused quite a sensation. Everything about her performance—Mrs. Paul told me—her appearance, movements, voice, diction—was exquisite. And her performance received special praise from two of the most distinguished members of the audience, Gladstone and Tennyson."[15] Apparently, Gladstone had forgiven Jane her cool reception of him at Newnham several years earlier. Looking back, Elinor regarded *The Tale of Troy* of 1883 as "rather an absurd affair," but recalled that she and Jane enjoyed searching the British Museum's collection of Greek vases for inspiration. It was all "a very amateur affair & rather laughed at as giving society ladies an opportunity for dressing up & displaying their beauty as they did in the groups. It was all so unusual then. But Jane's acting was beautiful."[16] Moreover, Jane undoubtedly reveled in being perceived as a society lady.

Despite her wide circle of friends, Jane once told Hope that she "never felt really in sympathy with any of the generations whose *florait* was in the nineteenth century. It was F. M. Cornford's generation she first began to feel in sympathy with."[17] When she returned to Cambridge, she gravitated toward the Bloomsbury-Cambridge group, composed of people at least a generation her junior. Jane's outlook clearly situated her between her own generation and the next. Shackled by convention that both limited her sphere because of her sex and marked her as solidly middle class because of her family background, Jane felt more at ease with the younger people who supposedly did not pay such close attention to these factors. A part of her, however, desperately craved acceptance into London's cultural establishment. After all, much more than two hundred miles separated London from Yorkshire, and Jane's conflicting feelings toward her background intensified her desire for a place in London culture.

By all accounts, Jane reached the height of her attractiveness during her thirties. She also seemed within striking distance of attaining the status to which she had aspired for so long. She made many friends among London's haute bourgeoisie. Her work captured her imagination while leaving her time to socialize in artistic and literary circles. But if in her "Reminiscences" she skipped lightly over her difficulties in this period, her acquaintances did not. One of her difficulties was a long and complex friendship with a woman referred to as "Get" Wilson, and Jane's friends provided the few sketchy details that survive. Get and Jane shared a series of living quarters for many of Jane's seventeen years in London. When Get moved to the city in 1882, she met Jane through Mabel Malleson, according to Hope Mirrlees, and the two women took a maisonette in Notting Hill Gate. Get worked at "procuring trained nurses for the workhouse infirmaries," and Hope Mirrlees asserted that they "had nothing whatever in common." Jane's later snide reference to the British Lionesses who "promoted Friendly Girls and Workhouse Nurses" conveys resentment that may have lingered from her London years with Get. Hope Malleson, who knew both of them, believed that Get's "great sense of humour" was "their only bond." Get grew ill and finally became an invalid, and Jane later told Hope Mirrlees that the London years had been a "great strain on [Jane's] constitution" because of the "continual train journeys, the very great strain of lecturing, continual dining out & people," as well as ultimately having to nurse Get. Jane obviously felt torn by her London experience, for although she reached dizzy heights in her work, she felt keenly the pressure of keeping up appearances in society. As Charles Newton perceived, she may well have been "too North-country" to maintain the pace.[18]

Jane and Get's living arrangement presents another curious aspect of this story. Generally, middle-class women who did not live at home sought the comfort and protection of women's communities such as clubs or other housing specifically designed for them, both of which blossomed in the late nineteenth century. Often, these women worked within institutions that provided them with alternative living places, such as colleges or settlement houses.[19] Late in the century, however, the educated, middle-class woman living on her own became an increasingly familiar phenomenon. This new style of living created a demand for new kinds of housing. For her sixteen years in London, Jane was not connected with an institution that provided her with a place to live or a network of support. Her need to live on her own in London reflected her attempted entry into the male world of classical study and the British Museum. Jane belonged for many years to London's Sesame Club, which opened in 1895 and catered to bourgeois working women.[20] Her frequent travels alone during these years rounded out a striking picture. The "continual train journeys" to lectures in the provinces would have been novel experiences for a typical provincial middle-class woman. The professional woman sharing an apartment with a friend and commuting to her work presents an interestingly modern picture.

This aspect of Jane's experience also raises the issue referred to earlier, that of the increasing number of women who remained unmarried in the late nineteenth century. They created two problems for society: first, understanding why they did not marry, and second, trying to decide what to do with them. Education played a critical role in women's choosing to remain single. Freed from economic dependence on men and increasingly aware of opportunities in the public sphere, bourgeois educated women shrank from relinquishing their chances at an interesting life by marrying. They lived in a time when the ideology of marriage had not kept pace with broadening opportunities for women. For the most part, they faced a clear-cut choice between an interesting and fulfilling career or a traditional role as wife and mother. As was shown in chapter 2, some of the academic women Jane had known at Newnham could combine the two since life in Cambridge made it easier to maintain an active part in the academic world while also being married. But usually women could not find a way to "have it all," in modern parlance.

Some observers argued vehemently that women did not choose single life. Moreover, many of them could be particularly nasty in their attacks:

> Be patient, fair and gentle readers . . . we are well aware that you, and you, and you, might, had you chosen it, have been married. . . . And why are you still single? We do not know; nor would you yourself, perhaps, find it easy to account for the fact with historical distinctness. One thing only can you and we alike predicate negatively, yet surely: whatever may have been the causes which induced or compelled you to remain unmarried, we can name one which found no place among them. It was not love for single life itself; it was not deliberate preference for an estate alien to the whole constitution of women's nature. You did not *intend* to be an Old Maid.[21]

If women responded defensively to discussion of their marital status, no wonder; this author's attitude could provoke no other reaction. Observers linked marriage to ideal womanhood and perceived the very real threat that education posed to the continued viability of bourgeois marriage. For the most part, the women did not deliberately set out to revolutionize gender relations, but their actions and society's hysterical reaction no doubt made some of them recognize the radical nature of their ambitions.

Other writers worried over how middle-class women would live on their own. Their distinctive needs prompted some writers to address the housing question. In an article in the *Contemporary Review,* Alice Zimmern pointed out that lodgings modeled on establishments for men would not suit women's needs.[22] They needed a more psychologically stable environment to call their own. Men could live comfortably in lodgings that required them to leave their belongings in lockers during the day, but women needed to have a place that resembled home. The Ladies' Residential Chambers at Chenies and York streets and Sloane Gardens House met this need, but demand far outpaced supply. Usually, the units consisted of small separate bedrooms and sitting rooms with larger areas available for communal use. Zimmern applauded these efforts but raised a revealing point. She urged future planners to arrange for housekeeping service, claiming that professional women had no time to perform the work necessary to maintain their middle-class standards. Her concern for this aspect of single life reflected the great disparity in tone between discussion of middle-class and working-class needs.

More conservative critics suggested that young ladies in London lodge in private homes.[23] Such arrangements would both protect the young women from the dangers of city life and reassure their parents at home, presumably, many of them in the provinces. No doubt parents would have felt more comfortable if they could persuade their daughters to take this route not only to assure their physical safety but also to keep them within a traditional family setting.

Seeking support in the face of a world that did not understand their ambitions, bourgeois women began to congregate around the ladies' clubs that sprang up in the 1880s. Initially, these clubs provided a safe, comfortable, inexpensive place for bourgeois working women to have their meals. The planned housing did not provide kitchen facilities, and although they usually had some sort of dining room, many women preferred the sense of community fostered by shared interests in the clubs.[24] For most of Jane's years in London, she followed the alternative housing route of taking unfurnished rooms. She had brought a longtime family servant named Joanna from Yorkshire, who presumably provided meals, housekeeping, and a suitable bourgeois standard of living.[25]

The mystery of Jane and Get's relationship deepens as a result of a curious letter Jane wrote to Hope Malleson on April 30, 1882. The letter is marked "Private," and the absence of any other surviving correspondence discussing the issue only makes this fragment more incomprehensible. Jane and Get had "talked over plans a great deal," the letter states, and "she has given up the idea of Richmond"; apparently they had contemplated a move. Jane pointed out that if Hope

> had been in town as in the old plan she [Get] would so have liked the amalgamated scheme but she feels what I have been growing to feel more strongly day by day that without you it would be too complicated and difficult—we should be 4 sets of people in the house and no one there to be an oiler of intricate wheels—we both have the feeling that it is just the presence of some one like you that would make all the difference. As to my own personal difficulty I took counsel with my friends and they think that the malicious (not the merely conventional) and it is only the malicious I fear would at once if they found out you were not always in town think that the chaperonage I pretended to was merely specious and would be more inclined to gossip afresh than if I faced them independently—I feel the justice of this knowing as I do the sort of tongues I have to dread but I do not expect you will understand it for you are so far removed from these villainies.
>
> At present then Get and I think of looking about for unfurnished quarters of a very modest kind and as she is obliged to be very oeconomical I shall be so too and try to get a good deal of time abroad for a few years at least so that my constant presence in London living alone may not keep me too much before the public eye. I feel as if I had given you a great deal of trouble and worry for no purpose but I think it is Fate who has altered plans not I.[26]

It is impossible to tell what sort of indiscretions she hinted at, but her concern for chaperonage and public perceptions of female behavior indicate that she probably meant sex. At the very least, the letter implies that some people reproached Jane for some aspects of her behavior. The letter throws a different light on her passion for travel during her London years. She went on trips as much to escape from wagging tongues as to fulfill her desire to explore new worlds. Nothing in Jane's papers sheds light on who would have shared the house with her, but whatever the circumstances she could not face the inevitable criticism. A resurgence of Yorkshire conventionality may also have fueled her reluctance. Certainly her parents would have disapproved of any arrangement that appeared improper, but Jane herself retained a strong streak of conservatism. Above all, this letter offers an instancc of a potentially revealing incident's being obscured by Jane's destruction of her letters, leaving behind only the mystery and no clues with which to unravel it.

Get's decline into invalidism coincided with yet another personal crisis in Jane's life: her failed romance with the art historian and critic D. S. MacColl. Jane attracted other admirers in the London period, but none to her liking and none very serious. Hope Mirrlees stated that "there had been a man in her life, whose name she would never divulge, who had an agonising passion for her." According to Hope, Jane "admired & liked him tremendously & did everything in her power to make it easier for him." She referred to the man only as "T.," but Bella Napier, a good friend of Jane's during these years, mentioned a Mr. Tatton, a suitor of Jane's of whom Bella used to say, " 'my dear, of *course* you can't marry a man with a face like a penny bun!' "[27] R. G. Tatton administered the Oxford University Extension Lectures in London. He thought Jane "perverse" because she disliked Bernard Bosanquet, who "was certainly one of the cleverest men she had ever met in her life." He attributed her dislike of Bosanquet to the fact that "she liked people to be warmhearted" and "felt something cold about Bosanquet." He also quoted Jane's description of her attempt to give up smoking: she felt " 'not so much a craving, but a *terrible* loneliness.' " But poor Mr. Tatton paled into insignificance beside the brooding Scot, Dugald Sutherland MacColl, who influenced both Jane's personal life and the future direction of her scholarly work.[28]

Sutherland, nine years Jane's junior, was the son of a Scottish Presbyterian minister. He was born in Glasgow, but the family moved to London's Kensington borough in 1873. He went up to Lincoln College at Oxford in 1881, placing in the second class in 1884. After inheriting a small income from his mother, he spent much of his time traveling, lecturing, and painting. When he and Jane met, he was traveling extensively. From 1890 to 1896 he was art critic for the *Spectator* and then until 1906 for the *Saturday Review.* He wrote on art and architecture, and in 1906 became keeper of the Tate Gallery. From 1911 to 1924 he served as keeper of the Wallace Collection, and then devoted the rest of his life to writing and painting.[29] Augustus John, whose first exhibit Sutherland reviewed favorably, characterized him as "pawky and didactic," an "accomplished writer" with "somewhat limited" perceptions.[30] He exhibited his didactic nature in his behavior toward Jane by denouncing her lecturing style as too aesthetic.

Although scholars have referred to the affair with Sutherland, none has fully explored its implications.[31] Consequently, the true nature of their relationship has remained shrouded in mystery. In her notes, Hope Mirrlees offered a skewed version of it. She warned that "one must not take the *crise* [of Sutherland's attack on Jane's style] *too* seriously. Without doubt it was very serious for one of the personages; but I am sure Jane bore it with the greatest equanimity. Jane's *ironeia* prevented her, & would prevent her taking any *crise* too seriously." Elsewhere, Hope admitted that it was "by means of this *crise* that [Jane] became a mythologist." In all fairness, even many of Jane's closest friends also denied or underestimated Sutherland's importance in her life. Helen Salter recalled that her mother, Margaret Merrifield Verrall, "at first considered

D. S. M. purely a passing fancy."[32] Alice Dew-Smith, who should have known better, told Hope Mirrlees that Sutherland "was a dear comic character to Jane," who "used to call him 'the old post' in the tone of voice she used when speaking about old dogs." Perhaps out of loyalty, Jane's friends refused to acknowledge how much the failed romance devastated her.[33]

The main facts of the case are that Sutherland accused Jane of being too aesthetic in her work; that he later asked her to marry him; that she refused; and that she fell into a deep depression when he married Andrée Zabé in 1897.[34] It appears that the damage caused by Sutherland's criticism of her work continued to affect her long after the immediate crisis had passed: she refused to marry him precisely because she could not reconcile herself to his intellectual and personal power over her.

Jane first met Sutherland at a luncheon in the winter of 1886 at Ashbourne, the home of her old friend Peveril Turnbull and his wife, Phyllis. Sutherland must have heard Jane lecture soon after they met, for the apparently scathing letter arrived sometime in late January or early February 1887. It no longer survives; Jane "tore it up in the fury of first reading," but responded in a letter dated February 6, 1887. She said in passing that his visit the previous night would not have been unwelcome "a month ago," for then he "had not written that—to me—fatal letter."[35] It is disappointing that the letter no longer exists, but the story seems to be as follows. Jane's lecturing technique attracted audiences, but Sutherland believed that her lectures were "performances of an overheated, sensationalistic and superficial kind and related them to her desire to live as intensely and beautifully as possible."[36] Certainly she adopted an aesthetic style. Aestheticism appealed greatly to a young woman raised in a strict Evangelical household, who rebelled throughout her life against the drabness and formlessness of her stepmother's religion. Her behavior, however, greatly displeased Sutherland, and his criticism so devastated her that she actually changed her style. This response alone seems ample evidence of how deeply she cared for him.

Her surviving letters to Sutherland from this time, though, reveal more. It is not clear exactly when he proposed to her, but even these early letters, written when they had been acquainted only a few months, indicate a growing intimacy. Some are charming, probably dating from the early days of their friendship, and others reveal Jane's growing trust in him. She frequently lets the mask slip and tells him things about herself that she does not want made public. Tracing their deepening relationship through the letters proves two things: that it was an intimacy of equals, despite Jane's surrender to Sutherland's criticism, and that it was a much deeper, more intuitive attachment than any that followed. Sutherland's background and temperament closely resembled

Jane's, and the surviving letters attest to a shared sympathy unequaled in any of her other relationships.

A sample of some early playful notes demonstrates how charming Jane could be, especially to those closest to her. Inviting Sutherland to the theater, she wrote, "God wills that I and three others of his chosen ones should go and see 'Partners' (Haymarket—Mr. Tree) Thursday or Friday. Will you be one of us? . . . The piece is, I believe, bad, and only Mr. Tree is much good—but the leading seems so plain I feel I must go and chance disgust. It is the last theatre I shall enter till I sit with Dionysos himself beneath the 'hill-top'—so please come." In a "left-hand invitation," she said, "should you not be too bored to try 'gringoire' Friday, Nov. 4, I am almost sure I have a spare ticket. I had asked another man, but have had no answer for 5 days so I conclude he is out of town." She asked forgiveness for her tactless wording by explaining that she thought he was "not available Friday." Just before the great aesthetic crisis, she invited him to tea at the Albemarle Club, to which she had once belonged. "I cannot play hostess to you, for I was turned out of that select club years ago, but I have suborned one selecter than myself to provide tea and muffins, and my Kensington Square playfellow [Lionel Robinson] is coming here to chaperone us and to meet a mere heiress—*not* a beauty, so no fasting is enjoined—you can come in your worst mood." The letters exhibit great charm and vivacity; unfortunately, soon after the last one, the great crisis occurred and they took on a new tone. They also began to illuminate the dark side of Jane's London experience.[37]

The letters are worth quoting at length, for they fully reveal the complexity of Jane's relationship with Sutherland. On February 6, 1887, right after receiving his criticism, she apologized for treating him rudely during his last visit.

> I think I had better tell you the real reason that your presence was so unwelcome last night, as I do not want you to credit it with any form of personal rudeness.
>
> A month ago I should simply have been a good deal gratified by your coming but then you had not written that—to me—fatal letter. I daresay you have forgotten its—rather strongly worded—contents, which have been rankling in my mind ever since—I tore it up in the fury of first reading but unfortunately that only made me remember every word of it. I knew from the first that my rage against you was caused by the simple fact that you were right & I was wrong—but it was not till I began my work again that it was borne in upon me *how* wrong—how much more wrong than you could possibly divine—The worst is that all the success I have had has been based on wrongness, I could always hold an audience—any fanatic can—not by the proper & legitimate virtue of my subject or its treatment but by the harmful force of an in-

tense personal conviction—I had grown into a sort of Salvationist for Greek art—probably a sort of educated decency withheld me from the constant obtrusion of my gospel or someone would before now have told me less politely—not more pointedly—that I was a fool—but none the less the faith in my gospel was the secret of my strength.

The practical proof of this is that I feel now that all virtue is gone out of me; lecturing this term has been nothing but a dreary mechanical struggle & if my hearers have not found it out as they soon will it is only that something of the manner of conviction clings.

Last night to this depression your coming added a hitherto unknown sensation, that of absolutely paralysing nervousness—I can only recall that I went on for an hour doggedly determined to make audible sounds—however the failure more or less matters very little & the term's work has to be got through somehow—

It will seem to you—with your sane mind—as absurd that the shattering of a theory should depress as that the building of one should inspire—& indeed it is not the shattering of any particular theory but the giving up of the habit of mind that demands a creed—I know by experience that one gets on much better in practice without a religious creed than with one, but it was none the less desolate at first to live without God in the world—art has to me taken & more than taken the place of religion & my work for it was I see only another form of an old & I thought long dead personal fanaticism—which is, it seems, hydra-headed.

I have added to this personal misery the depressing reflection that I have done a great deal of harm tho'—as you pleasantly point out—'not as much harm as I might.' . . .

At the present moment I feel that I shall never teach & certainly not preach any more after this term—, I tried indeed a wild plunge from theory into practice but with no relief. . . .

A right-minded person would be grateful to you & perhaps I should have been but that some of your arrows were dipped in a peculiarly irritating poison.[38]

Such an extraordinary outpouring deserves a closer look.

As Jessie Stewart and Robert Ackerman noted, this crisis resembled a religious conversion, a revolution in ethos on the purely intellectual level. In true Evangelical style, Jane overstated the error of her old ways and berated herself for indulging in such egotism. The conversion interpretation is sound, as far as it goes. The letters that follow chronicle a change from deep depression to a final acceptance of the new order. But Jane's self-awareness may be the most impressive aspect of this letter. In the middle of the crisis, she clearly recognizes her motives for studying and lecturing and struggles with her most terrifying demon: the need to believe ardently in something, to fulfill the religious impulse without resorting to theology.

The subtle but highly significant undertones of the series of letters are remarkable. Sutherland's influence and Jane's wholehearted acceptance of it are equally important. For one thing, they had been acquainted for only a few months, at most, half a year. Second, Jane had achieved enormous success with her extravagant style, which Sutherland found so objectionable, over a period of nearly five years, and she had reached many of her goals. It seems curious that one man's opinion so radically disrupted and altered her work. It appears that Jane was not only in love with Sutherland but so completely and uncharacteristically taken with him that his power over her threatened her autonomy. Sutherland shared Jane's North-country background and temperament, although he seemed more at ease in their London world. His Scottish Presbyterianism and taciturnity may well have reminded Jane of her father, thereby increasing her attraction to him. He played the role of mentor and therefore established an intellectual connection with her. The intellectual crisis, Sutherland's marriage proposal, and Jane's refusal are intimately connected. If the crisis over aestheticism had not occurred, Jane may well have married him and never produced her great works.

Ever resourceful, however, she threw up smoke screens to cover both the intellectual conversion and the refusal to marry. In her "Reminiscences," she indirectly excused her surrender to Sutherland's criticism by claiming that art was "a subject for which I had no natural gifts," and that since her reactions to art were "always second-hand," she was "docile and open to persuasion." She felt more confident about literature, where she was "absolutely sure" of her own tastes (RSL, 335). Judging by the ease with which she deflected the barbs of her later critics and the ferocity with which she defended herself and her colleagues, it is difficult to imagine her being persuaded by anyone.

In personal terms, she justified her refusal to marry Sutherland by citing an unnamed condition that prevented her from bearing children. Hope Mirrlees referred only vaguely to "fibrous tumors." In her early thirties, Jane learned "that she could never have children at risk of almost certain death" and "immediately decided that she could never marry." With characteristic denial of her emotions, she later told Hope Mirrlees that "it was not a really great tragedy." After Sutherland married, she said, "so far as was possible I kept clear of passion & threw all of myself into close friendship based on work. I starved the physical side of my nature & as sometimes happens with ascetics grew into a certain distaste for it." This extraordinary admission at least acknowledges her abhorrence of sexuality, but altogether ignores the enormous effort required to suppress the anger that led to it. After her passion for Sutherland nearly betrayed her self-control, Jane reined in her emotions and clamped the lid on all feeling. She sensed the value of the emotional life in her observations on ancient society, but only because of the price she paid of keeping her own emotions rigidly controlled.[39]

Her letters to Sutherland also reveal a depression much deeper than hitherto recognized. The next letter is undated, but its contents indicate that Sutherland responded to her outburst of emotion and tried to calm her fears. She wrote in return:

> Thank you more than I can say—you give me a sort of hope not that I have not been intensely wrong but that I may work right again—& not give everything up—my work is so absolutely my life that the horror of feeling it go as I felt on Saturday utterly unnerved me—
>
> The sting of your first letter was that you understood me & the helpfulness of your last is the same. I am generally so well supplied with *autarkeia* that I must own in self defence that I cannot sleep now except under drugs; but commit this secret to the grave as I would not have it known for worlds—I know in this state one cannot—if one ever can—distinguish between the moral & mental & the physical so I shall commit myself to nothing desperate till I can sleep—I wish I could think that all the remorse I feel would be resolved with sleeplessness but I cannot—probably your letter only lighted a long laid train of discontent, but it seemed to cast a sudden flash of light on every foolish thing I had said or written. I am horribly ashamed of the trouble I have given you—thank you again.

It seems remarkable that Jane confided her dependence on drugs for sleep—however harmless a habit it may have been—to someone she barely knew and who had just upset her whole world. Sutherland's criticism alone probably did not reduce her to this state. Clearly, the London period had not gone as smoothly as she would have had the world believe. Hope Mirrlees remembered hearing that Jane once became violently ill upon witnessing a torture scene in a play during these years and had to be helped from the theater. Such sensitivity to staged violence indicates a great deal of fear, anxiety, and repressed anger and provides more evidence that she suffered from depression in those days. She was unhappy, despite her triumphs, and Sutherland delivered the crushing blow.[40]

For all his audacity, Sutherland helped nurse Jane out of her despair. In response to a letter in which he must have suggested a new direction for her work, Jane wrote:

> I am not quite sure what I ought to say. I have decided . . . to give up entirely next year all lecturing that is purely lecturing, because I see only too clearly that it is the Epideiktikos Logos that has been my undoing—but I am not sure whether I need exclude Extension work in

> my Self-Denying Ordinance—&, if I can persuade myself I need not, new work for it would be a god-send as I shall have a good deal of spare time & energy on my hands—
>
> You would not so readily stand sponsor for me if you knew how badly—just because I lacked the sensational element—I have done my Wimbledon extension work—however, I do honestly think I can put all that behind me—
>
> The pay question happily does not matter to me next year—it is only when I have to be abroad a great deal that I am constrained to avarice.

The subtle jab at Sutherland connecting the lack of the "sensational element" with her inadequacy as a lecturer shows a resurgence of spirit. She envied Sutherland his ease before audiences and wrote after hearing him lecture that he had "found for lecturing the 'more excellent way' as remote from dulness on the one side as from sensationalism on the other." She thanked him for "forgoing sleep or smoke to 'exchange ideas' " with her.[41]

By November, Jane could write a more encouraging letter describing her return to lecturing.

> Don't write me down a confirmed egoist if I tell you that your good wishes *did* bring me good luck—I had a superstition they might that is why I asked for them.
>
> I was wretched & almost desperate about the Eton lecture & all the demons of last spring were camping about my bed but I was resolved, come what might to try your plan & trust the subject to its own value & rid myself of my hateful habit of trying to force upon it meretricious effects—& you were absolutely right. I felt directly I began to speak it all went ever so much better. . . .
>
> I wonder why you so often say just the right thing to me—I acquit you of all intention you must be an instrument of the gods—I certainly won't call you anymore a 'messenger of Satan'—happily I don't now mind the least being your debtor. . . . I have begun lately—only quite lately & perhaps too soon—to think of you as friend not foe—I think you must promise (as the candid friend)—if you see me falling into the old or any new form of lunacy to write me a thoroughly unpleasant letter. . . .
>
> Of course I feel all the more keenly what a knave or a fool (I am not sure which) I was last year & what dishonour I did to a peculiarly self sufficing subject but no remorse can mar the holy calm that has set in—a peace better even than that born of whiskey & soda.
>
> P.S. Do not answer this & do not laugh immoderately—you may laugh a little—but at yourself—cast for the double role of Paraclete as Convincer of Sin & Consoler in my miracle play—
>
> Is it that ministerial ancestry of yours that will out?

The crisis past, Jane and Sutherland settled into a friendship that lasted nearly ten years and led to the publication of a joint work, *Greek Vase Paintings,* in 1896. Jane's conversion was complete. For his part, Sutherland claimed merely to have "turned her attention to the folk lore & ritual side of Greek mythology." Hope Mirrlees credited him with introducing Jane to the mythological studies of Wilhelm Mannhardt and Theodore Best. Clearly, to Jane the experience held far more significance. There is a feeling of total collapse in the letters—a radical break with a very successful past. It is not clear when Sutherland proposed to her, but it is not so hard to understand why she refused him. He held tremendous power over her, and she gave up an integral part of her style to appease him. It seems as if the intellectual conversion frightened her; it was one thing to relinquish her style, but quite another to face losing her meticulously crafted self to another person.[42]

Sutherland's criticism touched other aspects of Jane's work, also. Her *Introductory Studies in Greek Art* (1885), which expressed her aesthetic infatuation with Greece, contains ideas that disappeared from her work after her "conversion." She remained passionate about Greece and the Greeks, but drastically changed her focus. Before 1886, the glory of Greece meant the Parthenon frieze and the Olympian gods; everything prior to the fifth century B.C. existed only to contribute to the greatness of Athenian art. After Sutherland's devastating letter, Jane abandoned ideality and kind words for the Olympians. Ironically, Sutherland himself sounded the aesthetic note in his preface to their *Greek Vase Paintings* in 1896. He cited the book's great virtue of making high culture accessible to a mass audience.[43] But he apparently failed to notice that Jane's first work, *Myths of the Odyssey in Art and Literature* (1881), contained hints of her later fascination with religion and ritual.[44] In this work, Jane took her first tentative steps toward religion. She immediately backed away from many of the issues she raised, but nevertheless lifted the veil that hid the archaic past from the classical age.

In the preface to *Myths of the Odyssey,* Jane justified examination of artistic works on Homeric themes by claiming that they shed light on the larger context of the myths and helped in tracing their origins. The search for origins became her primary quest after her conversion to the study of ritual, but her first book prefigures it. Commenting on the relationship between literary and artistic representations of Homeric myths, Jane wrote, "frequently we have plain evidence that it is not the artist who is borrowing from Homer, but that both Homer and the artist drew their inspiration from one common source, local and national tradition. Nothing perhaps makes us realise so vividly that the epics of Homer are embodiments, not creations, of national Sagas, as this free and variant treatment of his mythology by the artist."[45]

She later transformed the assertion that a group experience precedes literary or artistic representations into the belief that ritual emerges from group projection and precedes both mythology and religion. The difference lies in emphasis: she still followed principles of aestheticism and therefore focused on the artistic rather than the social or ritualistic. But she was already growing impatient with the traditional literary and rational approach to the ancient Greeks, dating back to the Greeks themselves; the "writings of scholiast and grammarian" lead to "much verbal intelligence of our poet, but perhaps attain to but little additional sympathy" (vii–viii). Early in her career Jane understood intuition's part in creating a picture of ancient Greece. Most telling, however, is her reason for not "dealing, except quite incidentally, in the questions of comparative mythology." Aside from her view that "the express object" of the study "forbade my treating of the several myths in their purely *literary* form," she believed "the materials for such treatment to be at present incomplete" (xii). She did not close the door on comparative mythology; she merely recognized that it remained in its infancy.

The aesthetic influence reared its head throughout the book. She stated her aim succinctly in the preface:

> I believe the educational value of a study of archaeology to consist far more in the discipline of taste and feeling it affords, than in the gain of definite information it has to offer. . . . the best gifts of archaeology,— the trained eye, quick instinct, pure taste, well-balanced emotion,— these we may be thankful if we gain in a lifetime; and each man must strive to attain them for himself. (xii–xiii)

She remained under the spell of the perceived rationalism of ancient Greece although the very source of her study, the Homeric epic, dated from the disorderly archaic period. Jane extricated herself from this paradox by examining later classical and Hellenistic representations of the myths.

Mainly in her comparison of classical Greek with Roman artists Jane gave full reign to her aesthetic prejudices. *Myths of the Odyssey* contains analyses of such myths as those of the Cyclopes, the descent into Hades, the Sirens, and Scylla and Charbydis. All offered horrifying tales warranting graphic depiction, but Jane consistently preferred the classical interpretations, which tended to soften their terror. In her discussion of a bas-relief portraying Odysseus' offering of wine to the Cyclope, Polyphemus, before he gouged out the giant's eye with a log, Jane attributed its popularity with classical artists not to its dramatic content but to its "scope for skilful grouping and posture," which "needed only some hint of horrors past and to come to make the picture dramatic and yet not disgusting." Late Roman artists portrayed the incident more graphically, but "Greek vase and Etruscan sarcophagus are alike free from this revolting realism" (5). Furthermore, in a footnote to this section, Jane praised Greek and Etruscan artists for portraying Polyphemus with two eyes, as opposed to the reprehensible Roman artist who insisted on giving him only one. Such "shameless realism" showed, in her opinion, a "most morbid craving after sensationalism" (8).

Her analysis of the Cyclopes also prefigured her dislike of the family, which reached its pinnacle thirty years later in *Themis.* First, she discussed their ambiguity as neither mortals nor gods and their association with nature deities:

> These wild nature-forces, whether of water or of fire, were in themselves, so to speak, neutral; they might be tamed to the service of the gods and of men; then we have Cyclopes for giving thunderbolts and uprearing masonry; they might expend themselves in lawless violence; then we have the giant-robber of many lands. (29)

But it is not their ambiguous status or natural power that made them so distasteful to the Greeks:

> The special characteristic of the Greek giant-robber is, as was likely, that he lacks *social* virtue; no more dismal, more barbarian picture could be presented to the mind of the city-loving Greek than that of a "froward, lawless folk, who have neither gatherings for council nor oracles of law." Thus the Cyclopes became for Greek political writers the type of primitive barbarism, *when the family was the only social unit.* (29; italics mine)

In Jane's view, archaic Greece denounced the family as the sole basis of society. Families only encouraged competition among members for limited attention and resources and worked against the interests of society at large. Ironically, the classical Greeks attached grave importance to the family unit, so much so, in fact, that they based social organization on family membership. Jane projected her loathing of her own family onto the ancient past and attributed to archaic Greece her own disdain for the family as the basis of society.

Etruscan artists' failure to maintain their distance from the horrors of Odysseus' descent into hell and its graphic portrayal in art prompted Jane to muse that "perhaps it was only for a few happy centuries, when beauty reigned supreme, that even the Greeks could resist the strong doctrinal impulse which besets mankind to people hell with horrors" (144). Ever mindful of her stepmother's rigid Evangelicalism, Jane knew firsthand of this irresistible impulse. Comparing the grotesque style of Etrurian to the earlier Greek depictions of hell, Jane mourned the loss of "that Hellenic euphemis, that quick instinct for beauty and limit, which prompts the true Greek artist to conceal deformity and soften terror" (141).

When she turned to the final chapters on the powerful female figures in the *Odyssey,* the treacherous Sirens and the grotesque Scylla, she changed her tune slightly. She switched rather abruptly from dogmatic aestheticism to a more subtle understanding of these portrayals, and the change can be explained only by a concomitant shift from purely artistic to more mythological-religious analysis. In the process, Jane exhibited the germ of familiarity with anthropological data and fascination with nature deities that became the hallmark of her later work. Her analysis retained the aesthetic belief in the moral uses of art, but also showed a glimmer of comprehension of the power that these symbols exerted.

The classical interpretation of the Sirens disgusted Jane, for it marked the failure of her beloved Greeks to live up to her expectations. One believed that, since the Sirens have a beautiful song, they must be lovely in form as well. But even the classical Greek artists, for all their love of serene beauty, knew that these temptresses could be simultaneously alluring and dangerous. Moderns like Jane might

> turn, perhaps with something akin to disgust, from these hybrid bird-women creatures with heavy wings and awkward flight, and ask almost indignantly, Why care to investigate an art whose sole purpose seems to be degradation? But a closer inquiry, here as elsewhere, will modify our views; we shall learn to see that our conception even of Homer's Sirens loses nothing, and by antithesis gains much; we shall feel that these quaint forms which at first so vex our imagination have a strange beauty, a deep moral and religious significance of their own, which the conditions of Homer's art and time alike forbade. (146)

Despite her ultimate need to fall back on the Sirens' "deep moral and religious significance," she implicitly accepted their mystifying natural force. The archaic literary vision and its classical representation agreed when it came to the power of these female figures who were so intricately connected to the natural world.

In discussing the artistic representations of Scylla, Jane appears to retreat from her temporary infatuation with the terrible Sirens and initially offers the reader a celebration of the classical triumph of artistic beauty over literary evidence. Quoting Butcher and Lang's translation of the *Odyssey,* she gives her readers a portrait of the fierce Scylla:

> Her voice is indeed no greater than the voice of a new-born whelp, but a dreadful monster is she; nor would any look on her gladly, not if it were a god that met her. Verily she hath twelve feet all dangling down, and six necks, exceeding long, and on each a hideous head, and therein three rows of teeth set thick and close, full of black death. (183–84)

She further asserts that such a grotesque figure would never find its way into Greek art.

> We can fancy that some Semitic craftsman might have attempted a faithful copy of this hideous sea brute . . . but the Greek artist refused almost from the outset to embody conceptions so unmeasured. If ever the great Homer sang of a hybrid beast too horrible for representation, the artist refused to produce a servile copy of the poet's picture. (185)

Then, just as she seems to be leaving the Scylla in the classical convention, she gives herself away: the Scylla's ferocity cannot be denied even in classical representations. Here, Jane betrays one of her rare preferences for the Hellenistic representations of Scylla, precisely because they tone down her viciousness, which Jane fears. A terra-cotta figure from Aegina and a rhyton from Naples depict her "in a calmer aspect,—symbolizing, one might fancy, the sea at rest, with all its hidden terrors lulled to peace for a while" (194). The rhyton gives "the final and more finished conception of Scylla: the monstrous elements are all present, but so softened, so skilfully combined, that their horror is abated, the general type has been preserved, but there is no rigid adherence to unsightly details" (195). For the first time, Jane admits the existence of a real terror beneath the serene facade, admits that it is the depiction of the "unsightly details," not their existence, that so offends her. Whereas she normally rejects claims that a time really existed when the Greeks were not rational, in her discussion of Scylla, she finally admits the possibility. She may accept a nature deity embodying the sea partly because of her familiarity with the Yorkshire coast; still, it is a breakthrough in her thought.

This breakthrough set Jane on the path toward Ritualist theory for it represented her acceptance of the primacy of the constant conflict between emotion and intellect. Recognizing their coexistence in herself enabled her to perceive them in the past. On one level, she began to discern the interrelation of intellect and emotion; on another, she connected those contradictory realms to similar contradictions within herself. Accepting such an integrated ethos opened new doors for her.

Jane had not yet become a Ritualist, however. While admitting that "Scylla, in a word, is the sinister aspect of the sea, with all its malignant forces of storm and rock and sea monster," and thus "in close connection with the daemons of the lower world," she emphasized that this explanation satisfied neither the ancient Greeks nor her. "The men of latter days were not content with a nature-myth so simple" and "the fierce rage of the sea-monster had for them no interest unless it were tinged with the bitterness of some more human frenzy" (204), so the Greeks created a love story to explain Scylla's unhappiness. Jane preferred this legend, as well she might. For it seems that Scylla had loved King Minos, who besieged her father's city, so deeply that she betrayed her father and cost him his kingdom. Minos, who had not asked her help, rejected her love out of horror at her treachery. Scylla's betrayal is depicted on a Pompeian wall painting, and Jane wonders "that the Pompeian could have cared to see painted upon his walls a scene so sad and shameful,—the daughter who, unasked, betrays her father" (205). Apparently, she could accept betrayal with provocation or upon request; Scylla's crime was to betray her father out of sheer willfulness. Furthermore, Jane leaves unclear whether the betrayal consists in sacrificing her father's kingdom or in falling in love with another man. In any case, the Pompeian who commissioned the wall painting shared Jane's fascination with the darker side of human nature.

Yet it is in her discussion of the Sirens that Jane comes closest to capturing the interplay between archaic and classical views of the world. The myth of a competition "in singing and in playing on the lyre and the lute" (166) between the Sirens and the Muses shows "the natural antagonism, the attempted revolt, of the new order against the old, of wild sensation against tempered emotion, raised in vain against the harmonies of high Olympos" (167–68). The Muses win, symbolizing the triumph of rational order, but the Sirens' portrayal reminds the Greeks of their hidden power.

> Never, perhaps, so keenly as in the conception of the Sirens are we made to feel how fluctuating, how almost antithetic, are the elements which go to form a Greek myth: the sinister daemon of one moment is the gracious goddess of the next, the boundary between good and evil is a soft shadow land to a people whose moral standard was in the main aesthetic. (165)

As with other figures, Greek artists replaced "devout symbolism" with "a conscious seeking after form" that incidentally suited modern tastes (168). But Jane understood that the Sirens represented something far more primitive. Discussing their appearance on funeral monuments, she states:

> It is hard for us, with our Christian associations, deepened to a gloomier austerity by Puritan training, to feel with the Greeks about death and funeral ceremonies; but if we wish to understand them at all we must activate this historical sympathy. . . . The Greek mind, in its early freshness at least, was little troubled by the dualism of this world and the next. Greek youths and maidens made no promise to renounce the wreath and wine cup, the mirror and bead necklace, and so they bear them to the grave—to the end a glory and a grace. No doubt this close connection of Bacchus and Aphrodite with the dreadful gods of Hades had a deep mystic significance, of which much is lost to us, only the lighter aspect remaining. We must not condemn as frivolity the outcome of a sacred joy, a glad religious confidence,—must not turn away

offended when we see the Siren standing as chief mourner by the tomb. (159–60)

Dionysos appears frequently in the chapter on the Sirens, and Jane exhibits a budding fascination with his disorderliness and lack of discipline. Decades later, Jane's experience helped her divine the "mystic significance" of the connection between Bacchus/Aphrodite and the "dreadful gods of Hades."

Although *Myths of the Odyssey* examined origins, Jane shrank from forsaking the gentility and aestheticism of the classical age for the graphic horror, as well as the unbridled joy, of the archaic period. But the legacy of her early Evangelical training, which made her dimly aware of the emotional potential of the religious impulse, piqued her interest. *Myths of the Odyssey* offers glimpses of topics that later consumed Jane's work. She had not quite overcome the shackles of the rational side of her stepmother's religion nor fully opened herself up to the mysteries of ancient religious experience. But the work foreshadows her later focus on the importance of group experience in religion and the primacy of the irrational.

After a few years in the London scene, Jane regained her self-control and became more aesthetic. Her *Introductory Studies in Greek Art* reflects the change. In her preface, Jane asked why civilization remains so fascinated by the Greeks, why we derive from them "not merely an impression of the senses, but also a satisfaction that abides and an impulse to growth, moral and intellectual?" She answered by citing "a certain peculiarity of Greek art which adapts itself to the consciousness of successive ages," which is ideality.[46] She relied heavily on Plato's doctrine of the ideal, characterizing Greek art as the best attempt to portray the true quality of objects in harmony with nature. True genius lay in idealizing an object, not substituting a symbol. "Doctrinally a symbol is good and useful, artistically it is a confession of weakness and incapacity" (51). Egypt, Phoenicia, and Assyria contributed to the development of Greek art by struggling to represent concepts later so important to the Greeks, but these cultures always fell short because they turned to symbolism when frustrated in their efforts. Jane admitted that "quality . . . is always abstract," but argued that "some nations are naturally of what I must term adjectival mind." Such nations "love abstractions" and "have a capacity for thinking in them" but can never be "in the best sense" artists because "form is to them secondary." The Assyrians, she asserted, suffered in this manner. Their carelessness with form meant their "demons always lack life," possessing "wings that do not fly, eagles' beaks that cannot devour." She valued Greek art more highly because it harmonized with nature rather than violated it (53–54).

In its attempt to "utter some thought of man's mind, which has no actual correspondent in the outside world," artistic expression can take two paths.

Scared at the difficult task before her, she perhaps takes refuge in adjectival symbolism, seeks to indicate what she cannot embody, draws no inspiration from the outside world of nature, and produces a monstrous figment which violates its laws. This is a broad and easy road, but for art it leads to death and destruction. Or, following a higher and a harder method, art may seek to express man's thought, not by violating nature, but by idealizing nature's own creations, producing what is above and beyond nature, but never impossible and contrary. This is a steep and narrow path, but it leads to artistic life. (54–55)

Ideality is achieved when the artist uses art to "transcend nature, yet never violate her laws" (4). The Greeks, building on the experience of earlier civilizations and influences carried through trade with other lands, reached a pinnacle of artistic achievement that united nature and morality.

Jane celebrated the Parthenon frieze depicting the Panathenaic procession as the centerpiece of classical artistry and therefore of her book. She rhapsodized over Pheidias, supervisor of the project, as a sculptor who "united beauty with greatness," whose work was "at once large, impressive, full of dignity . . . and yet characterized by the utmost delicacy and fineness" (196). The Parthenon's pediment, which bears Pheidias' mark, makes us "feel we are in a higher world" and is "still the marvel of the world" (210–11). Of the two works, though, she considered the frieze dedicated to Athena remarkable for its capturing of her spirit and "its beauty and calm gravity" (212). Jane felt a special affinity for gray-eyed Athena, the wise and masculine goddess who symbolized rationality and asexuality—an affinity later overthrown in favor of Dionysos, the unruly invader associated with unbridled emotion and passion.

Jane defended the Greeks from critics who attacked their love of physical beauty. She worried

because too often the Greeks are spoken of as a people who desired physical beauty to the exclusion of spiritual, who because they are artistic became immoral. In later days we have sorrowfully to own that art and morals alike did decay; but their fall is together, neither is to blame for the other, both have common causes. What we do notice . . . is that they seek the spiritual, but not to the exclusion of the physical; that they alone among nations have known, or rather instinctively felt, how to hold, if even only for one happy century, the just balance between body and soul. For a little while they showed the world the lovely picture of a nation living a sound and healthy life in the happiest of all

> faiths that the beautiful is the good. . . . This devotion was only possible to a race naturally beautiful; to an ugly race such a faith would have been akin to despair. . . . We are not however to suppose they were a nation uniformly beautiful. There were plenty of ugly and mediocre individuals, and this contrast would be necessary to stimulate the critical and appreciative faculty. (183–84)

Not only were the Greeks right-thinking, they exuded beauty naturally because they were a race of physically attractive people. Jane fully internalized aesthetic ideals and projected them onto classical Greece, and her obsession with beauty and its equation with goodness demonstrates her passion for those ideals.

Despite her infatuation with Greek art, Jane had no use for primitive religion. The ritual that marked the Assyrians, "a people addicted to magic, to obscure rites of divination and incantation, to elaborate and significant gesture and posture, to the letter with little of the life," resulted in "mechanical formularies rather than vital expression" (63–64). Although the Greek gods, especially Aphrodite, bore traces of Phoenician origin, one should not for a moment "suppose that the Greeks, the most human of all nations, had no indigenous goddess of love, that they must needs wait to borrow their loveliest conception from the fierce, inhuman East" (84). This sentiment is a far cry from the later work; in twenty years, she would denounce the Olympians as stale and lifeless, finding the true religious impulse in the "fierce, inhuman East."

Sutherland, then, persuaded Jane to abandon her love for art and the Olympian religion and to stand her entire ethos on its head. His interest in ritual and folklore indicates a similarity of thought that would have both attracted and repelled Jane. She relied on her rigid self-control to keep order in a chaotic and tumultuous world. Sutherland, equally calm on the outside and passionate under this veneer, appealed to her both intellectually and sexually. But Jane, so attuned to the coexistence of these two realms in theory, could not cope with them in reality. Accepting his intellectual supremacy meant rejecting him sexually. Jane's horror of male sexuality and its equation with both overwhelming power and the pain of rejection and separation doomed their chances for a fulfilling romance from the start.

In the spring of 1888, Jane had sufficiently recovered from the intellectual crisis of Sutherland's attack on her style to begin planning another trip to Greece. The Turnbulls were going, along with the Arthur Sidgwicks and Sutherland. Jane wrote to Sutherland from Ashbourne asking if he could "forego" his "paranymphic function [lectures]" and be ready to leave on March 29, promising him that he "could, by going overland, dance at Megara on Easter Tuesday."[47] The group agreed on an itinerary and departed as scheduled. Both Jane and Sutherland chronicled this often hilarious adventure, portraying it as an unqualified success. Most remarkably, the Sidgwicks and the Turnbulls dropped out of the tour at different locations, leaving Jane and Sutherland to traipse through Greece alone for the better part of two months. They suffered the typical mishaps of English people traveling abroad; as Jane said, "Greece in those days held many adventures" (RSL, 336).

Jane and Sutherland spent early April in Athens hearing the German archaeologist Wilhelm Dorpfeld lecture on his excavations at the Theater of Dionysos. On this trip, Jane visited museums and studied vase paintings, but she also made a "real archaeological discovery" in Athens. In a "rubbish-pile" in a corner of the Acropolis Museum, she "lighted on the small stone figure of a bear." Its "furry hind paw" captured her attention, and she "immediately had her—it was manifestly a she-bear—brought out and honourably placed" (RSL, 338). Jane admitted that she often became "maudlin" at "any mention of a bear," and indeed she did (RSL, 329). She possessed a "small endearing woolly bear called the Herr Professor, who lived in a sort of shrine on her mantlepiece" and had "spectacles and an umbrella but no other clothing." Bears were her totem animal, and it had "always been the dream of my childhood to sit upon an iceberg with a bear."[48]

Sutherland's diary of the trip skips to April 26, when he, Jane, and the Turnbulls left Athens for Thebes after a night-long "solemn farce" of bargaining with a carriage driver. Arriving in the late afternoon, they set out to explore the town. "At one point," wrote Sutherland, "we had got separated for a few minutes & Turnbull & I were attracted by a large crowd of people in one of the streets." Investigation revealed that

> the center of it was Mrs. T. and Miss H. A chorus of the women of Thebes were standing round & questioning them. How old were they? Were they married? How often? Had they children? If not married, why not? They pressed Miss Harrison Why did she not marry the other *kouros* (=lord=gentleman). On her answering that she objected to being married she was greeted with screams of laughter & followed the rest of the time by an excited & incredulous crowd.[49]

This reaction may not have been so different from that of her English contemporaries.

In early May, Jane and Sutherland traveled to Constantinople on an Italian steamer. Sutherland recorded that bad weather, a food shortage, and a plethora of American tourists made the journey unpleasant. On their return to Athens, Jane discovered that she had lost her passport and had to reenter Greece posing as Sutherland's wife. As bad as the trip was, Jane " 'forgot her sorrows in the sight of Troy.' "[50]

Sutherland's diary is a collection of impressions interwoven with details of the trip, many of which reveal the extraordinary difficulty of travel in the 1880s. Sutherland, who had taken charge of all the travel arrangements, haggled frequently over prices and grew impatient with the slower-paced Greeks. Both he and Jane described their visit to a monastery at Vurkano, which seems to have been the highlight of the journey. Jane had desperately wanted to "go to some other rock monasteries in Thessaly where the only way is to be pulled up by a rope in a basket," but the journey to Vurkano proved treacherous enough. Their trip from Sparta required travel on mules and took several days. The true Englishwoman, Jane had "most luckily brought from England a spirit lamp and compressed tea" which was "our salvation all through the pilgrimage and many a stream and mountain pass has seen us crouched round its feeble light." The mules were "wonderfully clever beasts" who seemed "to prefer going up or down the side of the house to anything less arduous." Sutherland wrote that Jane "could not believe in the safety of the proceeding and begged to be taken down," but that as the trip progressed "she soon got to look on it as a matter of course." At one stop along the way "some young fellows were eating and drinking and invited us to have some krasi." They accepted, and "drank and smoked and chatted with the men."[51] They finally straggled into Vurkano near sunset and were "hospitably received," according to Jane (RSL, 336). Sutherland remained a bit more skeptical.

The Hegoumenos, or abbot, took to Jane and fed her "with titbits from his own plate" (RSL, 336). Sutherland recorded that "he [the Hegoumenos] and Miss Harrison taught one another a good deal of Greek and English," and that "he kept her hard at it most of the time." When they asked if they might remain another night, "he at once invited Miss Harrison to stay three months and carry on the Greek and English lessons." Sutherland noted indignantly that "for the head of a monastery his conduct was really outrageous"; the Hegoumenos "softly stroked her hands at times and said they were whiter than snow," although Sutherland added acerbically that this "was not the case after a night spent in the monastery." Jane gave the Hegoumenos "a languishing Mendelssohn photograph of herself in ball dress which he stuck up in the room and said he would look at every day." No one seemed to think it strange that Jane should travel to faraway lands with such a photograph in her luggage.[52]

Jane showed remarkable restraint in her "Reminiscences" when describing this incident, for in her words, the Hegoumenos merely "placed [the photograph] below the Eikon of the Virgin and solemnly commended me to her protection against the spiritual dangers to which I was so obviously exposed" (RSL, 337). She described her gift of the photograph as occurring the morning after Sutherland had committed a terrible blunder that awakened the monk to her "spiritual dangers."

Sutherland offended the entire monastic community by bathing in the courtyard. In order to soothe the ruffled feathers this sacrilege caused (the monks believing it evil to wash above the wrists), Jane "ruthlessly sacrificed my kind protector. The 'Lord,' I said was young and ignorant; he knew no Greek letters (a gross libel); he had been born and reared not in Christian England, but in a strange barbarian hyperborean land, where raiment was scanty and Christian modesty unknown." She heard Sutherland "mutter to himself words to the effect that he would 'jolly well like to put the Hegoumenos under his own pump.' " Despite their handsome donation at parting, the "adieus were frigid" and they "left under a cloud" (RSL, 337). The less sensitive Sutherland remembered the parting differently. Rather than its being cold, he wrote that "the old Boss . . . pressed the boy [one of his servants] upon us to take with us to England and promised himself to come and see us there and lie on our sofas."[53]

Few middle-class Victorian women embarked on unchaperoned journeys through desolate country.[54] Jane's family's reaction is unknown, but she showed an acute awareness of conventional opinion of her actions in a letter dated soon after her return to England. On June 6, 1888, she wrote to Hope Malleson that she was back from "nearly three delightful months in Greece," working in Athenian museums and at excavations, "but I had also a beautiful and resting time in the Peloponnese." She added coyly,

> Who do you think protected me thro' those wilds? I know I may venture to tell *you* what I do not disclose to every British matron that Mr. MacColl and I ventured on that pilgrimage alone—and we have come back firmer friends than ever—he was a perfect traveling companion—not only poetical but to my astonishment—but then he is a Scotchman—also practical—able to deal with rugs and railway tickets steamers and worse still mules and Muleteers.

She went on to say that in "Arcadia" they "slept in monasteries and strange khans where half the village comes to drink with one and camp round one all night—it was a never to be forgotten experience but inconceivably primitive and savage." Given Jane's passion for things primitive, it would be hard to imagine a higher compliment.[55]

Despite her glowing description of her relationship with Sutherland, strains coexisted with intimacy. A month after their return, Jane wrote to him criticizing his poetry as "needlessly obscure." She added, "It is odd how your verses take me."

> Sometimes, I feel only rage against you, as against a creature to whom this live world is only a spectacle to say neat and curious things about, and to try and experience curious sensations towards—and then

before I know it I have 'gone soppy' (your own words, my poet) all of a sudden for just a line or a phrase.[56]

She sensed and criticized Sutherland's tendency, both in his poetry and in his life, to distance himself from the world, a tendency best exhibited by his denunciation of her aestheticism for signifying a passionate attachment to life and art. Not surprisingly, and more personally, Jane also considered her Yorkshire moors far superior to his Scottish moors.[57] Her praise of the beauty of her native land at his expense cannot be ascribed purely to aesthetic criteria.

In addition to the Greek trip, Jane and Sutherland traveled together on many other occasions, often with friends or members of Sutherland's family. In the summer of 1887, before the trip to Greece, Jane, Eleanor Butcher, Lewis Nettleship, and Alfred and Violet Hunt had vacationed at an inn on Robin Hood's Bay on the Yorkshire coast. Sutherland, his sister Elizabeth (Lizzie), and his mother lodged nearby, and "there were many walks along the coast & over the moors & lying about on beach & cliff." Hope Mirrlees later recalled that Jane viewed Mrs. MacColl as "the typical widow, very self-respecting marvelously clean, &, Jane said, with a wonderful refinement." Sutherland lectured on nursery rhymes, game songs and dance songs, ceremonial or ritual songs, and ballads at Ashbourne in the winter of 1888–89, and Jane, vacationing at Sandybrook, came to hear him. Sutherland believed that these lectures "gave [Jane] her impulse to study Greek ritualistic dancing." He repeated the lecture series at Oxford in the summer of 1889, and "JEH & Violet Hunt joined my sister Lizzie & me at Oxford, & tempered the lectures with picnics on the River." They spent vacations with other friends in 1890 and 1893, and two years later, Jane, Sutherland, Mr. and Mrs. Hugh Egerton, and Roger Fry journeyed to St. Pierre-en-Port.[58]

Although it is unclear when Jane turned down Sutherland's marriage proposal, her trip to St. Moritz in 1889 on the advice of her doctor suggests that she may have suffered another crisis then. Her "great breathlessness" led the doctor to suspect delicate lungs, but her condition may have derived from emotional distress. In any case, in 1896 Sutherland, while on a bicycle trip with Jane and some other friends, split off from the group to visit the Zabés, his future parents-in-law. Obviously her rejection of Sutherland as a husband did not diminish her enjoyment of his company; the blow came only when he actually married someone else. In a letter to Jessie Stewart in connection with her efforts to gather material for her collection of letters, Sutherland reminisced about the April 1896 bicycle trip.

Another excursion was bicycling in France (referred to in VW [Virginia Woolf's] life of RF [Roger Fry]. He, J.E.H., my sister and self were original members. Roger brought Helen Coombe [his future wife] who had

> been a fellow student with my sister . . . at SK [South Kensington]. J.E.H. didn't like this because wanted to further Roger's attraction to E.M.M. [Sutherland's sister, Lizzie] which had been noticeable at S. Pierre en Port (previous summer). Three of us were held up at a town by missing a train and spent night there. R. and H. had gone on together and I imagine fixed up things or went far that night. J.E.H. made herself conspicuous by wearing silk breeches and a Bishop's apron (she was proud of her legs. Here [*sic*] eyes were fine and her look of reverie smoking happily on a Yorkshire moor very attractive) and I had to ward off a small riot of French bystanders at St. Lazare. R. conveyed J. to Dieppe towing her against a strong wind. The rest of us bicycled from Fontainbleau to Paris. I spent two nights there and looking up the Zabé's (my future wife's people).

Commenting on this story, Hope Mirrlees added that a year after the bicycle trip, Jane "almost caused a riot when she appeared in this garb [her bicycle suit] at the Gare du Nord."[59]

It would be fascinating to know Jane's feelings on this trip, aware as she was that Sutherland would marry soon. She wanted to give him the Degas she had purchased on his advice as a wedding present, but he "refused to allow it to her and she said would leave it to me in her will." Later in her life, however, she sold it for desperately needed cash.[60] Hope Mirrlees, who arranged the sale of the painting, spoke more bitterly about it, accusing the Irish dealer who bought it of giving her "a bad deal because of the fact that the French hated the Irish."[61] It may also be that Hope felt hurt on Jane's behalf by such a painful memory of the past.

In a much later letter to Lady Mary Murray, Jane touched indirectly on the question of marriage and referred, presumably, to Sutherland. "I often reflect on the sorrows of being married to a genius," she wrote, "because genius is like God who belongs to everyone up to the limits of their power to comprehend. I long ago refused to marry a man I cared for because he was a genius and some instinct told me I dared not and tho I am an oldish woman and fairly lonely I have never repented." This statement reveals her fear of being engulfed by a man who was at least her intellectual equal and whom she perceived (as evidenced by her conversion) as her superior. Ironically, if genius did indeed mean belonging to the world as a whole, Jane probably also feared that she would not be the center of their circle. Yet the equality implicit in Jane's relationship with Sutherland sets it apart from all the rest and makes it decisive—literally crucial—to the course of her life and work. For Sutherland was everything a woman like Jane—intelligent, independent, creative—could want. He was interested in her work and knowledgeable about it, in love with her, and, most important of all, accessible. But for these very reasons, Jane refused him. He married Andrée Zabé, who was "elegant, witty, skilled in all the social graces," as well as "a noted beauty." Although Jane had her own unique, more unconventional attractions, it must have hurt her to see Sutherland turn finally to someone so unlike her, so much the antithesis of all that she represented.[62]

Despite Sutherland's attractions, however, he posed a threat. His ability to hold his own with Jane intellectually endangered her autonomy, and she feared being submerged to "genius" as one would be to God, especially in the Evangelical worldview in which she was raised. The mention of genius and God in one sentence to Mary Murray is no coincidence, and reveals the depths of dependence to which Jane feared she might sink if she allowed herself to fall in love with a man like Sutherland.

Whether or not Sutherland would actually have had such an effect on her is debatable. The important point is that Jane foresaw disaster if she married him. In all likelihood he would have been a good match for her. Evidence suggests that he possessed great strength and kindness, as well as a fine intellect. Late in her life she acknowledged some of her feelings more openly than usual. The Degas, she wrote years later, had become "less and less" to her. Two letters of 1903 and 1914 remarked on how "odd" it was that she should have heard from him at certain times because she had been thinking of him. In 1905, she wrote that "Violet Hunt appeared . . . last Sunday and reminded me of a long past." On May 30, 1909, she wrote to thank Sutherland for suggesting Augustus John as the artist to do her portrait for Newnham. In her touching final paragraph, she responded to what must have been a question as to why he had not heard from her.

> I quite admit that I am no good over that rather to me conventional business "*keeping up with*" old friends. I know it quite well. Either I have to live people's lives *with* them intimately, or I fall away. That is just me—the me you used to know well and I think once understood. It would interest me very much to know if we had anything really to say to each other nowadays. I think we might—I am *not* sure. My life has been tremendously rich and happy since we knew each other, so I am sure has yours; but whether we have gone quite different ways I do not know. I never see anything written by you now that gives me any clue as to where you are.

The evocation of intimacy long past makes this letter moving. Her conscious and absolute rejection of the one man who truly loved her and whom she could have married may have been the most tragic event of her adult life.[63]

Sutherland's marriage in 1897 capped a long series of disappointments. In 1888 and again in 1896, Jane had applied for the Yates Professorship in Archaeology at University College, London. An impressive list of scholars from Oxford and Cambridge, museum directors in London, and archaeologists from all over Europe provided testimonials on her behalf. Her references included R. C. Jebb, Henry Sidgwick, Henry Jackson, A. W. Verrall, and Walter Leaf of Cambridge; Henry Butcher and Arthur Sidgwick of Oxford; F. H. Middleton, director of South Kensington Museum, and Sir Edward Maunde Thomson, librarian of the British Museum; and Continental archaeologists Wilhelm Dorpfeld, Ernst Curtius, Wilhelm Klein, Otto Bindorf, and Cavalier Luigi Melina, among others.[54] Her three trips to Greece in the 1880s had put her in touch with the foremost archaeological scholars of her day who thought very highly of her, but her expertise could not conquer the fears of those who questioned the wisdom of granting the distinguished professorship to a woman. In addition, the hidebound world of classical scholarship had no room for innovative thinking. Classicists considered Jane's work far too unconventional to merit such a prestigious position. Finally, Jane hinted in a letter to Edmund Gosse that Reginald Poole, who also applied for the post, had persuaded Charles Newton and Sidney Colvin to recommend him rather than her. "I may tell you privately," she wrote, "that my candidature has given great offence to Mr. R. S. Poole who is also standing. When I thought the post was *not* open to a woman he constantly told me I was the fit person, & now he goes about saying I have turned against him." His candidature made it impossible for her to "get a single testimonial from the archaeologists of the Museum tho' Mr. Colvin and Sir Charles Newton are both *most* kind & urge me to stand. It is a question of colleague etiquette."[65]

Her personal and professional failures made her London years seem a defeat, despite her many achievements. She had made her own decision to refuse Sutherland's marriage proposal, but perhaps she regretted it; she had no control over the Yates Professorship appointment. These events and the wider conflict between her provincial background and London society made her view her London years, unconsciously if not consciously, as a failure. Years before, Jane had applied to become Newnham's first classical lecturer. The administration rejected her as far too unorthodox a scholar for a woman's college still in its infancy, and it chose the more docile Margaret Merrifield instead.[66] But in 1898, Newnham reversed its policy and offered Jane its first research fellowship. Feeling depressed, defeated, and disillusioned with London, Jane accepted Newnham's offer and returned to her old home.

4

SCHOLAR AND TEACHER: NEWNHAM COLLEGE, 1898–1922

The earliest Cambridge that I can remember must have been seen by me in reflection from my mother's mind. . . . In this, the first Cambridge in the mirror of my mind, the sun is always shining, and there are always ladies and gentlemen sitting in the garden under the trees, very much occupied with each other. It was quite a different Cambridge which I saw later on, when I looked at it with my own eyes.

—*Gwen Raverat,* Period Piece

Cambridge generally always makes a rather melancholy impression upon me now. So many of my friends are dead, or mad, or have turned old fogies, or taken to drinking, that I feel as if there was something unhealthy in the place.

—*Leslie Stephen to R. C. Jebb, May 12, 1875*

THE RESEARCH fellowship that brought Jane Harrison back to Newnham in 1898 had been created for former students and required the recipient to reside in Cambridge and pursue research in her field.[1] Jane's success in London outweighed her besetting sins of rebelliousness and unorthodoxy, and the college rectified its past neglect by risking her appointment as a fellow. By 1903, Jane's talents had so won over Newnham's administration that, after her fellowship ended, they asked her to stay on. She explained to Gilbert Murray, "the arrangement is that I live here for nothing, giving in return the blessing of my presence (no small thing) & lecturing for part II & on other things, like Kers, when I have anything to say." Her income would be decreased "by a third," but "it suits me perfectly & if I were decently economical (which I am not) I should still be quite rich." She declared a dislike of money as "so ugly & abstract & unmeaning" and believed that it "ought not to exist in a decent state," attributing the development of this "theory" to a period spent "studying bimetallism for the London Univ[ersity]."[2]

During Jane's twenty-five years at Newnham, she formed some of her most intense and satisfying relationships. Her friendship with Gilbert Murray began as an intellectual collaboration but rapidly developed into a warm personal bond. He and his family provided a base for Jane, a group in which she felt secure, even though she remained outside the family circle. Jane's return to Newnham also meant a return to old friends from her student days. Margaret Merrifield Verrall and her husband, the classicist A. W. Verrall, lived there; so did Ellen Crofts Darwin and her husband, the botanist Sir Francis Darwin. Jane found a sense of community at Newnham that perfectly suited her emotional needs. She stood out as a somewhat eccentric figure compared to the usual Newnham don, thus ensuring continual attention. Her students loved her and appreciated her keen intelligence and apparent disregard for many conventions. Newnham fulfilled the needs of the persona Jane had created for herself.

The larger university community also offered many intellectual attractions. Jane's years at Newnham coincided with the presence of some of Cambridge's towering figures, mainly associated with Trinity and King's colleges. Sir James George Frazer continued to puzzle out his view of the relationship between myth and ritual. During the period between the appearance of Jane's *Prolegomena to the Study of Greek Religion* and *Themis: A Study of the Social Origins of Greek Religion,* Bertrand Russell and Alfred North Whitehead collaborated on *Principia Mathematica.* G. E. Moore held a Trinity fellowship between 1898 and 1904. Although it is difficult to gain a sense of how much direct contact she actually had with these men, her correspondence refers to them often enough to indicate a certain degree of familiarity. No doubt she enjoyed her association with them as stimulating colleagues, although her enjoyment was probably tempered by other factors: Frazer eventually repudiated the Ritualists' theories, and Jane sided with Alys Russell during the breakup of Alys's marriage to Bertrand Russell. Nevertheless, the presence of such prominent colleagues made Cambridge a lively place to be, both intellectually and socially.[3]

Cambridge had changed considerably during Jane's twenty-year absence. In 1878, the university revised its statutes and allowed fellows of colleges to marry, whereas previously only professors and heads of houses could do so. This revision enhanced the growth of what Noel Annan has dubbed the "intellectual aristocracy" by encouraging intermarriage between sons and daughters of prominent academic families.[4]

Once romance became a legitimate concern in Cambridge, college life took a new turn. Not everyone wholeheartedly approved of the revised rule. Gwen Raverat, the daughter of George Darwin and Maud DuPuy and one of the "first hatching of Fellows' children," commented on her mother's vision of the university, claiming derisively "you would really think . . . that Unrequited Love—other people's Unrequited Love—was the only serious trouble." Her great-aunt, Cara Jebb, wrote to her sister in 1882 that "this new bill permitting Fellows of Colleges to marry makes a great matrimonial rush among those beings" and stated her hope that "it won't quite spoil the charm of the place by filling it with semipaupers." T. R. Glover feared that the tedium of everyday family life would deplete fellows' creative resources and make them much less interesting. Above all, the increase in numbers of families meant that unmarried female dons became a rarer and thus ambiguous type within the university.[5]

Although Jane put up a good front, she harbored fears about returning to Cambridge. Having failed to achieve her ambitions in London, she felt she had to settle for lesser ones. Her relationship to Cambridge was certainly problematic: "Cambridge thought her dangerous; & she, in turn, when she first came back to it, thought Cambridge provincial." Although Jane told Hope Mirrlees that she "adored provincial towns," Hope remembered that Jane kept her room at London's Sesame Club for several years after her return to Newnham "as a sort of hostage against a fear of stagnation & provincialism." Her uneasiness reflected unresolved conflict over her background. She certainly thought she had repudiated her Yorkshire roots but remained unconvinced that the rest of the world believed in her transformation.[6]

In addition, London society had encouraged her sense of style. She had surrounded herself with less stuffy people who, simply because they were Londoners, represented the height of her aspirations. Jane told Hope Mirrlees that "after the urbanity of the men who had taken her down to dinner in London, it was disconcerting to find the onus of starting conversation entirely on her own shoulders; also either not to be answered at all, or only by grunts."[7] She felt simultaneously superior and inferior, thus increasing her general sense of uneasiness.

Jane's flair for the outlandish in dress contrasted sharply with typical Cambridge expectations of female demeanor. Many of the Cambridge ladies, for one thing, found her dresses "too low." Her penchant for flaunting her friendships with male colleagues, often in front of their wives, also exasperated many Cambridge women. Florence Maitland deplored Jane's flirtation with her husband, the historian Frederick Maitland. " 'Jane Harrison has let herself go,' " she remarked to Virginia Woolf in 1904. Jane was " 'a great admirer of Freds' " and demonstrated her affection so openly that Mrs. Maitland " 'had to tell her she was positively indecent!' " The " 'repulsive woman' " believed " 'Fred so beautiful that she would go anywhere to see him.' " No doubt this incident increased Woolf's appreciation of Mrs. Maitland's willingness to "introduce me to the repulsive Jane," along with "all the other learned Ladies."[8]

As a recent observer has noted, "university life . . . provided a niche for the genuine eccentric, the scholarly recluse, the man who might find it difficult to secure congenial employment outside the cloistered courts," and "in such surroundings native eccentricities, vagaries of dress and behavior . . . flourished." His observation, however, applies only in the case of the male dons. Many "harmless madmen" amused generations of undergraduates. Cuthbert Shields, a nineteenth-century Corpus Christi don, appeared at the dinner table in the nude, and classicist Robinson Ellis cut holes in his boots "to give his toes more room." Cambridge frowned on such behavior among the female dons, who were generally "women of considerable personality, learned and rather masculine, not unlike the suffragettes, more given than their male colleagues to high thinking and austere standards of living." They "tended to be dowdy in appearance, intense and rather serious, though generally more conscientious than academic men." Conversely, some were "endowed with conspicuous charm and ability" and "would be ornaments to any society." If forced to choose between these two models, Jane would probably have felt more at home dining with Shields or debating the virtues of open-toed shoes with Ellis.[9]

In any event, having reconciled herself to her return, Jane blossomed in Cambridge's rarefied atmosphere. Not only did its intellectual possibilities satisfy her; the social distinction that accompanied an appointment gradually helped ease the ache of having failed to achieve her ambitions in London. Indeed, Cambridge proved to be the best choice for a woman with scholarly ambitions and a desire to identify herself with the educated upper class.

Jane nevertheless found the transition to Cambridge life difficult.[10] For a woman of her provincial merchant-class background, Cambridge represented a giant step up the social ladder, but embracing its values meant rejecting her past. Despite her outward ease, then, she found this process difficult.

On the other hand, she had good reasons for wanting to spend thirty years as both student and teacher at Cambridge, most of them intimately connected to her perceptions of herself and her place in the world. Sheldon Rothblatt's *The Revolution of the Dons* studies Cambridge's nineteenth-century reforms without mentioning women at all, but his work offers some otherwise valuable insights into Cambridge's role as preserver of the social status quo. He contends that

> one of the primary objects of the great nineteenth-century reforms was to guarantee that Cambridge did not lose its traditional connexion with the professions and professional men, especially clergymen. . . . This does not mean that dons wished to definitely close the university to non-professional groups; merely that they had no intention of making Cambridge in any way attractive to students from non-professional families who might prefer a career in business, or who were unprepared to accept *Cambridge values and style.* (italics added)

This style had attracted Jane as a student and drew her back as a teacher. Moreover, as Rothblatt points out, during the nineteenth century Cambridge "became more socially exclusive than ever before, a step in the climb of the parvenu bourgeoisie to status and influence." As a member of this "parvenu bourgeoisie," a part of Jane desperately wanted to leave her provincial and merchant roots behind, and Cambridge represented a means of achieving this end. Despite Rothblatt's focus on men's colleges, his conclusions about the attractiveness of Cambridge's style to young men desiring to improve their status certainly applies to Jane as well.[11]

Jane's interest in the classics was part and parcel of this subtle attraction. If a Cambridge education provided a springboard for upward mobility, study of ancient society further encouraged identification with the upper classes. Rothblatt discusses the mid-nineteenth-century attack on classics as the centerpiece of a liberal education because it was "narrow, one-sided, and illiberal." As with other aspects of university reform, some forward-looking individuals argued that the identification of classics with high social status did not sufficiently justify its continued emphasis. Its very status appeal, however, attracted many others to its defense. As Rothblatt states, "the attack failed intellectually to dislodge classical learning because of *its total identification with the elite culture of the period,* because of *its intricate relationship to the values of right living*" (italics added).[12] Those who were already upper class in status wanted to preserve classical education as a means of setting themselves above the middle and lower classes, while aspiring members of these classes desired to emulate their social betters by mastering the classics themselves.[13] I would add that Jane's experience introduces a third element to this debate: that of women aspiring to equality with male students and scholars by achieving distinction in classical study. This relationship is more subtle and complex, for the social status argument is complemented by one based on gender. Women like Jane, fighting both intellectual and social battles, tended to identify with male values as well as upper-class values. They valued classical study as a means of acquiring both social and sexual equality.

A. H. Halsey and Martin Trow emphasize even more clearly not only the superiority of both Cambridge and Oxford but also the distinction between these two universities and the newer British universities.

> Oxford and Cambridge were national universities connected with the national elites of politics, administration, business and the liberal professions offering a general education designed to mould character and prepare their students for a *gentlemanly style of life:* the rest were provincial, all of them, including London, addressed to the needs of the professional and industrial middle classes, taking most of their students from their own region and offering them a more utilitarian training for middle-class careers in undergraduate courses typically concentrated on a single subject. (italics added)

Cambridge's superior virtue consisted in its transformation of middle-class men into gentlemen, which represented the highest aspiration of many of its students. The promise of such a transformation could only have enchanted Jane, so eager to deny her Yorkshire heritage. No other place could satisfy her. But her background ensured a rocky path toward acceptance. Even in the eighteenth century provincials had a poor reputation at both Cambridge and Oxford. University students thought the northern clergy "course, illiberal, and ungentlemanly," and took "a distinct dislike . . . to the northerner who brought with him manners regarded as awkward, a dialect that was considered rude, and a personality avoided as prickly. The northerner named most often was the Yorkshireman." How could Jane fit in at a place that judged her kind so harshly?[14]

In one way, Jane answered that question by refusing to fit in. She donned the trappings of bourgeois culture while playing up the qualities that made her anomalous. She apparently dropped her Yorkshire accent early in her career, probably even as a student, and acceded to the basic demands of propriety upon her return to Cambridge. Using her innate intelligence as both defense and justification of her actions, however, she built a career based on her eccentricity. Having finally won her battle with Newnham and received her fellowship despite her dangerous ideas, Jane thumbed her nose at the established powers and went her own way. Her powerful personality, striking appearance, and often outlandish behavior thus reflected a deep-seated conflict over her ambitions and ultimate goals, but her students loved her for those very qualities and for her passionate devotion to her work and her teaching.

Jane felt closest to other women who shared her delight in eccentricity. She often visited Ellen Crofts Darwin, sometimes with Alice Dew-Smith, at Ellen's home, Wychfield. "They used to play games there: making rhymes about their friends, or comparing them to plants or puddings." Ellen's niece Gwen Raverat considered "Aunt Ellen and her friends . . . wonderfully up to date and literary." Jane found many ways to criticize people who strayed quite innocently across her path. A visiting speaker prompted the following complaint to Mary Murray:

> But the dear Miss Harriman is *too* much for me; we (Federation of University Women) have just been dining her. She spoke for ¾ hour & she could be funny without the faintest trace of humour & about what she called "the lords of creation" too. It was dreadful. However perhaps my exacerbation was chiefly caused by the fact that there was no time for me to deliver my own elegant oration!! She must be a fine woman but she should never open her mouth. Mrs. Sidgwick was in the chair, looking so sick & doing her duty, even to the point of smiling heroically.

Jane was passionate about people she cared for, but devastating in her criticism of others.[15]

Carol Dyhouse asserts that the female dons most frequently mentioned in students' memoirs were popular because they most closely resembled what students wanted to become. "These community-minded, middle-class women" served as "role models over a generation of young female university students." She claims that the more steady, less flamboyant dons appear more frequently and "are described more vividly in many personal reminiscences of student days than are most of the full-time women tutors." She attributes their popularity to their being "married (or widowed)," which reflected the students' vision of their own future. In other words, students distanced themselves from female teachers who had achieved academic success at the expense of marriage and family.[16]

Joan Burstyn too emphasizes the narrowness of the nineteenth-century vision of educated women's roles and reminds her readers that even those Victorians who favored higher education for women by and large "still believed in separate spheres for men and women." She concludes that "given the popularity of this vision, we should not be surprised that few women graduates . . . during the nineteenth century ventured into work in the male sphere." Although teaching at a women's college could have been viewed as a kind of retreat, Jane's participation in the scholarly battles raging in the classical field marked her as a powerful figure. Her uniqueness forces Dyhouse to admit that Jane was certainly a "notable exception" to the usual run of drab unmarried dons. Her popularity with students attests to their willingness to accept a combination of individuality with intellectual achievement: "these were the years of 'the wicked dangerous Jane Harrison,' " but her students loved her nevertheless.[17]

One early twentieth-century student described Jane simply as "our most brilliant resident don," but others cherished memories of specific incidents that demonstrated her eccentricity. E. G. Brown recalled a 1901 glimpse of Jane through her window. She saw her "wheeling a very old-fashioned pram in which was a Greek statue of a female figure," probably of a "goddess," with "an outstretched left arm." Since the figure "was on its back in the pram the arm was held up to high heaven and the effect was most extraordinary." Jane "had wheeled this through the streets of Cambridge completely unperturbed." F. M. Wilson, who came to Newnham in 1906, regretted living in Old Hall because Clough Hall, then Jane's residence, was "much superior to Old in my time, for the quality of both its students and its dons." Jane "with her originality and her penetration into the world of Ancient Greece brought glamour into scholarship."[18]

Others remembered Jane's smoking habit. Its frequent mention indicates how rarely women smoked in polite society. Newnham, in fact, maintained a prohibition on smoking through the early twentieth century, even though many faculty members and the principal, Blanche

Clough, smoked. Even the elegant Eleanor Balfour Sidgwick had once tried smoking, on a trip to Egypt. "At about eighty, being asked if she smoked: 'Once I smoked, in a harem,' was her reply." Jane and Arthur Sidgwick had once "smoked pipes together on the steps of the Parthenon." Jane's niece, Hilda Lane, wrote that "the first picture that I have of her is when I was about four. . . . She was sitting talking with my father [William Lane, the clergyman who had introduced her to cigarettes] in the verandah & they were smoking together so that I grew up as few of my generation did feeling that smoking was correct for women." In his private journal, Bertrand Russell described Jane as "envied for her power of enduring excess in whisky and cigarettes." Jane found many ways to defy convention and don the trappings of male culture.[19]

The high point of each day in college seems to have been dinner, at which Jane would hold court at table. F. M. Wilson remembered that "you had to go down to dinner early for the privilege of sitting at her table, but it was worth it." Students fought for a seat near her, and once when a Miss Jordan monopolized Jane's attention, a group of other students fought to get their own share of her conversation.[20] Competition grew so fierce that finally "a bodyguard was formed to protect her from bores."[21] One Newnham student recorded a vivid impression of Jane's presence in the dining room.

> The most cheerful person at the High Table was Jane Harrison who was always the centre of animated conversation. Her striking appearance and often unorthodox clothing, added to her reputation as a scholar, made her one of Newnham's outstanding characters of that period. At lunch soon after my arrival she and I were standing together at a side table helping ourselves to food. To my amazement I saw her add to a plate which already had a helping of soup, some hard stewed prunes and the light brown liquid which accompanied them. For good measure some meat from another dish was added. As she sat down at table with this extraordinary mixture she remarked, with obvious satisfaction, that this was an interesting combination and we should try it.[22]

She may not have served as a role model to conventional female students, but she left an indelible impression nevertheless.

Years later, Hilda Lane provided a glimpse of another side of Jane. Reminiscing about a village luncheon Jane attended near the Lanes' home, Hilda remembered that she could be a good listener as well as performer. Her "greatest gift" was "the power of enabling everyone to be their best selves."

> The luncheon was the greatest success not because she talked brilliantly but that she made everyone else do so—in the garden party everyone enjoyed themselves because of this gift of hers which enabled her to

draw out everyone. I used to be amazed at the interesting thoughts she enabled people ordinarily dull & boring to express. . . . At Newnham it was very apparent but not so wonderful as when you saw it exercised on unintellectual people. . . . She always made me feel that she reverenced everyone's personality & that everyone could be interesting. I always enjoyed so much her great courtesy to the young & she never made me feel my inexperience but helped without seeming to do so.

Jane may have chuckled more at the "unintellectual people" than Hilda knew, but she genuinely loved the young.[23]

The young women closest to her recalled that she was "exceedingly striking to look at in those days—tall, a little swaying, graceful, massive in build, a wonderful mixture of grace and ruggedness." She "dressed with individuality and sometimes very elaborately" and "held herself finely, but she did not walk well." In spite of Sutherland MacColl's criticism of her aesthetic style, Jane never totally abandoned it. She appeared particularly striking when lecturing. M. E. Holland, a classics student who arrived at Newnham in 1909, remembered how "often a visible effect would be produced when a glittering shawl, worn by Miss Harrison round her shoulders and shrugged off at an exciting moment of recital, would fall in shimmering folds about her feet." Jane's "small, snowy-white, nervous hands" figured prominently when she was lecturing. Francis Cornford offered the most detailed description of her style.

Her lectures were designed so that each new light should break upon the scene just when she would have it. I have a vision of her figure on the darkened stage of the lecture room at the Archaeological Museum, which she made deserve to the full its name of theatre—a tall figure in black drapery, with touches of her favourite green and a string of blue Egyptian beads, like a priestess' rosary. The rather low voice vibrated with the excitement that had been working in her for many hours of preparation.

The hushed audience would catch the nervous tension of her bearing, even before the simple conversational tones began to convey the anticipation of some mystery to be disclosed. . . .

Every lecture was a drama in which the spectators were to share the emotions of "recognition."

This description beautifully conveys the excitement that accompanied Jane's lectures. She retained the touches of color, contrasting with black, and the dramatic performance of her old aesthetic style.[24]

On a personal level, Jane lavished individual attention on many of her students. She favored Victoria de Bunsen and Jessie Stewart in the early days and then grew fiercely attached to Hope Mirrlees after Hope's arrival at Newnham in 1909. Victoria, one of Jane's Greek students between 1900 and 1903, reminisced about Sunday morning visits during which Jane sat in her big armchair: "I can see her lighting a cigarette, crossing her knees, fumbling with rather helpless fingers in a heap of quotations and inscriptions, and prints of Greek vases pasted on loose sheets of paper—and then the deep repose of the figure when once she settled down and gave one her mind." Hope Mirrlees recalled Victoria's confiding to her that "though Jane had never modified [Victoria's] beliefs nor influenced her actions, yet having known her was the greatest & most important thing that had ever happened to her." Jane mentioned Victoria in a letter to Gilbert Murray, who had come to speak at Newnham. Defining her relation to this "very dear pupil," Jane wrote, "I teach her the Greek I don't know & she gives me daily lessons in strenuous goodness." Perhaps Jane also appreciated their shared propensity for ill health. Jessie Stewart wrote to her mother that Victoria had to interrupt her studies as she had been put on "a very severe Salisbury diet & open air cure." In July 1901, however, Victoria returned, and Jane told Jessie that "it was delicious to have V back," as "her single mindedness always does me good. We have sketched out a beautiful plan for next term to be spent in a general survey of the universe." How far this ambitious scheme progressed remains a mystery, but Jane's playfulness generally signified good feeling.[25]

She did not always respond so positively to her students, however. Even her good friend Margaret Merrifield Verrall's daughter, Helen, elicited faint praise, mainly because she epitomized the second-generation Newnham student:

> She is a queer child—such an embodiment of pure reason & perfect decorum she makes one feel like a street-boy. I have to pull myself up & remember I am her maiden Aunt. Nothing impresses me so much in the modern young girl as their sweet reasonableness—they haven't the smallest desire to kick over the traces.

In many ways Jane may have envied Helen's detachment and submissiveness, but it rankled nevertheless. Years later, Hope Mirrlees commented on Helen's interpretation of the motives of early Newnham students. Hope dutifully recorded Helen's opinion that the early students (presumably her mother's generation) were "very conscious of the Movement" for women's education and thus aware of their success, a trait that distinguished them from her own generation. But Hope added critically that this belief was "*typical* of Helen Salter [her married name]: Her *grotesque* matter of factness & lack of understanding of all emotion is here well exemplified." Perhaps Hope overreacted out of jealousy of Helen's position as daughter of one of Jane's closest friends. She probably would have preferred a certain Miss Webtz, whom Jane thought "a slow & not a very accurate worker & a bad examinee," although, she admitted, she "always liked teaching her."[26]

The generation of women students that followed that of Jane's viewed their situation much differently than she had. Dora Russell, a member of the second generation at Girton, described herself and her peers as more "conscious of our ability and education and of our physical health and strength." Vera Brittain held a similar view about her cohort at Oxford. Their experience seems similar to that of any second generation; once the pioneers had broken the barriers, their followers accepted the new opportunities as their due. Memoirs take on a new cast in this second generation. Dora Russell's autobiography devotes much more discussion to the larger world and contains comparatively little on the intricacies of her educational experience. An extreme case is Josephine Kellet's memoir of her friend, Marguerite McArthur, which focuses almost exclusively on the camaraderie of sports. Although both Kellet and McArthur were Newnham students in Jane's heyday, coming down in 1911, Kellet never mentioned Jane. Her world consisted of field hockey games, friendly dinners, and Fire Brigade practices. These women, far less constrained by Victorian ideals of womanhood than their forerunners, did not see themselves as pioneers; therefore, they felt no need to "kick over the traces."[27]

Sometimes appearance redeemed an intellectually inferior student. Jane mentioned Kitty Marquessan, "who is so lovely that I can't bear her to go to Girton." She admitted to Jessie Stewart her "fear that like her dear mother the girl is brainless," but asked Jessie to "come and say a good word" for Newnham as Jane wanted Kitty to attend there. Finally, she asked rhetorically, "why do plain mothers have lovely girls?"[28]

Recalling her relationship with Jane, Victoria de Bunsen recognized the limitations to Jane's intimacy with students. Primarily, she took no interest in their family lives.

> She was not what is usually called sympathetic. I mean she showed very little interest in the subjects that were bound to concern her non-academic, especially her married, friends. She wrote to me about a bit of work I had done: "Oh I suppose it is inhuman but it does interest me a thousand times more that you should bring forth a book than that you should bring forth a child!" And that was her attitude always. She knew and cared nothing about my children, and I do not think family relationships meant much to her at any time. It was a relief to know that to one person at least one never became the married woman "living *in*" her children or her husband, nor yet the mentally middle-aged enchained by links & ties to other lives with very little of oneself left. To her one remained an individual, and so with her one could not grow old.

Victoria sensed that Jane had retained her dislike of the family and as a teacher continued to create a surrogate family in the college. During the course of some correspondence about a summer governess for Gilbert and Mary Murray's children, Jane wrote to Mary that "one gets to feel rather from the mother's point of view about the girls one wants to help." Although carefully avoiding placing herself in the role of their mother, she nevertheless emphasized that she saw them from a mother's perspective. In the same letter, she rejoiced in Denis Murray's happiness at school, stating that "I never had a peaceful moment till I got there—at the mature age of 17! I sometimes have a Platonic fit & foresee that we make all live in institutions renouncing the rank egotism of Home Life!" Once again, she presented the contrast between the selfishness of family life and the nurturing atmosphere of school. Her conviction prevented her from seeing her students as anything but students for all their lives. Such tunnel vision made their defection through marriage and motherhood difficult for her to accept and explains why she could not delight in other people's children.[29]

Yet while they were students, Jane devoted boundless energy to their training. More important, they benefited from her passion for her subject and her keen intellect. Jessie Stewart wrote that they "were plunged into whatever was engrossing her at the time." More than anyone, Jessie received Jane's undivided attention in these years. Jessie was in her second year at Newnham when Jane took over as director of archaeological studies for the new part II of the classical tripos. As Jessie tells it, Jane adopted her after "she had seen hanging in my room her favourite scene of initiation ritual from the Villa Fernesina ceiling which I had newly brought back from Rome." They remained close friends (although their relationship took on a new cast after Jessie's marriage to H. F. Stewart) until Hope Mirrlees supplanted Jessie in Jane's affection around 1912. Jessie, who never lost her admiration for Jane, wrote a loving and gentle biographical portrait, and she retained a special place in Jane's heart as one of her earliest students and her "first First."[30]

Jessie sat for part I of the classical tripos in June 1900, and for some reason Jane feared that Jessie might have done well enough only for a second. She wrote to Jessie the day the lists were to be published, saying "I am very much afraid this morning's list could be a disappointment to you but just look upon it as a good . . . basis on which to build archaeological distinction!" (Jessie faced archaeology in part II of the tripos.) Jane revealed her own disappointment at achieving only a second in her tripos and admitted that "it was a dreadful blow to me long ago when I had to face a second, but I have never found it made a bit of difference in one's life's work."[31] Although she may have found comfort in the thought of Jessie's replicating her achievement, it turned out that Jessie got a first after all, and Jane pronounced herself "bursting with pride."[32]

Jessie Stewart, 1902. Photo courtesy of Jean Stewart Pace. Reproduced by University Library, Cambridge.

In September 1900, Jane proposed that Jessie join her on a trip to Greece the next year and wrote to her with arguments in its favor. Jane had explored the administrative details and "ascertained that you need not keep your terms strictly this last year." She believed that "from the tripos point of view the time would be well spent" and that "from the general educational standpoint you could scarcely do better." She allowed Jessie plenty of time to consider the trip, but asked her to inform her parents that "if they entrust you to me I will do my best with a weighty responsibility!" Jessie's parents agreed to the trip, and she set out in the spring of 1901 to join Jane in Italy.[33]

Jessie wrote excitedly from various stops on their tour of archaeological sites, exclaiming over Jane's acquaintance with so many leading figures. From Athens, she told her father that "Miss Harrison gets all the great men to let us in everywhere!" Jane's old friend, German archaeologist Wilhelm Dorpfeld, was in Athens, and Jessie was "tremendously excited" by his presence.[34] She wrote from Petras that despite a rough trip and losing their luggage, everyone remained in good spirits. She called Jane "splendid" and remarked that Jane "feels responsible for Greece & shows off everything." She had introduced Jessie and the group to " 'resinous wine' " and they "had a procession round our beds" at the hotel. They attended a party hosted by Dorpfeld, which Jessie gleefully described to her family.

> It was such fun, all the greatest archaeologists in the world, & none of them on speaking terms! Dr. Dorpfeld brought Prof. Furtwangler & made him say How do you do to Jane & he looked so furious, I thought there was going to be a scene & Jane rose with her most gracious smile & shook hands—They all flock round her & appreciate her far more than the English.

The trip was a resounding success, and Jessie returned to Cambridge later in the spring to prepare for part II of her tripos.[35]

That same year brought Jessie's engagement to H. F. Stewart, which spelled the beginning of the end for real intimacy between her and Jane. Upon hearing the news, Jane wrote: "You always were meant to be married which doesn't the least to my mind mean 'flabbiness.' Only a certain human dependence which comes of keen sympathies. I shall burn all my bedroom candles for you both." Despite the distance Jessie's marriage created, Jane showed more interest in her family than in those of her other younger friends. In 1903, when Jessie had her first child, Jane wrote to Jessie's sister, Edith Crum, that "it is a great delight about Jessie" giving birth. But more than the baby, Jane wished "for a sight of the mother—babies are all very well but mothers are very much better." Jessie apparently suffered a miscarriage late in 1904, and Jane wrote anxiously about her health: "I am concerned about your letter. You are rather vague but—putting two & two together I fear it means a second & real misadventure. I am grieved at this for I fear it means that you are not as strong as you think . . . please send me a word as to how you really are." Jane's memories of her mother's death and her own fear of childbirth made her anxious throughout her friends' pregnancies and also help explain her unmistakable preference for mother over child. Always sensitive to forces pulling her friends away from her, Jane viewed each child as another wedge driven between them. The easiest way to neutralize their influence was to ignore them. As she confessed to Gilbert Murray, she could not help feeling that "this world is a splendid place but I am always *furious* when anyone comes into it."[36]

Yet Jane could be remarkably tolerant of and concerned for other people's children, partly because of her love for the parents (usually the mothers) and partly because of her own childlike appreciation of the world. Jane congratulated Jessie Stewart on the birth of her son in 1908 and commented on the behavior of Jessie's daughter toward him, saying "I think Jean will be a really good sister to this small son, she will keep him last & in his proper place." She then related that she had met Jean "the day after & she shouted after me 'I can't spare my little brother to you!'; I did not know that I was looking covetous!"[37]

Jane and Jessie stayed in touch beyond Jessie's marriage partly because Jane often asked her to make drawings for slides. Jane acknowledged her dependence on Jessie's help, calling her "the most able person I have ever known & the greatest comfort." Another request for drawings led Jane to add, "I know you are thinking how safe & happy you are—but—alas. There is no peace for the really competent." Jessie also had a gift for finding presents that especially suited Jane. A set of pencils elicited the following thank you: "I was much touched by the gift of the green pencils. It was a real inspiration. I *never* have a pencil, and no one ever before gave me one, and now I feel I have a real understanding friend as well as five green pencils."[38]

Jessie also owned two dogs that enchanted Jane and received more attention than Jessie's children. Hope Mirrlees observed that "Jane used to say that she had lived all her life on other peoples' animals" and that "as a result she had no sense of responsibility towards them." Jane accused Jessie's Dandie Dinmont terrier, Robin, of having "eaten most of my feather boa in a fit of emotion," but she loved him nevertheless.[39] She mentioned his death in a letter to Mary Murray when she sent Mary a photograph of herself taken with him. She mourned the death of "my best friend here" who was "buried with a letter from me in his grave." She exalted him as "the only Christian I have ever met" and "just a perfect thing in one's life, all beauty and gentleness and love."[40] Jane rarely bestowed such praise on any human friend. In response to a letter containing news of Kapi, Robin's replacement, Jane wrote, "it was beautiful to hear of Kapi. It's very sad for in desponding moments I sometimes fear I shall never hold his black paw again. Kiss his still blacker nose for me."[41] Eventually poor Kapi's "depradations on the hen-roost led to his disgrace and banishment to a farm in Scotland," and Jane composed an inscription detailing his exploits in cuneiform done by Francis Cornford. She translated the inscription as follows: "Kapi whom I love like my life, precious, the hero mighty, girt with terrors to slay the fowl of heaven, the black one, with her blood he dyed the mountain like crimson wool. I was distressed—my countenance was troubled. But he came—he kissed my feet. I had mercy on him." Such playfulness marks much of Jane's correspondence during these years when she surrounded herself with admiring students and congenial colleagues.[42]

Newnham in this period most closely resembled the "learned community for women" Jane envisioned in her "Reminiscences," for it now suited her vision of such a community in many ways. It fulfilled her needs as an established scholar differently than it had when she was a student. During those early days, Jane had still had to contend with rivals and the fact of her provincial background. Eccentricity could either enhance or detract from her image in her fellow students' eyes. As an established scholar, however, she could flaunt convention without fear of antagonizing either students or colleagues. Instead of being in the position of one of many siblings, as she had been while a student, she could become the center of attention by assuming the role of surrogate mother.

Despite her avowed preference for a community for women, she insisted nevertheless on having the best of both worlds. Except for an early collaboration with Margaret Merrifield Verrall on *Mythology and Monuments of Ancient Athens,* she never worked closely with female colleagues. They were a fine audience, as were her women students, but she would share the stage only with male colleagues. Newnham provided an outer circle, a safe personal haven from everyday life. There she could protect herself from the hazards of personal relations with men. Newnham also released her from the obligations of family life and responsibility for men's needs and demands while simultaneously providing emotional warmth and support. When it came to the life of the mind, however, she preferred the company of men.

Although Jane did not think so, marriage and teaching were not necessarily incompatible. Mary Paley, Margaret Merrifield Verrall, and Eleanor Sidgwick, for instance, combined service to Newnham with marriage to fellow Cambridge scholars. The essential difference between their careers and Jane's, however, lay not in their teaching but in scholarly production. None of them remotely matched her record of publication and breadth and depth of research. She did, of course, have somewhat more time to devote to research and travel because of her early fellowship, but she also lectured and supervised students. Jane's immersion in her work distinguished her from her married colleagues in a variety of ways and for several reasons. Her books were the children she never had, and she nurtured their growth and endowed them with human characteristics. Perhaps more important, she channeled the energy she might have devoted to a husband and marriage into her scholarly work. Believing as she did that art springs from unsatisfied desire, Jane sensed that her imperative need to make sense out of a chaotic universe could not tolerate many diversions and, conversely, that she felt inexorably driven by that need. The reasons for this need were complex, but continued to revolve around the sense of betrayal that lingered from her childhood. Her scholarly work was a journey to understanding, and in some ways she knew it had to be a solitary one.

In other ways, Jane desperately wanted a fellow traveler. But her extraordinary intelligence and unique character clashed with the idea of romance in a society that devalued smart, independent women. Those of her classmates who married happily and lived the usual academic life were competent teachers and adequate scholars, but they lacked the burning intensity that infused Jane's life and work. Even Cambridge men such as A. W. Verrall and Alfred Marshall who married educated Newnham women respected Jane's intellect but seemed not to regard her as a woman. While puzzling out the relationship between knowledge, power, and love for her 1914 essay "Scientiae Sacra Fames," Jane asked "a really thinking man" what "a man expected to get from the intellectual companionship of his wife that he could not and did not get from a man friend." This unnamed man made the revealing reply that "a man doesn't expect his wife to really understand his work, though she will be interested in it because it is his." Her true purpose was to "keep him in touch with things and people in general" that he might not become lost "in his own specialism." Wives served a social purpose, in his mind and doubtless in the minds of most other academic men as well. Men assumed their inferior intelligence but expected their unfailing support and lively interest in their husbands' endeavors.[43]

Despite her reservations, Jane came close to marrying the Pembroke College philologist R. A. Neil soon after her return to Newnham. His role in her life has been defined as "friend and . . . helper" and "probably the soundest, most critical of her advisors," but Hope Mirrlees's notes tell another story. Jane met Neil soon after her return to Cambridge, and their common scholarly interests brought them together. He was born in 1852, the son of a Scottish clergyman, and graduated from the University of Aberdeen in 1870 at age eighteen with a first class degree in classics. After toying with the idea of becoming a doctor and then spending four years as a fellow of Peterhouse College, he became a lecturer in classics at Pembroke College. He supported women's education and lectured at both Newnham and Girton in his early days at Cambridge. Neil also shared Jane's interest in Sanskrit and Buddhism. Jane herself rarely referred to him in print, but described him fondly when she did. He was the friend whose "sympathetic Scotch silences made the dreariest gathering burn and glow" (RSL, 332), and "almost the best & quite the oldest of my friends here" whose "Sunday luncheons were to me the best intellectual thing in Cambridge." According to Elinor Ritchie Paul, however, they had once been much closer than that. In fact, Neil asked Jane to marry him, and she agreed. But his sudden death from complications following an attack of appendicitis in 1901 put an end to their plans. Her sorrow at losing him was evident when she wrote "every scrap of my present work [the *Prolegomena to the Study of Greek Religion*] has been discussed with him and simply aches with remembrance." Jane was otherwise reticent about her feelings toward Neil, however, making it difficult to discern the motives behind her acceptance of his proposal. More than likely, at the age of fifty she felt that she would not have another chance at making a match, and they shared an intense interest in and devotion to similar kinds of work. No doubt respect for both his kindness and his intellect would have contented Jane, but she seems not to have had the complex, passionate feelings toward him that she had earlier shown toward Sutherland MacColl. Nevertheless, his proposal of marriage is the only one Jane ever accepted. Unfortunately, precious little evidence about the nature of their relationship remains. Very possibly, Jane agreed to marry him precisely because he did not evoke a passionate response and therefore seemed less threatening to her autonomy.[44]

It is interesting to speculate on what course her life would have taken if Neil had lived. Recognizing that "the role of wife and mother is no easy one," Jane feared that "with my head full of other things" she "might dismally have failed" at both (RSL, 345). It is equally plausible that her work would have suffered. Clearly, at age fifty she did not need to fear the prospect of pregnancy. If she had truly succeeded in suppressing the physical side of her nature, as she claimed after her failed romance with Sutherland MacColl, she may not even have had to fear the power of sexuality. Perhaps she and Neil had agreed to base their marriage on a desire for companionship rather than sex. Whatever the situation, Jane's perception of the demands marriage placed on women indicates that she feared failing in the family setting or, conversely, being consumed by it.

Jane's frequent forays into her friends' family homes belie her inner conflict between a need to belong and a need to maintain her independence. The Verralls, the Murrays, and the Darwins all welcomed her into their homes, but in those family circles she remained an outsider. Jane's Newnham students and friends loved and admired her for her intellect, but as a visitor in a family home she felt on shaky ground. Her close relationships with Jessie Stewart and Hope Mirrlees provided the best of both worlds: the intimacy of two people devoted to each other but without sexual entanglements.

The most enduring of Jane's relationships with students was that with Hope Mirrlees, who was Jane's companion from her arrival at Newnham in 1909 until Jane's death in 1928. They met when Jane became her Greek teacher, and they were soon fast friends. Their correspondence, partly letters written during periods of separation but largely notes exchanged when they both lived at Newnham, reveals an extraordinary devotion. For her part, Hope admitted that she owed her "whole picture of the universe to her, & everything about me that is not ignoble," although she later tempered this statement by noting that "I wrote this before I became a Catholic." She bore striking similarities to Jane: bourgeois family, northern provincial origins, uneasiness among the cultured elite of Cambridge and London, propensity for ill health, sharp intelligence, and a certain eccentricity. Above all, Hope shared with Jane a problematic relationship with her mother, which worsened after her father's death in 1924. By that time, Jane had retired from teaching and gone to Paris with Hope. After Hope's father died she brought her mother to Paris, and Jane wrote to Jessie Stewart that her visit did not "contribute to a quiet & regular life." Lina Mirrlees was "quite at loose ends as to what to do & where to go," but it quickly became "quite clear & very tragic" that "mother & daughter can never make a home together—how little love does towards making compatibility." Jane had learned that lesson through bitter experience.[45]

Like Jessie Stewart, Hope's family owned a dog that Jane adored; in contrast to the more likely canine names of Jessie's dogs, Hope called hers Cranmer. At one raucous family dinner, Jane ignored the commotion and "wearing the rather stern expression her face assumed when abstracted from her surroundings, she went on quietly feeding Cranmer with chocolates . . . Cranmer standing on his hind legs at her side, a furry confident pillar." Cranmer would, "according to Jane . . . say to her from time to time in a condescending tone, 'I've a little spare time, so you may scratch me under the chin.' "[46]

The notes from their early Newnham days reveal that Jane and Hope created a little world for themselves in which they shared a cast of characters and let their imaginations run free in peopling their little universe with anthropomorphized stuffed animals. Jane's love of bears became almost an obsession at this time, although her room, which she usually called her "cave," contained stuffed sheep and dogs as well. According to Hope, the business of the bears started when three students, Agnes Conway, Helen Verrall, and an unnamed woman, gave Jane the stuffed bear that became "Herr Professor," or the "Old One," or

Jane Harrison and Hope Mirrlees in Paris, 1915. Postcard sent to Gilbert Murray. From JEH Papers, Newnham College. Reproduced by University Library, Cambridge.

simply "the Bear."[47] Much of their correspondence revolved around or was carried on through the Bear, and Jane often used it to express feelings she preferred not to articulate herself.

Jane referred to Hope as the "Young Walrus" and herself as the "Elder Walrus," and often to the Bear as husband to them both. This bizarre use of an inanimate object could be construed as indicating that Jane viewed her relationship with Hope as a sort of marriage, and indirectly this interpretation may be partly true. Martha Vicinus believes that "Hope Mirrlees appears to have been sexually attracted to Harrison, but it is unclear to what extent Harrison reciprocated." I would argue that their relationship was certainly erotic but not sexual. First, although Jane had a very sensual element in her nature that could not escape unnoticed, she also possessed extraordinary self-control. Such control exacted an enormous psychological cost, but in her everyday life she had indeed mastered her physical side. Second, all the evidence paints Jane as determinedly heterosexual. For complex reasons, she greatly feared sexuality, but she reserved her greatest passions and attachments for men. Although she shared many intense and rewarding relationships with women, no evidence indicates that she had a sexual relationship with Hope or any other woman.[48]

Hope commented that "it is certain that Jane, although much *more* sensible to the attractions of men, was by no means insensible to those of women—if she considered them beautiful. . . . She certainly was slightly, & quite unconsciously, slightly flirtatious in manner both to men & women." Virginia Woolf read Hope's 1919 novel, *Madeleine: One of Love's Jansenists,* and pronounced it "all sapphism so far as I've got—Jane and herself." But Woolf often made hasty and inaccurate judgments about even those people whom she liked. I do not find any of this evidence sufficient to conclude that Hope and Jane had a sexual relationship. Despite her avowed detachment from intimacy, Jane craved affection and attention. She found both in her relationship with Hope. Frustrated in their dealings with the world at large, they turned to each other for emotional sustenance.[49]

Hope proved her fidelity early on when she broke off her engagement to a young man in 1910. The man's name and the actual circumstances of their engagement have never surfaced, but it is known that Jane approved of Hope's action and rejoiced over her return to Newnham. In a letter postmarked July 3, 1910, Jane sent her condolences on the breakup, saying she was "relieved it is ended—for tho' 'pedestrian love' is a good & great thing it is not quite enough I think on which to climb the steep stair of marriage." In saying this, she may have had in mind many of her own relationships with men. She was "truly glad" Hope planned to return to Newnham, as well she might be: unlike the other members of Jane's circles, Hope had consciously rejected marriage and returned to the fold of the college community. Jane told Hope's mother that she "felt from the way she spoke that the engagement might not be a lasting one" and that she did not "feel that the hour has struck for Hope yet." As Jane undoubtedly hoped, it never did, and after the one possibility of marriage fell through, Hope seems to have given up the idea altogether. Some time after the engagement ended, Jane wrote cryptically to her, asking that she "think of North & his widder & you—if you hadn't been so stand-offish might have been the happy mother of his many children." Whether North was the man Hope earlier intended to marry is unclear, but obviously Jane did not think she should regret her decision.[50]

Jane often used the Bear as a means of inviting Hope to visit or go places with her. A note from the Bear headed "To my Wives" requested that "my young Wife [Hope] do dine in Hall tomorrow with my elder Wife and go to the young Ladies' Revue." The Bear insisted that Hope "is *not* a comic cub she is my young wife" and solemnly recorded that the message was "given in the Cave—in the presence of Mrs. Mutz & the Glass Horse." The identities of the two witnesses remains a mystery; most likely, they were other members of the stuffed menagerie. On another occasion, the Bear asked that "if you happen to be free tomorrow afternoon Wednesday about 6 do come & meet the Grey Hare. Something extraordinarily solemn is going on in the Cave." Along with this message, Hope's "Husband" sent her a "red carnation with His Love."[51]

The Bear could both suffer illness (presumably Jane's) and sympathize with others' illness. Once while recuperating from sickness, Jane invited Hope to tea and promised "you will find Ursula much stronger, the old Bear has turned a Xian Scientist & is [illegible] along her with his front paw." Another time, when apparently both were ill, the Bear thoughtfully sent Hope a companion to cheer her up. "The Bear (his temperature is lower but he is still *very* weak) sends Mr. Velvet Brown with his compliments to stay with you till you are better. They are very close friends drawn together by a close analogy in furs paws high moral tone etc." Mr. Velvet Brown, named after Jane's sister's cat and presumably a fellow feline, had unfortunately "lately 'passed away' but 'he being dead yet speaketh' as the Psalmist says." When Hope fell ill on a visit to Gloucestershire, Jane sympathized over her "crise" and exclaimed that it must have been "perfectly horrid" for her to be "all alone"; then she caught herself, remembering "I mustn't say that for One was with you—'One there is above all others.' "[52]

Hope looked after the cave's inhabitants while Jane traveled. Before leaving for Greece in April 1912, Jane wrote to Hope, then traveling in Germany, asking her to take care of the Bear upon her return. "When you get back will you take him up into your room as he will be lonely?"

Familiar surroundings were very important to Jane, and she expressed her anxiety in another undated message written soon after her return from perhaps the same journey.

> Thank you so much for looking after the old Bear & most of all for putting him back so beautifully into his cave. I flew across the garden the moment I got back but a "pale green fear" got hold of me lest you might have forgotten & the cave be empty. It was faithless of me for you never do forget *really* important things like that. He looked so wonderful leaning his head against the wall-eyed sheep.
>
> But it's rather serious for he firmly tho' quite politely refuses to move into Sidgwick Hall he says you never lived there & it isn't a place for a Bear of his standing—& that the W.E.S. agrees with him. So there's nothing more to be said.

Sometimes, though, the Bear had to remain in Hope's room until Jane's return. On Christmas Day, 1914, Jane wrote that she had not found the Bear until that morning, when he was "sunk in sleep when I came over to Peile at screech of dawn—he had made himself a hot drink, mulled mead I think it was in his Victorian way & he had such a heavenly look of warmth & peace on his old face."[53]

Some letters show that the Bear also shared Jane's prejudices. In 1913, as she worked on her essay "Scientiae Sacra Fames" she wrote to Hope in Paris that "the old Bear is busy forming an anti suffrage league. It is since my discourse on Woman & Knowledge. He says She Bears are getting out of hand." Commenting on Hope's absence, she added, "he still can't understand your leaving Home & Duty." Like Jane, the Bear believed that acquiring knowledge conferred more power than simply acquiring the vote. In the same year, the Bear "had a great compliment paid him: the Berne bears are having an Esperanto Congress & they sent a deputation to ask him to take the chair—he won't go because he is a really Sound scholar but he thinks it a very proper attention." Jane wrote this letter when Hope was away and included an obvious dig at her friend for deserting her. The Bear was "much upset by your not coming back" and claimed that "Ursula like all young people is fickle—so he has got a new love a large & splendid Yorkshire Ram not wall-eyed at all." He grew impatient if Hope remained out of touch for long or neglected his desires. Jane wrote that "the Bear is in a fearful fuss to have his portrait fixed—He says I am to write 'lest she forget—He is muttering a great many things about 'Tempora mutantur' (he is a sound scholar), & 'Young people' & 'want of proper consideration for old bears of position' & many other really fresh & original thoughts." Through the medium of the Bear, Jane conveyed her dependence on and affection for Hope.[54]

Like Jane, though, the Bear reserved his deepest contempt for Christmas. Jane explained his behavior while she visited Alice Dew-Smith in Rye over a Christmas holiday.

> Just to tell you the Real Truth. I couldn't tell it when Alice Dew-Smith was in the room for fear it might seem a reflection on the Hutch [the name of Alice's Rye home]. The Old Bear wouldn't come because he likes a traditional Xmas in his own Baronial Halls—with his retainers round him & a boar's head brought in & mummers & things—it *isn't* snobbishness—but just a very deep down & beautiful feudalism.
>
> If you will take the cock to see him when you get home you will find him keeping Xmas on the second shelf of the middle cupboard in my room with all his retainers revelling round him. The cock cannot be a retainer but he might be the Holy Ghost brooding over Bethlehem (proleptically) there was in the Middle Ages a muddle (I mean a calumnatio) between cock & dove.

The Bear preferred to emphasize the social rather than the theological aspect of Christmas, despite his being "L. C. [Low Church] & thoroughly conservative"—so much so that he once requested "a set of bands—such as your father (& distinguished clergymen) wear when royalties are about" and refused to "join the Fabians or be dans le mouvement at all."[55]

Hope responded to Jane's anxiety during her absences by keeping in close contact with her, often sending her the postcards that Jane so treasured as part of a long-standing rebellion against her family's distrust of the innovation of the penny post.[56] The Bear either often traveled with Hope or influenced her telepathically because, according to Jane, he chose some of Hope's postcards. "The old Bear has the most wonderful taste in post-cards," she wrote to Hope in Paris; "please thank him very much. He must always help you to choose things—he might even choose your chiffons his touch in art is so sure." After Hope set off for a visit to Gloucester in the summer of 1915, Jane complained, "here I am pining to know how the Old One bore the journey & never a word—Only a pc is wanted to say if all goes well with Him & you & if you are finally under way? Don't attempt a letter a picture pc is what I yearn for with the print of his paw on it." Hope responded with two postcards, and Jane "was glad to get news of the Old One and you. . . . the B 'bless you & keep you' & make you to walk in the print of His footsteps."[57]

The Bear could also dote on his "wives." When Jane returned from a visit to London in 1918, the Bear greeted her with pleasure: "The OO [Old One] is in his cave—he never [illegible] yelled—not a sound—he only smiled very sweetly & said as long as his two wives were safe all was well with his world—& he sent a soft stroke with his right paw to his young wife." Hope remained in London, and Jane included a rare message directly to her without the Bear as intermediary. "This will find you I hope when you are having your walrus breakfast . . . eating it slowly I hope & not overeating—you must have been a worn out walrus by the time you got there."[58]

Not surprisingly, Jane's very intense relationship with Hope created distance between Jane and Jessie Stewart, particularly since Jessie had "deserted" Jane for a husband. The full implications of this rivalry did not emerge until well after Jane's death, but hindsight shows clearly that they occupied the position of two daughters competing for their mother's affection. Hope's decision to remain at Newnham with Jane gave her the edge in the competition, and Jane voiced her hopes for the future to Mrs. Mirrlees. "It is sad to think my last class with Hope is over," she wrote after Hope had completed her studies, "but that is only the end of one chapter I hope. Some ways when the relation of teacher & taught is past it is easier to get to know one another."[59] Jane and Hope certainly proved this statement true.

That these two women shared a special bond is both undeniable and understandable. They came from similar kinds of families and reacted in similar ways to the elite world in which they found themselves. The most significant difference between them is that Jane attracted people to her, whereas Hope, self-conscious and abrasive, antagonized them. But if Hope lacked Jane's charm and vitality, she compensated for it, in Jane's eyes, with her dutiful and deferential behavior. Jane referred to Hope as her "ghostly daughter" (RSL, 346) and their relationship was primarily a mother-daughter one. They had all the benefits of such a relationship without the inherent conflicts and tensions, and Hope conformed to Jane's vision of what college life could do for both students and teachers by creating a community of women. Most important, their friendship was unscarred by rivalries concerning men; both having rejected marriage, they could devote their energies to maintaining the relationship that offered them support in a world that considered them anomalous.

Although Jane took an active interest in some of her students, she rejoiced, like all academics, in the vacations that brought peace to Newnham. As the September lull approached in 1904, Jane wrote joyfully to Mary Murray, "now I am back at work & in two days I shall have the college to myself—oh the peace of it! I know I am a hermit gone wrong." Earlier, she had told Jessie Stewart that "the approach of term fills me with horror" because she had "come to regard the College as my own exclusive preserve & every fresh arrival is a personal insult." She could do "more real work in September than in the whole of the rest of the year." Even in the best times Jane jealously guarded the very small circle of her world against intruders. Her concern for her students never wavered, however, and she proved her passionate devotion to their welfare by her efforts on behalf of the only women's issue that ever interested her: the granting of university degrees to women.[60]

Jane's support of degrees for women represented much more than a political view. She knew that a university degree would greatly increase a woman's marketability in the work world. But more important, she understood that education and knowledge conferred power. Her intuitive perception of the social and cultural values attached to a university education and the importance of status and power to both reformers and critics enabled her to understand, perhaps more fully than many others, the intricacies of the reform movement.

An essay that appeared first in the *New Statesman* and then in *Alpha and Omega* illuminates Jane's views on the power of knowledge and its relation to women. "Scientiae Sacra Fames," initially published in 1914, offers a wealth of autobiographical information that helps explain her meshing of political and intellectual justifications for the granting of degrees to women.

The essay begins by recognizing the Victorian tradition that young women should be educated primarily in order to provide good conversation for their husbands.

> But the dear delight of learning for learning's sake a "dead" language for sheer love of the beauty of its words and the delicacy of its syntactical relations, the joy of tracking out the secret springs of the human body irrespective of patient or doctor, the rapture of reconstructing for the first time in imagination a bit of the historical past, that *was,* that in a few laggard minds still obscurely *is,* unwomanly.[61]

Jane recalled an incident from her childhood that conveyed her own rebellion against these oppressive values.

> Some half-century ago a very happy little girl secretly possessed herself of a Greek grammar. A much-adored aunt swiftly stripped the gilt from the gingerbread with these chill, cutting words: "I do not see how Greek grammar is to help little Jane to keep house when she has a home of her own." A "home of her own" was as near as the essentially decent aunt of those days might get to an address on sex and marriage, but the child understood: she was a little girl, and thereby damned to eternal domesticity; she heard the gates of the temple of Learning clang as they closed. (117)

Domesticity equaled sex: she could neither separate nor reconcile them. Acknowledging that the "temple of Learning" had since opened to women, she addressed the question of the nature of knowledge and explored why men feared the result if women acquired it. She concluded that "it is not that any particular knowledge or information is denied as unsuitable" but that "unstinted knowledge begets a habit of mind, an atmosphere, an attitude deemed unwomanly." The imminent danger, in Jane's view, was that "between feeling and knowing there is a certain antithesis; the province of women was to feel: therefore they had better not know." She was too smart to deny the radicalizing potential of women's acquiring knowledge, admitting that in men's attempts to deny them education and access to knowledge, "as in all the most poisonous falsehoods," there exists "some grain of muddled truth" (118). In her view, the "muddled truth" lay in education's potential for freeing women from dependence on men.

Jane contended that the limitations imposed on women's knowledge, reducing them to students of only those things that are of practical use, resulted not from men's innate selfishness but rather from women's exclusive devotion to the home. Through a complicated process of mutual reinforcement, man's fear of losing the support of a being who catered to his needs and woman's "family egotism" created the Victorian family, which Jane posited as a nearly universal institution. Women were already possessed of " 'knowledge by acquaintance,' " knowledge that could be related only to the self or to its "immediate surroundings." They needed to acquire " 'knowledge by description,' " which men had and which enabled an individual to be "conscious not only of the thing *felt*, but . . . conscious of its relation to other selves than our own self; conscious, too, of the relation of the thing to other things" (120–21). Women's exclusive focus on the family was an "old virtue . . . fast rotting into a vice" whose destruction would be "clear gain" (122). Jane criticized women's inability to relate to things outside themselves. Knowledge would serve primarily to draw them out. Indirectly, Jane called on women to engage actively and constructively in society: not so much politically as psychologically.

Women's knowledge of religion proved equally pernicious, for "the emotion of religion . . . may be the deadliest danger unless informed and directed by a knowledge of the ways of God—i.e., the nature of the universe and that part of it which is man" (123). Women needed to make sense of the universe, to understand and replicate its order, and religion worked directly counter to that purpose. Moreover, this ordering of the universe had always been a distinctly male undertaking. With a vision of her stepmother before her, Jane decried a purely personal religion by claiming that "a religious woman without knowledge is like a lunatic armed with an explosive" (123).

Advances in education for women occurred when men finally admitted what women reformers hinted at: that educated men were ultimately dissatisfied with poorly educated wives. At first, man "created a demand for fools . . . whose interest was focussed on himself." He got what he wanted and deserved but remained unhappy, so "the prayers of the congregation are now asked on behalf of the husband who is sick of a wholly devoted wife" (124). But Jane did not attribute steps forward to men's whims. Women's increased freedom benefited society as a whole. Restricting women to the home did not serve society's best interest. "What is really wanted for the home is, we are beginning to find out, a little more wide human knowledge and a little less egocentric sentiment" (125). Jane compared men's and women's rooms in the home, citing the quiet, "inviolate" study where "man thinks, and learns, and knows" versus the drawing room, ordinarily the wife's preserve, the "room in which you can't possibly settle down to think, because anyone may come in at any moment." The wife "must be able and ready to switch her mind off and on at any moment, to anyone's concerns." But "one of the most ominous signs of the times is that woman is beginning to demand a study" (128).

Despite her belief in women's potential, Jane freely admitted that she preferred the intellectual company of men. She believed in sex differences in the intellect, resulting from a "difference in focus," although she advocated cooperation as "fruitful." She based her ultimate optimism on a belief that "intellect is never wholly and separately intellectual," but rather "a thing charged with, dependent on, arising out of, emotional desire" (140). What she called the "holy hunger after knowledge" represented "but the latest, rarest utterance of the Will to Live" (141). And from the universal, Jane extracted the particular. Humanity as a whole recognized the validity of women's claim to greater knowledge, so this step could be considered a healthy one. Women could achieve the insularity of mind that Jane valued so highly in men only if they broke the bonds of family obligations and true womanhood. In a roundabout way, she renewed her attack on the family, based on her own childhood experience, from a different direction. As in many other writings, the family loomed as obstacle to any intellectual achievement, but she also exhibited an underlying current of resentment toward the family's exclusiveness. She acutely sensed the divide between each family and the outside world and the definitive way in which her status as a single, educated woman excluded her from the world of family. If she could not become part of that world, her only alternative was to call for its reform. Her vision of the family as engaged with the larger world both allowed her emotional intimacy despite her singleness and made that alien world of the family conform more closely to the world in which she lived.

Jane also urged the granting of degrees on practical grounds. Cambridge moved even more slowly than Oxford on this question, and the campaign stirred much angry debate. Jane perceived the concrete disadvantages caused by women's exclusion from degrees and worked actively to change the university's policy. The struggle began virtually with the founding of women's colleges in the early 1870s, and it was not resolved at Oxford until 1919 and at Cambridge, incredibly, until 1948.

Many works, both contemporary and recent, have chronicled and analyzed the campaign for degrees. Briefly, the good showing that early Newnham and Girton students made on their examinations and in the tripos prompted reformers to ask that the university Senate consider granting degrees to women on an equal basis with men. In 1881, upon the first request, the Senate recommended admitting women formally only to the honors examination, without granting degrees, and the publication of a separate class list that would indicate their rank in the general list without placing their names with the men's. The separate list was designed to appease those who feared that, as with allowing women to take the same examinations as men, direct competition would result. Subsequent attempts at reform came in 1887 and 1897. The first action failed miserably, but in 1897 the university formed a syndicate to investigate a compromise. It devised a plan offering women B.A. diplomas and the use of that title if they had completed nine terms in residence and passed the tripos, but stopped short of granting membership in the university. All degree recipients became members of the university and were thus entitled to vote on university policy. Not surprisingly, the members (all of them, of course, male) overwhelmingly voted down this plan. The debate continued during Jane's next two decades at Cambridge and beyond. Her letters frequently referred to the status of various schemes to give women both degrees and membership in the university, especially around the time of a vote in 1920.[62]

By 1900, debate had shifted in focus from the 1860s and 1870s. The opposition to degrees for women arose more from fear of allowing them to become voting members of the university than from doubts about their ability or the seemliness of such a step. Degree holders set university policy, and the old guard who made up Cambridge's alumni hated to give up this privilege. It had been their university for centuries, and they had no desire to see what women would make of it. They feared that if Cambridge granted degrees to women, the best young men would flock to Oxford, while female dons feared that if Cambridge refused degrees, the best young women would flock to Oxford, especially after 1919.[63] The standoff endured until 1948.

Jane recognized the influential role that public perceptions of womanhood played in the degree struggle. Because she had been raised with the specter of propriety always at hand, few knew better than she that men feared more than anything else an "unwomanly" female. She remarked to Gilbert Murray after hearing an archaeological lecture that it had depressed her because of the recognition that "women tend to 'inhibit' horns—men are showy & exhibit them—I mean in the Sheep class—now how *can* we hope for votes & degrees if nature condemns us to this inhibition?" She allowed him to "tell this to Mary tho it will depress her too, but do not let Percy Gardner [brother of her rival for the Yates Professorship, Ernest Gardner] get wind of it for I hear he thinks a diploma in archaeology might endanger our modesty—he will use it as an argument." The lecturer displayed a picture of "an old She-Sheep," and Jane "nearly wept she looked so womanly" with her "inhibited" horns.[64]

Practical problems arose because of women's ambiguous status at the old universities. Jane asked Gilbert Murray for advice on dealing with a problem pitting a female student against the British School in Athens. Miss Hardie, the student, had applied to go on an archaeological dig, but since she was not officially a Cambridge graduate, the British School tried to keep her out. Apparently Mrs. Sachs, wife of the classicist Gustave Sachs, had founded a studentship in her husband's memory for "*a graduate of an English university* for Greek Studies in Athens." As Jane pointed out, these terms made Cambridge and Oxford women ineligible, and she implored Gilbert to speak to Mrs. Sachs about changing the definition of eligibility. The outcome was never revealed, but this incident illustrates Jane's concern about the concrete problems that women faced without degrees. The issue resurfaced in 1922 when the British School in Athens gave preferences for studentships to "*duly qualified members of the University.*" By this time, Oxford women were eligible, along with women from every other British university. Only Cambridge women were excluded.[65]

The debate over degrees for women culminated in the unrest sparked by a 1921 proposal. In May 1919, Oxford finally admitted women to membership and agreed to grant them degrees. Fearing a mass exodus of the best women students to Oxford, Newnham dons began to agitate for another bid at degrees for women. After fruitless years of placating Cambridge men who feared the terrible vices that might be spawned by educating women, Jane wrote dispiritedly to Gilbert Murray.

> I don't suppose you realize how convention & all the conservative virtues are canonized in a woman's college necessarily I suppose until we are free & get membership—sometimes I feel that *the* virtue fostered among us is conformity—it is simply priceless to have someone like you to raise the standard of living for ideals instead of living to propitiate captious & ever vigilant critics. I don't think it is quite our own fault that our virtues are mainly those of slaves but they *are*—nice well educated slaves but still slaves. Of course the education that is being got will in the end stop all that—but meanwhile much of our ingenuity & energy goes in cringing—I feel it constantly myself.

She spoke for a generation of women who had struggled against enormous odds. They believed they had paid their dues and deserved better treatment from the university. Yet, being proper ladies, they controlled their anger and frustration, trusting in Cambridge's essential fairness. Jane, however, had begun to lose hope, recognizing that years of playing by men's rules had made Newnham (and Girton) women subservient. After an exodus of women students during World War I, Jane wrote to Gilbert, commenting briefly on the differences she saw in her students. She wanted to ask Mary "about Somerville [College at Oxford] & self-government & no chaperones—our young things come back from the land etc. rampant—do yours?" She found it "very interesting" but declared their situation would be "a bit difficult till degrees are got." She closed by referring to opponents in general as "monastic *cave*-men!"[66]

Once Oxford had granted degrees, Cambridge's position became even more unacceptable to the women staff and students. "I gnash my teeth when I think of all your Somerville young women preening it in cap & gown," Jane wrote to Gilbert; "so like Oxford & so low to start after us & get in first." As the 1920 vote drew closer, Jane grew more pessimistic. "We have no chance I believe," she wrote, and added, "I am sick of strife—of course if we fail the Commission or Parliament will eventually step in—but I hate to get it from the outside." Members of the university descended on Cambridge, and soon it was "full of voting guests." Jane lamented that she could not "get at what your American friends call the 'psychology' of the difference between Oxford and Cambridge." Interestingly, she declared that "the mischief is all local—the country clergy come up thinking it is a foregone conclusion that Cambridge follows Oxford. Some adorable old pet lambs have come up to see their old Colleges never doubting of the issue." The rural clergy, traditionally looked down upon by their fellow students from the cities, shared the women's sense of disfranchisement, and their perspective on what was morally and ethically best for the university differed from that of the typical upper-class undergraduate or graduate.[67]

When the plan was rejected in December 1920, Jane drearily anticipated the next term when "the old weary struggle about the vote" would "begin again and all the fierce young disappointed ones come seething back and it is all, as you say, so 'silly' and so small." She felt cheered, however, by those alumni who had supported the plan for degrees and membership for women: "old clergymen (that *I* should live to say it!) who came up with shining faces and shabby old threadbare coats to vote for 'A' just because it was right and just in a fine Old Rat-ish fashion [a term of endearment]." Unfortunately, the debate sparked some bitterness and division among Jane's friends. A. B. Cook, a classicist and peripheral member of the Ritualist circle, sided with the conservative classicist William Ridgeway against the plan. Cook's defection hurt all the more since by opposing Jane's position, he was supporting that of her bête noire, Ridgeway. Jane fought scholarly and ideological battles with Ridgeway, one of Cambridge's staunchest conservatives, throughout her career. She mourned to Gilbert, "alas alas there is ABC [Cook] on the wrong side St. George fighting side by side with the old dragon Ridgeway." But even in her disappointment over Cook's stand, she defended him in the next breath from an attack on his scholarship: "all the same Mr. Halliday's letter enclosed makes me boil with fury—who is he that he should speak of ABC as 'a nice little enthusiast'—what has happened to Mr. Halliday? Is his wife a reactionary or who is it that has poisoned him of late?"[68]

Remarkably, the situation worsened. Nearly a year after the Senate rejected degrees and membership for women, a compromise plan proposed granting titular degrees but not membership in the university. Not only was this plan rejected, but when the results were announced, a group of undergraduates marched from Cambridge to Newnham and stormed the college gates, destroying them. Jane wrote to Gilbert that the event had

> been all so disgusting. I stood by and saw those young wild beasts break down the beautiful gates. I am glad though that the other right-minded undergraduates have been really nice, as you would see in the papers. They are apologizing and raising a fund. Of course we refused any money from the guilty ones. . . .
>
> Unless we get membership quickly, we are doomed. Parents will not send their girls to Cambridge to be looked down upon. Even worse, the best young women will not come to us as lecturers. The position is too galling. We older ones have suffered enough, but we are brought up on it; the young simply won't stand it. We have waited fifty years for it. The University hasn't done it. Parliament must. We are in real danger, and the smashing of gates is a trifle to this.[69]

This outburst of anger demonstrates just how heated and ugly the struggle between the women's colleges and the university had become. Male undergraduates particularly, sensing the winds of enormous change after the war, clung desperately to one of their few remaining bastions of power. They saw their entire style of living threatened if women gained voting privileges, although it would obviously take years for the numbers of women to reach the point where they could exercise even a negligible influence on university policy. The men's obstinacy was but a symbol of upper-class resistance to the rapid disintegration of the social fabric that had begun in the Edwardian age. While society eddied furiously around them, they strove to maintain Cambridge as an island of the old order. They could not hold back the tide forever, of course, but they thought they could slow it.

This sense of retrenchment gradually convinced Jane that the time had come for her to leave Cambridge. Sheldon Rothblatt cites a contemporary comparison of Victorian and Edwardian Cambridge that helps explain Jane's disillusionment with the academic community. Henry Sidgwick's time, corresponding to Jane's tenure as a student and her years in London, "was an heroic undefiled and golden age which valued character and intellectual virtue to an extraordinary degree. By contrast the later Edwardian or Bloomsbury period is called an age of decline, in which frivolity, conceit and superficiality replaced the sensitivity and responsibility of the earlier period." Jane echoed this statement. In her "Reminiscences," she said that she left Cambridge "with measureless regret" for she "began to feel that I had lived too long the strait Academic life with my mind intently focussed on the solution of a few problems" (RSL, 346). She "wanted before the end came to see things more freely and more widely." Privately, she confided her doubts about the university's future to Gilbert.

> We are just recovering from praelections or as they are now called Expositions. I am so relieved that we escaped [J. T.] Sheppard—I dread the actor-manager in Classics—also I think he is barely sane. Pearson is quiet & kind & "unexceptionable." FMC [Cornford] gave a beautiful sermon quite over their heads—the row of old cabmen who were electors looked bothered.
>
> It looks as if this would be my last year in Cambridge (not public yet)—I retire forcibly the year after & I think it is better not to wait till one is booted out. Old Cambridge is gone I felt that so at the praelections.

Jane thus started on yet another journey feeling defeated and out of date, making a bonfire of her correspondence and taking only a few personal possessions with her when she fled to Paris with Hope Mirrlees as companion. But these twenty years at Cambridge had been the most fruitful and productive of her intellectual life, as well as the most wrenching and disruptive of her personal life. The two strands were intricately interwoven during these years. Her relationships with Gilbert Murray and Francis Cornford directed the course of both. Having canvassed the larger picture of Jane's life in Cambridge, it is time now for a more detailed examination of these years.[70]

5

THE SECOND CIRCLE. THE CAMBRIDGE RITUALISTS: GILBERT MURRAY

We had better not talk of debts. My cup of gratitude brims over. It was a good God that sent us into the world in the same century.

—*Jane Harrison to Gilbert Murray, May 16, 1927*

IN ORDER TO understand fully the nature of Jane Harrison's Cambridge years, her relationships with Gilbert Murray and Francis Cornford must be explored more deeply. They formed an inner circle that guided her intellectual development during her tenure at Newnham. Gilbert Murray actually spent his academic career at Glasgow and Oxford, but he met Jane through Arthur and Margaret Verrall. After their initial meeting in Cambridge in 1900, Jane and Gilbert embarked on a collaboration that lasted for twenty years. Francis Cornford was a Trinity student when Jane met him in the late 1890s, and his casual question at one of her public lectures led them into an intense friendship. During her twenty years at Cambridge, Jane produced her most significant scholarly works: the *Prolegomena to the Study of Greek Religion* (1903), *Themis: A Study of the Social Origins of Greek Religion* (1912), and *Ancient Art and Ritual* (1913). All testify to the influence of the Ritualist circle, and of Gilbert Murray in particular, for he, more than Francis Cornford, shared Jane's concern with ancient religion. Francis's interests lay more in philosophy than religion. Although Jane destroyed her letters from Gilbert, he saved all of hers to him, and they offer eloquent testimony to the value and endurance of this most untroubled of Jane's relationships with men. She also wrote frequently to Lady Mary Murray, Gilbert's wife, and these letters further illustrate the complexity of the friendship this remarkable group shared. Gilbert's stated preference for the Olympian gods of the classical age and his disdain for the archaic age that Jane so loved makes their friendship all the more extraordinary.[1]

Photographs of Gilbert show a meek-looking, slightly built man of gentle appearance. Virginia Woolf described a 1918 luncheon with the Murrays. When Mary opened the door, Leonard Woolf "was half inclined to think her an untidy but cordial housemaid." Virginia Woolf disliked

Gilbert Murray. Photo courtesy of Jean Stewart Pace. Reproduced by University Library, Cambridge.

the tea-party atmosphere, but asserted that "it was the respectability that weighed me down, not the absence of intellect." She continued:

> There are certain dun coloured misty days in autumn which remind me of the Murray's [*sic*] atmosphere. The cleanliness of Gilbert was remarkable; a great nurse must rub him smooth with pumice stone every morning; he is so discreet, so sensitive, so low in tone & immaculate in taste that you hardly understand how he has the boldness to beget children. [Mary] is a wispy elderly lady, highly nervous, a little off hand & much of an aristocrat in her dashing method, kindly, fussy, refined too—O yes, they are all refined.

E. R. Dodds, who followed Gilbert Murray in the Regius Professorship at Oxford, cited George Bernard Shaw's opinion of him. Shaw, " 'who had known a younger Murray,' " used him as the model for Adolphus Cusins in *Major Barbara* and described Cusins as " 'a most implacable, determined, tenacious, intolerant person who by mere force of character presents himself as—and indeed actually is—considerate, gentle, explanatory, even mild and apologetic, capable possibly of murder, but not of cruelty or coarseness.' " Bernard Berenson, who met Gilbert while traveling in Florence in 1903, pronounced him "so gentle, so sweetly reasonable—almost the ideal companion." Conversely, Arnold Toynbee, Gilbert's son-in-law until his marriage to Gilbert's daughter Rosalind ended in divorce, accused Gilbert of speaking to Toynbee's mother and sister "about religion in a cruel way, which made them cry." J. A. K. Thomson, relating this story to Jessie Stewart, remarked, "can you imagine G. making a woman cry? This sounds to me like some nonsense from Jocelyn (who would be the sister)." Certainly Jane saw the steel behind the benevolent exterior, for she would not have been the least interested in anyone so blandly good. Nevertheless, Dodds agreed that "the immediate impression made by Murray's personality was one of gentleness, serenity, effortless control and perfect balance." As such, he made a perfect foil for Jane.[2]

In many ways, Gilbert's background prepared him to react to Oxford as Jane did to Cambridge. He was an Australian by birth, the son of an Irish family living in New South Wales. Gilbert was born on January 2, 1866, in Sydney and came to England at age eleven to be educated at the Merchant Taylors School. His father, president of the Legislative Council of New South Wales, died when Gilbert was only nine, and the family grew progressively poorer throughout his childhood. Gilbert stated that he and his family "tended to be 'agin the government' whatever the government might be" and that they "were apt to be rather passionately on the side of those likely to be oppressed." As a member of an Irish family living in a far-flung corner of the empire, Gilbert felt an outsider to the cultured elite among whom he found himself at Merchant Taylors and, later, at Oxford.[3]

Gilbert admitted that Oxford "disappointed" him. "I had expected so much; new lights on life, new learning, enlightenment and philosophy. I found, on the contrary, much the same influences as I had felt at school." Nevertheless, he distinguished himself there as a classical scholar, and at the age of only twenty-three he was offered and accepted the chair of Greek at the University of Glasgow. A few years later, he once again found himself at odds with those around him when he supported the Dutch settlers in the Boer War. Within ten years, he had overworked himself into a state of ill health and resigned, spending the next decade translating and editing the dramas of Euripides and writing *The Rise of the Greek Epic* (1911). In 1908 he was appointed Regius Professor of Greek at Oxford, where he remained for the rest of his academic career and lived until his death in 1957.[4]

Gilbert, whose family background prepared him to oppose not only political but academic trends, was a liberal in a conservative climate. According to E. R. Dodds, he was also a great lecturer who fulfilled his ambition to bring the past to life and transmit a sense of its atmosphere to others. Certainly Jane shared this desire to cultivate a respectful attitude toward the past. She also shared his antagonism toward William Ridgeway, who seized every opportunity to blast away at the Ritualist theory. On one occasion, Ridgeway chaired a meeting of the Cambridge Classical Society at which Gilbert spoke. Gilbert's premise, according to a member of the audience, was that "all Greek tragedy was to turn on the 'tearing up' of somebody or other in the process of it." Ridgeway, who abhorred anything irrational, tried his best to be civil, but his speech of thanks to Gilbert repeatedly erupted into "a burst of controversy quite irresistible" and an attack on Gilbert's ideas. Ridgeway quietly labeled the lecture "damned rot" and assumed Gilbert did not overhear his judgment, but the member of the audience recounting the story had "a pleasant recollection of his twinkle on one occasion when he recalled Ridgeway's 'vote of thanks.' " Gilbert's background had made him rather an iconoclast, and he often clashed with Ridgeway over scholarly issues.[5]

Francis Macdonald Cornford and Arthur Bernard Cook made up the rest of the small Ritualist circle. Francis, born in 1874 the son of an Eastbourne clergyman, spent his life at Cambridge writing on classical topics ranging from drama to philosophy. He became a Trinity fellow in 1899, assistant lecturer in classics in 1902, and lecturer in 1904. Just as Jane and Gilbert sought proof of the ritual origin of myth, Francis sought the ritual origin of philosophy. Of his many works, *Thucydides Mythistoricus* (1907) and *From Religion to Philosophy* (1911) bear the clearest imprint of the Ritualist circle. A. B. Cook was born in 1868 in Hampstead and educated, like Francis, at St. Paul's School and Trinity College, Cambridge. He received a fellowship at Trinity in 1893 and married Emily Maddox, also of Hampstead, in 1894. He was professor of Greek at Bedford College, London, 1893–1907, and then returned to Cambridge as reader in classical archaeology. His magnum opus, *Zeus,* appeared in three volumes in 1914, 1925, and 1940. He was only a peripheral member of the Ritualist circle, unwilling to accompany Jane and her associates on some of their more outrageous forays in the world of scholarship, but Jane appreciated his innate kindness and always spoke fondly of him.[6]

Robert Ackerman rightly claims that each of the three men in the group was closer to Jane than to the other men. In his view, Jane "was the center of the group because she always seems to have had a broader conception of their common subject matter than any of the others." Because of her wider view, "she was able to afford each of the others an important intellectual stimulus."[7] Her need to live other people's lives intimately with them also contributed to her central position in the group. Whereas the three men had family responsibilities that limited their personal interest in each other, Jane combined professional collaboration with intense personal attachments.

Above all, Jane placed herself at the center of the group because she, more than any of the others, needed to be the focus of attention: she made her colleagues revolve around her in the same way she had done with her fellow students at Newnham. In order to function and maintain the self-image that allowed her to create, she had an overwhelming psychological need for attention. She dominated the Ritualist circle and made it as much a family to her as the men's own families were to them, while remaining free of burdensome family obligations. If she could not marry them, she could command a large portion of their time and energy by encouraging them to work as a group.

Although it is partly true that "the reason for the group's coming-to-be was that Jane Harrison had a need for making passionate intellectual friendships," the group's interaction and Jane's perceptions of male-female relations tell a more interesting story.[8] Her friendship had an important intellectual component, but the connection she made between intellect and emotion meant that these relationships were much more complex than scholars have recognized.

"Scientiae Sacra Fames" is the most informative of Jane's formal works on the relation between intellect and emotion. "Body and soul are indeed hard to sunder," she says. "We may talk as we like of spiritual friendship that is purely Platonic, as though the intellect were a thing purely discarnate; but who does not know that spiritual jealousy is as sharp and as hot as any physical pang?"[9] We can easily discern the "physical and emotional sides of knowledge" (140). "Anyone who makes even a very small mental discovery can note how, at the moment of the making, there is a sudden sense of warmth, an uprush of emotion, often a hot blush, and sometimes tears in the eyes" (140–41). Finally, she asks, "who can say that a process so sensual and emotional . . . is insulated from a thing as interpenetrating as sex?" (141).

One cannot achieve these discoveries while leading a fragmented life. Women are distracted by families and children in a way that men are not; so Jane relied on men for intellectual companionship. She accepted their help "as a good and pleasant thing in life, perhaps the best and pleasantest, the purest pleasure life has to offer" (130).

> Now, emphatically, I never looked to man to supply me with new ideas; he might accidentally or, as oftener happened, we might flash them out together; but that was not what I wanted. Your thoughts are—for what they are worth—self-begotten by some process of parthenogenesis. But there comes often to me, almost always, a moment when alone I cannot bring them to the birth, when, if companionship is denied, they die unborn. The moment, so far as I can formulate the need, is when you want to disentangle them from yourself and your emotions, when they are sending out such a welter of feelers in all directions, setting up connections so profusely and recklessly that you hold your sanity with both your hands, and yet it seems going. Then you want the mind of a man with its great power of insulation. That is why a man's mind is so resting. To talk a thing over with a competent man friend is to me like coming out of a seething cauldron of suggestion into a spacious, well-ordered room. (130–31)

Male intellect helped Jane perform her most important task: imposing order on chaos. She chose male companions who were well suited to the task, who could balance her emotional reactions to ideas by remaining serenely rational. In a footnote to her 1909 essay "Homo Sum" Jane quoted Gilbert's views on intellect:

> The love of knowledge must be a disinterested love; and those who are fortunate enough to possess it, just in proportion to the strength and width of their love, enter into a great kingdom where the strain of disturbing passions grows quiet, and even the persecuting whisper of egotism dies at last completely away.[10]

This remark certainly springs from a restful, insulated mind. It also shows why Jane's work, regardless of its validity, is so much more appealing to readers. Although she herself may at times have sought a cooler serenity, her lively interaction with her subject results from her ability to infuse it with passionate intensity.

Jane's longing for men's intellectual companionship reflected other needs as well. Clearly she viewed her colleagues, particularly Gilbert and Francis, as more than merely intellectual friends. Her perception of the nature of knowledge indicates that a sexual element coexisted with the purely intellectual one. The sensual process of mental discovery, experienced with male colleagues, imbued their relationships with a degree of sexuality, even if never overtly acknowledged by any of the group. Whether the men perceived or understood the sexual component of their relationship is debatable. Their few surviving remarks on the nature of the group make it seem unlikely. Nevertheless, Jane derived much more than purely intellectual satisfaction from them. Only understanding the complexity of her interpretation of the word *intellectual* explains how much she needed the group and the reasons she placed herself squarely at its center.

Gilbert Murray gave the most insightful comments of the three men on the nature of the group. Writing to Jessie Stewart about a talk she gave on "those old exciting days," he agreed that she was "quite right in emphasizing the "group" Jane, FMC [Cornford], me and, I think, A. B. Cook. She had the power of making us feel that we were all working in common and not considering who should have credit for what." Eighteen months later, he examined the impetus behind the ritual theory and how it served to unite the Ritualists against other scholars.

> About the Group: do you remember what I said about Jane always looking out for the religion—or new light on religion—that was behind a ritual or an art form etc.? Well, I think that was common to the group and was what annoyed the "Sound Scholars" so much. We were—perhaps foolishly—young. We expected to find a great light which our elders had not seen. FMC was always looking for it in his Pre-Socratics, and finding it; I was the same in Euripides; JEH was doing it everywhere. We all wanted to see what things "really meant;" we were not content with merely construing or cataloguing them. ABC was a great help to us, but not one of us.

Gilbert seems to have missed the deeper implications of the group's revolving around Jane, but he put his finger directly on the central theme of their quest, which was the search for origins. The members' motivations for this search differed, but more than anything else they desired to get at the very root of an integral part of human experience: the religious impulse.[11]

Jane strove to find the source of the emotional life her culture seemed to find so distasteful by concentrating her search on the religious impulse. She equated the emotional life with a feeling of belonging to a group, and the most intense group experience she could imagine was a shared religious experience. The religious impulse was a primary source of emotional connection, and therefore she believed she could glimpse the origins of the emotional life by studying primitive religion. Only the primitive would do, for since the Olympian age, religion had steadily lost its emotional content through internalization of control. Jane's intuitive understanding of the emotional content of the Ritualists' studies gave her the most insight into ancient ritual and religion, thus providing a center from which the circle's scholarship could radiate.

Gender also played a critical role in forming Jane's scholarship. She believed that men's and women's minds were different, and scholars have occasionally remarked on the effect of her gender on her work. For instance, Jacquetta Hawkes, reviewing Jessie Stewart's *Portrait from Letters* in 1959, remarked that "what was most splendid about the collaboration was that Jane Harrison participated essentially as a woman. Her greatness lay in creative imagination of a deeply intuitive feminine kind." Her talent, however, cannot be reduced to the mere fact of her sex. As Patricia Meyer Spacks has argued, "the mind has a sex, minds *learn* their sex—and it is no derogation of the female variety to say so." The problem lies not in recognizing or admitting differences in the ways that men and women view the world. The problem traditionally has lain in the superior value attached to men's view. Of course, Jane "participated" in the Ritualist circle "essentially as a woman"; she could scarcely do otherwise. But her vision of the world around her came not only from her sex. It came also from her experience as a female in a society with rigidly constructed views of womanhood.[12]

Jane's need to create a self played an equally important role in her scholarship. She carefully designed a persona to present to the world. Thus her scholarship represents, and can be studied as, not an unconscious welling up of feminine intuition and imagination finding its full expression through an innate sense of understanding, but rather a conscious decision to define her self, through her subject matter and method, as different from male scholars. Her flagrant disregard for conventional ideas about the ancient world and her alliance with carefully chosen like-minded men reflected her view of her place in the world. Her work demonstrated more than imagination. It also represented her attempt both to carve a niche for herself in a man's world and to order the chaos of her own life.

Jane's letters to Gilbert Murray provide a privileged view of her special blend of intellectual and personal concerns. In 1900, they began a correspondence that quickly moved beyond formal discussion of points of textual criticism to a delightful and lively interest in each other's lives. Their letters combine serious discussion of new ideas, defenses of colleagues and criticism of outsiders, and gossip about family and friends. More important, they show Jane's dependence on Gilbert for support and her appreciation of his friendship and abilities.

By 1902, perhaps sensing that their letters might one day be useful to other scholars, Gilbert apparently asked Jane to date her letters, which she did not often do. She responded,

> I did it once "to oblige a Lady" [Mary Murray] & may continue the custom to Her but I'm blessed if I'll be bullied by you—so there—Be good enough to remember that I am not a Bank Clerk nor yet—thank Heaven—your private secretary nor yet a Pragmatical Pedant who thinks all his remarks are Epoch-making. While you're at it why don't you mention the Year & the Day each time you deign to *speak?*

Except for rare occasions, she remained true to her word.[13]

Jane's first letter to Gilbert, although formal in tone, revealed a great deal about her. She wrote, "I think I must confess to you that when your Greek literature book [*A History of Ancient Greek Literature,* 1897] first came out in the first fervour of enthusiasm I wrote an impulsive letter to tell you how it had rejoiced me, & then on second thoughts burned it as an impertinent indiscretion!" She feared exposing her emotional reaction to the work to possible criticism. But her need to curb her enthusiasm soon faded as their correspondence continued. When she asked A. W. Verrall for help on a particular Greek phrase, he referred her to Gilbert, which "was most indiscreet of him for he knows the fell curiosity of this particular Eve." On behalf of herself "and the hungry young sheep [her students] who look up & are not fed" and who "would all burn incense to you forever," she begged Gilbert's help in translation. Before long, he was making trips to Newnham to read his translations, and there would be "a great atmosphere of excitement during the reading." Jane often arranged visits so that her students could, with his help, "get at the *real* & not merely the conventional beauty & value of classical things."[14]

Jane's first chance to visit the Murrays in Surrey arose in December 1900. Mary Murray must have indicated a desire to meet her, for Jane asked Gilbert to "thank Lady Mary very much for her kind message." She could not make the trip, but added, "it would have been delightful to come & see you as I should then have had the chance—long denied—of getting to know her too." Her first visit to Barford, the Murray home, in February 1901 proved eventful indeed. On her last evening there, Jane fainted and had to be carried to her room. She left for the Continent soon after that visit and wrote an apologetic note to Mary Murray from Bologna.

> I longed to write you before I left but I felt too much of a gibbering idiot to face pen & ink. I am afraid it is cheap to be contrite for unwilling & unwitting offenses, but I must say how grieved I was to lose the end of my evening & be such a harried bother to you—& if possible a worse

one to poor Mr. Murray—No doubt he made light of my weight but I am deeply & painfully conscious of a good nine stone—it was a hateful fate that just when I wanted to "crown him with many crowns" I should set him so hateful an *athlon*—My stern stepmother used to say "No one faints but the kitchen-maid." I am not in a position to share her social prejudices but I *do* feel that people who reel into ditches should be left to lie there—by the by please tell my kind preserver that I would rather have been left lying in a ditch than have to be told next morning that I was "an over-worked failure." That hurt badly & rankles still, but I was too weak & meek . . . to resent it at the moment—my better self would have hurled the bad books on the hall table at the admonisher's head.

I wonder what happened on Monday & oh—dare I ask? Would you be very kind once more & send just a post-card to say how Andromache goes on the 24th [the staged version of Gilbert's translation]. I meant to ask Mr. Murray but I shall never dare to ask him anything again.

She recovered from this crisis, but plainly the stress of visiting Barford and meeting the Murray family proved too much for her.[15]

Two years later, Jane expounded on her theory about fainting and inadvertently shed light on the 1901 incident. In response to a fainting spell that Mary described, Jane wrote, "I believe in fainting as a blessed dispensation of providence to break the threads of consciousness, just for a moment when they are spun too fine & taut—& all your threads moral & physical are spun many degrees too fine, as is patent to the nearest observer!" She expected that Mary's were "moral faints," while her own were "grossly physical." Jane probably misinterpreted her own tendency to faint, but understood that anxiety and nervousness could underlie it. During Jane's first visit to Barford, Mary may have exhibited some jealousy toward her for receiving so much of Gilbert's attention and thereby unsettled her. If so, Jane was neither the first nor the last woman to arouse Mary's jealousy. According to Murray's biographer, Francis West, Mary feared Gilbert's interest in any woman who shared his extrafamilial interests such as classical study or the theater. Hope Mirrlees believed that Jane invariably overcame any doubts that jealous wives might have and developed lasting friendships with many of them, but Jane could be exceedingly flirtatious.[16]

She carried on much of her correspondence through Mary, but despite the cordial tone they were not, at least initially, the best of friends. Perhaps Mary resented such intrusions as a letter Jane wrote from Naples in 1903 while she and Gilbert were studying Orphic tablets. It would be an unusually patient and understanding woman who could bear the implied criticism and Jane's wifelike concern for Gilbert's health without reacting angrily.

I have a theory about his health in general which, at the risk of being called an ignoramus & a nuisance I will impart—I think what he wants is a long, quiet stay in a *warm* climate—it seems to me half his rather small stock of vitality goes in keeping warm. he reminds me in so many ways of Mr. Maitland, who has nothing in the world the matter with him but that he just shrivels up at the touch of cold—& the warmth they both need is not artificial heat but shaded sunlight. It is quite pathetic to see how he thaws & brightens when his feet are in a spot of sun!

I wish oh I wish so much—that next winter you would let Barford & take him to Sicily or Tangiers—or somewhere where there is no struggle with cold—I feel he is quite able to work moderately & in good conditions—& indeed that he is all the better for doing things, if they can be done with no strain—I think the little time he has been away will have done him good as a break & a change—he says travelling about with me is a "worry-cure" not a rest-cure! but I feel sure what is really wanted is a *long* quiet stay, a whole winter in real warmth. . . . You would have to pack up the children & root yourself up—for he would never settle unless you were there, he is restless now to be back. . . .

Here I am yarning on—but I *do* so want him to get well.

Part of Jane's concern grew from her morbid fascination with the state of her own and other people's health, but her proprietary feeling about Gilbert is highly significant. Since Gilbert lived to be over ninety, he clearly had no life-threatening health problems, but Jane delighted in sharing her health woes with others and playing up their illnesses. Mary Murray probably resented her interference, especially since Jane ended her letter by admitting rather condescendingly that "I feel by sympathy other peoples aches & emptinesses [presumably Gilbert's for his family] & have some human longings of my own after you—& yesterday, when we went to the Aquarium, I even longed for the children!" Jane bowed to the supremacy of family life but asserted her own superiority in the intellectual realm.[17]

Although complicated by Jane's and Mary's mutual jealousy, Jane's love for the Murrays ran deep. Even her cynicism and distrust of most people could not blind her to their essential goodness and decency, and she spoke of them in a manner reserved for very few of her friends. Moreover, she often expressed her fondness openly and directly. They had many differences of opinion, chiefly regarding religious and social questions, but Jane accepted their views with more tolerance than she usually displayed. As she wrote to Gilbert,

Quite seriously you are both bad for me—Lady Mary I think worst because she is best but you are both so hypermoralized & super-spiritualized that you force me to think of "righteousness—Temperance, & judgment-to-come" &, in the words of my own Baptismal Service I have by a healthy instinct of self-preservation "renounced them all." Everything is a danger to me that cannot be instantly translated into hard thinking. . . . As I said to Lady Mary I say to you that you have done me good in one way, I will never set my influence as I have done in the past, against good things because I see in you two how beautiful it all is—but I will not think about these things or try to practice them, because for me that way madness lies and in my family we are already liberally supplied with lunatics! It is all right for you because you were made like that & can preserve thro it all a holy calm that makes me sometimes want to send books . . . at your head.

She showed even more uneasiness in a letter to Mary at approximately the same time. Jane apologized for some incident that remains unknown, but went on to vent feelings about the Murrays in general and Mary in particular.

It is on my mind that I teazed you with questions when you were tired last night & ought to have read Clarissa—but I did so want to know what you thought at first hand. I can't tell you how upsetting & bewildering it is to me to find all these things that I have labelled "fads" held steadily as principles by you two—who—much against my will—I am forced to feel are far away above & before me. I have never known anyone before you held these views—I mean anyone I took seriously—people like my dear Alys Russell & the Marquessons I *can't* take quite seriously. I don't know the least whether you are right or wrong, but if you are wrong your wrong is something that makes me more ashamed than any right. . . . But the worst is that I know with a horrid certainty that you have let me get to know you on false pretences. I never shall be like that—it isn't in me—all I can say is that some things will be different ever after, I mean I shall never again sneer or laugh at the things that are sacred to you.

Well it is no use repenting on paper & I am glad I did get to know you even on false pretences! I never felt so happy & at home in anyone's house before—how do you do it? perhaps after all as the hymn says "Heaven is my Home"—I doubt it tho!

Presumably this letter refers to their political differences. The Murrays were liberals, while Jane, despite a half-hearted attempt at liberalism, remained a Tory virtually all her life. Initially, political differences caused friction, and Jane later disagreed with Gilbert when he enthusiastically supported England's participation in World War I. These were still early days, though, and the series of letters stretching out over the next twenty-five years demonstrates that Jane and the Murrays settled into a friendship that remained remarkably tranquil—especially considering the smoldering rivalries—until the end of Jane's life.[18]

Jane relied on Gilbert for scholarly help, and they often discussed their work at Barford. After a January 1902 visit, Jane wrote Gilbert asking him to inform another guest that "I hate him for he is sitting at this moment in *my* seat smoking *my* cigarettes in your study." She thanked him for his kindness and explained, "I was too dumb to say any polite things, besides I inwardly felt all the time that you were longing to tear up my untidy mind & put it neatly into its proper place—the waste-paper-basket." In 1904, she sent the following list of grievances "To the Complaints Committee, The Study, Barford":

re—*Waste paper basket*—
Housing conditions for poor-translations cramped. Ventilation fairly adequate but system out of date.
re—*Rack on Writing-Table*
Class distinctions between half-sheets of paper too rigidly enforced.
re—*Stamp-box*
. . . empty
re—*Ink-Pot*—jarring note in otherwise harmonious & elegant environment.
re—*Chimney piece*—Poison exposed unlabelled—result: total moral collapse of—Temporarily Resident Ker
Remedies suggested—Flight.

Other visitors shared amazement at the "harmonious & elegant environment." Pernel Strachey, Jane's Newnham colleague, visited Barford in 1911 with some of her family members, and Jane wrote that "they are all quite hysterical (a rare thing in Stracheys) about the spring-freshness of the house & your arch-angelic goodness in heavy books unlocked up, & the symmetry & rhythm with which the clean towels are arranged each in its own house."[19]

When Jane left Barford after her last visit before the Murrays moved to Oxford, she "felt . . . like a dove leaving a nice kind ark. You do make your home very like an ark for all sorts of strange weary beasts and birds." She vowed she would "always keep the two white feathers [a gift from Rosalind Murray] in their silver casket for a charm to bring me back" and predicted that "wherever you set up that Ark it will be a blessed Tabernacle."[20]

To one seeking order as Jane was, Barford and later the Murray's Oxford home seemed an oasis of calm and serenity. The Murrays extended their kindness so far as to allow Jane, over her protests, to sleep in their bedroom during at least one visit. She viewed this "turning out" as "disgraceful," and insisted that "if I had had a spark of spirit I should have set to & had an internecine pillow-fight with you & driven you back dead or alive to your own place." But she gave in easily as "a poor backboneless woman with no Free Will & what is worse no Proper Pride."[21]

Gilbert's visits to Newnham did not always go as smoothly as Jane's to Barford. After they began to collaborate, Gilbert often planned visits either to lecture or to discuss scholarship with Jane and usually stayed with his old acquaintances, the Verralls. Jane's letters, however, indicate that his plans frequently changed at the last minute and, furthermore, that she could become quite incensed at his cancelations. She shared her nervousness with him, writing before one planned lecture to discuss the most suitable sort of desk for him to use when he spoke.

> As usual I have left out the only important thing—what sort of a desk do you like? I have a great big thing against which I can bear up in moments of emotion, but a lecturer the other day swore at it & had it removed before he began—also is it high enough? I am 5 ft 6½ (the perfect height for a woman) but it can be built up higher if you like—a wrong sort of desk paralyzes me with nervousness—but if you are above these details of course don't bother to write.[22]

Gilbert's response, if any, has not survived, but it is unlikely that he was quite as compulsive about lecturing arrangements as she.

Planning for the same visit, Jane wrote to tell Gilbert, "as a 'confirmed habitual' philanthropist you will remember—won't you? that if you fail me [by not coming to visit] you will just spoil the day I most look forward to in the whole year." He did let her down by falling ill just before the lecture, which was scheduled for February 14. Jane responded to the news in the most charitable manner Gilbert would ever see, urging him to cancel because of his illness. "I am going to be a real Xian—for the first & I sincerely hope the last time—& suggest that you give it all up & not come at all. But I shall arrange this with your lawful *despoina* & you will not be consulted at all so don't write & argue but just lie still in bed & get well." She continued, saying, "I knew for certain yesterday morning some disaster was impending for I had a fearful fit of the blues about nothing," but unable to diagnose the problem, she had "resolved to cheer up & go to Girton. . . . I came back to find the fallen bolt your telegram."[23]

On some visits, Jane had to defer to Gilbert's interest in politics. She resented a scheduled discussion on political issues because "I shall have to sit meekly in a corner listening while you & Mrs. Sidney Webb reconstruct the Liberal Party in your loud dogmatic way—I shan't like it, but 'I know my station.' " Immersed in the *Prolegomena,* Jane knew that she would "be seething with Orphic eggs & Wild Bulls & really important things." She was not above jealousy in other ways as well. Before a November 1902 visit, she tried to cover a very real irritation with a playful tone. When Gilbert arrived he would "be met by a Shut Door," for he was "in deep & dire disgrace: you have been & gone & read at least 2000 lines of your dull epic to Bertie [Bertrand Russell] & never a line to me—The blood of many (& wild) Bulls will stain this river—& in vain—in vain." She signed "yours more in anger than in sorrow—*much more.*" Jane thought he had neglected her and fiercely resented it.[24]

Before long, she stopped being charitable when Gilbert canceled. Her responses varied. On one occasion, she joked, "I am going to assassinate all your relations."[25] On another, she claimed, "I knew you couldn't come, all the time—but I toiled away finishing my lecture prematurely to be free for a little converse about Moons & Milky Ways—& now alack—alack." She sympathized with him over this particular bout of ill health, asserting that "the only thing that matters is your resting as much as you can & saving your strength & giving the lie to that ominous Hell-hound [her name for his doctor]." She urged, "don't be depressed—you have a thousand beautiful things to do in the world yet."[26] She brightened at the prospect of an impending visit by all the Murrays, "tho of course I never expect to really see any one bearing your holy name until I *do* see them—I am therefore armed for the reception of telegrams all day with a fresh disease in each which you will have carefully caught to annoy me." They were to meet at Jane's favorite retreat, the Suffolk coast town of Aldeburgh, and Jane promised Gilbert that "there is a balcony sheltered from every North & East wind waiting for you, it was built for you from the beginning of time."[27]

Her close friendship with Gilbert and Mary allowed her free rein in speaking on some of her favorite topics: ill health and the problem of children. All three seemed to be chronically ill, although the seriousness or legitimacy of some of their complaints is dubious. Nevertheless, the letters provide evidence of how Jane worried over her health and discussed it endlessly with a true hypochondriac's enthusiasm. She suffered real symptoms, but they were probably brought on in part by her inability to confront her feelings of anger and anxiety. Discussion of illness provided one avenue of interaction with Mary, who was not particularly interested in scholarship, as did Jane's thinly veiled mixed feelings toward the Murray children.

At times, Jane could be positively gushy toward Mary. When Mary could not accompany Gilbert to a lecture at Newnham in 1902, Jane wrote to her proclaiming, "I was so bitterly disappointed, I wanted it all to be quite perfect—& it just wasn't because you weren't there. . . . Also I want you so badly this morning to talk over the lecture with & tell all the things that people have said to me, which would be simply indecent to repeat to the lecturer." The lecture was "a brilliant & beautiful success," although Jane "raged inwardly thro the first half which was solid politics [on the Boer War]—exquisitely done, but still politics." Ten years later, she expressed gratitude for all the occasions on which Mary "allowed incursions on Mr. Murray's time & strength which your wifely & guardian angel self must have disapproved."[28]

Jane could also grow lyrical over Mary's appearance and demeanor. Writing from Chinon during a visit to France, Jane advised Gilbert "for the sake of educating your family you ought to take a chateau in Tourraine." She had "seen several that would just do, one especially with a wonderful door-way, coming out of which Mary would look simply perfect—Mary ought always to be standing in a beautiful door-way welcoming guests." After Mary suffered a spell of illness, Jane speculated, "perhaps it was partly your beautiful white gown that made you look more like a tired angel than a sick mortal," and asked that she "never wear a scrap of colour when I am in sight—it spoils the . . . effect: but I think I can remember it, even without that photograph *which has never been sent.*"[29]

When speaking to others, however, Jane could be less kind in her appraisal of Mary. When Mary arrived for a visit in Aldeburgh, Jane wrote to Jessie Stewart that "Lady Mary has been and after the usual drains-v[ersus]-milk Sturm and Drang period she has actually taken a small house for her babies and nurse." On another occasion, when Mary came to join Jane, Gilbert, and Frank Darwin at Aldeburgh, Jane mourned the end of a perfectly good vacation. "Tomorrow Lady Mary comes & we shall all have to sit up—till then we are very slack." Gilbert and Frank were such good company to her and to each other that she wished "it could go on much longer."[30]

Whatever Jane's private opinion of Mary, she wisely never expressed it to Gilbert. She always referred lovingly to his family in her letters and showed interest in their lives. She lived largely a family life through the Murrays, and her mixed feelings about families emerged in her relationship with them. She tempered her desire to belong with a need to maintain distance. The Murrays served several functions for her. Gilbert was her intellectual companion; Mary a friend whose abilities and personality did not threaten Jane; the children, especially the daughters, young people with whom Jane could identify. They opened their home to her, and she enjoyed the warmth of their family circle. She had no desire, however, to play any of their roles or to carve a larger niche for herself in their lives. She had rejected family life as too stifling and appreciated the freedom that choice had given her. Jane would not trade her intellectual companionship with Gilbert for Mary's position as his wife. Their friendship flourished largely because of the geographical distance they maintained, which mirrored their emotional distance. The Murrays lived far enough away for Jane's visits to be special occasions. Any closer contact might have changed the nature and course of their friendship.

Jane was at her playful best showing concern for the Murray's health.

She thanked Gilbert for helping her with work when he was ill with "that large sore throat too." She blamed his illness on "Jahweh" who was "a beast I always knew it." She wanted to see him, but knew that "if Jahweh caught you starting he would make you all one long throat. . . . The Lord bless you & keep you—but he's never any use."[31] When Gilbert had to be admitted to what Jane referred to as "that accursed 'Home,' " she wrote, "it is monstrous of whoever arranges these things to send this curse upon you—The only good thing that can come out of it is that you will be quite quiet in bed for a few days—but then what is the use when you will be sick with ether & chloroform & things—Will it make you really much better & do you mind it horribly? please answer all these questions." But Jane added an affectionate postscript, insisting that he "tell the fiend of a doctor that you are of more value than many humans."[32] She herself eventually concluded that Mary was "a heart case" and that Gilbert's "extreme weakness" was "an almost certain sign that your *chiffre* (blood pressure) wants raising."[33]

Jane enjoyed discussing her own illnesses at length as well. She advised Mary to try a drug called Kola, which "pulls one together astonishingly & even takes away the sick horror of nervousness. I believe it is *non* alcoholic," which would be important to the teetotaling Murrays. Her often light tone covered up concern for a chronic and rather serious nervousness. A letter to Gilbert soon after one of his visits to Newnham revealed its extent. During that visit, he must have helped her fight off an anxiety attack.

> I was brutal to ask you, but you were very kind to come that night. I get so frightened when I cannot sleep—& now these three nights oh how I have slept! a great well of sleep at the bottom of a green sea—so I must send my blessing tho I laugh aloud at my absurd self—& to think that this magical thing whatever it is (Mrs. Verrall has been in to explain that it is super-auto hyper aesthetic, subliminal-something, which is of course illuminating & convincing) roused in me such a "sourde antagonisme" that I almost decided to drop the acquaintance—it was only sleep after all! as gracious & harmless a gift as the small white paper knife—But I did so hate the idea that I was sub-dominant! I thought it was unwholesome but it can't be for I wake up feeling like a new-born lion (no mere kid).

Her insomnia dated at least from the 1880s in London, and clearly the anxiety that provoked it ran like a current throughout her life.[34]

The pressure of writing infused Jane's academic career with bouts of anxiety. This pressure was not external but internal and surely derived from the displacement of her anger at family and society that she did not confront directly. She herself required that writing be painful and stressful, and her most energetic scholarly exertions produced her worst periods of ill health. Jane's association of creative work and stress was overdetermined by her use of writing as a response to personal crises. The complex bonds between her personal and intellectual lives guaranteed that she would live in frantic vacillation between despair and calm. In her "Reminiscences" Jane described the psychological state that produced her works and stressed the unconscious but irrepressible need to release energy through work.

> One reads round a subject, soaks oneself in it, and then one's personal responsibility is over; something stirs and ferments, swims up into your consciousness, and you know you have to write a book. That may not be "hard work," but just let me tell Professor Murray it is painfully and pleasantly like it in its results; it leaves you spent, washed out, a rag, but an exultant rag. (RSL, 335)

Jane relied heavily on her scholarship to defuse her anger over her mother's death, her father's betrayal, her failed romances, and her inability to reconcile love and work, all of which contributed to her rejection of the structure of Victorian society. And "once her theories had turned into a book she ceased to be interested in them." Having dealt with a particular crisis by channeling her anger or frustration into a book, she could become indifferent to it. Each work evoked painful, if unconscious, memories that she preferred to forget. Although Jane herself believed that she "had never written anything that was quite literature," Gilbert Murray unknowingly put his finger on the appeal of her scholarship. He "used to tell her that he could never read anything by her without being seized with happy laughter—it was always so exactly like herself." He correctly identified its appeal—it was "like herself" because she threw her essence into every page. In her own way, she lived intensely and fully experienced her life. Her writing helped her make sense of all that had happened to her, and therefore she infused it with great passion.[35]

After Jane completed her *Prolegomena,* she had more to say about her health. A month after finishing it, she was "a deeply dejected Ker" with what her doctors diagnosed as a thyroid condition. She often referred to herself as "Ker," a Greek term akin to "ghost" or "spirit" but with a rather more sinister aspect as Keres were believed to bring disease and other evils. She hoped that her "local Vet" would "say he need not excavate my throat," preferring him to "those London swells . . . always so ready & handy with their knives." The doctors believed her "thyroid gland accounted for everything, short breath, nervousness, fainting, & that, but for it, a great strong cow like me would have no nerves at all—for my heart is as the heart of a wild bull." In addition to the thyroid condition, her symptoms may also have been related to the stress of working and her grief over the death of R. A. Neil, which occurred during the period in which she wrote the *Prolegomena.* She cheered up at the thought of her doctor's wanting her " 'on no account to be worried' " and admonished Gilbert to "remember this & accept all my theories & emendations unquestioned henceforth."[36]

Only a few days later, however, Jane wrote to Mary about her heart problems and a new treatment. "I expect I am making a fearful & unnecessary fuss & probably you have borne heart-symptoms twice as bad without saying a word," but she wanted to tell Mary about a new treatment with a drug called strophanthus, which was "the drug they are experimenting on with 'confirmed dipsomaniacs.' " On Jane's next visit, Mary would have to "have a big bottle of strophanthus on the table & withdraw that hospitable & much too superior whiskey of yours." Another of the drug's miraculous powers was that it would "help one to bear not smoking." Apparently her doctor, "who luckily is a smoker himself," had urged her to quit. She felt better, but remained worried.

> It is a wonderfully soothing drug & has eased my "beating heart" not a little already—he says there is no disease in the heart at present but the thyroid mischief would easily set it up if not checked—& at present my poor old heart is doing all its work twice over.
>
> I am so relieved that he doesn't want to operate—I am a horrid coward & I have seen so much of the resulting shock from operations.
>
> It is such a blessing I am allowed to do my normal work here, in fact allowed to do anything that doesn't make me nervous.

Part of her anxiety about facing an operation may have arisen from the memory of her good friend Eleanor Butcher's death after a successful operation in 1894, for Eleanor's death had hit her hard. It is ironic that Jane's doctors allowed her to work—that made her more nervous than anything else.[37]

The appearance of the *Prolegomena* (the "Fat One") in November 1903 should have cheered her, but instead she grew more despondent.

> I will tell you at last about doctors I have been too sullen to write about them. Macalister says the abatement in the heart's action from one fortnight's akaprica & strophanthus is little short of incredible—he gives up all thought of operation & I ought to be . . . relieved. I *am* in a way for I am a contemptible coward about physical pain, but yet I feel I would screw myself up to any operation rather than face this dreariness—it is a daily hourly misery that one cannot even dignify by the name of pain—just to be told to get over a bad habit—ugh—If giving up drink is like the wrench from a lover—who all the time you half-despise—giving up smoke is like parting from the best friend who always comforts & never torments—Also I hate asceticism & am compelled to practice it. All my life I have meant to behave handsomely to my body & it has done the like to me & now it goes & plays me a low trick—& I have to

> paint my throat a bright orange & take vile drugs—& I have no work to interest me & the Fat One at last sits on my table & grins at me & I don't care enough for him even to turn over his horrid pages.[38]

Clearly, curtailing her smoking and drinking bothered Jane. And as frightening as the prospect of surgery had been, she felt better when she could attribute her illness to a physical cause. Without that excuse for her misery, and with the *Prolegomena* finished and no new projects in the wings, she felt depressed and at loose ends.

Jane derived some pleasure from experimenting with different remedies of dubious value. In 1904, she was "rather seriously ill" with "a germ," but she fought it off with "a new medicine given me by Mrs. Sidgwick 'as supplied to her by the Prime Minister [Eleanor Sidgwick's brother, Arthur Balfour]' " and imagined the Murrays "would rather die than take it." Two years later, she advocated a new "germ bread" as medicine. "All mortals' ills are cured by eating the new germ bread. . . . some one has discovered that anemia & all other sins are owing to machinery that grinds out the germ—The Mills of God grind slowly—for vegetarians—which I am almost one—it really is important & it is so nice." She directed the last comment to the Murrays, who were vegetarians. The "cholera germ" attacked Gilbert, which was "hybristic of it—it is the same germ I expect that nearly slew AWV [Verrall]. . . . it attacked all sound scholars—it tried even me but was routed immediately—when Ker meets Ker." But her greatest joy was meeting other people who were willing to discuss their problems or, better yet, listen to hers:

> I also met at the Vice-Chancellor's a gentleman called Marcus Aurelius has he been to Oxford? his other name is Dr. Stein—I loved him—he had lost several toes in a snow-storm in central Asia & he was very sympathetic about my great toes being excavated—it is so seldom one can pour out about one's toe joints at dinner. I am sure you would like him.

Sir Mark Aurel Stein, the Hungarian-born explorer, had other traits to recommend him to Jane. In addition to his health woes, his archaeological expeditions in Asia and his interest in Buddhism would have intrigued her. She must have felt an immediate kinship with him on many levels.[39]

In addition to her own illness, Jane frequently alluded to Mary's several pregnancies and displayed her old conflicting emotions about children and childbirth. In 1901, on hearing of Mary's latest pregnancy, Jane wrote anxiously: "Your news has completely taken my breath away. . . . I am glad for one thing that it explains your not being well & that will only be for a time, only it is a long & worrisome time I am afraid—I can't think how you can think of anything or anyone except yourself." She then added her own perceptions of what pregnancy must be like: "I always feel when it happens to anyone one knows that it must put everything & all the world out of focus or rather into a new focus—I should feel like God when he made the world." Unfortunately, her experience of watching sisters and friends undergo childbirth had opened her eyes to its pain and discomfort, and "from being much with many sisters who suffer untold miseries I know too well there is another side—it is part of the horrible tangle of things that it should be so & always makes me want to curse." The real specter looming over the issue of children, of course, was her own mother's death as a result of childbirth.[40]

Once the Murray children were born, Jane showed interest in them despite her professed disdain for babies. She wished that Basil "could have been a 'horned thing' but perhaps his mother likes him best as he is—mothers are so scareful." She offered to take him "out for a ride in my bicycle bag," claiming that she "did take a baby once & he has never given his mother a moment's anxiety since." Once she saw "that great big Basil smiling I think I feel he was worth while." A year later, Mary resumed her study of Greek, a step Jane applauded. "I am glad you have gone back to Greek, which you never should have let lapse—It is worth all the mere children in the world. Such is the mind of this spinster." The birth of another son, Stephen, led Jane to predict that "the new Baby will be as great a joy to you as Basil has been and is." Stephen also prompted her to say, "you know I don't love babies as babies—but he is himself." Stephen took to Jane as well, giving her "for my very own a white rabbit & a sheep" during a visit to the Norfolk coast, leading her to assume that she "must be in favour."[41]

Rosalind, the eldest daughter, seems to have had pride of place in Jane's heart. On hearing of her engagement to Arnold Toynbee in 1913, Jane responded joyously to Gilbert.

> Oh what a letter of excitements—I went quite dizzy when I got it. . . . Your own Rosalind engaged—she who has been more & *so* sometimes less than any daughter—& it all coming so swiftly & strongly—my goodness he sounds something like a man to hold himself like that & run such an awful risk he clearly thinks of something more than developing his own individuality all over the place. He sounds just the right tower of strength.
>
> And you & Mary believe in him I am *so* glad—It almost makes me believe in God almighty—it is so like a deus ex machina—saving the whole situation—I have ached with longing to save Rosalind from the pain of living & now—at least for a time—it is all done.

Privately, however, Jane had her doubts. In a rare burst of concern expressed directly to Gilbert, she commented on her own impressions of Toynbee gleaned from his writings.

Oh but reading his stuff gives one furiously to think about the marriage—it will be one of the [illegible] contraries type—which I never understand—but I am learning to know they are possible. There is no literary touch in him—it is all science & good thinking—& R. has literature in every bone—in a way I can't help being glad because there will always be great spaces when she will need you—but won't she find empty spaces in him—well who knows—it *may* be all right—he has the scientific imagination which is precious near art—I don't yet know where the dividing line is.

It is impossible to know if Jane sensed what would eventually lead to the breakup of the Murray-Toynbee marriage, since there is no way to determine conclusively what makes any marriage fail. The fact that Jane feared the marriage would not last is less important than her recognition of the strength of the father-daughter bond. She believed that Toynbee's inadequacies would ensure a strong tie between Gilbert and Rosalind and keep him from supplanting Gilbert in Rosalind's affection. Jane rarely admitted the significance of the father-daughter tie, but in this letter she implied equal concern for both parties.[42]

Jane's devotion to Rosalind ran deep enough for her to show concern for Rosalind's health when she had her first child. After Arnold Toynbee wrote to give her the news, Jane admitted to Gilbert that "I am quite inhuman & take no manner of interest in the newly born—but till I got his letter I scarcely knew how I had trembled for Rosalind." She remained troubled over Rosalind's health, for a month later Ruth Darwin told her that "she had come across Rosalind in a bathchair 'looking deliriously happy but not at all well.' " Jane did not typically display this kind of concern, and it demonstrates the depth of her feeling for Rosalind.[43]

Another way in which Jane displayed her great affection for Gilbert was to bestow various names on him. In most of her letters after their first year of correspondence, she addressed him as "Cheiron" or "Ther." Cheiron was the centaur who tutored the heroes Achilles and Jason, and the use of that name reflected Jane's perception of her indebtedness to Gilbert as teacher. "Ther" is a trickier but perhaps more fitting term. It is derived from "therion," or "beast." A theriomorph signifies an animal or creature identified with an individual. Jane's theriomorph, obviously, was a bear, and Gilbert's, because of his Australian origin, was a kangaroo. Perhaps more important, it denoted an intimate connection with the natural world. Finding the perfect name for her friends meant a great deal to Jane, and both of Gilbert's names suited him well. When illness forced her, on her doctor's advice, to take a rest in sunny Algiers early in 1904, Jane wrote to Gilbert, "how absurd it is for this Polar Bear to be sent sun-wards & a thin Kangaroo to be leaping about in the snow." In one of her birthday letters, a long-standing tradition, Jane, who "never understood before why [Gilbert was] born at the beginning of the Year," finally recognized that it was because his "theriomorph is a kangaroo" and he "came leaping into the world," thereby making him the spirit of the new year.[44]

As their collaboration progressed, Jane increasingly depended on Gilbert for help in her work. She often expressed her wish that they lived nearer to one another so that they could work together more easily. She showed great diffidence in her letters, generally deferring to Gilbert's judgments and always proclaiming, either directly or indirectly, his superior scholarship. Jane's work clearly shows the livelier imagination and breadth of vision, but insecurity about her position in the academic world prompted such self-deprecating remarks as "I should soon be such an elegant scholar if you lived here." Perhaps it was better all around that they lived apart; Jane complained that "whenever Mr. Murray looks over a paper of mine he always says at the end, 'This is quite admirable, every word of it,' then sits down & softly re-writes it all!" She joked that "that is how I should like my life to be—to sit reading & writing stuffage all day & every morning you to walk in for about half an hour & say it was all wrong!" Her joking probably hid some resentment, but his criticism, although sometimes making her feel unhappy, did not affect her train of thought. Gilbert offered his criticism constructively and in an egalitarian manner. Jane was much less likely to change her ways at the age of fifty or sixty than she had been at the age of thirty, when she reacted so angrily to Sutherland MacColl's criticism of her style.[45]

Jane's and Gilbert's collaboration was mutually enriching and marked by deep respect and genuine affection on both sides. Remarking on an upcoming social engagement, Jane wrote, "I am going to meet Mr. Mackail [classicist J. W. Mackail] at AWV's Sunday—I wish I soon met you anywhere at anything." After just missing him somewhere, she admitted that "sometimes when ages & ages go by & I don't see you I am tempted to—well—doubt the goodness of God. I know I should work just twice as well if you were here to do all the real thinking for me—or rather the imagining—I was so sick that evening [of a lecture] with nervousness that when the light went out I felt like going out too & then I said to myself—The only creature in the room that I am really afraid of has read it what do the rest matter—& they didn't really matter any more." The Ritualist circle was a small and exclusive one, and Jane derived her self-image from her participation in it. In a way, her deference to Gilbert testifies as much to her gratitude for his support as to her insecurity.[46]

This gratitude stemmed in part from his encouragement when she moved tentatively in new intellectual directions. His interest in classical literature and drama opened new doors by giving Jane fresh fields to examine for the connections among ritual, drama and literature. Gilbert's translations of Euripides struck her with their beauty and revealed new insights into the ancient world's relation to its gods. "When you first say those lovely verse-things to me I feel dazed & a little frightened—you see I am moving about in worlds half-realized—hence the obstinate questionings!" She felt unsatisfied with her work, as if somehow she never managed to capture exactly what she wanted to express. After praising his translation of Euripides' *The Bacchae,* she confided to him,

> You will laugh I know & well you may but I think the reason why your verses give me such intense & almost immeasurable delight is that they are just what I would have given my soul to do myself—As a quite young girl I had a dream of being first a poet & next a scholar & tho both dreams faded swiftly & completely they have always left a sort of empty ache of something never found. . . . I think at first I half-jealously resented it, but now I don't the least mind it being you not me—It is more resting so!

She went so far as to comment, when Gilbert's translation of Sophocles' *Oedipus Tyrannus* seemed stiff and unnatural, that "I am sure it is the fault of Sophocles if you can't translate him save with a sense of labour."[47]

Jane admitted that she felt her mind moved "at snail's pace" by comparison with other scholars. Gilbert, however, found her a great source of inspiration. In one of the few letters to her that survive, he wrote,

> You make me feel rather intoxicated, which is not good for Beasts, only for grown up men. But the inspiration really comes from yourself, as anyone who knows you at all knows. You only need a dry stick or two, to make a fire, & naturally the barking of the Theres round about you adds to the excitement of the blaze.

For her part, Jane recognized that Gilbert's calm detachment and serenity spilled over into his scholarship.

> You *are* strange—you sit like some great creating Spider & let all of us second rate flies buzz about & then when the tangle is hot & furious enough you begin weaving your web & it straightens out to your pattern & you chuck out our corpses—Just now I am thanking God that I happen to like you & so can learn from you, it's the merest chance—if you had had auburn whiskers like Menelaus I should have listened to nothing you said.

She cared deeply for Gilbert, but could express herself only humorously and indirectly.[48]

Jane may well have confused her feelings for Gilbert's work with her personal attachment to him. Although her work was far more imaginative than his, she often praised his writing for its intuitive understanding of the past. She seems to have ignored his pronouncements when they ran contrary to hers, as any true friend would, and focused solely on the part of his work that complemented her own. She advised him to read J. A. Stewart's *Plato's Doctrine of Ideas,* which she believed "explains why thinking is no good at all unless one feels & is excited—it gives one the psychology of ecstasy—& of beauty the same thing." Its greatest value consisted in its explanation for "the difference between [Gilbert] & almost every other scholar & why everything you write excites one all over & everything your pet lambs Percy [Gardner] & Mr. [Lewis] Farnell write is so much dead lumber."[49] Gilbert's main value, however, lay in his "insulated" mind. Jane knew that "when I have shot a rubbish heap down at your door you will build me a shining palace out of it."[50] She welcomed his advice but often felt a "cold fear" that he would not approve of her work and credited him with the ability to "subdue the natural vulgarity within me."[51] His painstaking research served as a counterweight to her impatient intuitive method. She "never understood till I knew you what taking the right sort of fruitful pains meant—one sees so much barren classical effort that I had let myself grow to despise minute work—& take a sort of stupid pride in splashing round inaccurately & superficially, & now you show me the beauty of all that burrowing."[52] Jane's research entailed more discipline than she admitted, but the structure of her relationship with Gilbert required a certain amount of diffidence.

Although she could be "the usual Doormat," Jane was capable of pouncing on Gilbert's scholarship. Early on, she chided him for his translation of "Skirophoria," a Greek festival name.

> Oh dear, dear! How can you expect an S. S. [Sound Scholar] like me to "visit with" a person who thinks that Skirophoria means carrying "parasols"! Just look into your heart as I looked into mine & see if you cannot find some other meaning more "consonant with the Greek spirit."

Jane insisted that the *skira* referred to sacred objects made of gypsum, perhaps combined with flour paste, which women carried in processions during both the Thesmophoria and the Skiraphoria. Scholars generally accepted the translation of *skira* as "umbrella" or "parasol," but Jane adhered to her theory of the importance of ritual objects invested with an aura of sanctity, remarking that "a white umbrella is a slender foundation for a festival." Later she threatened Gilbert that their "acquaintance must cease" if he insisted on using another particular translation.[53]

Gilbert's criticism could send her into a despondency similar in kind, although not in degree, to her reaction to the earlier criticisms from Sutherland MacColl. Now, too, she voiced doubts about the validity and originality of her work. While writing the *Prolegomena,* she sent chapters off to Gilbert for evaluation. When he approved, she was "relieved" because she "had begun to feel it might be all inflated nonsense & would disgust" him. Knowing that he believed "the main issues are worth stating," she could find "faith & courage to pull it more into shape & to look at details—drunkenness & things." In a less confident moment, Jane wrote sadly that she was "so deeply conscious that like S. Paul I know nothing 'by' myself. I always owe what the prefaces call 'the inception of my work' to someone else & it gives me cold misgivings as to whether such second-hand stuff is worth doing at all."[54]

Gilbert's criticism could make her feel "second rate & cheap all over" and as if she were behaving "like the thing I most despise in the world, a half-educated scholiast—piling up odds & ends of information & not taking the time or the trouble to see what they are really worth & how things really were." She asked why she could not

> behave with dignity, recognize my limitations of mind & training & keep my second rateness to myself? Something that I have struggled against all my life compells me to write books but at least I needn't inflict my proofs on you. . . . I should like to begin everything all over from the beginning & pray to the Lord for a new mind—My heart is all right—it's my head damn it, & that's the only thing that really matters.

The *Prolegomena*, the cause of this anguish, would be finished "somehow because I am caught in the Wheel of Things," but she had reached the nadir of her confidence in it.[55]

Predictably, her unhappiness touched Gilbert and he responded quickly with encouragement. Jane thanked him for the "kind & most comforting letter" and admitted she may have been "rather morbid" as the result of a "sleepless night" which made things look "black." A. W. Verrall's criticism on another point in the work had hurt as well: "tho he was, as always, angelically kind, I could see that he thought [her discussion of the Erinyes] was all a much ado about scarcely anything, & was puzzled as to why a sane or fairly sane person should write such stuff." She regretted making Gilbert set her "right where I never ought to have gone wrong" and promised not to impose on his time in the future.[56] The next day, however, having "thought about proofs—or rather—which is more to the point . . . slept about them," she sent another batch. "The simple fact," she wrote, "is that your help is too valuable to be given up for conscience sake." She blamed him playfully for the fact that "the whole centre of gravity of the book has shifted"; having begun "as a treatise on Keres with a supplementary notice of Dionysos—it is ending as a screed on Dionysos with an introductory talk about Keres."[57] Furthermore, she feared he would force her to "rewrite most of Dionysos tho' I have watered him down till Semele herself wouldn't know him." Although Jane appreciated Gilbert's aid, unsolicited advice from Frank Darwin led her to remark sulkily that "my book it would seem is being written by everyone except me."[58]

Jane's doubts about her scholarship stemmed from an only vaguely recognized tendency to project her personal conflicts onto her sources. She knew half-consciously that her view of the past and her intuitive understanding of ancient religion and ritual often resulted in less than objective scholarship, which accounted for her doubts about the work. She failed to see, however, that this quality of imaginativeness made her the most interesting and foremost scholar of the group. Because of her empathy for earlier peoples living in an age filled with vague terrors, she evoked more skillfully than the others the liveliness and intensity of the religious experience. Moreover, she synthesized contemporary scholarship, giving her work more depth and breadth than Gilbert Murray's and Francis Cornford's. But scholarship infused with intuitive perception, a quality that her critics associated with women, offended many other scholars and caused Jane a great deal of nagging doubt. Her refusal to recognize how much her own experience shaped her view of the past made her work utterly unselfconscious and therefore both fascinating and relatively easy to interpret, but it also made her uncomfortable during its writing by filling her with nebulous, paralyzing doubts about its validity.

One observer has praised Gilbert Murray as "both [Jane's] master and her pupil" and for his "authority to curb some of her more fantastic flights of fancy." Gilbert himself recognized that she was "a woman of genius." Their mutual respect and admiration made their relationship rewarding both personally and professionally. But another figure cast an even greater shadow over Jane's life and work: the Trinity philosopher and fellow Ritualist Francis Cornford.[59]

6

THE SECOND CIRCLE. THE CAMBRIDGE RITUALISTS: FRANCIS CORNFORD

It is [Phaedra's] tragedy that she knows spiritually that the only salvation is the utter blank of the shut door, just the thing intolerable to her passionate temperament. I suppose that was why she fell in love with Hippolytus whose strength was to shut doors.

—Jane Ellen Harrison to Gilbert Murray, December 1900

FRANCIS CORNFORD was nearly twenty-five years Jane Harrison's junior when they met in the late 1890s. He wrote asking her a question about a point made in one of her public lectures, and their friendship—begun so auspiciously on an intellectual plane—grew from that exchange. Jane appreciated his interest in her work and their shared background in the classics, but such attention from a much younger, attractive man probably pleased her as well. Francis was twenty-six years old when they met, a tall young man with curly dark hair and strong features, just exotic enough in appearance that he could not fail to attract Jane's attention. Gilbert Murray, who met Francis through Jane, remembered seeing him in her rooms, "listening intently to the lively discussions, meditative, admiring, & critical, seldom arguing but always—so one felt—taking ideas away with him to think over and consider, & re-examine." Francis's main scholarly interest turned out to be philosophy, but at an early stage he studied the origins of drama. Since he and Jane both lived in Cambridge, they were able to work together easily. They also spent much of their free time together, either taking the long bicycle rides that became almost legendary events or traveling together through Britain or on the Continent.[1]

Frances Darwin recalled images of those bicycle rides:

How well I remember the sight of them passing up the Madingley Road in great leisure (for Jane's health was already not what fifty years of trading on a magnificent constitution had led her to expect) on their high old-fashioned bicycles: Francis very upright, with his usual rather Spanish dignity, she with her sibyl-head (which yet always had an indefinable look of a sailor about it) thrown back and a long sea-green or

H. F. Stewart, Gilbert Murray, Francis Cornford (l. to r.), and Jane Harrison in Malting House Garden, Cambridge. Photo by Jessie Stewart. Courtesy of Jean Stewart Pace. Reproduced by Michael Manni Photographic, Cambridge.

silvery scarf blown about her, that somehow managed never actually to be caught in the mudguard.

Although Cambridge folk thought these outings amusing, Jane treasured them. Francis entered her life at a critical time: their friendship deepened after R. A. Neil's death. Margaret Verrall considered Jane "rather silly over FMC—sentimental & undignified," but he filled the void left by Neil's sudden death.[2]

Jane and Francis traveled extensively together in the early years of their friendship. Letters to Gilbert Murray and Jessie Stewart from the coastal towns that Jane so enjoyed or from various European cities indicate that they spent a good deal of time roaming and exploring favorite places and working on their respective subjects. Jane spent July 1904 in Surrey, having found "a clean little lodging" with "just room for me & Mr. Cornford." They traveled to Teckenham for part of the long vacation in 1905 and worked on some of Jane's Orphic studies. She joked with Gilbert Murray that "I taught Mr. Cornford Hebrew & Phenician that he might keep *me* straight—& now he is ten times madder than I am—sometime I must have a long talk with a sane person." That spring, she and Francis had traveled to Athens, and "the voyage from Marseilles was like a beautiful dream." On that trip, Francis was "a great comfort—as much as anyone merely human could be."[3]

In 1906, they visited Chartres and Chinon, where Jane found striking scenes to describe to Gilbert Murray. He was translating *Medea* then, and Jane found its violent passion disturbing. She hoped her visit to medieval sites in Chinon would help her "feel better about Medea" when she returned.

I expect it is mere physical weakness that gives me such a horror of any sort of thing involving physical cruelty—I have felt it badly here—you are shown an exquisite oratory which is all peace & loveliness & before you know where you are, the guide is showing you instruments of torture & subterranean dungeons & you feel sick for the rest of the day—I should like to have every monument of a cruel deed razed to the ground.

Once again Jane's own tangled emotions, simmering beneath her outward calm, made her unusually susceptible to the presence of evil and cruelty, even when buried in centuries of history. But she also rhapsodized over "the portal of the collegiate church of the Holy Bear—who is Saint-Ours" and praised the Roman Catholic church for being "catholic in her canonizations."[4]

This idyllic existence began to disintegrate in 1907, when both Jane and Francis suffered periods of illness. In February, Margaret Verrall informed Mary Murray of Jane's becoming ill and speculated that it resulted from a general sense of overwork and unhappiness. Jane was about to leave for the Continent and did not want her condition to interfere with her plans.

> Miss Harrison was much better by Monday afternoon & after a good night went off on Tuesday with a friend. She swore by all her gods—and she has more than most of us!—that if she were the least ill on the way she would stop at Dover. Sea air always sets her up. But as no post card has yet reached me, I take it that she was not ill & has gone on to Lucerne at least or perhaps Milan. She has a large & competent companion [probably Francis] & I expect all has gone well. The friend will stay with her till she joins the others, so I feel quite happy. I believe the change is what she really wants; Cambridge does not suit her for long & she had been working very hard to get things finished.[5]

Most interesting is her mention of Jane's unhappiness in Cambridge. After a decade, she still had not resigned herself to her exile from London and spent months on end away from Cambridge. Although her research interests generally justified these lengthy absences, she also used them to protect herself against the threat of stultifying provincialism and the often scurrilous attacks on her scholarship and personal style.

A letter to the Murrays during their visit to the United States in the spring of 1907 chronicled what must have been even more terrifying bouts with illness, although Jane described them good-naturedly enough. "I have been beset by evil Keres since you went," she wrote; "first they brought blindness to my eyes—just like them & the doctor has cut me clean off from Hebrew & hieroglyphics & Sanskrit & forbids me to read by artificial light." Even a temporary deprivation of work disrupted her life. What is more, this mysterious ailment recurred in June 1907 during a visit to Southwold with Francis. He recorded the memory of "coming in one summer afternoon at Southwold, when she had been lying in a long chair looking out at the sea. She told me she had been totally blind for perhaps an hour and she was wrought up by a visionary experience which she described." These eerie incidents are the more fascinating because, although they were probably hysterical in nature, there is no immediate connection to a specific event by which to explain them. This year should have been a relatively peaceful one for Jane. Her only major scholarly work consisted of preparing the second edition of the *Prolegomena*, and the Ritualists were working steadily at important books: Murray on *The Rise of the Greek Epic* (1908) and Francis on *Thucydides Mythistoricus* (1907). At age fifty-seven, Jane may have been suffering the effects of menopause, which could account for some of her symptoms. The other serious illness of this period, though, may also have provoked such a dramatic response.[6]

This, in its way, more sinister occurrence was Francis's sudden attack of appendicitis in May. Jane thoroughly depended on him by now for intellectual and personal companionship, and his illness undoubtedly raised the specter of R. A. Neil's death from the same ailment six years previously. Jane reported Francis's illness lightheartedly after the fact, but she must have been terrified at the thought of his dying. She jokingly rebuked men in general for being "so melodramatic in their illness—they go a long bicycle ride with you one day & the next you find them in bed with doctors & a trained nurse," but concluded thankfully, "he is out of danger now." The Southwold trip in June was designed partly to allow Francis to regain his strength, and Jane altered her plans for a visit with the Murrays in order to accompany him. "It *was* a wrench tho; changing my Oxford date—but it had to be done for you might as well send a cave-bear into lodgings by himself as this poor Mythistorical Man—he is picking up now with this air." Her cheerfulness notwithstanding, Francis described her as "alarmingly nervous sometimes."[7]

Despite Francis's illness and Jane's bout with temporary blindness, the trip did provide some amusement, primarily in the form of a visit from Jane Bury, wife of the classical scholar and King's College fellow J. B. Bury. Francis described her intrusion and gloated over his ability to escape her clutches while Jane bore the brunt of her incessant complaining. They had arrived at Southwold safely, only to find

> that Fortune has raised up an evil spirit to torment us in form and voice—especially the voice, ceaseless, unmerciful—like unto Mrs. Bury, who arrived last night with a "migraine" just at dinner time & went to bed. Thereby Jane sits, fast held by the creature's claw, & listens, as a passive bucket, to a whole Iliad of woes, past & present, pumped into her by the remorseless voice which the "migraine" has no way enfeebled. Today the monster has descended to our lower sitting room; and thence Jane emerges from time to time, like a jaded & hunted fish coming up to breathe a mouthful of silence. . . . I am understood to be too weak to bear human society & so have escaped—so far.

It is difficult to imagine Jane so completely at the mercy of another human being: clearly Mrs. Bury's was a personality to be reckoned with. September 1907 found Jane and Francis back at Southwold again, but after that, their travels together not only became more infrequent but also took on a new character.[8]

Jane's relationship to Frances Darwin, who married Francis Cornford in 1909, was of longer standing and greater depth. Ellen Crofts Darwin, Frances's mother, had been Jane's closest friend as a Newnham student and a Newnham fellow and lecturer in English literature until her marriage in 1883. Francis (Frank) Darwin, Frances's father, was one of Charles Darwin's sons and "always apt to suffer from fits of depression," especially after the death of his first wife, Amy Ruck, in childbirth. Jane was evidently fond of Frank Darwin, often referring to him as an "old bear," but she loved Ellen Crofts even more.[9]

Gwen Raverat, Ellen's niece, described her as "reserved," observing that "it seemed to be difficult to Aunt Ellen to be warm and open to the ordinary lowbrow inhabitants of the world." She had cut her hair short, always looking "picturesque and charming," and smoked cigarettes with Jane and Alice Dew-Smith. They often played games like "making rhymes about their friends, or comparing them to animals or plants or puddings," and "seemed . . . wonderfully up to date and literary." But Ellen Crofts possessed an air of melancholy that neither her close friends nor her family could explain. Nevertheless, Jane called Ellen "the friend whom I chose for myself" and their friendship lasted until Ellen's death in 1903.[10]

Jane frequently visited Wychfield, the Darwins' Cambridge home, so she watched Frances grow up. Frances recalled,

> I can hardly remember a time when "Aunt Jane" was not a part of my existence. It became a custom for her to lunch with my parents almost every Sunday in term. Even as a child I felt she gave roast beef and Yorkshire pudding a particular glow and she went to the head of any intelligent adolescent like champagne.

But, virtually from the beginning, rivalry and competitiveness shadowed their relationship. In her collection of notes on Jane's life, Hope Mirrlees recorded some extraordinary passages from Jane's letters to Frances, the originals of which are not among Jane's correspondence. In one very moving letter, Jane described an incident from Frances's childhood that proved how early in her life Frances began to feel threatened by Jane's ubiquitous presence in the Darwin home.

> One afternoon I went in to see your mother when she was reading to you & she told you to wait because it was business—& you went off & lay under the piano & literally glared at me. Your mother took it very hardly, she came out to the door with me & said what *am* I to do Frances is jealous of you—it is terrible—& I laughed (I was very breezy & unmorbid in those days & I said)—It's quite clear what we've got to do, we must never let that adorable little mite suffer on my account—& I never came again at those hours.

This touching excerpt illustrates both Frances's pain and jealousy and Jane's defeat at the hands of yet another family circle that steadfastly refused to revolve continually around her. Ellen reacted to this incident as if both Frances and Jane were her daughters, and Jane may well have designed their relationship that way. She spoke of Ellen Crofts in terms she reserved for descriptions of her own mother. Ellen may have represented the good mother to Jane, and she would be reluctant to share her good mother with Frances. That dynamic had been established before Frances's birth, and it is hard to tell from Jane's memory of the event who felt more jealous of whom. The Darwins provided safe haven for her, as did the Murrays. The main difference is that whereas she felt jealous of Gilbert's wife, in the Darwin case she felt jealous of Ellen's daughter. In the competition for Ellen's affection and attention, her daughter won. Family ties once again proved stronger than intellectual and spiritual ones.[11]

The weekly dinners at Wychfield continued until Ellen's death when Frances was seventeen. The shock proved too much for both Frank and Frances Darwin, who "fled to London to escape a home without her." Frances " 'started vehemently working at an art school.' " The frenetic pace could not divert her attention for long, however, and she suffered a total breakdown that seems to have lasted for four years. Jane bore Ellen's death with a resigned stoicism. She told Gwen Raverat, " 'I could not be sorry when Ellen died, because she was so unhappy; though I don't know why. She loved her husband and child, and had everything she wanted in the world.' " Frances had a much harder time coming to grips with her mother's death, but after several futile remedies and a rest cure, she returned to Cambridge at Christmas, 1906, apparently recovered. With renewed vitality Jane found "almost frightening," she threw herself into the study of Greek as Jane's pupil. While awaiting Frances's return, Jane had written to her:

> Very soon you will be back & I shall see you face to face & that will be great joy. . . . What a long bad time you have had—but it is nearly over—I sometimes wonder how much of you, the old you is left, there will certainly be a new you to get to know after all this—but that will be a fresh joy.

Jane, no stranger to depression, understood the trauma Frances had faced, but Frances's return to Cambridge set off a chain of events that culminated in the most profound depression Jane ever experienced.[12]

In the spring of 1907, Jane had given a "small tea-party" to introduce Frances to Francis, whose *Microcosmographia Academica,* a satirical look at academic life, she had read and enjoyed. After Frances's miraculous recovery later that year, the two began to see more of each other. In Frances's memory, "Jane Harrison seemed determined to thrust us together. I was her newest human discovery and plaything and she was delighted that it should entertain him as well." Jane probably did mean to thrust the two together, albeit unconsciously. She sabotaged her relations with men all the more efficiently the more they meant to her, and Francis meant a great deal to her. He also remarked rather bitterly on Jane's propensity for directing other people's lives. "I often thought she did not know what I was really like. Did she ever know what any of her friends were really like, or did she rather see them as symbols and assign them parts in the drama of her life?" Whatever Jane's motivation, she surely had not foreseen her own feelings when the two young people fell in love.[13]

Passages from Jane's letters to Frances Darwin collected by Hope Mirrlees offer the closest look at the actual events leading up to Frances and Francis's marriage in 1909. More letters to Gilbert Murray and other friends provide mostly oblique references to her actual despair, but they offer evidence of how long she suffered with her great unhappiness and its concomitant ill health. For the most part, she remained extraordinarily reticent about the specifics of her love for Francis and the sense of betrayal she felt when he married Frances. Even her letters to Gilbert Murray rarely referred to either of them by name. But Hope Mirrlees's notebook and the extracts of letters to Frances Darwin give concrete evidence that Jane was in love with Francis and felt devastated when he married Frances.

Although the notebook contains only fragments of letters in Hope Mirrlees's own writing and makes no direct mention of their recipient, clearly they were written to Frances Darwin. The letters, despondent, angry, and forgiving by turns, trace the chain of events leading up to the marriage and give a clear idea of Jane's attitudes toward work and love.[14] When Sutherland MacColl married, Jane had convinced herself that she could put aside all emotional and potential sexual attachments to men. She admitted later, however, "When I came back to Cambridge . . . I met a man over my work again & fell deeply in love with him more hopelessly & intensely than ever before." Presumably this statement refers to Neil. The details are murky, but some unnamed "disaster" intervened and "it was more & more imperative I should be separated from the man I did love & more & more I took refuge in the new friendship with ———." This blank must stand for Francis, whose relationship with Jane began as an intellectual friendship. She does not seem to refer here to Neil's death, but perhaps the intervening decades had clouded her memory of the exact order of events. She continues: "Then somehow I drifted into the most beautiful happiness I have ever known—I never consciously fell in love but bit by bit I came to depend entirely on him." He wrote her a letter that "made me feel that things were on a different footing & that he would never marry & that our sort of unmarried-married life would be for always." Hope Mirrlees added that Jane "thought of suggesting they should marry, but just then gossips began to talk & things at Newnham became a little difficult for her—& from sheer pride she wouldn't." One can easily imagine what the Cambridge ladies would have to say about a middle-aged woman nursing a passion for a man nearly twenty-five years her junior. But when Francis fell ill (presumably the appendicitis attack), Jane discovered that her feeling for him was "not friendship but the deepest love." In her words, "I seemed to have found myself married in spirit before I woke up to love."

As Frances and Francis grew closer beginning in early 1908, Jane became increasingly anxious and depressed. Her doctor, Christopher Wheeler, failed to perceive that her poor health resulted from an emotional trauma and advised her "to take more & more exercise," scheduling her for surgery to correct a podiatric problem to facilitate such activity. However, "more & more the frightful nameless nervousness that comes with sclerosis grew on me—till I could sometimes scarcely bear Francis to leave me even to go for a walk." Hope claims that "it was at this stage (i.e., her frightful nervousness soothed by F. [Francis] yet very trying for him) that ——— [Frances] came back [from treatment in Switzerland]."

Jane expected Frances to require a great deal of care because of the long time it took for Frances to cope with her mother's death. But within a year of her return from Switzerland, the rest cure (or rather, an internal psychological process) healed her and allowed her to resume an active life. Jane wanted Frances, in Hope's words, "to be a spiritual daughter to them both," stating, "I felt that F. [Francis] would help me to help you. . . . I always felt as if F. was years older & maturer than I am." The crisis reached a peak when Frances and Francis discovered they were in love.

Hope Mirrlees described the crisis tersely in her own words and with excerpts from Jane's letters to Frances. Jane was to have surgery and "before operation writes letter in case of her death under ether telling him [Francis] F. loves him. After operation destroys the letter & writes another, she feels he must find out for himself that F. loves him." In a letter to Frances, Jane admitted that she "lied even to him & said I did not know whether you cared—I put it on him I said I felt almost sure he cared (which was *not* true) & that he must not let the tie between us ever hamper him." After the operation, Francis escorted Jane to Devonshire, but Jane "gradually feels more & more that his heart is elsewhere & that she is only a duty," as Hope described it. Jane recalled that she "had had the foolish dream that love of one woman need not diminish the closeness of friendship with another." Although Francis "was always about me nursing me & helping me yet he was somehow gone. . . . I seemed to have come back from Death to great weakness just to find the man I always called my 'Rock of Ages' slipping away from me." Once Francis discovered Frances's feelings toward him, Hope asserted, Jane decided to "play providence" as she feared Frances "might go mad." In Jane's own words to Frances, "I was thinking of you then far beyond myself, far beyond him—perhaps as regards him & me I felt we were too closely linked for anything even his marriage to separate us." Jane described her feelings toward Frances: "three parts of one's love is an instinct of protection—a feeling that at all costs one cannot hurt that it is mean to hurt a thing weaker & younger than oneself." As Jane would discover, she herself, although older and unafflicted by an instability so obvious as Frances's, was in reality more vulnerable than the young woman she wanted so desperately to protect.

The final heartbreak occurred when Francis wrote a letter proposing to Frances. After he sent it off, Hope stated, Jane "breaks down & tells him that she herself loves him." No evidence of Francis's response survives, but the hopelessness and fear that drove Jane to make such a futile gesture cannot be overstated. Again, it was uncharacteristic of her to reveal such emotion, and the fact that she actually admitted to a love based not on intellectual compatibility or mutual interest but on genuine passion proves that even she could not deny the strength of her emotions. Up until his engagement, she did not regard the twenty-five-year difference in their ages as an obstacle, for she identified so closely with his generation and had always surrounded herself with younger friends. It was only after the engagement and marriage that Jane began to address questions of age and youth. Along with Francis's rejection, her failing health and her menopause undoubtedly contributed to her finally coming to grips with her age: when Frank Darwin sent word to Francis that Frances would soon be accepting his marriage proposal, Jane suffered her first attack of "pseudo-angina."

Frances Darwin gave her own interpretation of the triangle in 1908. She was a talented artist and presented as a Christmas gift to Francis a drawing modeled on a Greek vase painting (see illustration). The drawing shows four figures, clearly identifiable as Frances, Francis, Frank Darwin, and Jane. The young woman stooping ostensibly to sacrifice a pig is Frances. Francis stands behind her, holding a pig roughly in his outstretched hand. Frank Darwin follows, cuddling a pig lovingly in his arms. Jane brings up the rear of the procession, holding her pig tightly on a leash. All the members of the group would have been familiar with the Greek use of the pig as a symbol for female genitalia, and Frances's drawing provides a wry commentary on each person's attitude toward female sexuality—more specifically, toward her own sexuality.[15]

Hope Mirrlees commented at the beginning of her collection of the letters from Jane to Frances that Jane "had always hoped that Sir F. [Francis Darwin], he [Francis Cornford] & Frances & she would all go off on holidays together, & sometimes he & she alone." In the passage that follows, Jane explained to Frances Darwin how difficult it was for her to comprehend Francis's willingness to relinquish their common work and focus instead on a wife.

Drawing by Frances Darwin, presented as Christmas gift to Francis Cornford, 1908. Courtesy of Christopher Cornford. Reproduced by Michael Manni Photographic, Cambridge.

It was very hard indeed to me at first to realize that there could be anything worth calling a marriage with a community of work—I mean actual specialist work. . . . Even after you were engaged my dream of the solution of the difficulty was to teach you Greek & for us all three to work together.

Jane then wrote poignantly that she felt "that thing after thing had been wrenched from me or offered to me on condition I shared them." This single sentence evokes the image of a much younger Jane, a frightened little girl desolate at her father's second marriage, which required her to share him with a stepmother and, eventually, a large family. Decades later, death had claimed R. A. Neil immediately following their decision to marry. Even her mother had been "wrenched" from her by death: the pattern had persisted from the earliest days of her life.

Frances's response is unknown, but whatever it was, it led Jane to make an uncharacteristically direct attack, incidentally making a striking point about her nature and Frances's.

Of course you understand ———, you & she are by nature birds of prey, you pounce straight down on what you want & eat it up & the devil take the other birds—isn't it so? I knew it was. Well if we are two birds of prey, the Old Eagle, & the Young One shall we try at least not to prey on each other? The Old Eagle would like to try—for she loves her Young One.

In a "later letter," Jane recognized the reality of the situation and steeled herself to become reconciled to the new order.

So we must face both of us, all three of us, the fact that my loneliness may be for life. It isn't I know that I am specially weak in moral courage, it [is] just that life is ebbing & with it the power to change & grow new spiritual tissues—One's life lives longest in one's brain & so my only life is really there now. . . . And also tho the loneliness is there & almost always aches, all the bitterness went in that miracle & has never come back—it has tried to once or twice, mechanically I have felt the old misery against you but it goes now directly—& that is due in part to the miracle but also in part to you—to the faith I have in you & your tenderness towards me.

Hope Mirrlees closed this section of her notes with Jane's attempt "to find consolation in work." Jane wrote to Frances that "I began to have horrible nightmares of you dancing with lights & flowers—coming to fetch ———, & me left all broken & desolate." The dream symbolism was wrenchingly clear, but Hope gave the story a happy ending. "After [the] marriage, things improved for her. Once more he [Francis] became interested in work & she felt that he wanted her again . . . & soon *Themis* was under way & things began to open out in the wonderful way they do." Jane's other correspondence tells a different story: one of incessant pain and anguish relieved only by driving herself to work more frenetically.

Augustus John divined the full measure of Jane's grief over the Darwin-Cornford marriage and incorporated it in his portrait of her which now hangs in the Senior Combination Room at Newnham College. Unlike the distinguished founders who appear in traditionally stiff poses and glare ominously from the walls of the Fellows' Dining Room, Jane languishes full length on a sofa with her Wilson Steer painting "Yachts," symbolizing her love for the sea, hanging in the background. It is a sad, tired face that gazes out from the canvas, and Jane is clothed not in her customary blue-greens or shimmering colors but rather in black, with a green shawl draped around her neck and flowing to the floor. John painted the portrait in the summer of 1909, his unconventional appearance and personality providing the only highlight in the otherwise unendurable summer of Frances and Francis's marriage. He remembered that, while sitting for the portrait, Jane "smoked innumerable cigarettes and talked learnedly with Gilbert Murray." Jane's old friend, Sutherland MacColl, had suggested John as the artist for her portrait, and Jane thanked him for his advice while invoking memories of a time long past. "I remembered how you used to scowl over something that was amiss with the drawing in the corners of my eyes, and so I thought you would know who could best cope with these ineluctable difficulties." She approved of John because "he has seen the vision of the Beauty of Ugliness, and, which is still harder, of Plainness." Even at sixty years of age, Jane was anything but plain, but well-bred modesty combined with great despair made her downplay her own worth. She joked, "I *am* now just what you used to amuse yourself by *making* me into some 20 years ago!"[16]

Later that summer, Jane expanded on her opinion of Augustus John. She "felt spiritually at home with him from the first moment he came into the room." His presence cheered her considerably:

> He came to Cambridge in two vans with 6 horses, 7 sons, and I was never quite clear how many wives. I asked the chief one to come and see me, but she couldn't or wouldn't. . . . He was perfect to sit to; he never fussed me or posed but did me just as I lay in the chair, where I have mostly lain for months. I look like a fine distinguished prize-fighter, who has had a vision and collapsed under it. . . . He wanted a background, so I suggested my Steer. He seized it and spent two days working away at it in utter oblivion. I now look as if I was an episode in its career.

She described herself aptly, for despite her striking appearance she was clearly in both physical and psychological pain.[17]

Jane demonstrated her conflicting emotions toward Francis through her difficulty in finding the right name for him. Frances Darwin asserted that his private name was "Zeus," but Jane herself expounded on her inability to arrive at the all-important name. She had tried "Frank," "Comus" (for his role in the 1908 Newnham production of *Comus*), and "Francis," but found all of them unsatisfactory. Before Frances appeared in the picture, Jane had come close to discovering the name that would give her a sense of control over him, but those days were gone. The following letter to Frances Darwin, which dates from late 1908 or early 1909, indicates that Jane had begun to reconcile herself to their engagement.

> "Francis" will do quite well as a label for Francis—Comus cannot go on & "Frank" I always flatly declined to call him. I don't like the name *in itself* & all its associations for me are round yr father—tho it expresses him as little as it expresses "Francis." In time I daresay I shall get used to saying the label name, & he had better label me in the family "Jane" tho he has never called me that in his life. Long ago as I daresay he has told you he announced by letter (he always announces everything by

letter) that he meant to call me Shvah, which is Hebrew for the Queen of Sheba. It was because . . . but you know yr Bible [*sic*]. So then I fell into calling him Shlomoh (accent on the last syllable) which is Hebrew for Solomon. So if you want to understand our signatures you will have to learn one Hebrew letter . . . he *is* very wise. Long before that when we were in Greece together he got called the Bear—I will show you some-day the photograph that will explain why he was called that—& then Shlomoh became the name of the he-Bear because it is soft & padding & fumbles and shuffles—but these names & great truths are known only to me & him & you.

This touching chronicle of the naming process shows just how far Jane and Francis had drifted apart after such promising beginnings. The transformation from "the Bear" to "Francis" reflects the growing distance between them.[18]

Her difficulty also in finding a proper name for Frances illustrates the extent of her conflicting emotions toward her, which resulted from continual competition for attention from the same people. The tension between them transcended even that between Jane and Francis because, unlike the latter, Jane and Frances had no history of knowing, however briefly, each other's "totemic" names. In the letter to Frances cited above, Jane pursued the logic of naming to its inexorable conclusion:

I think you & I have felt about for names for each other & never found them. Frances doesn't somehow mean much to me. I think that is why I shorten it to F. But it means a remembrance as it was a great deal to yr mother. I shall perhaps some day find the right beast for you but it certainly isn't a bear. You haven't a scrap of one in you, wch is odd because yr father has.

Yet Frances remembered a time when Jane had identified her with bears. Jessie Stewart quotes Frances as saying, "it is odd now to recollect that she very often called me Old One, which was also her nickname for . . . the small endearing woolly bear . . . who lived in a sort of shrine of her mantelpiece." Jane once viewed Frances benevolently, but after she intruded on Jane's relationship with Francis, she quickly replaced past kindly identification with chilling distance.[19]

Jane's relationship with Francis Cornford proved the most spectacular failure of all her complicated attachments to men. The depth of her feeling replicated her emotional tie to Sutherland MacColl, but she acted out the experience on a far grander scale. Moreover, she was much more vulnerable and less resilient in her fifties than she had been in her thirties, and the great betrayal devastated her. Francis compounded the injury of never reciprocating her affection by the insult of marrying the daughter of her closest friend, to whom she had introduced him. Hope implies that Jane experienced her illnesses first and that Francis withdrew from her and gravitated toward Frances because of the strain of caring for Jane. It is just as likely that Jane unconsciously drove him away by engineering his romance with Frances. Her own great passion for him did not prevent her from encouraging his attraction to Frances in order to protect herself against feeling so intensely about him. In fact, she may have deliberately encouraged their relationship in order to destroy her fantasy herself, before Francis had the chance to do so. Regardless, Jane's physical health remained so poor for so long during and after the Darwin-Cornford courtship that her illnesses must have been related to the stress of genuine grief.

Jane counted as her greatest agony the end of her intellectual partnership with Francis. Although she loved him desperately, she knew unconsciously that the strongest bond between them lay in their mutual interest in each other's work. She believed the intellectual bond to be the strongest, and Francis's betrayal shattered the small universe in which she resided at the center and watched her colleagues revolve around her. Nevertheless, the fact remains that Jane ultimately experienced Francis's marriage to Frances as a betrayal less because of their intellectual friendship than because she was very much in love with him herself.

The ultimate reconciliation between Jane and Frances should not be taken as evidence of a final, peaceful resolution of the matter. Betrayed and abandoned, as she thought, and still unconsciously angry over her mother's death, her father's remarriage, and a succession of failed romances, Jane could no longer contain her anger against Francis. To see the extent of that anger, one has only to look at her most impressive work, *Themis,* which she wrote while trying to face up to the reality of her new status as maiden aunt to the man whom she loved so deeply. Letters and reminiscences testify to Jane's conscious attempts to come to grips with the great betrayal; *Themis* offers proof that for Jane, as she had claimed for Phaedra, "there were some facts you must *not* face, still less repent of."[20] Her refusal to face her anger head-on, while causing her almost unendurable anguish, drove her to create her most absorbing work. Turning her anguish into scholarship required prodigious mental effort, but Jane was not yet finished with Francis. *Themis* is not so much a study of Greek religion as a repudiation of the Victorian society that had thwarted her every desire and taken from her every close relationship she had ever had. *Themis* derives its power from the extraordinary energy that infuses every page. The next chapter explores the work itself; for the moment, the complex psychological process that turned personal rage into both chronic illness and innovative scholarship must be examined.

After the vague but unsettling ailments of 1907, Jane began to suffer from more serious complaints in the next year. Jessie Stewart often could not date letters any more precisely than by the year in which they were written, but since Frances and Francis started courting in 1908 it is relatively safe to assume that Jane's illness coincided with the growth of their mutual affection. Early on, she was in high spirits, and she described encounters with doctors and their advice lightheartedly to the Murrays. She made light of her symptoms, warning Gilbert not to "think I am a malade imaginaire or otherwise," but evinced concern by stating her intention "as soon as I can get my head above business to see an *all* round doctor to try [illegible] if he can cure me of extreme shortness of breath &—I believe the two are the same—attacks of abject nervousness. . . . I have leisure to get well in next term if I knew how—talk of egotism."[21]

Gilbert recommended his own osteopathic physician, Christopher Wheeler, to her. She thanked him for the reference, saying she had "to bless your holy name—I did like your Dr. Wheeler." Wheeler suspected a heart ailment, and Jane announced to Gilbert that "it is my heart that is playing the fool—I thought it was—he talks of Nanheim [for a rest cure] but I am to see him in 3 weeks again & then something I suppose will be decided." She confided that "he says I am to drink rather less than more whiskey!" Jane wanted to avoid a visit to Nanheim and had "high hopes I shan't be sent"; the "two drugs" the doctor prescribed enabled her to report that "the last two mornings I woke up *not* fainting," and she expressed hope that the medication would prove effective. It must have done, for Dr. Wheeler did not send her to Nanheim for a rest. Jane told Gilbert, "I *do* like Dr. Wheeler—& I am sure his multitudinous drops & tabloids are doing me good—I am sure he takes extra trouble with me because he has a Murray-cult!"[22]

Dr. Wheeler referred her to a Dr. Robert Jones for the operation on her feet that would enable her to exercise more.

> How fierce & violent are the sons of Aesculapius—Mr. Robert Jones wants my two great toes for his own—I wish they would be content with just playing on the lyre like your namesake.
>
> It seems I have rheumatoid arthritis in them & the joints are "cusped"—I swell with pride at this because it shows that in temperament I am like AWV—but it *is* a nuisance because I must either have them both operated on which means not walking for 6 weeks or I must have eternal iron bars below all my boots & shoes & even then never be sure it won't get worse.

By the end of the letter her tone had changed considerably from the eager description of her exotic ills:

> I shall have it [the operation] done if Dr. Wheeler will let me but he rather shook his head over chloroform—I am afraid he is not satisfied

with me. I am "flabby" with a flabby heart—it is disgusting. . . . Well my vile body *is* disgusting. . . . Do tell me something nice I feel so sodden and depressed.

She frequently expressed such melancholy thoughts over the next four years. Her increased reliance on medication probably played some part in her despair, although the root cause appears to have been her emotional turmoil.[23]

In May, Jane's heart had responded to treatment and her improvement averted the rest visit to Nanheim. Dr. Wheeler pronounced her "heart performances" as "most creditable & even distinguished" and discovered that her only problem was "an 'area of leakage' in a valve which makes me have to do most of my work twice over." In a revealing note to Mary Murray, Jane praised Dr. Wheeler as "the only doctor I have ever met who took a real interest in making one better when one hasn't anything very particular the matter. Generally doctors are so bored with that." She credited him with having "quieted down my heart a bit" and made her "considerably less nervous—I find that I don't dwell on tiresome things half as much & I even sometimes forget them!" This passage is noteworthy as a rare instance of Jane's admitting both that her ailments were subordinate to the general sense of fear and anxiety she often experienced and that these ailments may have been psychological as much as physiological in origin.[24]

Jane's growing depression coincided with the production of *Comus* at Newnham, in the summer of 1908, that drew Frances and Francis together. Francis acted the part of Comus and Frances helped behind the scenes. This production was the first by a new dramatic society at Newnham that Jane described as "fathered by Mr. Cornford & maiden-aunted by me." In June, Jane again thanked Gilbert Murray for sending her to Dr. Wheeler, reiterating her belief that "he has done something to stop my heart & nerves playing the fool—I no longer feel that if I am going out to dinner I must commit suicide before I dress." Although this letter reveals a precarious mental state, she usually hid the depths of her despair very effectively.[25]

As she prepared for the operation on her feet during July 1908 by composing the letter to Francis telling him of Frances's affection for him, she also wrote to Gilbert Murray of Margaret Verrall's interest in observing her under anesthesia for purposes of psychical research. "May Verrall is going to be with me when I come *to*—she is going to suggest things to me when I am subconscious & see what occurs." She worried over being anesthetized and told Gilbert she was "steadily remembering that you said taking ether was your one blissful chance of getting drunk & I shall see if I can look at it in the same light."[26] Soon after the operation, after which she destroyed the original letter to Francis and substituted one in which she disavowed knowledge of Frances's feelings toward him, she admitted to Gilbert that "taking the ether was quite a nice treat, tho' I didn't feel as if I was getting drunk." Francis wrote this letter for her from the hospital, since she was still too weak to write. "I could write today," she asserted, "but they won't let me, because, when I was doing my back hair this morning, I dissolved into floods of tears—not because it was sparse & grey . . . but for the sheer pathos of the thing." In addition to her anxiety and uncertainty about Francis and Frances, her gray hair must have reminded her that at her age she could not hope to compete with the young Frances. It is no wonder she could not hold back the tears.[27]

Despite her misery, Jane wrote cheerfully to Jessie Stewart, passing along encouraging words to a friend of Jessie's who faced an operation and also feared anesthesia. With Francis and A. B. Cook working on proofs with her while she was still in the hospital, she appeared content.[28] Francis escorted her to Devonshire to convalesce and Jane wrote a sprightly postcard to Frances Darwin from Braunton. "I know Comus sent you news so this is only one word in my own paw. I wish all day you were here. I can walk from room to room proudly rejecting all proffered paws but upstairs is still a poor business." She was working on a paper on " 'divine dickie birds' for the Oxford Congress. I dictate it to Comus & he sniffs & groans at every other word." Gilbert Murray presented another view of Jane's progress, writing to Jessie Stewart that "Miss Harrison seemed to me at first a good deal pulled down; but since she has begun to get about in a bath-chair she has improved. . . . To-day she seems very bright." Gilbert may have had a better idea of Jane's experience simply because she seems to have confided in him more than in anyone else.[29]

Once again Jane's destruction of her personal papers frustrates the search for her feelings during this period. Her letters to Gilbert Murray tell only part of the story of her despair over the Francis-Frances affair, and her feelings on the matter can only be extrapolated from her somewhat cryptic writings to the Murrays. The letters do reveal, at least, how greatly she suffered and the extent to which anxiety, depression, and rigidly controlled anger damaged her health. As Francis and Frances created their own circle, Jane wrote thanking Gilbert for what must have been a kind response to a sad letter. "I wrote in great despondency, everything seemed crumbling away—but I know you will *not* crumble." She craved work to take her mind off the painful present and admitted that if some unnamed group would request work from her "it would compel me to write & work & I seem only to be able to do it now under compulsion." As the autumn of 1908 approached, Jane had to face the inevitable loss of Francis: in October, he became engaged to Frances Darwin.[30]

Frances described the engagement in a letter to Mary Murray as "the best thing in all the world that could happen to me, it's like suddenly coming to life. . . . I didn't know it was possible to feel so happy or so sure. It is very wonderful." The engagement proved so traumatic to Jane that she fled Cambridge for Yorkshire, which turned out to be a mistake. She "escaped here to a parsonical sister's [Elizabeth Lane's home in the Yorkshire coast town of Bridlington]" as she "felt I could not bear to be a blot on the sunshine—& now they are gone together to Hunstanton [a seaside resort on the Norfolk coast] & all is well with them." However, "for me coming here was a mistake—the feeling that I belong to no-one, least of all to my own kin is so keen." Her only remaining tie seemed to be to Gilbert Murray, to whom she wrote:

> I go back next Tuesday the 6th & then to work that is my one hope—Oh *how* I miss you—coming in twice a day bringing sanity & gentleness with you & above all the sense of a steadfast friend—I cannot be quite lonely while the Ther lives on in his chthonic cave & lets me babble of mimes & magic. . . . I like to have postcards just to make me feel you are there. I can't *write* about things. I shall worry on.

Once again, Gilbert satisfied Jane's need to belong without making her painfully aware of the distance between them. Distance from Gilbert seemed appropriate and necessary. Visiting her family, though, only reinforced her awareness of how far she had traveled beyond them and Yorkshire.[31]

Jane brooded over the irony of having introduced Francis to Frances and offered two strikingly different interpretations of her role to Gilbert Murray and to Frances's cousin, Ruth Darwin. She wrote as cheerfully as possible to Ruth:

> Yes it is a most blessed thing & very blessed to have been cast for the part of deus ex machina. I don't think my own child could be dearer to me than Frances & I know now she is safe as human strength & goodness can make her—I know him far better than I know her & of course the whole thing from his side is ancient history to me as ancient as Comus himself! that makes it none the less perfect to have it settled. Of course when they are married they will be lost to this world—that we must be prepared for—I do hope this my first triumphant appearance will not turn me into a chronic "deus ex!"[32]

Jane tried to protect herself from her own emotions by distancing herself from Frances Darwin, toward whom she then felt her greatest anger. She had known Frances from her childhood, and she was lying brazenly to Ruth when she denied their long history. She sounded an old theme here, one she revived in later essays appearing in *Alpha and Omega.* Just as her father's remarriage had turned his attention from her because of the "blinding sex delusion," Francis would be lost to her through his marriage.

If Jane managed to put on a good face for Ruth, she let down her guard to Gilbert. "Letters of congratulations begin to pour in upon me & I must take up my role of *deus ex machina,*" she wrote; "I never felt it an inspiring part but you will help me to understand it."[33] Needless to say, the confusion and sorrow she expressed more clearly described her true feelings over the dubious distinction of having brought the happy couple together.

A week later, Jane wrote morbidly to Mary Murray: "I am much better for chronic [illegible], but I still shun hot rooms & in fact all evening things. I don't feel as if I could ever face a long proper dinner again & indeed why should one? They are vile inventions." Her only solace lay in bicycling, to which she had returned after recovering from her operation. Resolving to put the past behind her, Jane would the next day "begin interviewing 'first year' archaeologists—& then turn with a clear mind to put things in order for my new book." Despite her ambition, the next month found her still in "constant *slight* physical pain—it is only slight but none of Dr. Wheeler's medicines so far touch it." She was strong enough to visit the Murrays in Oxford, but begged "no dinings out *please* for me."[34]

Jane reacted emotionally to another event of November 1908, when Gilbert Murray decided to forgo the honor of presenting the Gifford Lectures in Edinburgh. He had intended to talk on "Ancient Religion and Modern Anthropology," but his duties as Regius Professor at Oxford demanded too much of his time and he abandoned the plan. Jane, who had been delirious at the prospect of the boost the series would give their common work, was crushed.

> What *can* I say? I hoped the Professorship would give you more leisure for other work not less—It is such a crushing disappointment that you should give up the Gifford lectures that I cannot look at it with clear eyes—but that is just rank selfishness just the wish that for a time you should be looking at things more from my angle so as to help *me!* . . . The gist of the disappointment is to me—that I feel you will drift away from mythology & religion & *origines*—you see there are only two people who are scholars & with literary minds who understand that these things are at the back of everything—FMC here for Cambridge—& I hoped you for Oxford—The specialists don't count—they grub up the facts but don't see the relations—& it would have been so splendid that you as Professor should give those lectures.
>
> But again I say I can't see clearly perhaps there are tears in my eyes. Follow your own conviction of what is best for work & I will not uselessly lament.[35]

With Francis rapidly losing interest in their joint work, Jane could barely face the future if Gilbert withdrew from the circle as well. At this bleak juncture, she fell back on a familiar pattern of response to crisis: she fled Cambridge for her beloved coastal retreat of Aldeburgh in Suffolk. During her several months away, she sank into a profound depression and then gathered strength to channel her deep anger at Francis's betrayal, never directly articulated, into the work that was taking shape in her mind.

Judging by her letters to the Murrays, it is astounding that Jane recovered at all. Before leaving Cambridge for Aldeburgh in mid-December 1908, she wrote to Mary that her condition kept her confined to bed. "I am in bed still & am to be till Friday—Rogers [a new doctor] will not let me stir till the last heart pain is gone." Dr. Rogers "diagnosed me exactly the same as Dr. Wheeler," but prescribed instead "rest rest & take a long course of Iodide of Potassium." Jane longed to leave Cambridge, being "sure I want sea." She wrote from the Darwin home at 13 Madingley Road, and without doubt, having Frances Darwin as her nurse exacerbated her illness. Moreover, the "most excellent parlour maid," who was helping to look after her, along with the "equally excellent cook" were "carefully training Frances in housekeeping." Small wonder that Jane could barely wait for Rogers to pronounce her fit enough to travel to Suffolk.[36]

In mid-December, Jane finally escaped to Aldeburgh with her close friend Alys Russell. Jessie Stewart described Jane as retiring "wounded, after physical and mental strain, to Aldeburgh," which understates the severity of her depression.[37] She did not mention the immediate cause, which was the impending marriage. Jane, trying to derive solace from her visit to the usually replenishing Aldeburgh haunt, wrote Gilbert Murray about her discovery of "the Great-good Place—a huge balcony sheltered on 3 sides where I lie all day long." In this idyllic setting even he "would be warm for the sun is shining brightly & white gulls are flapping." She urged him to visit there during the summer, for "there is just room for you & me & Rosalind," obviously the only company she could bear.[38] Despite the fine weather and her propinquity to her "great sea-mother," Jane did not recuperate.[39] Christmas, traditionally an unhappy time for her, found her "ordered another fortnight complete inertia" and "at the bottom of a pit of exhaustion," although she had "no pangs." She ended wearily, "shall I ever get my head up."[40] Her annual birthday letter to Gilbert, written on December 29, 1908, for his birthday on January 2, 1909, touched on the power of work to heal one's soul.

> I heard a Darwin story the other day that I liked—the butler was overheard saying to a visiting [illegible] "Master thinks he's ill but it's my opinion if he had something to occupy his mind with he'd be all right."

It is a great thing to be a butler & *have* to clean the silver however sick you feel—but I am feeling less sick—only I seem to have dropped into a pit of exhaustion where there is nothing within reach—that is one's vile body I suppose.

Thankful for his friendship, she closed wistfully, "I believe life for you is pretty full now & I am glad of that," and with the wish that he "live as long as I do & much longer."[41]

Her illness left her time to brood over the abrupt changes in circumstance, and she began to steel herself to the reality of Francis's engagement and his diminishing interest in their work. Still unreconciled to his betrayal, however, she lashed out at him indirectly in a letter to Frances Darwin.

About work. Yes the world *is* a ruthless place & sex the most ruthless thing in it. Thank you for seeing that. I am just now faced by the blank unâlterable fact that for more than 6 months Francis has not cared & could not care at all for the work that has been for years our joint life & friendship—but I have faith to believe it may not always be so. While it *is* so it is better that he & I should not be together. I also absolutely believe that you reverence work—tho' you could as yet not understand nor can he how—late in life—work & friendship come to be the whole of life.[42]

At this stage, Jane still clung to the belief that Francis would eventually regain his interest in their work, a necessary illusion. If "work & friendship" were to be the whole of life, she could not face the loss of her closest colleague, even if he had failed at the other roles in which she had cast him.

In an effort to overcome her illness, Jane launched a campaign to convince herself of its physiological root. While apologizing to Mary for her "disgraceful behavior" during a visit to the Murrays' in early 1909, she admitted the strain she had been under but attributed her condition to physical causes. The letter is lengthy but bears close scrutiny, for it demonstrates the supreme effort required to deny the depth of her depression and the force of her anger to transform anxiety into illness.

I wanted to tell you—partly to apologize for my really disgraceful behavior when I was with you—that I am now convinced that the whole business of the heart pain was far more physical than I or Dr. Wheeler thought. What has convinced me is that I had a very bad return of the pain after Alys left me at Aldeburgh—so bad that I was frightened & should have called in a local man only I was so sick of all that I thought for *every* one's sake I had better die if there was a chance—but one night, after not being able to touch food for about 9 hours [illegible] faintness, I felt relief—being hungry in the morning I gulped down my breakfast in a hurry & in about a quarter of an hour back came the old anguish—I can call it nothing else—then at last I said to myself "this is body, not soul" & it must have to do with food & digestion. I halved my meals & ate them like a snail & began bit by bit to get better.

She continued, explaining that "once you have a heart pain there is no distinguishing it from a very bad ordinary heartache—which everyone I should think has to bear sometime in their life." Simultaneously Jane advanced reasons for depression and denied their validity.

Of course the pain was *first set going* by severe mental anxiety, the sort of original attack I had after waiting five days for the telegram [Frances's acceptance of Francis's proposal] was the beginning—but what I mean is that had it been treated physically, rest & care about food from the beginning, I believe, whatever mentally I might have suffered, & for however long the mental pain might have lasted, the *physical* pain would have been over in a few days. The mistake I made was in being too frank. I always feel it is wrong to humbug a doctor—so I told Dr. Wheeler I had had great mental anxiety & he always advised work & going about & getting [illegible] one's general health. He was kindness itself—but after trying various drugs—I think he stopped looking for a physical cause. Rogers to whom I told nothing ordered me instantly to bed. I am eternally grateful to him—it was the first step. . . . I only slowly began to see that it was the pain (set up by mental misery) that was recalling the mental misery—not the mental misery causing the pain.

This triumph of denial of emotion and the power of depression to cause illness represented the height of Jane's refusal to face the depth of her anger toward Francis. Ironically, the second half of the letter revealed other causes for unhappiness and serves only to emphasize how depressed and abandoned she felt during this crisis.

When I came to stay with you I thought the pain was mentally caused & I thought if anything would distract me & help me get over it, it would be the change & delight of being with you. To my despair it got worse—then when you said & most rightly that I must not go abroad with Mr. Murray I was in desperation because I felt my last hope of relief & distraction was gone. I also felt that you thought I was giving way & *causing* myself pain by useless regrets. I began to accuse myself & feel unfit to live—in reality I know now that I had no more power to stop the pain than Prometheus had to stop the vulture gnawing at his liver.

With a herculean effort, Jane began to submerge the emotions that threatened to get out of control. She accomplished this task by channeling her fury into work. "My despair was that with that gnawing pain I could not work or think except under a fearful strain. Now that the pain is practically gone I *can* work & can think & assuredly, could I have done that before I should never have burdened my friends with my groans. So long as you can *work* life is abundantly worth living." Life is particularly worth living when one has a score to settle. It took time, but the anger that threatened Jane's life, paradoxically, became transformed into the force that saved her.[43]

Believing Cambridge to be "the worst place in the world for me the next 6 months," as she wrote in January 1909, Jane resolved to avoid it. Dr. Rogers foiled her plans by refusing to allow her to travel. Despite occasional setbacks, she slowly began to regain her health, come to grips with the impending marriage, and, most important, start thinking about her next book. Although in February 1909 the "fierce weather" gave her "pains again," Dr. Rogers reported encouragingly that she had "gained ground sclerotically" and advised her "to spend all day lizarding in the sun as soon as there is any sun." In April she decided to go to Aldeburgh for the next term, believing that the sea air would keep her from feeling "the depression that they say is inevitable with iodine so much." Occasionally, though, she could not help but let slip some of the old sadness. Gilbert Murray visited her in Cambridge, and she gratefully acknowledged how much he had cheered her.

> It was good of you to come up that last day—I knew it was to help me & I was oh so grateful.
>
> For all this time I cannot say any thanks but I do want to say just this—It *has* helped me—this way—it has made me feel that as long as you let me be your friend I cannot & will not sink lower into any pit of self-abasement.

Jane went to Aldeburgh in the early summer and remained there until after Francis's wedding, which took place in July 1909. She returned to Cambridge later in July and began sitting for Augustus John, who painted the portrait that fateful summer. Upon returning to Newnham, Jane wrote an entirely unconvincing letter to Gilbert Murray, resolving to put the past behind her and focus on the present.

> My cave feels very lonely, but it is a good deal less lonely when a letter comes from you—& there is Thursday coming soon. I have resolved to follow your counsel & not to think of the endlessness of the lonely years to come but just to try & go on mending up my life with lots of work from day to day—the thing that helps me most is thinking of the patient lines about the mouths of some people.[44]

Relapses into illness and despair punctuated the next three years, during which Jane worked on *Themis,* but gradually she returned to her usual routine. In October 1909, Dr. Wheeler told her that "having made so much advance I ought to make more." A visit with the Murrays had been "refreshment & delight" that enabled her to "plunge in to work with fresh courage & put thro' my lecture without any undue strain—which shows I must be really strong."[45] But in November she lapsed again into despair, as she confessed to Gilbert Murray: "And here comes your letter. Thank you—did you know O Cheiron how badly I wanted consolation. You see too clearly—I *was* in a good deal of pain—I had been doing rather much I suppose—& a dreadful loneliness was on me at having to go." She asked him to thank John Galsworthy for comments that, although unrevealed, gave her

> great inward joy. . . . I did not quite see that Sex was force & that therein lay not only its strength but its terror & its ignominy—& that in balance—which I shall never get—lies peace. . . . I am here—& have a clear fortnight for work—& the stress of the Kouretes is over—& just because I have no such compulsion I simply can do nothing but sit & think of the utter loneliness of things—Please send me a word to give me strength to begin—for I *must* work.

She signed this letter, "your desolate Ker."[46]

The sadness crept into her minor works as well. In December 1909, she delivered a lecture called "Heresy and Humanity" to the Cambridge Society of "Heretics" in which she extolled the virtues of collectivism. Having been disappointed so often in close personal relationships, she became almost strident on the superiority of the communal life. The ferocity of her attack on individualism reached its pinnacle in *Themis,* but she refined her thoughts while brooding over its plot. In this lecture, she provided a glimpse of the pain caused by a close friend's betrayal and offered proof of individual treachery: "A close companionship withdrawn is a wound to our actual spiritual life: if our egotism and self-sufficiency be robust, we recover from it; if weak, we go maimed and halting, with minished personality." During these years, Jane appeared "maimed and halting" despite her inner strength.[47]

April of 1910 found her in rather better spirits. She had heard Gilbert lecture and visited with him. She still worked at her writing, but admitted that "sometimes I do want just to be happy & enjoy myself thro & thro for an hour." She especially welcomed his visit because she had "felt almost sure that old Harpy Providence was somewhere round—she always is nowadays—to snatch the feast from my lips." That summer brought more ill health, and Jane tried escaping to Yorkshire and even a Swedish resort to recover, but other than diagnosing her pain as "intercoastal neuralgia" the doctors could not cure her. Jane's Swedish excursion provided at least temporary diversion, as she went off with Lytton Strachey and his sister, Pernel, in July 1910. Although several weeks at

Saltsjöbaden did not improve Jane's health as it did Lytton's, she still cut a colorful figure. Lytton confided to his mother that Jane and Pernel "both find the place very singular . . . and I should think the place returns the compliment so far as Jane is concerned—she makes a strange figure among the formal Scandinavians, floating through the corridors in green shawls and purple tea-gowns, and reciting the Swedish grammar at meals." The third week of August brought cold weather that proved too much for Jane and Pernel, prompting them to leave and Jane to vow, "this is the last anyone will hear of my health." Despite her resolution, her friends continued to hear of it.[48]

At the same time, the ideas for *Themis* were fermenting in her mind and beginning to take on a life of their own. After a casual conversation in which Jane mentioned some of her ideas on the connection between art and ritual, Gilbert Murray urged her to begin work on what would later become *Ancient Art and Ritual,* but she refused to work on it then. She was "just embarked on the Epileg [her early working title for *Themis*] & it absolutely *must* be done this year." She could not "bear it in my head any longer" and needed to put her thoughts on paper. Three weeks later she sent summaries of chapters and an outline of *Themis* and concluded, "I hope & trust—unless I lapse in my vile body—to get it all written out rather quickly now—I am in the stage now that bad or good I have got to get rid of it before I can think in any other form." Her ideas became obsessions, and she envied Gilbert that "this never happens to you—you always command your material—mine commands me."[49]

Her euphoria did not last long. She added a rather morose postscript to her birthday letter to Gilbert Murray on December 29, 1910, having spent another Christmas alone at Southwold in Suffolk, a town she had often visited with Francis Cornford in happier days. She apologized for a "petulant letter" sent earlier and explained:

> I was cross because material blessings were being heaped upon me & a happy healthy Xmas was being organized for me at Littlehampton by telegram & that—when the one thing needful is withheld—exacerbates me—but I broke loose & now I am better. After all tho my measure is much minished it is all laid up in heaven now where neither moth . . .[50]

Once again, the old sorrow crept into her correspondence. Over the next eighteen months, the loss of an old friend prompted further expressions of despair.

Late in October 1910, Henry Butcher suffered a stroke and died on December 29. His death prompted a very sad yet strangely chilling letter from Jane to Gilbert Murray, who had sent his condolences. After the conventional lines about his death's being all for the best under the circumstances, Jane gave her reaction to reading the obituary notices of the man she had loved so many years before.

It is so strange & chill to read about all the apparatus of public life when one knew that life from the inside—it all sounds so unreal—& yet it was real in a way—I ought to feel much more sad—sometimes it frightens me that I feel so little—I believe there are just two things in the world that could really hurt me now & only two. I am oddly numb.

After this confession of emotional and spiritual numbness, Jane mused over Gilbert's recent forty-fifth birthday.

Forty five is the very best age to be—only it seems to me—at 60—a frivolous & irresponsible age—at 45 it seemed to me impossible that one should ever die or grow old. Now I always think of what you once said to me—I thought it so amazing—that whenever you heard any one was dead (it was Sir Richard) you couldn't help being rather glad because anyhow there was one person who couldn't hurt or be hurt any more.

Beginning to feel the effects of poor health and her age, and suspecting that Gilbert Murray was losing interest in the Ritualists' labors, Jane grew increasingly morose. Still brooding over his forfeiture of the Gifford Lectures, Jane complained that "now all my stuff is so outside your real work that, tho you are infinitely patient & good, I always feel it is an effort to you to refocus your attention on it—I shall not come again that way at the end of term—tho it was beautiful to be with you." She attributed her petulance to "pain & loneliness" which made an "egotist" of her, and recalled that she "used to be too happy to fuss consciously about myself or my work."[51]

Jane failed to recognize that when her circle had revolved faithfully and cheerfully around her, she had no need to fuss about herself; when the circle began to fall apart, however, she experienced terrible anguish. Furthermore, family problems surfaced. Jane stated that "this damnable season of peace & good will makes it all worse because I have all I can do not to hate two of my sisters." She could "hate them both comfortably & fiercely" if she had "never known" Gilbert, but his gentle influence dissuaded her from such harshness.[52]

Jane continued brooding and feared the loss of still more friends. A few letters from 1911 and 1912 illustrate her unhappiness. Mary Murray's father, Lord Carlisle, died in April 1911, and Jane wrote morbidly to Gilbert of her fear that "you will probably catch cold at the funeral & die too—people always do—but don't if you can help it." Her fear is not so remarkable as the fact that she felt frightened enough to make such a tactless remark in a letter of condolence. But Gilbert remained a staunch friend, who always seemed to know just how to cheer her up when she felt most despondent. She appreciated his writing on one occasion when he "made a tired & always rather sad Ker feel new life & strength in her old bones—& a great confidence in her new theories." Christmas of 1911 prompted her to write another unhappy letter, noting an unnamed tragedy descending over the Murray household and observing, after a visit with Alys Russell, "what a horrible scar a broken marriage leaves." Understandably, Jane closed the letter by remarking that "the world is a horribly sad place."[53]

The world did not improve much in the winter of 1912. A performance of *Oedipus* in January drove Jane into a rage over the portrayal of Jocasta, who was "noisome to me all thro & most in the 'great tableau' of the dominant mother, overhanging him, I nearly fled—its womanliness made me sick." Jocasta's tragic love for the much younger man who turned out to be her son struck too close to home for Jane, who had not yet recovered from the Francis-Frances episode. She experienced an anxiety attack during a visit with the Murrays in March and apologized for her behavior. "I am afraid I was a bad visitor. I have been told that when I am nervous I simply 'exude' nervousness & am intolerable."[54]

These letters, conveying the strain of successive tragedies, tell her story up to 1912, the year in which she finally completed and published *Themis.* The difference between her *Prolegomena* and *Themis* reflects both the personal influence of Gilbert Murray and Francis Cornford and the intellectual influence of contemporary scholarship. Primarily, though, the two works illustrate Jane's different ways of coping with the world around her. In them, she used her scholarly work to make sense of her own experience. A comparison of these two fascinating works demonstrates the intimate—and inevitable—connection between life and work.

7

THE *PROLEGOMENA*, *THEMIS*, AND THE FURIES AT BAY

In my own specialist work of Greek religion my friends have brought against me of late a serious charge. They tax me with some lack of reverence for the Olympian gods, for Apollo, for Athena—nay, even for Father Zeus himself. My interest, I am told, is unduly focussed on ghosts, bogies, fetiches, pillar-cults. I pay to them and to such-like the attention properly due to the reverend Olympians. Worse still, in matters of ritual I prefer savage disorders, Dionysiac origins, the tearing of wild bulls, to the ordered and stately ceremonial of Panathenaic processions. In a word, my heart, it would seem, is not in the right place.

—*Jane Ellen Harrison,* Alpha and Omega

The study of mythology need no longer be looked on as an escape from reality into the fantasies of primitive peoples, but as a search for the deeper understanding of the human mind. In reaching out to explore the distant hills where the gods dwell and the deeps where the monsters are lurking, we are perhaps discovering the way home.

—*H. R. Ellis Davidson,* The Gods and Myths of Northern Europe

JANE HARRISON brought her fascination with primitive religion to its height in her two central works, the *Prolegomena to the Study of Greek Religion* (1903) and *Themis: A Study of the Social Origins of Greek Religion* (1912). This fascination served many purposes. Overall, she used the ancient past to work out her complicated feelings about both her own life and the society in which she lived. She chose the ancient past because of its distance from the present. Her own emotions continually threatened to get out of control, and distancing herself from them was a safe way to deal with them. She addressed issues of sexuality and emotion through her work by focusing on the chthonic cults, while strenuously denying their power in her own life. She also wrestled with her anger at the nature of Victorian family life by projecting the structures she saw around her onto the past. Her criticism of the Olympian pantheon reveals her own prejudice against bourgeois Victorian family life. She envisioned a more hospitable world through her defense of the historical existence of matriarchy. But perhaps the most interesting as-

Jane Harrison at Newnham College, ca. 1905–10. Photo by Jessie Stewart. Courtesy of Jean Stewart Pace. Reproduced by University Library, Cambridge.

pect of her work lies in its illustration of the fundamental contradiction in her life—her attitude toward emotion. Although in her work Jane railed against the denial of emotion, she devoted much of her strength to keeping her own potentially explosive emotions under rigid control. Finally, Jane re-created the past as a means of rebelling against society in general and easing the pain caused by her lifelong experience of intense attachments that ended in abandonment.

Jane's scholarship can be considered a part of the intellectual movement described by H. Stuart Hughes as the "revolt against positivism."[1] Disillusioned by scientific thought and its sweeping effects on society and ideology, many fin-de-siècle intellectuals sought spiritual comfort in the study of the irrational. Although the Cambridge Ritualists alienated many classical scholars, they kept distinguished company in their quest for the origins of the religious impulse. Belief in the benefits of collectivism connected Jane to wider intellectual trends. In an increasingly depersonalized world in which rapid social change routinely destroyed interpersonal bonds, she looked back fondly to the dim past. In those days, she believed, group interest took precedence over individual interest. She also idealized the primacy of emotion that held the group together. Above all, she posited the historical existence and superiority of matriarchy. Although she marshaled evidence to support her theories, she ultimately strove to recast Victorian society in a primitive mold.

Jane closely followed and relied on the work of scholars whose ideas meshed with her own. In the *Prolegomena,* she drew on Friedrich Nietzsche and J. J. Bachofen, borrowing from Nietzsche the concept of the duality of rational and irrational, and from Bachofen evidence of the historical existence of matriarchy. Ten years later, she frequently cited Emile Durkheim and Henri Bergson in her footnotes. Durkheim's British disciple, A. R. Radcliffe-Brown, brought his work to Cambridge in a 1909 lecture, which Harrison attended and cited in a footnote in *Themis.* She also referred directly to *L'Année sociologique* and praised Durkheim's papers "The Definition of Religious Phenomena" and "The Incest Taboo and Its Origins"; his work with Mauss on "Primitive Classification"; and Hubert and Mauss's "Nature of Sacrifice." Durkheim's *Elementary Forms of Religious Life* (1912) buttressed Harrison's arguments about the nature of primitive religion, although his scientific rationalist approach probably alienated her. She found Bergson's ideas far more congenial, for he seemed to her to get at the root of human experience. His *L'Evolution créatrice* struck a responsive chord, and she asserted that it marked a stage of her own thought.[2]

Many anthropologists contributed to Harrison's vision, but in the general sense of capturing, as she did, a feeling that was brewing in intellectual circles; a sympathy for the irrational and an interest in primitive religion. William Robertson Smith, Edward Burnett Tylor, and Sir James George Frazer all influenced the direction of her work. Their vast accumulation of data gave her the base on which to build her theory. She herself attributed the growth of Ritualist theory to Frazer's *The Golden Bough,* the culmination of years of research and innovation that finally challenged conventional wisdom in classical study. She wrote:

> We Hellenists were, in truth, at that time a "people who sat in darkness," but we were soon to see a great light, two great lights—archaeology, anthropology. Classics were turning in their long sleep. Old men began to see visions, young men to dream dreams. I had just left Cambridge when Schliemann began to dig at Troy. Among my own contemporaries was J. G. Frazer, who was soon to light the dark wood of savage superstition with a gleam from *The Golden Bough.* The happy title of that book—Sir James Frazer has a veritable genius for titles—made it arrest the attention of scholars. They saw in comparative anthropology a serious subject actually capable of elucidating a Greek or Latin text. Tylor had written and spoken; Robertson Smith, exiled for heresy, had seen the Star in the East; in vain; we classical deaf-adders stopped our ears and closed our eyes; but at the mere sound of the magical words "Golden Bough" the scales fell—we heard and understood. (RSL, 342–43)

However, Durkheim, Bergson, and later in her experience, Freud were much more sympathetic than were the anthropologists and classicists to the unconscious motives that lay behind this need to explore the irrational. Despite Frazer's work on early religion and ritual, he rejected the primacy of emotion that became the cornerstone of Harrison's contribution to Ritualist theory.[3]

Ironically, Harrison's most concise exposition of Ritualist theory appeared in a work that Gilbert Murray "never thought . . . was among Jane's better books," namely *Ancient Art and Ritual.*[4] Although *Art and Ritual* falls chronologically at the end of her most productive period, it offers the best introduction to Ritualist theory. It provides a succinct summary of the theory and thus sheds light on the more richly developed *Prolegomena* and *Themis.*

The *Art* of the title refers to drama, which Harrison considered a "clear historical case of a great art, which arose out of a very primitive and almost worldwide ritual."[5] She linked ritual and art because "it is at the outset one and the same impulse that sends a man to church and to the theatre" (9–10). But the Ritualists looked beyond classical drama to the murky origins of ritual dance that preceded it. The classical model alone offered inadequate material for study because "in the case of drama," ritual was "swiftly and completely transmuted into art" (14). Harrison recognized that "Greece is often too near us, too advanced, too modern, to be for comparative purposes instructive"; a clear rejection of conventional Victorian classical scholarship (15).[6] By this time, Harrison understood the seductiveness of the classical period and how its dizzy heights of achievement deliberately obscured the past and dazzled the researcher looking for origins: "So fair and magical are their cloud-capp'd towers that they distract our minds from the task of digging for foundations" (14). The only way out of this muddle was finally to work backward into primitive society.

Once arrived in the distant past, Harrison reconstructed the early connections between art and ritual. "In ritual, the thing desired . . . is acted, in art it is represented" (18). Both were essential because they denoted two levels of emotional expression.

> At the bottom of art . . . lies, not the wish to copy Nature or even improve on her . . . but rather an impulse shared by art with ritual, the desire, that is, to utter, to give out a strongly felt emotion or desire by representing, by making or doing or enriching the object or act desired. . . . This common *emotional* factor it is that makes art and ritual in their beginnings well-nigh indistinguishable. (26)

She could hardly have come further from the ideality of the London period. Calm detachment had finally given way to keenly felt and freely expressed emotion.

At its best, "ritual . . . involves imitation; but does not arise out of it. It desires to recreate an emotion, not to reproduce an object" (25–26). If ritual lost its emotional content, only a meaningless rite would remain. "Because a rite has ceased to be believed in, it does not in the least follow that it will cease to be *done*" (27). Art became the visible representation of a collective emotion, for "though the utterance of emotion is the prime and moving, it is not the sole, factor. . . . We must not only *utter* emotion, we must *represent* it, that is, we must in some way reproduce or imitate or express the thought which is causing us emotion" (34). In primitive society, where group interest subordinated individuality, ritual became especially significant.

> Collectivity and emotional tension, two elements that tend to turn the simple reaction into a rite, are—specially among primitive peoples—closely associated, indeed scarcely separable. The individual among savages has but a thin and meagre personality; high emotional tension is to him only caused and maintained by a thing felt socially; it is what the tribe feels that is sacred, that is matter for ritual. (36–37)

Emotion, particularly repressed emotion, provided the moving force. "Art and religion, though perhaps not wholly ritual, spring from the incomplete cycle, from unsatisfied desire, from perception and emotion that have somehow not found immediate outlet in practical action" (41).

Primitive society focused emotional energy on the desire for food and the sexual instinct.

Harrison's discussion of the connection between ritual and drama explained the nature of both religion and art. In Greek drama, "there is no division at first between actors and spectators; all are actors, all are doing the thing done, dancing the dance danced. . . . No one at this early stage thinks of building a *theatre,* a spectator place" (126). When spectators became separated from the actors and dancers, ritual and art differentiated as well. Ritual required the entire group's participation to be efficacious, and it directed the collective emotion toward a specific end. Art allowed one to become a spectator: "The difference between ritual and art" is that "the *dromenon,* the thing actually done by yourself has become a *drama,* a thing also done, but abstracted from your doing" (127). Ultimately, religion acquired the same distance from ritual as art did. Both acted as intermediaries to placate gods that had been transformed from embodiments of nature into images more structured and human. Harrison succinctly summarized the Ritualist theory of myth by using the example of the primitive armed dance.

> There is, first, the "actual necessity of war." Men go to war armed, to face actual dangers, and at their head is a leader in full armour. That is real life. There is then the festal re-enactment of war, when the fight is not actually fought, but there is an imitation of war. That is the ritual stage, the dromenon. Here, too, there is a leader. More and more this dance becomes a spectacle, less and less an action. Then from the periodic dromenon, the ritual enacted year by year, emerges an imagined permanent leader; a daemon, or god—a Dionysos, an Apollo, an Athena. Finally the account of what actually happened is thrown into the past, into a remote distance, and we have an "aetiological" myth—a story told to give a cause or reason. (196)

This example explained the social origin of ritual and mythology. A natural component also figured in the case of the drama.

Harrison saw a close relation between drama and the religious impulse. The structure of Greek drama emerged from ritual and reflected primitive concern for the food supply and propagation of the tribe.

> A *chorus,* a band of dancers there must be, because the drama arose out of a ritual dance. An agon, or contest, or wrangling, there will probably be, because Summer contends with Winter, Life with Death, the New Year with the Old. A tragedy must be tragic, must have its *pathos,* because the Winter, the Old Year, must die. There must needs be a swift transition, a clash and change from sorrow to joy . . . because, though you carry out Winter, you bring in Summer. At the end we shall have an Appearance, an Epiphany of a god, because the whole gist of the

ancient ritual was to summon the spirit of life. All these ritual forms haunt and shadow the play, whatever its plot, like ancient traditional ghosts; they underlie and sway the movement and the speeches like some compelling rhythm. (138–39)

The first spirit the primitive mind recognized was the spirit of life, of the new year, of renewal and growth and plenty. The Ritualists called this spirit the "Year-Spirit" or "Year-Daimon."

Harrison's fascination with the ritual origin of mythology and religion marked a radical change from her London period. *Art and Ritual* illustrated how far she had come in twenty-five years, but her *Prolegomena* and *Themis* marked transitional stages in her thought. Sympathy for the group experience of the archaic period gradually replaced her aesthetic appreciation of classical religion and culture. The *Prolegomena,* however, shows that she kept a foot in both camps before finally and dramatically rejecting traditional classical scholarship and individualism in *Themis.* The Olympians in her *Introductory Studies in Greek Art* (1885) were idealized human beings, the end product of anthropomorphism. At this early stage, she did not view them as remote and detached, because they retained some kinship with their human creators. They "are as strong and fair as the sons and daughters of men, nay, stronger and fairer, sometimes as frail. They love and hate, they hope and fear, they feast and dwell in goodly houses, they are weary and would fain sleep—they are human, in a word, and nothing human do they account alien." The Greek defeat of the Persians in the early fifth century B.C. ushered in the greatest period of classical civilization, but as the century ended, the Peloponnesian War "turned the best thoughts inward from the state to the individual, from politics to philosophy; and in so doing it exalted the individual, his thoughts, his emotions, even his passions; he was no longer to lose himself in serving his country, rather he must live his own life to the fullest, knowing of no other."[7]

The Greeks had early on rejected emotional religion, but in 1885 Harrison admitted its existence. In her London years, she had written scornfully of it: "I do not mean to say that the Greeks never had their period of grosser religions. . . . But what the Egyptians could never free themselves from, the Greeks shook off for the most part in almost prehistoric times." She referred to the pre-Olympian stage then as the " 'seamy side' of Greek religion," which

undeniable as it is, serves only to point more emphatically its generally beautiful and human character. When we consider to what a flood of Oriental contagion of hideous forms and still more horrid practices the Greeks were exposed, we wonder only that they remained so steadfastly devoted to the pure and the beautiful, that they threaded their way in art, as in religion, so delicately through such a mire-stained region.

To a disciple of aestheticism, the Olympians appeared a great cultural achievement.[8]

Fifteen years later, Harrison's view of the ancient world had changed considerably. Her *Prolegomena* reflected the influence of two scholars whose work demonstrated a similar sympathy to the intuitive and the irrational: Friedrich Nietzsche and J. J. Bachofen. Nietzsche's appreciation of the Dionysian elements of Greek culture in *The Birth of Tragedy* (1871) and Bachofen's defense of matriarchy in *Mutterrecht* (1861) captured Harrison's imagination and gradually permeated her work.

Nietzsche's paean to intuitive perception sounded a note similar to Harrison's work. His preference for the "immediate certainty of intuition" over "logical inference" (*BT,* 21) would have seemed familiar to Harrison. Like her, Nietzsche perceived the terror that lay under the veneer of civilization. "Indeed the man of philosophic turn has a foreboding that underneath this reality in which we live and have our being, another and altogether different lies concealed, and that therefore it is also an appearance" (*BT,* 23). Dionysian ritual and religion drew out this irrational, terrifying element, the strength of which Nietzsche fully understood. The attraction of Dionysian festivals "lay in extravagant sexual licentiousness, the waves of which overwhelmed all family life and its venerable traditions," and also in the "detestable mixture of lust and cruelty" that they inspired (*BT,* 30). Moreover, Nietzsche divined the real purpose of the Olympian pantheon. It did not exist merely as a group projection; it served a far more essential function. "The Greek knew and felt the terrors and horrors of existence: to be able to live at all, he had to interpose the shining dream-birth of the Olympian world between himself and them" (*BT,* 34–35).

The main difference between their philosophies lay in their attitude toward the horrors that lurk beneath the surface. To Nietzsche, human beings could recognize the horror but not live with it—hence their construction of the Olympian pantheon. He believed humanity incapable of surviving without the lid on, although he played dangerously close to that border himself. In his view, Dionysos and Apollo had to coexist. Harrison banished the Apollonian and elevated the Dionysian. For this reason, she set down *The Birth of Tragedy* when she reached Nietzsche's discourse on Euripides. Instead of seeing Euripides as the rationalist, she saw him as the one playwright capable of loosening the lid on the emotions. She also appreciated his skepticism about the gods. Whereas Aeschylus and Sophocles justified the Olympians' ascendancy and applauded their supposed justice, Euripides reminded his audiences that things are not always as they seem.[9]

Harrison expressed greater faith in Bachofen, whose work she appreciated. She believed that his *Mutterrecht,* in "spite of the wildness of its theories, remains of value as the fullest existing collection of ancient facts." The root of her sympathy with Bachofen lay in his exaltation of maternal love—an idea sure to appeal to a woman who had lost her mother after only a month. Bachofen, writing under the compulsion of his great love for his mother, ascribed to the mother-child bond an almost mystical nature.

At the lowest, darkest stage of human existence the love between the mother and her offspring is the bright spot in life, the only light in the moral darkness, the only joy amid profound misery. . . . The relationship which stands at the origin of all culture, of every virtue, of every nobler aspect of existence, is that between mother and child; it operates in a world of violence as the divine principle of love, of union, of peace.

They parted ways over the superiority of matriarchy. Despite his intuitive preference for matriarchy, Bachofen attributed the development of civilization to patriarchy, which Harrison considered an inferior system. That they both confused matriarchy with matriliny is immaterial. Anyone reading their work critically and thoughtfully knew exactly what they were talking about. Turning patriarchal culture on its head required a whole new vision of the world. Primitive societies and academics alike had devoted enormous energy to proving women's association with nature, believing that this association made them inferior. Harrison strove to make such an association a sign of superiority. Moreover, she softened the distinction between nature and culture.[10]

Like Harrison, Bachofen also searched for origins. His journey took him back beyond the classical age to the archaic period that Harrison found so fruitful. He based his theory of the universality of matriarchy on "the universal qualities of human nature," insisting that it represented a stage in any society's growth. Harrison agreed with his assertion that societies experienced stages of growth as individual human beings did, but she did not agree that "the beginning of all development lies in myth" or that "myth contains the origins." For the most part, however, she adhered to his views.[11]

In the *Prolegomena,* Harrison began to doubt the Olympians' supremacy and the virtues of classical culture. Although tentatively accepting the chthonic deities as superior to the Olympians, however, she could not yet throw over great classical literature for ritual formularies.

Literature as a starting-point for investigation, and especially the poems of Homer, I am compelled to disallow; yet literature is really my goal. I have tried to understand primitive rites, not from love of their archaism, nor yet wholly from a single-minded devotion to science, but with the definite hope that I might come to a better understanding of some forms of Greek poetry. . . . A knowledge of, a certain sympathy with, the *milieu* of this primitive material is one step to the realization of its final form in tragedy. It is then in the temple of literature, if but as a hewer of wood and drawer of water, that I still hope to serve.[12]

Even a cursory reading of the work shows how dismally she failed at her task. She rapidly transformed the desire to shed light on ancient literature through the study of ritual into an effort to prove the ritual origin of drama, myth, and religion through the accumulation of textual and anthropological evidence. The *Prolegomena* stopped just short of a full-scale attack on Victorian society, but it contained the genesis of her critique. The themes of the historical existence of matriarchy, rejection of the Olympian pantheon as a sterile relic, and the primacy of emotion emerged tentatively in the *Prolegomena*, but still lacked the passionate conviction that marked *Themis* a decade later.

Harrison posited the historical existence of matriarchy by connecting matrilineal descent and the presence of early pre-Olympian earth goddesses. She straddled the fence by being neither overly lyrical about these goddesses and the matriarchy they represented nor overly hostile toward the patriarchal structure that Olympianism reflected. She still groped for the source of the imbalance between male and female in social relations and focused primarily on the more obvious role of ancient goddesses as sexual playthings to the gods. Recounting the story of Pandora, Harrison traced her career from an original earth goddess to a creation of Zeus.

Zeus the Father will have no great Earth-goddess, Mother and Maid in one, in his man-fashioned Olympus, but her figure *is* from the beginning, so he re-makes it; woman, who was the inspirer, becomes the temptress; she who made all things, gods and mortals alike, is become their plaything, their slave, dowered only with personal beauty, and with a slave's tricks and blandishments. To Zeus, the archpatriarchal *bourgeois*, the birth of the first woman is but a huge Olympian jest. (285)

Moreover, Zeus was an intruder from the North, a conventional interpretation of the development of Olympianism, but especially significant for Harrison. Northern culture, whether in archaic Greece or Victorian England, represented patriarchy and the subordination of women.

Her outbreak on behalf of Pandora may sound inspired enough, but she followed it with a curious admission. This shift from matriarchy to patriarchy, in

spite of a seeming retrogression is a necessary stage in a real advance. Matriarchy gave to women a false because a magical prestige. With patriarchy came inevitably the facing of a real fact, the fact of the greater natural weakness of women. Man the stronger, when he outgrew his belief in the magical potency of woman, proceeded by a pardonable practical logic to despise and enslave her as the weaker. The future held indeed a time when the non-natural, mystical truth came to be apprehended, that the stronger had a need, real and imperative, of the weaker. (285)

She implied a dialectical relationship between matriarchy and patriarchy, leaving open the possibility of a reconciliation between the two that would admit their interdependence. She quickly abandoned such optimism, though, and never again sounded so forgiving and hopeful.

The old demon of the "blinding sex delusion" reared its head in the *Prolegomena,* but only briefly and only to be countered by a temperate appreciation of Aphrodite as representative of the impulse toward life. Under patriarchal religion the "woman goddesses are sequestered to a servile domesticity" and "become abject and amorous," but she found their increasing remoteness even worse. "Artemis becomes unreal from sheer inhumanity; Athene . . . becomes a cold abstraction; Demeter, in Olympus, is but a lovely metaphor." Only Aphrodite, by personifying "the mystery of life, and love that begets life," thus "keeps her godhead to the end" (315). With R. A. Neil and Francis Cornford part of the circle around her as she worked on the early stages of the *Prolegomena,* Harrison subdued the old anger at and fear of the awesome powers of sexuality to create divisions. Two years after its publication, however, with Neil dead and her feelings toward Cornford growing more complicated, Harrison wrote to Gilbert Murray with a new idea about the goddesses. "The dread thought has long been forcing its way into my mind that Athena is the armed Aphrodite," she wrote. "She *could* not have been home-grown—she is the *Libyan* form—but it rather frightens me." Her fusion of the sensuous Aphrodite and the rational Athena signified an awareness that the old duality she feared could be reconciled. On a personal level, this possibility surely terrified her, as it forced her to admit the complexity of her own feelings. On an intellectual level, it showed recognition of the goddesses' power.[13]

The triumph of patriarchy over matriarchy meant creation of a pantheon that reflected the new social order. Like Durkheim, Harrison viewed the Olympians as such a group projection. Remarkably, she remained comparatively neutral about the transition from matriarchy to patriarchy, showing only an occasional sorrow at the loss of some manifestations of primitive religion.

In the Homeric Olympus we see mirrored a family group of the ordinary patriarchal type, a type so familiar that it scarcely arrests attention. Zeus, Father of Gods and men, is supreme; Hera, though in constant and significant revolt, occupies the subordinate place of a wife; Poseidon is a younger brother, and the rest of the Olypians are grouped about Zeus in the relation of sons and daughters. These sons and daughters are

> quarrelsome among themselves and in constant insurrection against father and mother, but still they constitute a family, and a family subject, if reluctantly, to the final authority of a father. (260)

Without openly declaring hatred for patriarchy, Harrison still made it clear that she recognized its inherent tensions and power struggles. The Olympians were a typical Victorian family that lived with the lid on, as did Harrison. Ten years later she looked at that same family with the lid removed.

Harrison could afford to be so generous in assessing the Olympians because her story had a happy ending. After a period of worshiping sterile, remote gods, a new religious impulse swept out of the North, enticing the faithful back to joyous primitive cult practices. This new savior was Dionysos. For all her avowed distaste of overt emotional displays and her sweet reasonableness in graciously accepting the triumph of patriarchy, she enthusiastically embraced the essential elements of Dionysian religion. She may have been timid and easily sickened by violence in her private life, but she vividly described archaic rites of animal sacrifice and oath taking, the latter of which entailed the oath taker's standing on the butchered bodies of sacrificed animals (66–67). In the fifteen years since her conversion from aestheticism, Harrison had fallen under the spell of the "strange fierce loveliness that lurks in rites of ignorance and fear," rites that were "stark and desperate and non-moral as the passion that prompts them" (139).

Dionysos, the son of Semele before his rebirth from Zeus, returned both signs of the earlier matriarchy and an appreciation of the natural world to patriarchal, Olympianized Athens. To Harrison,

> the interesting thing about Dionysos is that, develop as he may, he bears to the end, as no other god does, his matriarchal origin. He can never rid himself of the throngs of worshipping women, he is always the nursling of his Maenads. Moreover the instruments of his cult are always not his but his mother's. (562)

In addition, his ascendancy brought "a 'return to nature,' a breaking of bonds and limitations and crystallizations, a desire for the life rather of the emotions than of reason, a recrudescence it may be of animal passions" (445). Dionysian religion, arising out of protest against the chill remoteness of Olympianism, represented the ultimate triumph of the mother-child bond and recognition of the importance of the emotional life. At this time in her career, Harrison still remained optimistic for the future and projected her hopefulness onto the ancient world. For the moment, Dionysos triumphed over the patriarchal Olympians.

The Dionysos cult derived its power from its intimate connection to the real, mysterious powers of life. It was not merely a rational projection of a particular social order. Dionysos' relation to the irrational and emotional life gave him his great strength and ensured his followers' loyalty. "The essential thing, the factor which recurs in story after story, is the rage against the dominance of a new god, the blind mad fury, the swift sudden helpless collapse at the touch of a real force." The resistance to his conquest of Greece represented "the mirrored image of a human experience, of the passionate vain beating of man against what is not man and is more and less than man" (370). In an effort to make an ultimate religious gain, humanity sometimes needed to "retrace [its] steps," and the resurgence of the Dionysos cult exemplified this process. "The Greeks of the sixth century B.C. may well have been a little weary of their anthropomorphic Olympians, tired of their own magnified reflection in the mirror of mythology," and thus embraced the new religion as a welcome relief (445).

As enthusiastically as Harrison accepted Dionysian religion, however, the religious impulse reached its apotheosis not with Dionysos but with Orphic mysticism. Truly ambivalent about the savagery of Dionysian rituals and repelled yet fascinated by the wanton destruction of animal life and the total abandon of the rites, she sought refuge in Orphism, which "took an ancient superstition, deep-rooted in the savage ritual of Dionysos, and lent to it a new spiritual significance" (474). Orpheus' "great step . . . was that he kept the old Bacchic faith that man might become a god" and "altered the conception of what a god was, and he sought to obtain that godhead by wholly different means. The grace he sought was not physical intoxication but spiritual ecstasy, the means he adopted not drunkenness but abstinence and rites of purification" (477). This curious combination of ambivalence toward Dionysian religion and avowed preference for Orphism makes Harrison's work interesting, mainly because the ambivalence rings much truer than the professed admiration for Orphic asceticism. She could powerfully portray the seductiveness of Dionysian ritual because she sensed its awesome potential energy. In a lengthy passage Harrison described Orphic religion as a sort of compromise between the wild abandon of Dionysian religion and the perfunctory, formulaic nature of Olympian religion, incidentally revealing her own dual nature. Reflecting her sense of her own conflicts, she broke humans into two types. To some,

> by natural temperament the religion of Bromios, son of Semele, is and must always be a dead letter, if not a stumbling-block. Food is to such a troublesome necessity, wine a danger or a disgust. They dread all stimulus that comes from without, they would fain break the ties that link them with animals and plants. They do not feel in themselves and are at a loss to imagine for others the sacramental mystery of life and nutrition that is accomplished in us day by day, how in the faintness of

> fasting the whole nature of man, spirit as well as body, dies down, he cannot think, he cannot work, he cannot love; how in the breaking of bread, and still more in the drinking of wine, life spiritual as well as physical is renewed, thought is re-born, his equanimity, his magnanimity are restored, reason and morality rule again. But to this sacramentalism of life most of us bear constant, if partly unconscious, witness. We will not eat with the man in hate, it is felt a sacrilege leaving a sickness in body and soul. The first breaking of bread and drinking of wine together is the seal of a new friendship; the last eaten in silence at parting is more than many words. The sacramental feast of bread and wine is spread for the newly married, for the newly dead.
>
> Those who derive from wine
>
> no inspiration, no moments of sudden illumination, of wider and deeper insight, of larger human charity and understanding, find it hard to realize what to others of other temperament is so natural, so elemental, so beautiful—the constant shift from physical to spiritual that is of the essence of the religion of Dionysos. But there are those also, and they are saintly souls, who know it all to the full, know the exhilaration of wine, know what it is to be drunken with the physical beauty of a flower or a sunset, with the sensuous imagery of words, with the strong wine of a new idea, with the magic of another's personality, yet having known, turn away with steadfast eyes, disallowing the madness not only of Bromios but of the Muses and of Aphrodite. Such have their inward ecstasy of the ascetic, but they revel with another Lord, and he is Orpheus. (453–54)

Harrison's skillful transformation of sexuality into creative intellectual energy tempts one to accept at face value her commitment to Orphic asceticism. She soon proves the folly of this notion, however, by her comments on Orpheus' death at the hands of a frenzied Maenad, representing "the intimate and bitter hostility of things near akin" (462). After describing a red-figured vase depicting Orpheus' death, she concludes, "Orpheus was a reformer, a protestant; there is always about him a touch of the reformer's priggishness; it is impossible not to sympathize a little with the determined looking Maenad who is coming up behind to put a stop to all this sun-watching and lyre-playing" (462). At the end of it all, Harrison refused to cast her lot solely with Orphism, which only replaced subservience to lifeless gods with subservience to internalized control and denial of emotion.

Control still seemed possible to Harrison in 1903, and therefore she could discuss Orphism in a generally positive way. Keeping the lid on her own emotions also prevented her from launching all-out attacks on patriarchy and the Olympians. She was not then ready, or angry enough, to reject the social structure that surrounded her and played such a formative role in ancient religion. In addition, she clearly had not altogether abandoned hope for a religious revival that would bring social change in its wake. A resurgence of the irrational could mean a concomitant shift away from patriarchy. Thus themes that appeared in *Themis* were prefigured here, but without its anger and passion, they are not nearly so compelling.

The *Cambridge Review*'s reaction to the *Prolegomena* shows how tentatively she presented her theory. The reviewer appreciated her imaginativeness, which clearly indicates that she had not gone too far. Furthermore, he praised her ability to bring the past alive. "Even if it should be thought that at times the writer's fancy outruns the warranty of facts, yet Greek religion, as handled by Miss Harrison, has this supreme merit, that it lives." He especially liked her "treatment of the worship of Dionysus: the foundations of argument are more surely laid; and the interpretation of all that was best in those ecstatic rites is wonderfully sympathetic."[14]

Harrison's fellow Ritualists did not necessarily agree with her in applauding the Dionysos cult. Gilbert Murray especially, preoccupied with classical dramatists and influenced by his own religious beliefs, added a moral dimension to the natural one.

> The renovation ceremonies were accompanied by a casting off of the old year, the old garments, and everything that is polluted by the infection of death. And not only of death; but clearly I think, in spite of the protests of some Hellenists, of guilt or sin also. For the life of the Year-Daimon, as it seems to be reflected in Tragedy, is generally a story of Pride and Punishment. Each Year arrives, waxes great, commits the sin of Hubris, and then is slain. The death is deserved; but the slaying is a sin: hence comes the next Year as Avenger, or as the Wronged One re-risen.[15]

This difference of opinion over primitive religion and Greek drama only begins to scratch the surface of her divergence from Murray's views, which, despite their opposition, did not threaten their friendship.

Harrison's and Murray's reactions to the ancient past were greatly determined by their perceptions of the world in which they lived. Harrison, the perennial outsider, challenged traditional views of the Greek world because of her uneasiness about her position in her own world. Although something of an academic maverick, Murray's personal convictions and his natural identification with traditional male-defined scholarship kept him aligned with the larger world. Whereas Harrison appreciated the vitality of primitive religion with its emphasis on emotions, sexuality, and nature, Murray ultimately sided with more conventional scholars who ignored those aspects of primitive society in favor of the rationalism of classical Greece.

The Ritualists based their theory ultimately on the preexistence of ritual and its role as precursor of myth and theology. Harrison upheld the Darwinian view that ritual preceded theology on the intellectual evolutionary scale. At the last minute, though, she stood Darwin on his head by affirming the superiority of the earlier stage.

> The ultimate and unchallenged presupposition of the old view was that religion was a *doctrine,* a body of supposed truths. It was, in fact, what we should now call Theology, and what the ancients called Mythology. Ritual was scarcely considered at all, and, when considered, it was held to be a form in which beliefs, already defined and fixed as dogma, found a natural mode of expression. This, it will be later shown, is a profound error, or, rather, a most misleading half-truth. Creeds, doctrines, theology, and the like, are only a part, and at first the least important part, of religion.

In primitive religion, "ritual is dominant and imperative." Although moderns tended to believe that humanity first "believes in a god or gods, and then worships," she asserted that in reality, man "worships, he feels and acts, and out of his feeling and action, projected into his confused thinking, he develops a god."[16]

After surviving the emotional crises of the years between 1903 and 1910, Harrison mulled over her original ideas and reworked them in the light of those experiences. The main difference between the *Prolegomena* and *Themis* is the passion with which she promulgated her view of the entire world in the latter. Criticisms of Victorian society implicitly expressed in her *Prolegomena* became explicit in *Themis.* The two works resemble each other in their vast accumulations of anthropological data dedicated to the service of illuminating the origins of Greek religion, but the resemblance ends there. In *Themis,* getting at the root of the religious impulse was only a secondary task. Her central purpose was to attack the structure of Victorian society in general and its rigid control of the emotions in particular. The *Prolegomena,* in contrast, offered a relatively mild criticism of the society in which she lived. Only in *Themis* did she fully develop the contemporary themes. Having suffered, so she perceived, her worst pain and betrayal at the hands of the men in her life, Harrison recast society in a matriarchal model, looking back nostalgically to the days when society placed a high premium on women and their nurturing role. In re-creating this past, Harrison harshly judged Victorian society's denial of the primacy of the emotional life and its repression of sexuality. She also signaled the end of her patience with male treachery.

One of the most remarkable aspects of *Themis* is the speed with which Harrison produced it. Francis Cornford wrote that "week by week" she produced "a new chapter almost in its final shape. The mood of inspiration would last as long as the words were pouring out upon the paper." He could not tell "whether this method of work" was "characteristically feminine," and he felt "she credited my slower mind with masculine qualities which she at once ridiculed and valued as a counterweight to her own." Cornford showed no sign of comprehending the spiritual agony that produced this work. Harrison's overwhelming need to redirect her anger at Cornford into an acceptable channel explains her frenzied authorship, and her anger gave birth to the principal themes of *Themis*.[17]

Its overriding principle is the primacy of emotion, and Harrison addressed this question both by exalting primitive religion for its celebration of the emotional life and by denigrating the Olympian pantheon for its sterility and remoteness. She defined her present task as differing from that of the *Prolegomena* in that, whereas the *Prolegomena* proved that Olympianism was not primitive, *Themis* explored the roots of Olympianism in the chthonic cults, thereby getting at the origins of the religious impulse. Her research for the *Prolegomena* led her to conclude that the Olympians "seemed . . . like a bouquet of cut-flowers whose bloom is brief, because they have been severed from their roots."[18] In *Themis*, she intended to "burrow deep into a lower stratum of thought, into those chthonic cults which underlay their life and from which sprang all their brilliant blossoming" (xi). At the beginning of the work, Harrison left the door open to admit at least "brilliant blossoming" on the Olympians' part, but five hundred pages later, their bloom had decidedly wilted.

Themis represented Harrison's shift from a "sense of the superficiality of Homer's gods" found in the *Prolegomena* to a "conviction that these Olympians were not only non-primitive, but positively in a sense non-religious" (xi). Despite its "errors and licenses," the "cultus of Dionysos and Orpheus seemed . . . essentially religious" (xi). As she brooded over Cornford's betrayal, her original distaste for the Olympians evolved into downright aversion. All the demons of her past rose up before her, and in asserting the primacy of emotion she took on her stepmother's rigid Evangelicalism, the implacability of positivistic science, and the conventions that prohibited Victorian society from acknowledging the power of love, hate, and anger.

Harrison drew heavily on the work of Emile Durkheim and Henri Bergson in *Themis*, borrowing chiefly Durkheim's idea of the god as group projection and Bergson's impassioned plea for the necessity and goodness of change as the basis of life. To Durkheim's arid formulations Harrison added her own conviction of the supremacy of the group; to Bergson's ideas she added an almost mystical appreciation of the interdependence of things. She utilized concepts that were in the air, but viewed them with a unique perspective and infused them with new life and vigor, thereby transforming them into something novel.

Harrison cited Durkheim's articles appearing in his *L'Année sociologique* at various points in *Themis*. His 1898 "Definition of Religious Phenomena" figured prominently, as did the work of his colleagues, Hubert and Mauss, on "The Nature of Sacrifice." Classicist S. C. Humphreys states that Jane Harrison and Francis Cornford soon tempered their enthusiasm for Durkheim's theory, and Harrison, at least, probably did so because she found his rationalist approach offensive. His *Elementary Forms of the Religious Life,* which appeared in 1912, demonstrated a keen awareness of the duality of human existence, of the presence of both an individual and a collective life. Unlike Harrison, however, Durkheim kept his distance from the past. He kept his true feelings toward primitive religion under rigid control, whereas Harrison asserted her distaste for the chaos of the past but proceeded to revel in it for hundreds of pages. But Durkheim knew from the start what Harrison learned only through bitter experience: that group cohesion, which she called "herd-suggestion," could be fiercely destructive if turned to the wrong use.

Henri Bergson exerted a more direct influence over her work, and she cited his *L'Evolution créatrice* as marking a stage of her own thought. She discovered his work at a time when philosophy did not appeal to her, and it appeared as a revelation. "Off and on I had read philosophy all my life, from Heracleitos to William James, but of late years I had read it less and less, feeling that I got nothing new, only a ceaseless shuffling of the cards, a juggling with the same glass balls, and then suddenly it seemed this new Moses struck the rock and streams gushed forth in the desert" (RSL, 342). She wrote to Gilbert Murray in 1908 that she was reading *L'Evolution créatrice* and warned him that "it is likely that I may be a nuisance about it when I come." She acknowledged that "there is going to be a boom in Bergson & I already begin to loathe him—but all the same he's splendid." Nothing made her more cross than to have her favorite authors appropriated by the world at large. She recovered from her bad temper, though, and remained faithful to Bergson because he seemed to her to get at the root of human experience. "It is odd but when I read Bergson he seems to me just to be telling one of what really *is* & happens & when I read BR [Bertrand Russell] or [George] Moore or any of them they seem to be saying fearfully clever things about life, but not the least telling one what really goes on." When Bergson visited Cambridge in 1911, Harrison heard him lecture and pronounced him "exquisite & really instructive," and so "civilized & attenuated" that "he made every Englishman look unlicked." She recommended *L'Evolution créatrice* to Sutherland MacColl, saying, "it is the biggest book I have read for a long time, and I know it has to do with art, only I cannot quite make out how."[19]

Building on the theory of the god as group projection, Harrison added her own perceptions of this role.

> Now it has of late been frequently pointed out that the god in some sense always "reflects" the worshipper, takes on the colour of his habits and his thoughts. The morality of a god is not often much in advance of that of his worshippers, and sometimes it lags considerably behind. The social structure is also, it is allowed, in some sense reflected in a god: a matriarchal society will worship a Mother and a Son, a patriarchal society will tend to have a cult of the Father. All this is true, but the truth lies much deeper. Not only does the god reflect the thoughts, social conditions, morality and the like, but in its origin his substance when analysed turns out to be just nothing but the representations, the utterance, the emphasis of these imaginations, these emotions, arising out of particular social conditions. (*TH,* 28)

The god turns out not to represent anything as concrete as a social order. It represents an even more intangible thing: the chaotic, irrational elements lurking behind social organization. She credited Durkheim with making her see "why Dionysos, the mystery-god . . . is, alone among Greek divinities, constantly attended by a thiasos, a matter cardinal for the understanding of his nature" (*TH,* xiii). He expresses the group's most basic instincts, which are directed toward its own preservation.

Dionysos also represented a larger concept as well. Bergson named it "durée," and it consisted in the ceaseless change that constitutes human experience. While admitting that Bergson did not set out to study or define the religious impulse, Harrison revealed that

> when, four years ago, I first read his *L'Evolution créatrice,* I saw, dimly at first, but with ever increasing clearness, how deep was the gulf between Dionysos the mystery-god and that Olympus he might never really enter. I knew the reason of my own profound discontent. I saw in a word that Dionysos, with every other mystery-god, was an instinctive attempt to express what Professor Bergson calls *durée,* that life which is one, indivisible and yet ceaselessly changing. I saw on the other hand that the Olympians, amid all their atmosphere of romance and all their redeeming vices, were really creations of what Professor William James called "monarchical deism." Such deities are not an instinctive expression, but a late and conscious representation, a work of analysis, of reflection and intelligence. (*TH,* xii)

Thus Harrison achieved a reconciliation between the theories of two avowed enemies. She accepted Durkheim's vision of the god as group projection, but favored the projection of only specific kinds of groups.[20]

As long as the projection reflected her own view of the world she found it acceptable. When a projection offended her, as the Greek Olympians did, she became an implacable foe. Ultimately she took her stand with Bergson's romantic and intuitive view instead of Durkheim's rational and oddly chilling one.

Dionysos still figured in *Themis*—although he did not loom so large—as the triumph of the resurgence of the primitive religious impulse. His connection with fertility and nature still endeared him to Harrison. His failing, she concluded near the end, was his masculinity, both literal and figurative. In a fit of anger, Harrison denounced the phallic element of chthonic religion, but her rejection stemmed from her inability to separate individual, personal hurt from the general notion of masculine power. In the *Prolegomena,* she favored Orpheus over Dionysos because of his mysticism but still respected Dionysos' embodiment of the emotional life. By the time of *Themis,* Dionysos' sex clouded Harrison's appreciation of his value. By rejecting the unabashedly male Dionysos in favor of the ascetic mystic Orpheus in *Themis,* she rejected Francis Cornford, her father, and a host of other men who had betrayed her. But because of his close association with the emotional life and his cult's indirect proof of the historical existence of matriarchy, Dionysos remained vastly superior to the Olympians.

Harrison considered the emotional life superior because it represented an aspect of group experience. "A high emotional tension is best caused and maintained by a thing felt socially" (43). She expounded on the supremacy of the group.

> The individual in a savage tribe has but a thin and meagre personality. . . . Emotion socialized, felt collectively, is emotion intensified and rendered permanent. Intellectually the group is weak; everyone knows this who has ever sat on a committee and arrived at a confused compromise. Emotionally the group is strong; everyone knows this who has felt the thrill of speaking to or acting with a great multitude. (43)

The Dionysos cult represented a revival of a projection of a group that still conceived of itself as a monolithic whole, not as an aggregate of individuals. In chthonic religion, the god is a projection of the irrational; in Olympianism, it becomes a projection of the intellect. But "Dionysos with his *thiasos* is still—Comus, still trails behind him the glory of the old group ecstasy" (48). Yet "the Olympians are . . . the last product of rationalism, of individualistic thinking," and once "cut off from the very source of their life and being, the emotion of the *thiasos,* they dessicate and die" (48).

Commenting on Hobbes's dictum that " 'the feare of things invisible is the naturall seed of Religion,' " Harrison posited that more than purely fear, the "naturall seed" is "fear felt together, fear emphasized, qualified by a sort of social sanction" (64). She also distinguished among fear, awe, and reverence, pointing out that these emotions held many levels of meanings.

> Fear does not quite express the emotion felt. It is rather awe, and awe contains in it the element of wonder as well as fear; awe is on the way to be reverence, and reverence is essentially religious. It is remote entirely from mere blind panic, it is of the nature of attraction rather than repulsion. . . . Moreover the fear which has gone to the making of religion is at least as much social as physical. (64)

Rather than accepting the religion of her upbringing and its terrifying vision of the individual soul defenselessly awaiting judgment before a remote God, Harrison described a more integrated approach to the undeniable powers of the world. She wanted to believe in a concept of religion that allowed appreciation of the natural world, and she found it in primitive religion.

Harrison's belief in "ceaseless change, which is the very essence of life" and best captured by Bergson's concept of durée formed the basis of her preference for the nature gods (477). The life force, ever striving for survival and fulfillment, could never be represented by such static and departmentalized figures as the Olympians. The gods of archaic Greece, whose essence survived into the nineteenth century in primitive societies in remote parts of the world, fit much more closely into her conception of the unity of humanity and nature.

> There were gods before the Olympians of Homer and Hesiod, but they were without titles, they were undistinguished in their functions, undiscriminated in their forms. We know now what manner of beings these pre-Olympian potencies were; they were Year-daimones, all alike in shape and function, all apt to take on plant or animal shape, the business of each and all monotonously one, to give food and increase to man and make the year go round. (466–67)

Not satisfied with this routine, the Olympians assumed a more glamorous life on Olympos and demanded more from their worshipers in return for fewer favors. But "the god like the man who substitutes privilege for function, for duty done, is self-doomed," for "the gods to whom the worshipper's real heart and life goes out are the gods who work and live, not those who dwell at ease on Olympos," or, for that matter, in the Protestant God's heaven. Harrison's aversion to the Olympians was also a thinly veiled aversion to her stepmother's God, who demanded ardent faith and gave only threats of eternal punishment in return (467).

Like most intellectuals of her era, Harrison cut her teeth on evolutionary theory and could therefore scarcely avoid taking an evolutionary view of religious thought. The inevitability of the change from primitive religion and its acceptance of the irrational to the modern denial of the irrational made those early days even more attractive. They represented the childhood of the human race, the happy times before the rise of the patriarchal family destroyed the one bond that should have been inviolable: that of mother and child. When the group was still an undifferentiated mass, it could neither separate itself into individuals nor distinguish itself entirely from the natural world surrounding it. Nothing epitomized this state more than the practice of totemism.

> Totemism, then, is not so much a special social structure as a stage in epistemology. It is the reflexion of a very primitive fashion in thinking, or rather feeling, the universe, a feeling the realization of which is essential to any understanding of primitive religion. It is not a particular blunder and confusion made by certain ignorant savages, but a phase or stage of collective thinking through which the human mind is bound to pass. Its basis is group-unity, aggregation, similarity, sympathy, a sense of common group life, and this sense of common life, this *participation,* this unity, extended to the non-human world in a way which our modern, individualistic reason, based on observed distinctions, finds almost unthinkable. . . .
>
> That outlook on the universe, that stage in epistemology which we call totemism has its source then not in any mere blunder of the individual intellect, but in a strong collective emotion. (122–23)

Harrison's respect for the primitive mind and her intuitive appreciation of its complexity, despite her occasional denials of these qualities, set her apart from many Victorian anthropologists who wrote disparagingly of their subjects. Her own keen sympathy for the link between nature and the emotions enabled her to appreciate these people.

She demonstrated this sympathy through her love of animals. Only someone who imagined herself as spiritually connected to bears and who wrote letters to be buried with her favorite dogs could even begin to understand the primitive identification of gods with animals and of animals with various kinds of natural power. One of the loveliest passages in *Themis* expressed Harrison's sorrow at the gradual exclusion of nature from religious thought. Discussing the Olympians, Harrison pointed out that although in artistic representation they shed the natural forms generally associated with chthonic deities, "sometimes the animal form of the god lives on as in mythology; more often perhaps it survives in the supposed 'attribute' of the god" (449). For instance, Zeus is often represented in mythology as a bull, and Athena frequently depicted with her owl. Harrison, however, mourned the loss of the mode of thought that integrated nature and religion.

The shedding of plant and animal form marks of course the complete closing of anything like totemistic thinking and feeling. It is in many ways pure loss. The totemistic attitude towards animals may, as based on ignorance, beget superstition, but it is full of beautiful courtesies. There are few things uglier than a lack of reverance for animals. . . . In art this exclusion of animal and plant life from the cycle of the divine is sometimes claimed as a gain. Rather it leaves a sense of chill and loneliness. Anyone who turns from Minoan pottery with its blossoming flowers, its crocuses and lilies, its plenitude of sea life, its shells and octopuses and flying fish, anyone who turns from all this life and colour to the monotonous perfection of the purely human subjects of the best red-figured pottery, must be strangely constituted if he feels no loss. He will turn eagerly for refreshment from these finished athletes and these no less accomplished gods, to the bits of mythology wherein animals still play a part . . . and he will turn also to the "attributes" of the humanized Olympian. . . . The mystery gods it should be noted here . . . are never free of totemistic hauntings, never quite shed their plant and animal shapes. That lies in the very nature of their sacramental worship. They are still alive with the life-blood of all living things from which they sprang. (449–50)

Harrison left no doubt about which mode of thought she preferred. Moreover, she clearly believed that, given a chance, her contemporaries would come to agree with her. She keenly sensed the persistence of primitive thought and recognized, in a truly Freudian sense, the power of this irrational undercurrent. As she said, "the oldest things lie deepest and live longest" (134). She referred specifically to sacrament, but her words also encompassed the whole range of human emotion and experience.

Unfortunately, even Harrison had to recognize that the elemental joy of pre-Olympian archaic religion could not be fully recaptured. The vestiges of mother worship demonstrated a horrifying side that offended her most deeply felt sensibilities with regard to primitive thought. Lucian and Pausanias described sacrifices to the earth mother and to Artemis, whom Harrison regarded as a primitive earth goddess relegated to the role of Apollo's sister, which included the burning alive of wild beasts (504–05). In *De Syria Dea,* Lucian recorded the existence of a festival in honor of a mother goddess at Hieropolis that culminated in the burning alive of tame, consecrated animals. According to Lucian, worshipers

cut down great trees and set them up in the courtyard. Then they bring in goats and sheep and other live beasts, and hang them up on the trees. They also bring birds and clothes and vessels of gold and silver. When they have made all ready, they carry the victims round the trees and set fire to them and straightway they are all burned. (504)

Harrison viewed this "sacrifice of all living things" to an earth goddess as "manifestly, if hideously, appropriate" but found a similar account of such a sacrifice to the Olympian Artemis "sad reading" (505). Pausanias recorded that at Patrae,

> they bring and cast upon the altar living things of all sorts, both edible birds and all manner of victims, also wild boars and deer and fawns and some even bring the cubs of wolves and bears, and others full grown beasts. And they lay on the altar also the fruits of cultivated trees. Then they set fire to the wood. I saw indeed a bear and other beasts struggling to get out of the first force of the flames and escaping by sheer strength. But those who threw them in drag them up again onto the fire. I never heard of anyone being wounded by the wild beasts. (505)

This powerful description offended Harrison's deepest intuitive perceptions about the archaic world, particularly with regard to the fate meted out to her favorite bears. She saw these rites, however, merely as corrupted practices of a dying mode of thought and refused to dwell on them.

Once primitive groups and their members began to understand their separateness from each other and the world around them, the stage was set for the advent of individualized, anthropomorphized gods. Harrison disapproved of the term *anthropomorphic* as "too narrow," but it still serves best in the context of the discussion (447). The gods who once mirrored human unity with nature came to mirror human individuality. As the shift from artistic representations of nature to those of humanity could not be counted a gain, neither should we "assume off-hand that the shift from nature-god to human-nature god is necessarily an advance" (447). In fact, the "Olympian is . . . in the main the negation of an Eniautos-daimon" and if the Eniautos-daimon is by definition good and superior, the Olympian must be evil and inferior (447). Harrison criticized the juxtaposition of individualistic rationalism with religion, not the religious impulse itself. "It is when religion ceases to be a matter of feeling together, when it becomes individualized and intellectualized, that clouds gather on the horizon" (487). Most of all, she could not bear to think of rational projections being equated with moral good.

> It is because religion has been regarded as a tissue of false hypotheses that it has commanded, will always command, the animosity of the rational thinker. When the religious man, instead of becoming in ecstacy and sacramental communion one with Bacchos, descends to the chill levels of intellectualism and asserts that there is an objective reality external to himself called Bacchos, then comes a parting of the ways. Still wider is the breach if he asserts that this objective reality is one with the mystery of life, and also with man's last projection, his ideal of the good. (487)

The rational thinker could accept the validity of the religious impulse only by seeing it for what it was: an example of the strength of the irrational, emotional life. By a convoluted process of approaching the irrational rationally, Harrison believed it possible to reconcile them.

On one level, then, the emergence of Olympian gods signaled a momentous change in thought: the triumph of intellect over emotion. Despite their swaggering brashness, Harrison intended to show the Olympians "for what they are, intellectual conceptions merely, things of thought bearing but slight relation to life lived" (xxi). Drawing on psychological theories, she ventured that "it could almost be said that the Olympians stand for articulate consciousness, the Eniautos-Daimon for the sub-conscious" (xxi). Harrison seemed to be wrestling with the concepts that Freud later set forth so powerfully in *Civilization and Its Discontents.* Like Freud, she sensed the potential force that smoldered beneath the veneer of civilization and feared its release. The central difference between them was that Harrison took much longer to come to grips with the necessity of keeping the lid on those primal forces. Unlike Freud, who understood from the start that civilization could not exist without rigid control, Harrison railed against the denial of emotion, all the while, of course, refusing to admit her monumental struggle to deny the validity of her own potentially explosive emotions.

The greatest hubris of the Olympians consisted in their exclusivity. The Olympians, "in their triumphant humanity, kicked down that ladder from earth to heaven by which they rose," thereby denying entry to any other deserving deities (446). Harrison discussed several heroes and chthonic deities who made futile attempts at Olympian status, achieving at best only half-divinity. Herakles and Asklepios, hero and healer, were in their spheres "greater than any Olympians," but failed to enter Olympos (384). These two figures retained their power because they remained rooted in the earth. "Their function is to make us feel how thin and chill, for all their painted splendour, are these gods who live at ease in the upper air, how much they lose when they shake off mortality and their feet leave the earth who was their mother" (384). The powerful Titans, the giants of earth, required even more effort to be kept in their earthly place. "The violence and persistence with which they are sent down below shows that they belong up above. . . . Their great offence in Olympian eyes is that they will climb up to high heaven, which the human-shaped Olympians had arrogated to themselves" (454).

Harrison heatedly attacked the Olympians for so sharply delineating themselves from nature and from their worshipers. She could not hide her intensely personal interest in this question. The reader gets the unmistakable impression that she often forgets her own professed belief that the gods do not really exist and that they are only group projections. They often take on a life of their own and seem real enough to act of their own volition. The Olympian "renounces" the things that make up "life and reality—Change and Movement," opting instead for "Deathlessness and Immutability—a seeming Immortality which is really the denial of life, for life is change" (468). In addition to "this conception of a dead and barren immortality there grew up the disastrous notion that between god and man there was a great gulf fixed, that communion was no more possible." Bridging this gap was "*hybris,* it was *the* sin against the gods" (468). Furthermore,

> In a fashion more sad and dreary and degraded still the complete separation of man and god utters itself in another and, to sacramentalism, a blasphemous thought. The gods are jealous gods. . . . The gods begrudge a man a glory that may pale their own splendour. (469)

Not only do the Olympians chill the soul by their distance and unattainability; they "positively offend that very intellect that fashioned them" by their "claim to have objective reality" (477). At the end of this argument, she once more blamed the gods' actions on humans themselves by recognizing that people manipulate the gods in accordance with their own level of thought.

> Man feels rightly and instinctively that a god is a real thing—a real thing because he is the utterance of a real collective emotion, but, in progress of time, man dessicates his god, intellectualizes him, till he is a mere concept, an *eidolon.* Having got that *eidolon,* that *eidolon* fails to satisfy his need, and he tries to supply the place of the vanished *thymos,* the real life-blood of emotion, by claiming objective reality. (477–78)

The circle was complete, but humanity remained dissatisfied with its projections. Harrison offered no solution to the muddle. The only clear point is that the religious impulse, the need to create a group projection in one way or another, is inexorable.

Finally, Harrison came full circle and damned the classical Greeks for what a quarter-century before had been their greatest achievement: their aesthetic sense. The final blow came when the Olympians crystallized into objets d'art. "We feel instinctively that, however much we may quarry for the origin of Greek religion, and strive to reconstruct it, and see its influence on life and literature, the broad fact remains that the strength of the Greek temperament lay rather in art than in religion" (479). Art had become empty and lifeless, and the Olympians, who reached their height in artistic representation, were wholly inadequate as nurturance for the soul.

Ironically, having recited her litany of grievances against the Olympians for two chapters, Harrison relented at the end and admitted that at least their humanity made them more recognizable than the old

Eniautos-daimones. They did, after all, represent, for better or worse, the stage of the group that projected them. Even Harrison, despite her love for the emotional and the natural, could more easily comprehend an intellectual projection than an irrational one. "We feel instinctively that in some ways an Olympian is more vivid, more real than any shapeless, shifting nature-daimon. If we met Zeus or Apollo in the street we should know them and greet them. To put it simply, the Olympian, for all his negations, has personality, individuality" (469). Although she favored the chthonic deities, she also rejected a central element in the old fertility daimones. Having during the past three years turned her back finally and irrevocably on the prospect of marriage, she could no longer endure the ostentatious masculine sexuality of primitive Greek religion; rather, she had come to identify her own state with that of the "advanced" stage of civilization, which no longer concerned itself with such things. She specifically rejected male sexuality and focused on the figures of the gods. The goddesses hardly appear at all in her discussion.

> The Olympians then stand first and foremost as a protest against the worship of Earth and the daimones of the fertility of Earth. So far they command our respect and even our sympathy. As long as man is engaged in a hand to hand struggle for bare existence, his principal focus of attention must be on food. The magical inducement of the recurrent fertility of the earth is his first and well-nigh his last religious duty. But, as civilization advances, and he is freed from the more urgent necessities, his circle of needs enlarges and the focus of his attention widens. The old interest in food and fertility slackens. Moreover a worship of the powers of fertility, which includes all plant and animal life, is broad enough to be sound and healthy, but, as man's attention centres more and more intently on his own humanity, such a worship is an obvious source of danger and disease. Instinctively a healthy stock will purge its religion from elements exclusively phallic. This expurgation ranks first and foremost among the services Olympianism rendered to Greece. The fight of the Gods against the Giants had right as well as might on its side. (459–60)

In Harrison's eyes, this new religion reached its zenith in Orphism, which combined the best appreciation of nature found in the old religion with the rejection of phallic elements. Orphism "reformed the religion of Earth, but by strengthening the powers of Heaven, not by disallowing them" (462). This astonishing statement, in the light of her previous contempt toward the Olympians, proves her confusion and conflicting emotions toward her subject. Harrison brooded over Orphic asceticism at the end of her life, and her preoccupation with it grew from her rejection of the phallic elements of primitive religion.

Hope Mirrlees's notes contain the most damning proof of Harrison's enormous anger. She described her as "passionate but very pure"; she remembered Harrison telling her that she found "a naked body hideous; a phallus the most degraded of all objects. And she couldn't bear to think that even the noblest and purest of men were disfigured by it." This startling statement reveals not only that Harrison feared male sexuality but also that she emphatically rejected all masculine power and authority as symbolized by the phallus. Since sexuality seemed such a dangerous force, she went one step further and denied her own sexuality. Mirrlees recorded Harrison's explanation that she based her decision not to marry on a doctor's warning that childbirth would kill her. Mirrlees referred vaguely to "fibrous tumors," but neither of them ever satisfactorily explained the condition that made childbirth so dangerous to Harrison, and she may well have invented or exaggerated the story out of the horror and guilt induced by her role in her mother's death. Whatever the reason, Harrison avoided the whole question of sexuality by repeatedly falling in love with inaccessible men, a well-devised strategem: she could thereby succumb to love without invoking the specter of sexuality.[21]

Harrison's attitude toward sexuality had always been problematic at best, and years of reconciling herself to Francis Cornford's marriage and her own loneliness caused a pain that could be appeased only by purging both her scholarship and her inner emotions of phallic elements. Obsession with sexuality and fertility marked both individual and societal youthfulness. Once she attained later middle age in her own life, along with the human race in general, Harrison recognized that it was time to close the door on that obsession—or rather, Cornford played the all-important role of the person who shut the door. For her part, Harrison finally had to stop trying to reopen it. Before relinquishing her role in the drama, however, she threw one last parting shot through a door carelessly left ajar.

Above all, the Olympian ascendancy marked a pitched battle between the old social order and the new, the triumph of patriarchy over matriarchy. The chthonic deities, mystery-gods, were closely identified with the worship of the earth and therefore the mother, which Harrison asserted indicated the prior existence of matrilineal, if not matriarchal, order. She freely equated women with nature and men with rational thought by delineating the systematic subjection of the Olympian goddesses, originally as potent as the gods, to their male counterparts. Furthermore, that association appeared in both primitive ritual and modern consciousness. The myth of Dionysos' birth through Semele, his mother, and then rebirth through Zeus reflected the same fear of female sexuality present in initiation ceremonies for young men. "The birth from the male womb is to rid the child from the infection of his mother—to turn him from a woman-thing into a man-thing" (36). Such a process deprived women of much of their power as a creature "at once weak and magical, to be oppressed yet feared" because of her "powers of childbearing denied to men, powers only half understood, forces of attraction, but also of danger and repulsion, forces that all over the world seem to fill [men] with dim terror" (36). Moreover, vestiges of this primitive fear surfaced in her own society, where the "attitude of man to woman, and, though perhaps in a less degree, of woman to man, is still to-day essentially magical" (36).

The logical extension of rationalism to defining gods meant inevitably that the mystery-gods would be idealized into "blessed, ageless and deathless" deities (xxi). From there, "it is only a step further to the conscious philosophy which will deny to God any human frailties, any emotions, any wrath or jealousy, and ultimately any character whatever except dead, unmeaning perfection, incapable of movement or change" (xxi). Once again, Harrison referred not only to the Olympians but to the Jehovah of her own religious training, who was only another projection of a later patriarchal culture.

Harrison approached the question of matriarchy from an anthropological angle, examining primitive ritual in the light of research into initiation ceremonies.[22] At the root of the rituals she discovered an age-old preoccupation with the mysterious power of female sexuality. In the beginning, earth worship represented a matriarchal order later replaced by sky worship, representing patriarchy. "The shift of attention, of religious focus, from Earth to Sky, tended to remove the gods from man; they were purged but at the price of remoteness" (xx). Athens, like the rest of Greece, had once been a matriliny, but the rise of the Olympians obliterated nearly all traces of it. The enormity of the effort required to subjugate matriliny to patriliny appeared most clearly in the myth of Athena's birth through Zeus. Unlike Dionysos, Athena had no mother at all, and the story reflected the patriarchal tendencies. "The outrageous myth of the birth of Athena from the head of Zeus is but the religious representation, the emphasis, and over emphasis, of a patrilinear social structure" (500). Harrison, however, examined mythology and ritual to find evidence of the older order. Matriarchy represented to Harrison, as it had to Bachofen and other believers, a golden age in which mother love nutured all humanity and protected society from the conflicts all too present in the modern world.

Her research led her to conclude that matriarchy lurked behind every myth or legend of the classical period. She studied the myth of the Athenian hero Cecrops, who had supposedly civilized Athens. He revealed his matriarchal roots by appearing in artistic representations with a serpent's tail instead of human legs. Euhemerists explained his appearance by having his dual form symbolize his two languages: his native Egyptian and acquired Greek. Harrison asserted, though, that he was "twy-formed . . . because he instituted marriage, the union of two sexes" (262). She traced his decision to require "patriarchal marriage" to the contest between Poseidon and Athena for the city's loyalty and the role of patron. The women, who outnumbered the men, voted for Athena, and Cecrops punished them by instituting marriage (262–63). The festival of Apatouria, "the Same Fathers," as she called it, offered ritual evidence of its matriarchal origin. Despite its title, women performed the requisite sacrifices, among them, one to the mother, which Harrison viewed as proof of a matriarchal origin (498–99).

Harrison assumed marriage to be a patriarchal institution. Furthermore, it always symbolized a punishment or victory of some kind. Zeus and Hera, the archetypal married couple, represented the tensions of the male-female bond. "In Olympos Hera seems merely the jealous and quarrelsome wife. In reality she reflects the turbulent native princess, coerced, but never really subdued, by an alien conqueror" (491). The female self always faced the danger of subjugation, although a strong female personality could defend against it. But marriage on these terms, the only terms Harrison could conceive of, seemed unpalatable. She preferred the mother-child bond, which she perceived as serene and peaceful compared to that of husband and wife. And she saw the mother-son bond as the strongest and even the most desirable. This vision helped determine her attraction to men much younger than herself. Not only did she posit the mother-son bond as standing for the group; she projected her own dependence on the figure of the mother onto sons and saw this dependence as a way to bind people to her.[23]

Harrison professed to believe in the existence of a matriliny but freely displayed her fondness for and belief in a matriarchy. She cautioned readers against confusing the two orders but seemed to ignore her own advice.

> It may seem strange that woman, always the weaker, should be thus dominant and central. But it must always be observed that this primitive form of society is matri*linear* not matri*archal.* Woman is the social centre not the dominant force. So long as force is supreme, physical force of the individual, society is impossible, because society is by co-operation, by mutual concession, not by antagonism.
>
> Moreover, there is another point of extreme importance. In primitive matrilinear societies woman is the great central force or rather central focus, not as woman, or at least not as sex, but as mother, the mother of tribesmen to be. . . . The male child nursed by his mother is potentially a *kouros,* hence her great value and his. (494)

Patriarchal culture, by emphasizing the importance of fatherhood, robbed women of their most indisputable distinction and doomed society to the inevitable result of men running the show. The soothing, nurturing quality of matriarchal culture, which of course existed only in Harrison's imagination, disappeared. As patriarchal society had denied her both her mother's and her father's attention by emphasizing the male-female bond, so had it made all women suffer the same fate by overthrowing the close mother-child tie for the sex tie between man and woman. Ignoring the "motherhood of the mother" was even more unjust than denying fatherhood, "for the facts of motherhood have been always patent" (500). Harrison divined the connections among sexuality, gender, and power and perceived that the social struggle entailed more vital issues than mere tracing of descent. At the end of *Themis,* when she lashed out in great fury at men and patriarchy, she became even more vehement. First she castigated the classical age for its infatuation with sterile Olympians; then she praised the revival of primitive earth worship through the Dionysos cult, which threatened to destroy both the carefully designed Olympian patriarchy and the social system it mirrored. Her comparisons to contemporary society reflected her own dissatisfactions with family life and the patriarchal order in general.

If gods are a projection of the social structure that creates them, what do the Olympians tell us about Greece?

> Undoubtedly they represent that form of society with which we are ourselves most familiar, the patriarchal family. Zeus is the father and head: though Hera and he are in constant unseemly conflict, there is no doubt about his ultimate supremacy. Hera is jealous, Zeus in frequent exasperation, but none the less finally dominant. The picture is intensely modern, down to the ill-assorted, incongruous aggregate of grown-up sons and daughters living idly at ease at home and constantly quarreling. The family comes before us as the last forlorn hope of collectivism. Its real original bond is a sex-tie between husband and wife; its real function the rearing of helpless children. For this rearing the husband is, save for the highest forms of civilization, useless at home, his function is to be a food-seeker abroad and to come back with his beak full of worms. Once the children [are] grown up, and the sex-tie grown weak, the family falls asunder for sheer lack of moral molecular cohesion. (490–91)

After losing her father to a second marriage, watching the second family grow and deplete her father's emotional and financial resources while the stepfamily lived "idly at ease at home," and finally abandoning all hope of marriage, Harrison unleashed decades of pent-up anger through her study of Olympian religion. Clearly she directed her remarks to the society around her, despite the smoke screen of the Olympians as target. Once she had shown the barrenness of Olympianism, she could re-create the matriarchal past and describe her ideal world.

In order to get at the root of this past, Harrison finally had to deal with the concept of *themis,* which represented social order. Themis' value lay in her role as the only one of the archaic deities to survive into the Olympian age. A product of the matriarchal culture, she imposed order on the chaos of the upstart deities. Themis was female and lived on in Olympian myth as Zeus' second wife. But unlike Harrison's stepmother, this second wife was a good mother who embodied all the virtues of the conquered matriarchy. "If then we would understand the contrast between the Olympians and their predecessors we must get back to the earlier Themis, to the social structure that was before the patriarchal family, to the matrilinear system, to the Mother and the Tribe, the Mother and the Child and the Initiated young men, the Kouretes" (492). Mythology and art provided proof of the matrilineal order. A relief from the Capitoline altar depicting mother, child, and the two young men proved that "these are the factors of the old social group. The father, Kronos, is . . . nowhere" (493; Harrison's ellipses). Other artistic representations tell the same story. Thus,

> the conclusion is very clear. The myth is a presentation, a projection of the days when, at first, the facts of fatherhood were unknown, and later, but little emphasized; when the Themis of the group was the mother, as mother of the initiate youth to be. Themis as abstract Right or as statutory Law, sanctioned by force, would surely never have taken shape as a woman; but Themis as the Mother, the supreme social fact and focus, *she* is intelligible. (493–94)

Once Kronos appears he does not become immediately distasteful, for he "stands always for the old order, before Zeus and the Olympians; he hates his father Ouranos but reverences and takes counsel with Earth his mother." Kronos also avoids the title of "father"; "he is not father but 'king,' king upon earth in the other Golden Age" (495). Father figures per se were not suspect, but Harrison despised their inevitable insistence on dominance.

> Kronos as a father is respectable, even venerable. But patriarchy, once fully established, would fain dominate all things, would invade even the ancient prerogative of the mother, the right to rear the child she bore. . . . The man doing woman's work has all the inherent futility and something of the ugly dissonance of the man masquerading in women's clothes. (495)

Patriarchy stands for rigid control of the emotional life and of women's agency and power. It denies women the right to be dominant in the home. But worst of all, because of its identification with sexuality and the importance of the sex tie between man and woman, it deprived Harrison of her mother. Paradoxically, if she had not been born, her mother would not have died. Harrison attacked patriarchy largely as a means of relieving herself of her guilt at having caused her mother's death. By bringing the argument around to the unhealthiness of the primacy of sexuality, and the sanctity of the mother-child bond, she could blame her father rather than herself for her mother's death. Obviously this argument is not the product of a rational examination of the evidence, but it illustrates the intricate connection between personal experience and scholarship.

Ultimately, *Themis* lauded the supremacy of the group as the only means of reinstituting the old nurturing values of matriarchy. Harrison's fascination with the Dionysos cult resulted partly from her approval of Dionysos as a revived nature god challenging "civilized, Olympianized, patriarchalized, intellectualized Athens," which had once been a matriarchy. Its contribution to culture was its becoming "the seed of the drama" which grew from Dionysian ritual. Its overwhelming power, however, came not so much from Dionysos himself as from his role as the son of his mother, representing the mother of all that Harrison considered good. His worshipers, the Maenads, "are the mothers and therefore the nurses of the holy child; only a decadent civilization [like her own] separates the figures of mother and nurse" (39). The greatest mother of all, if one could not focus on one's own mother, would be the mother that represented the unity of the group. In Harrison's eyes, Themis filled this role because she represented the spirit of the community.

> Here the social fact is trembling on the very verge of godhead. She is the force that brings and binds men together, she is "herd instinct," the collective conscience, the social sanction. She is *fas,* the social imperative. This social imperative is among a primitive group diffuse, vague, inchoate, yet absolutely binding. . . . Themis was before the particular shapes of gods; she is not religion, but she is the stuff of which religion is made. It is the emphasis and representation of herd instinct, of the collective conscience, that constitutes religion. (485)

Themis reigned serenely over the group, as Harrison presided over the Ritualist circle, representing cohesion and unity. As part of a group, Harrison believed, one could be secure. In fact, she resembled Themis in her relation to the male world immediately surrounding her. *Themis* expressed her complete faith in the collective as a source of emotional strength. Disappointment after bitter disappointment had driven Harrison to shift her allegiance from the individual to the group, and *Themis* marked the most dramatic statement of her new convictions.

After *Themis* appeared in 1912, Harrison sent Gilbert Murray a review of it from the *Oxford Magazine* and asked if he knew who had written it. His response is lost, but the review survives as a typical example of the attacks on Harrison and is probably the work of the Oxford classicist Lewis Farnell. The following excerpt touches on all the major themes that made critics and scholars nervous: her imaginativeness and the liveliness of her interest in the subject. Critics had accepted these qualities in the *Prolegomena* ten years earlier, but *Themis*'s forcefulness made them uneasy.

> The book on the whole will appeal rather to the easy-going amateur than to the trained expert in anthropology and religion. The trained scholar will complain of the uncritical and indolent handling of texts, and will shudder at an amazing emendation on p. 147; the archaeologist will feel that Miss Harrison can no longer be trusted to interpret monuments; the historian will wonder at her elementary perception of historical evidence; the anthropologist will hope that in the future she will accept the more cautious method and limitation of range that the most modern anthropologists are imposing on themselves; while all who possess the scientific spirit will regret that the scientific effect of study should be so marred, as in this treatise it is, by the heat of the propagandist temper.
>
> Miss Harrison's work has always a freshness that is at first attractive; but the freshness is often found to be as that of the dew on cobwebs.[24]

Aside from the overheated nature of the attack, it is interesting to note that scholars took Harrison's work seriously enough to savage it so thoroughly.

Considering the pervasive interest in the irrational and the general revival of interest in collectivism led by such respected theorists as Durkheim and Bergson, one wonders that the Ritualists created a stir at all. Nevertheless, classicists reacted angrily to their work and were particularly vituperative toward Harrison. As a woman scholar and the group's most enthusiastic explorer of the dangerous, chaotic archaic age, Harrison served as a target for many traditionally minded male scholars who resented her treatment of the past, the imaginativeness of her work, and her thinly disguised attack on Victorian society. The nature of their criticism makes it clear that they sensed, even if only vaguely, the depth of her anger and had no idea how to deal with it. Harrison defended herself and her colleagues with generally good-humored references to critics in her personal letters, aside from her scholarly ripostes in letters to journals. She also praised other scholars whose works buttressed her own arguments. In either case, she maintained a rather benevolent view toward other scholars in her informal correspondence, telling Gilbert Murray that "God *is* good, whatever BR [Bertrand Russell] may say, who made Ridgeway & Ernest Gardner & you & gave me eyes to see his human comedy."[25]

Murray defended the Ritualists in the preface to his *Four Stages of Greek Religion* by commenting on the battle between classical literary scholars and anthropologists over the interpretation of Greek culture.

If ever the present differences resolved themselves into a simple fight with shillelaghs between the scholars and the anthropologists, I should without doubt wield my reluctant weapon on the side of the scholars. Scholarship is the rarer, harder, less popular and perhaps the more permanently valuable work, and it certainly stands more in need of defence at the moment. But in the meantime I can hardly understand how the purest of "pure scholars" can fail to feel his knowledge enriched by the servants who have compelled us to dig below the surface of our classical tradition and to realize the imaginative and historical problems which so often lie concealed beneath the smooth security of a verbal "construe."[26]

Murray focused the argument clearly. Traditional classical scholarship refused to admit the validity of anything other than Homer before the golden age of Greece, and the Ritualists and their allies in other fields challenged this stance. While the exchanges in columns of journals could be scurrilous, the private exchanges could be riotous.

When discussing people who were either not so well known or who were not direct participants in the ideological battle, Harrison could be scathing. After hearing Murray's comments on a "Miss Stawell's screed," Harrison wrote expressing agreement on his disappointment. "She is one of the people who make me hate morality & views & everything I shouldn't: she preaches so insistently that I long to go quietly to hell, but she is a real SS [Sound Scholar]. The only one we ever raised at Newnham." Miss Stawell apparently staged an Oedipal rebellion against her Newnham teachers, and Harrison felt no compunction about criticizing her perfidy. Years later, Harrison asked Murray "how long is 'literature' going to be left to that besotted owl old [John] Sandys—he gives a full page to Professor Seymour's stuffed emptiness & seems to think the only safe thing to say about you is that you 'have been favourably received' by [J. B.] Bury—& this is to guide the young!'[27]

She did not always spare the well known, either. During a 1901 visit to Rome, she complained to Mary Murray back in England that "Mrs. Frazer [J. G. Frazer's wife], (your double!) has been sitting by my bed for two hours, telling me 'who not to know' i.e. who has not paid Mr. Frazer 'proper attention!' This is the price I pay for a few shy radiant moments under the Golden Bough." Although still a "good conservative," she proclaimed herself "ready for any reform in the Game Laws for the preserving of Eminent Husbands." She seemed impatient with both Mrs. Frazer's backstage managing of her husband's career and with Frazer's indulgence of it.[28] Harrison saved her most acerbic comments, however, for her avowed enemies Lewis Farnell, Andrew Lang, and especially William Ridgeway.

Farnell's monumental work *The Cults of the Greek States* in part supported the work of the Ritualists, but Harrison did not think much of his intellectual ability. Faced with reviewing his two volumes on cult practice, she told Gilbert that she longed to be "spiteful—those two huge volumes are just *nil* & now I shall have to try & be kind & Xian just because woe is me—I have the fear of you before my eyes." His kind word on Farnell's behalf prompted her to threaten, "if you say Mr. Farnell is 'important' I should send for my neo-lithic club—he is essentially insignificant." Later, she "had to review Farnell twice" and did not find that he improved with age. "I didn't think it was possible for him to grow duller but with academic officials all things are possible." She defended herself against his harsh review of *Themis* in the *Hibbert Journal* by saying "I don't mind what he says of me a bit" and claiming that "a good deal of the book he simply doesn't understand & never will—& nearly all of it he temperamentally hates which is what one would expect." Her most significant comment on her critics, though, lay in her assertion that "unless I care about people they are quite powerless to hurt me, I suppose that is for worse not for better." She wanted to convince Murray that Farnell did not matter in the least, but his criticism likely hurt more than she cared to admit.[29]

Andrew Lang angered her by writing "enormous screeds to say I am wrong about the All Father. He seems to have reviewed [*Themis*] three times." His behavior at a dinner party also provided her with a charming vignette for her "Reminiscences."

> Our hostess brought him up to me and, with a misguided desire to be pleasant, said, "You know Miss Harrison, and I am sure you have read her delightful books." "Don't know Miss Harrison," muttered Andrew, "never read her delightful books, don't want to," etc. (Oh, Andrew, and you had reviewed those "delightful books" not too delightedly!) "Come, Mr. Lang," I said, "we're both hungry, and I promise not to say a single word to you. Be a man." Alas! I broke my word. It was an enchanting dinner. (RSL, 334)

Despite her intellectual differences with Lang, Harrison could ignore them in the interest of a peaceful meal.[30]

By far the most implacable of her critics was the classicist William Ridgeway, whose antics provoked her into a good deal of vituperative rhetoric both in public and in private. Their antagonism dated from her earliest days at Newnham, and Harrison often expressed mock fear that Ridgeway would one day come at her "in full shillelagh." He appears to have been an arrogant, gruff curmudgeon, always ready to take on the Ritualist circle. Ironically, Harrison often quoted Ridgeway's work on early Greece approvingly in her major works, but their basic views diverged and Charles Seltman rightly doubted "very much whether Ridgeway had much influence on her work." In a classic understatement,

Seltman admitted that "I am afraid he sometimes spoke a little unkindly about her—an indication that something she had published was in conflict with some of his pre-conceived notions." She footnoted him respectfully in both the *Prolegomena* and *Themis,* but otherwise they regularly exchanged insults.[31]

As early as 1901, Harrison wrote to Jessie Stewart with a complaint about Ridgeway. She had "had a long letter from Professor Ridgeway pointing out that the really strong points in his new book [probably volume 1 of *The Early Age of Greece*] were lucidity of statement, attractive presentation and a too amicable tone in controversy with what he elegantly and pacifically terms 'vermin.' This is all I get for my tactful admonitions!" She toyed with the idea of developing an archaeology seminar with Jessie Stewart in order to "get archaeology into shape, have every part of it properly taught—& avoid the growing scandal of the lectures of him who shall be nameless."[32]

After an anonymous review of his work in the London *Times,* Ridgeway was "out on the warpath in full shillelagh." Harrison wrote to Gilbert Murray that "he burst out to one of my archaeological students—he really has no decorum—'Read the review of me in the Times. It's Murray & Miss Harrison—I spotted them—Them & their initiation ceremonies—I'll initiate them.' " Apparently they only lightly veiled their identity, for A. W. Verrall spotted their style, too; "but F.M.C. [Cornford] was very dull. He said 'it's an admirable piece of justice. I suppose it's by some Oxford fellow for I don't recognise the hand.' He is dense—with 'year-gods' dancing round but it shows the general public won't detect you." Ridgeway created a scene after one of her lectures in 1911, and "there was a great to-do . . . between Ridgeway & ABC [Cook]. ABC was splendid so Xian but so incisive."[33]

Harrison did not always treat her critics so caustically, however. For some reason, she took a definite liking to Percy Gardner, whose status as a "sound scholar" should by rights have driven her around the bend, and she could be kind to people whom she liked. In 1907, with Gilbert Murray lecturing in the United States, Harrison wrote a review that got her into trouble. She chided him for going away and reminded him that "if you had been this side of the pond I should have sent you proof of my intemperate review (or rather I should never have dared to put you into it) & you would have *re*written it in words of one syllable & terms of the Xian religion & now here I am embroiled with 'old Percy' whom I adore . . . & his dear foolish head is stuffed with cotton wool." Despite his intellectual inadequacy, she found Percy's work "delicious" and was "glad" Murray was "getting to love him, I have always loved him because he makes me consume away with inward laughter & that shows he is really nice." His comments on a paper she read in 1910 delighted her, and she recounted the evening to Gilbert Murray.

Oh why weren't you there on Tuesday—Old Percy was *so* sweet & adorable I believe you are turning him into one of your Golden Lambs—he gave an impassioned address on my illness & recovery. . . . it was most moving—we wallowed knee deep in Xian charity—then Mr. Farnell got up & preached—O Lord how he preached & patronized—he said my theory reminded him of some words Professor Murray had "let fall" at the Anthropological Society & then pulled himself up in the clumsiest way & said of course he did not mean to imply that Miss Harrison's able paper was not entirely original! I believe really they were all convinced but of course they couldn't say so without "grave considerations" & old Percy said "before giving our adhesion that such a theory might lead us far in many directions"—awful thought.[34]

The Cambridge years were intellectually exciting, and the group provided Jane with many opportunities to exercise her sharp wit on her adversaries and grow closer to her colleagues in the fight. She took full advantage of chances to jump into the academic fray while the group provided the security she needed to create her works on Greek religion. But successive tragedies, besides that of her failed romance with Francis Cornford, overshadowed her most productive years at the university.

Nearly fifty years of age when she returned to Newnham and with many of her closest acquaintances several years older yet, Jane lost some of her most valued friends through death during these years. The death of Arthur Verrall, her classical colleague and husband of her old friend, Margaret Merrifield Verrall, especially affected her. Although Verrall often disagreed with her theories, they worked closely in classical studies, and she occasionally traveled with him and Margaret. In 1904, for instance, they had all journeyed to Algiers so the Verralls could recuperate from various ailments. When in 1901 Jane had returned home from a trip to Greece, she wrote to Gilbert Murray, "it is so beautiful to be home & see green things, after the horrible glare and those dreadful clean-cut-lines people rave about. I am still in the newly-home-stage when one gets hysterical at the sight of every lilac bush—but it will pass." She turned to work immediately on an article, and Verrall acted as an inspiration. "I should die of depression but Mr. Verrall comes in from time to time simply gurgling over with fresh classical indiscretions invented in the intervals of tripos papers," and she pronounced him "more refreshing than any lilac bush & quite as perennial."[35]

When Gilbert Murray sent Jane a copy of his memoir of Verrall, she wrote fondly about some of the memories his words evoked.

His criticising you as he did was a beautiful thing that makes the world better to have happened. I think I tried him there too because I rubbed in your views—he read that Bacchant preface to me with a sort of school boy glee & with occasional winks when he came to "wans" & "dims"—once I got rather cross & said—but surely you see how beautiful it is—don't you care for it—& he said—"Of course I care for it, why it's pure Gilbert—Gilberterrim"!! & then we clasped hands over the great truth that you can't possibly love anyone unless they make you laugh at them sometimes consumedly—I suppose I believe in God worse luck still for I know there is something I can't forgive for hitting him down & taking him away.

She mused in a postscript over why Verrall never became close to Francis Cornford and concluded, "probably he would have been bored by me if he hadn't taken me loyally on at first as his wife's friend—how queer things are." His death was a great sorrow to Jane, both because she would personally miss him and because of the sadness of Margaret's being widowed.[36]

During these years, the emotional cost of converting anger and pain into creativity took a tremendous toll on Jane's physical health, but in large part her effort succeeded. In 1912, she reconciled herself to Frances Darwin's role as Cornford's wife through the curious mechanism of a dream. Jane claimed to have had only two "significant" dreams in her life and surely this was one of them (RSL, 341). She described it to Gilbert Murray in a letter written in September 1912 while she was undergoing treatment at a clinic in Geneva.

And now I must tell you a strange thing. I was wondering if I should tell you or not when your letter came and now, though I am a little afraid, for you know so well the deceitfulness of the human heart and may dash my hopes. Do you think a blasphemous Ker could be converted? Do you remember contending with me on the cliffs and maintaining that there was more in religion than the collective conscience? I think I know now at first hand that there is. Last night I was awake all night with misery and utter loneliness such as often comes upon me now that I have to go about alone—only it was worse than anything I had ever felt—like a black despair, and I was full of hate against Frances, unjustly of course, as the cause of my loneliness. I fell asleep at last and woke about six bathed in a most amazing bliss and a feeling that all the world was new and in perfect peace. I can't describe it—the "New Birth" is the best—it was what they all try to describe, and it is what they mean by communion with God. Only it seems senseless to me to give it a name and yet I do not wonder for it is so personal.

Something physical has happened for when I went to Röthlisberger [her doctor] the moment he put his instrument to my pulse he said "Why this is all better" and seemed astonished—but something not physical too for all the hate against Frances was gone. For the last two years I have scarcely seen her. He found out by my face, he said, that every time I saw her it brought back the pain in my heart, so he begged me not to see her and I didn't. But I felt mean and wretched. Of course I cannot be sure till I do see her, but I have no fear. It seems to have gone away clean. I can't put it into psychology yet. What I feel most is that a wall of partitions is broken down and a whole crust of egotism gone, melted away, and that I have got hold of something bigger than me that I am part of. But it was all done in my sleep—not by me at all. What is it? I will never call it God—that name is defaced, but it is wonderful and you were right as always.

Jane's hatred for Frances disappeared in her sleep in both a literal and a figurative sense. Her dream, the content of which she never revealed, represented one of the ways in which Jane diverted her anger into productive channels and resolved her tension with Frances, at least. It was a telescoped version of a process that had taken four years. Jane admitted that the anguish sometimes returned, but her hatred of Frances had indeed disappeared. The two women shared a long relationship, which was sustained even through the bleakest times by their mutual affection for Ellen Crofts Darwin.[37]

Unfortunately, Francis was not so lucky. Although late in her life Jane came to grips with her past and reconciled herself to its failure to meet her expectations, she seems never to have forgiven him for not loving her. The wound was too deep and festered for too long to be easily put aside. Because of her long-standing love for Frances and the Darwin family, Jane needed to lay aside her hate for a young woman who, by her own admission, although "not a scholar, with [Jane's] genius, or her passion," attracted Francis's attention "partly through the simple accident of being more than thirty years younger than she was." Frances understood more than her husband did that "Jane had been like a key for him which unlocked the closed door of his personality" and that Jane's only reward was that Frances "was now able to turn the handle and walk straight in." Jane herself used similar imagery in a veiled reference to the whole Francis-Frances affair in her 1914 essay, "Crabbed Age and Youth." In it, she mused over the differences between young and old while striking out bitterly at Francis.

Age dominates, possesses Youth, uses Youth for its own selfish purposes, demands its sympathy and adulation, and then expects Youth to be grateful. Youth does not make the like demand on age. This word "grateful" is always a danger-signal; it means a certain denial of friendship and equality. Youth is pathetically "grateful," and therefore it is difficult for Youth and Age to be friends. The relation is that of helper and helped, not of mutual comradeship, where help is given and taken without account. I once knew a tutor who, rash man, thought he had made a friend of a pupil. The pupil wrote, as it happened, to announce

> his marriage, and used the occasion to say how "grateful" he was and for what. "I owe you eternal gratitude: *you have helped me to find . . . myself*—that self which I am now about to dedicate to another." The tutor's face was old and grey as he laid down the letter. But the young man was quite sincere: his tutor had been to him, not a friend, but a door by which he might enter, a ladder by which he might spiritually climb. The friendship between Crabbed Age and Youth is always beset on both hands by the fiend of megalomania; the younger enhances himself through the skill and knowledge of the elder, the elder feeds his vanity on the open-eyed admiration of the younger. Only very delicate souls can live unhurt in such an atmosphere.

Thus, she perceived, long after the fact, exactly what had been the basis of her relationship with Francis. Indirectly she blamed herself for not having recognized it, but she made no effort to hide her resentment of both his reliance on her to create his own sense of worth and the ease with which he changed his allegiance.[38]

For his part, Francis explained to Frances Darwin that he and Jane "were both rather lonely people, we foregathered and made friends and we have been a good deal together. Now she is feeling that someone else will be more than all friends to me henceforth—and that someone she loves very dearly." He hastened to add that he would "care for her more than ever" because she had "brought them together." Jessie Stewart remarked of Francis that Jane "treated him, he told Frances long after, as if he were a lover who had abandoned her. 'And did it never occur to you,' Frances asked, 'that she might be in love with you?' 'No, never,' he answered naively and in absolute sincerity. 'She meant a great deal to me, but she was old enough to be my mother.' " Despite her declaration of love for him, Francis never seemed to appreciate fully the depth of Jane's attachment to him. This misunderstanding colored their relationship for the rest of her life.[39]

Jane filled the three years between the completion of *Themis* and the start of World War I with travel and further attempts to deal with vestigial anger at Francis. Her physical health improved dramatically, but emotionally she still suffered a sense of not belonging anywhere. In the spring of 1912, she informed Frances Darwin that she was soon off on a cruise to Greece as she found it "more & more impossible to work." She required a "desperate remedy" as "there seemed no other chance of complete change & it may be that a crowd will do what solitude cannot." She wrote cheerfully to Gilbert Murray that "the deck of this absurd ship is simply strewn with copies of the Rise of the Greek Epic" and that she was " 'very jealous for' the lady Themis." Arthur Pickard-Cambridge was on board, and she sat "by his side a good deal while he softly reads old Themis, marking all the indiscretions with a beautifully pointed pencil." The methodical Pickard-Cambridge planned "to read it once on the way out, & again on the way back that he may come to no rash conclusions."[40]

A year later, Jane fled again, this time to Venice, announcing to Gilbert that she was "quite done—not overworked nor ill in body but just dead utterly in mind—I am going to be 'sensible' & try change . . . but in my heart I believe I am just played out, mere wreckage, & I don't care." That summer saw another Murray daughter engaged and Jane wrote to Mary with halfhearted congratulations. She felt "first & foremost the peril when I hear of an engagement." She recognized that that was "an odd thing to feel & simply means that one has seen scores of radiant engagements die out into greyness." As she grew older, however, she began to think "risks should be taken & every happy hour seized is a treasure forever—even when it is gone out of one's hands." No doubt she had Francis in mind as she pondered the wisdom of taking chances with one's emotions. Jane was "very lonely" that summer in Cambridge and particularly put out that although Gilbert was vacationing in Overstrand on the Suffolk coast, she could not visit him. Her letter implied that propriety alone kept her from rushing off to join him. She also hinted that he worried more about appearances than she did. "Well if you can't invite me I can't come—that is clear." His decision not to come to Cambridge upset her, and she concluded, "oh damn it all why am I not a man & then I could fly to Overstrand & hear about Euripides." In a postscript, she suggested rather wistfully, "if you ever found I might come a telegram would being me & I could live in that big hotel if it wasn't proper to be in your cave."[41]

Jane spent Christmas of 1913 at the Hutch, Alice Dew-Smith's home in Rye. The Mirrlees family had "taken the next rabbit-warren," as Jane put it to Mary, but the holidays remained, as usual, a gloomy time for her. "I am prostrate trying (& failing) to flee from the Eniautos-Daimon—How I do *hate the* Herd & the communal dais when it comes to real Turkey & Plumpudding." The year 1913 was particularly stressful because Jane plunged into *Ancient Art and Ritual* as soon as she completed *Themis;* she then had to spend the better part of the next year trying to regain her health. Letters and postcards she sent to the Murrays indicate that she spent a great deal of time in Paris undergoing electric treatment for her heart, which she claimed made her "feel a very marked calming of the nerves—less tension all over—during the week it was going on I felt as I haven't felt for 5 or 6 years." As the First World War drew closer, however, treatments became harder to obtain, and the disturbing issues raised by the outbreak of hostilities weakened Jane's tenuous hold on her emotions.[42]

Writing in the year after Jane's death, Francis touched on their intellectual collaboration and remarked that he believed he had "failed in the role for which she had cast" him. He described this failure in intellectual terms:

> Where I was expected to furnish a touchstone of sober criticism, I was too often captivated by the play of her imagination and afraid to cavil at intuitions of genius backed by a knowledge far greater than my own. I ought to have faced a truth I obscurely divined—that intuitions charged with emotion of subjective origin are as likely to project a mirage as to penetrate a mist. It was of little use to tell her, as a general proposition, that she did not, like the ideal man of science, make the truth of fact her first consideration.[43]

Although he never seemed to understand it, Francis failed actually in every role in which Jane cast him. In all fairness, she harbored unrealistic expectations of their future, but her lack of realism does not invalidate either her love for him or her sorrow when he married. The compelling question remains why she fell in love with him at all. He was, by his own admission, not her intellectual equal, nor could he identify intuitively with her view of the world or her complex personality. He lacked the emotional depth she valued so highly in her close friends, as she pointed out to him in a chilly letter of November 24, 1918.

> As to your religion—that is very interesting, because I see that between our religions there *is* a real and rather substantial difference. Your relation to human beings doesn't content my religious instinct at all; it seems to me just a refined socialism. There is something about us so enormously bigger, though not wholly better, than any human goodness, and also so hugely more interesting and beautiful. Partly I suppose I am more what you call Wordsworthian—things like sea and moor *do* bring the sense of God to me more than human goodness—partly I have perhaps more intellectual passion: the world of things to be known is my good. I *value* them intensely; so they become my religion. The purely human always cloys, always has brought a certain lassitude and left me hungry.[44]

Most of Jane's personal relationships had been profoundly unsatisfying, and she learned not to invest too much of her energy in them. Ultimately Francis, her greatest hope, became her greatest failure. She probably understood that such a result was inevitable. Francis was the perfect Hippolytus to her Phaedra in her interpretation of the tragedy. As attractive and intelligent as he was, his greatest strength lay in shutting doors.

The one door that was left ajar and represented Jane's faith in the collective as embodied by the historical existence of matriarchy was slammed shut by an ideological betrayal: the perversion of altruistic collectivism into destructive patriotism at the outbreak of World War I. With the war following closely on the heels of romantic tragedy, Jane sat out the war in Cambridge, brooding over the destruction of all her old ideals. When the dust settled, she broke entirely with her past, both personal and intellectual, and fled Cambridge for the neutral environment of Paris. This self-imposed exile marked the final stage of Jane's attempt to wrestle with her own history and brought the circle back around to its beginning.

8

The Circle Completed: World War I, Paris, and the Return to London

Real old age . . . should never be crabbed. These actors have first masqueraded, rehearsed life in imagination, then lived to the full, and last, discharged from life, they behold it. It is the time of the great Apocalypse. It is one of the tragic antinomies of life that you cannot at once live and have vision.

—*Jane Ellen Harrison, "Crabbed Age and Youth"*

And here I may be allowed to break off these autobiographical notes. The public has no claim to learn any more of my personal affairs—of my struggles, my disappointments, and my successes. I have in any case been more open and frank in some of my writings . . . than people usually are who describe their lives for their contemporaries or for posterity. I have had small thanks for it, and from my experience I cannot recommend any one to follow my example.

—*Sigmund Freud,* An Autobiographical Study

WORLD WAR I coincided with Jane Harrison's attempt to reconcile herself to the past and shattered her last remaining illusions about the superiority of herd instinct. After the war obliterated her belief in collectivism, Jane got along as best she could at Newnham until 1922, when she destroyed her papers and left for Paris with Hope Mirrlees in order to impose distance between herself and her past. Having burned her bridges, she spent four years in exile constructing a new bridge that would lead back to London in 1926.

After a lifelong search for the origins of the most fundamental human emotions, Jane during these four years dug even deeper by studying languages, believing they would reveal the common thread running through all human experience. Beyond the religious impulse, languages opened the door to the very soul. Despite her disclaimer to the contrary, the Russian soul particularly intrigued her as it had when she was very young, so that by mastering the Russian language she completed a circle begun in childhood. Finally understanding that the circle of one's life could not revolve forever around oneself, she opened up to kinship with the larger circle of humanity and pondered the connection between the individual and the race.

Her essays collected in *Alpha and Omega* had expressed her prewar philosophy, with the final essay, written just before publication in 1915, revealing a radical change from belief in the positive power of the group to conviction of its destructiveness. One of her last acts now in Paris was the writing of a brief autobiography, an undertaking that expressed her willingness finally to come to grips with her age and to reconcile herself to an unhappy past. In "Reminiscences of a Student's Life" (1925), Jane passed lightly over some important incidents and ignored others completely, but she generally presented a picture of a woman trying to make sense out of the life she had lived and to impose order on the chaos of seventy-five years. The "Reminiscences," as well as her personal letters, also chronicled her development between her flight from Cambridge in 1922 and her return to London in 1926.

For decades, Jane had opposed individualism for what she saw as its roots in the divisiveness of sexual attraction. In November 1912, she had expanded on this theme in a paper read before the Cambridge Society of Heretics. "Unanism and Conversion" offered a brief but fierce attack on lovers, who "long to make a holocaust of everyone and every thing on the altar of passion." This dual passion is not akin to the emotion produced by religious fervor because "we know it for what it is—the egotism, the megalomania, imposed by the fierce divinity of the group [of] two, exclusive, anti-Unanimist." Religion marks a major step forward since it draws human beings out of themselves and makes them aware of their place in a large group. Although "we must remember that many men and women never do and never can get beyond the group [of] two . . . the worship of even this rudimentary god is a step, and a big one, out of the prison of self." Nevertheless, progress is only relative, and the egotism of lovers suffers by comparison to the altruism of religious impulse.[1]

Jane's most succinct discussion of collectivism appeared in the 1909 essay "Heresy and Humanity," which she had first presented as a lecture to the Society of Heretics.[2] In primitive society, she says, collectivism is a positive force because "at the outset, what draws society together is sympathy, similarity, uniformity. In the fierce struggle for existence, for food, for protection, the herd and the homogeneity of the herd, its *collective*, unreflecting action, are all-important" (29). Ironically, Jane sometimes appears to have rejected the very herd instinct in modern society that she praised in the primitive, for she revised this essay between its delivery as a lecture in 1909 and its publication in 1915. In 1909, for example, she was still espousing collectivism in opposition to the selfish egotism of lovers, represented in this case by Frances Darwin and Francis Cornford. Still recovering from the pain their marriage caused her, she attacked them by flying the banner of the group. But by the time of World War I, she was presenting trenchant criticisms of the collective instinct. She pointed to "that noblest of latter-day survivals, the 'good soldier,' " who "does not, and may not, reflect and make personal choice." His orders are "sacrosanct" and "be it contrary to reason, be it contrary to humanity, [they] must still be obeyed." Collective beliefs, then, "are not rationally based, though they may be rationally supported" (29).

Although she praised science for drawing "ever clearer distinctions," she recognized that "by neither individual sense-perception nor ratiocination alone do we live" (33). The herd provided "our keenest emotional life," and "hence it was that, at the close of last century, the flame of scientific hope, the glory of scientific individualism that had blazed so brightly, somehow died down and left a strange chill. . . . It seemed an *impasse:* on the one side orthodoxy, tradition, authority, practical slavery; on the other science, individual freedom, reason, and an aching loneliness" (35). As society changed from the "multiplication of homogeneous units" characteristic of primitive society to the "differentiation of function" of modern society, we were left with disorder and disorientation (35). She believed that "we live now just at the transition moment; we have broken with the old, we have not quite adjusted ourselves to the new. It is not so much the breaking with old faiths that makes us restless as the living in a new social structure" (35–36). Her most grievous error in understanding was her failure to see that the world is always in transition, that all humanity is forever caught in a wrenching state of flux.

Her argument is at once unconvincing and intriguing because she tried to combine two fundamentally contradictory views of life. She could never quite make up her mind whether the collective life or the individual life is more satisfying. She defined humanity as "sympathy with infinite differences, with utter individualism, with complete differentiation" (p. 38–39). But in the end, the "old herd-problem remains of how to live *together,*" which is certainly an aim antagonistic to her old nemesis, egotism, which also takes its lumps in this essay (41). She advised that "whenever the old tiger-cat egotism snarls within us, we should resign our membership of the Society of Heretics, and go back for a season to the 'godly discipline' of the herd" (41). Heresy equals individualism, humanity collectivism, and it is not hard to see where Jane's deepest sympathies lay, at least until the upheaval of 1914.

In that year, in "Crabbed Age and Youth," Jane was still exhorting the young to reject their natural egotism and join the larger human race.[3] Youth seemed to her "a small, intensely-focussed spot, outside a great globe or circle," a spot that "believes itself the centre of the great circle" (16). As one grows older, the "little burning, throbbing spot that is oneself is sucked in with thousands of others into the great globe" where it "learns that it is no centre of life at all; at most it is one of the myriads of spokes in the great wheel" (16). Life events break the power of individualism: "through marrying, through having a bad illness, through accepting a 'post,' through any bit of actual work or responsibility, Youth takes a *part* in life, becomes a real part, instead of claiming a theatrical whole" (14–15). Youth is busy "rehearsing" while Crabbed Age lives, "and living, if sometimes less amusing, is infinitely more absorbing" (10). Not only is the collective superior; it is inescapable. If one attempts to evade one's responsibilities by remaining unmarried, by avoiding "the lure of passion for the individual . . . there is society waiting with its artificial lure—waiting to catch you and make an official of you" (11).

Despite the consolation of belonging to a group when all individuals had failed to fulfill her needs, even Jane could not ignore the events of 1914. When the war first began, she accepted the word of her friend Logan Pearsall-Smith, who informed her "on the authority of the Secret Service that all will be over in September."[4] As the war dragged on, however, Jane grew disillusioned. More than anything else, the ease with which her male colleagues abandoned their academic posts for the battlefield and cheerfully set out for war opened her eyes to the dark side of collectivism.

The "Epilogue on the War" (1914), the final essay in *Alpha and Omega,* grew from Jane's recognition that collectivism bred conflict in the modern world.[5] When, as in primitive society, the group was small enough to live together peacefully within itself and sedentary enough to avoid encounters with other self-sufficient groups, collective emotion bound it together. But when the group was subverted by appeals to patriotic fervor, which elevated one group's status at the expense of all others, confrontation loomed. Jane slowly recognized that her collectivist ideal could not survive in modern society.

Her initial dilemma consisted of the paradox that whereas she herself, "with every fibre of body and mind," stood for "Peace," the typical male don "turned soldier, and proudly, if a little shamefacedly, parade[d] the uniform which, ten years ago, would have been to him *anathema*" (223). This particular war seemed unavoidable, but she fervently hoped for the day when any war would be unthinkable. True peace could be attained only when all humanity accepted its interdependence and respected all others' autonomy, in a moral more than a political sense.

She was mystified that her fellow dons joined up so readily. The reversal of social values did not worry her so much. "War upsets every value; the beam is suddenly kicked and down falls the scale of learning" (228). Although soldiers can be expected to welcome war, which justifies their existence as military men, the dons' "temple of learning war lays in ruins—ruins not only material, but spiritual" (228). In wartime, learning loses all value and the life of the mind must be subordinated to the life of action. Paradoxically, "this very upset . . . is positively welcomed just by the man who might be expected to resent it: the scholar and thinker." Jane was shocked at how many of her colleagues "went, not reluctantly, but with positive alacrity" (228). She attributed their eagerness to an instinctive recognition that the solitary life of the scholar required the emotional boost that military service, the quintessential experience of brotherhood, would provide. "Into the seething cauldron they stepped as though some healing angel, and not some devil, had troubled the waters, and the cure they found was just the bond of a common fellowship" (231). In this respect, the war could be a positive influence, a compulsory collective experience for those who lived their lives in the rarefied atmosphere of the university. It frightened her that although she perceived it as "a savagery—a setback to civilization," war appealed to the modern imagination (231). She suggested an extraordinary explanation for this phenomenon: the emergence of collectivism as a popular philosophy.

So long as Jane constructed collectivist societies only in the dim past and in the pages of books, collectivism seemed a possible force for good. Once the ideal became reality, however, she turned against it. "The watchwords of my generation . . . were Knowledge and Freedom," and she reproached the young now for favoring "emotion and collectivism" (235). With the dark side of collectivism emerging around her, she no longer wanted to discuss it, saying, "frankly, just now I am rather bored with it" (235). Having "preached collectivism" for "five long years, in season and out," she abandoned it (235). She justified her action by claiming that "Nowadays, collectivism is not only becoming a fashionable dogma; it is—a conquest far more significant—astir in every man's heart. A dogma once boomed is, intellectually, stale, and therefore useless; but a lived experience may remain vital long after the dogmatic death" (235). Still, she longed for a collectivism based on rejection of the exclusivity of sex—the kind of collectivism she had initially created as a model out of her own experience. Her collective ideal had no political basis. In fact, if anything, her conservatism made her suspicious of any political collectivism. She used the vocabulary of her era, but she invested it with entirely different meaning. No one in the larger world could understand her ideal, of course, since it bore such an intimate relation to her personal life. Therefore, her brand of collectivism failed miserably to catch on and was superseded by a vulgar form that led to war.

Jane's wartime letters show a growing disillusionment with the war and its betrayal of her collective ideal. She viewed it as "horribly exciting" at first, but could not "*live* on it—it is like being drunk all day & I want some hot milk clean & feeding."[6] Her heart condition forced her to Paris in October 1914 for treatment. She found it "wonderful to be here

& somehow less unbearable for the nightmare becomes real." Her doctor greeted her as an ally, and she found it "very upsetting to be adored for one's group's sake."[7] She believed so strongly in the folly of war that "down in [her] deepest heart" she felt "we ought . . . to have marched out all of us to meet the German army & said 'we withstand you—shoot us down if you wish.' I wonder if they could have done it."[8] Her longstanding acquaintance with Bertrand Russell also made her sympathetic to pacifism. She asserted that "militarism is the offspring of fear—Germany is brutal because she is frightened—we are humane—as yet, because we are safe." A meeting with a refugee Belgian minister prompted her to accuse her country of being "deep dyed in the spirit of sport," which had led it to "look on war with the same eyes—what we care for is the fair playing of the game."[9] These insights impelled her to write a pamphlet called "War and the Reaction," which elicited some negative response. She even scolded Gilbert Murray for failing to appreciate her sentiments.

> Well I never. I don't know what young Thers of forty are coming to, mocking at a respectable old Ker over 60 in a cap & spectacles—Am I really so absurd? Each one of those things was written under dire compulsion, they forced their way out & seemed at the moment of tremendous importance—& even now I feel they have to be said—One thing you ought to remember—till I knew you I never thought or wrote about anything except—Pelasgians. & I suppose I ought to have gone on like that—but you came & muddled me up & made me turn an over focussed mind on practical things.

Like all the other matters on which she wrote, the war had taken hold in her mind and gave her "no choice" but to write about it.[10]

Jane was not totally immune to the war's seductiveness, however, and chafed at her inability to participate in it. She wished "for the first time in my life" that she was "a man and a young one . . . largely because the tension of inaction is almost unbearable, and thinking very difficult."[11] The Scarborough raid of December 1914 particularly upset her because of both the massive destruction of a place in which she had once lived and the death of Joanna, her old servant from the London days. The suffering of animals during the raid deeply touched her, and she cited stories in the Yorkshire *Post* "about the horses & about one old dog who went out to see how he could help & was lost." Their pathos caused her "a complete nervous breakdown" despite her pride that her "bit of coast has borne some real hurt."[12] She visited Yorkshire because her "native land pulled so hard" at her, and it was then that she learned of Joanna's death.[13]

When the war did not achieve its predicted rapid end, all of Europe dug in for an indefinite period of conflict. On January 1, 1915, with the war only five months old, Jane was "beginning to be bored" by the blackouts and the silencing of clocks and church bells. Still, she could not "hate the Kaiser I can't help loving him a little. I have laughed at him so long & so loud & you know my principles." But Jane's principle of loving anyone who made her laugh could not protect her from the war's effects on both her intellectual work and her health. In 1915, "the world" was "one great disillusionment," and she lamented that she was "dying quietly of want of health. . . . I just have no health." She planned to travel again to Paris for treatment in the spring of 1915, but the war forced the cancelation of her plans. She grew despondent and asked wearily, "oh—will it ever be all over. & will one have any life left in one to live with if it is." Circumstances, however, allowed her to visit her Parisian doctor later that spring, and she announced that his treatment for hardening of the arteries "puts new life into one." He expected "a complete cure now that will be permanent," but she had to continue treatment sporadically throughout the war.[14]

Her recurrent ill health may have resulted largely from the difficulty of working at academic research when the world was so focused on larger and more pressing issues. She blamed herd instinct gone awry for interrupting her work and creating this new, hostile atmosphere. She began to see some justification for the war, but reacted with sorrow and anger that humanity misunderstood and misused the power of the group. Jane wrote to Gilbert Murray:

> I think the safe thing for others & perhaps for oneself is *never* to say this war is right without adding one's deep sense of humiliation as a human being that war should be—one gains by the herd's power of intense feeling, one loses by its awful stupidity & savagery—& in so far as one is part of it one has to mourn & repent for that stupidity & savagery. & the test is does one hate Germay—I saw that in France. Even the civilized men hate Germany & are not ashamed to say so—even my doctor the best & gentlest of men—said cést la haine Mademoiselle . . . & I feel in my heart if they came here it would be "la haine" with me.

Jane thanked Gilbert for pointing out in one of his wartime tracts that "to hate Germany was both a stupidity & a sin—for the hate is growing—& is beginning to be made into a herd duty."[15] For decades, Jane had mistakenly assumed that any group would foster only positive, unifying emotions. She had failed to discern until now that hatred and fear could generate new and divisive forces within the group. Her response to another of Gilbert's tracts revealed how irrevocably she had turned against the herd.

> It is interesting about the ruthlessness of the really herd creature like the bee. Their polity makes one cold with horror also I am glad you

> show that pack feeling is quite diff[erent] from affection—The *size* of the herd & the relation of the small to the bigger herd is difficult & no one seems to have worked it out fully. . . . of course the more civilization progresses the more intensively a very big herd can act—by telephone etc.
>
> The negative self-feeling of obedience is important. . . . combined with herd feeling it may generate abysses of abjectness. I am very glad you put clearly how much herd emotion *deadens* individual sympathy—people positively use it as a pretext for their own callousness.
>
> Altogether your paper makes me feel more clearly than ever how literally I hate & despise the herd! it is so stupid—so bore-ing—& so idle.

These were not altogether new thoughts, but nevertheless represented a gradual rejection of her old ideals.[16]

Jane considered England's treatment of its conscientious objectors and pacifists the most distressing aspect of collectivism gone wrong. She valued independence of thought above all else and grew angry at the vociferous attacks on those who criticized the war. She was dismayed at the treatment of Gerald Shove, fiancé of her young friend Fredegond Maitland. She also sided with Bertrand Russell in his objection to the war, despite a long period of coolness on her part brought about by his divorce from her friend, Alys Russell, in 1911. On the one hand, Jane defended Gilbert Murray against detractors who abhorred his support of the war, although she did not entirely agree with him; on the other, she supported the right of individuals to oppose the war.

In a 1917 letter regarding Gerald Shove's case, Jane agreed with Gilbert Murray that "a man can have a conscience without belonging to a sect" and criticized the determination of prosecutors to be particularly harsh on the "poor lonely thinker" who opposed the war on philosophical and moral grounds. Fredegond Maitland informed her that "the small lower middle class fanatic too uneducated to state his case" suffered the most from the tribunal that tried Gerald Shove's case. This experience moved Jane to remark, "that awful herd do you remember how I used to enthuse over the herd—give me a hermit crab now."[17]

In order to escape these troubling issues, Jane plunged into the study of languages, especially Russian. This study, along with her contacts with East European refugees, led to a romance with Russia and its language that occupied nearly the rest of her life. She believed that that country cared "more than any other nation for the things of the spirit & that is priceless," and that "the words even seem like Greek to seek for the things of the spirit."[18] The Russians appealed to her from the start of the war because of her romantic association of the country with bears and forests and the Russian soul as seen through its great nineteenth-century authors, and she rejoiced over the March revolution as well. She tolerated Bolshevism largely because conservative Cambridge decried it, but her heart belonged to Old Russia. Her earliest memory, according to her "Reminiscences," was of a family dog symbolically named "Moscow"; her first toy was "a box of bricks and soldiers called 'The Siege of Sevastopol,' given by a patriotic uncle" as a reminder of the Crimean War (RSL, 312). Her father's timber business had brought him into contact with Russian merchants who sent "caviare and cranberries and reindeers' tongues" every Christmas; the tongues had tasted "not only of reindeer, but—but of snow-fields and dreaming forests". These memories formed Jane's vision of Russia that remained intact through the 1917 revolutions and beyond (RSL, 312). This vision probably prevented her from traveling to Russia except for one brief journey to St. Petersburg in 1886 to examine Greek antiquities housed at the Hermitage.[19] She blamed her avoidance of the country on her being too focused on Greece to think about it, but she probably knew that to make a reality of one's ideal would destroy it.

Her romantic view of Russia influenced one of the two significant dreams she claimed to have had in her life. A dream of the Russian forest contained all her favorite images and demonstrated her association of the nation with bears.

> One night soon after the Russian revolution I dreamt I was in a great, ancient forest—What in Russian would be called "a dreaming wood." In it was cleared a round space, and the space was crowded with huge bears softly dancing. I somehow knew that I had come to teach them to dance the Grand Chain in the Lancers, a square dance now obsolete. I was not the least afraid, only very glad and proud. I went up and began trying to make them join hands and form a circle. It was no good. I tried and tried, but they only shuffled away, courteously waving their paws, intent on their own mysterious doings. Suddenly I knew that these doings were more wonderful and beautiful than any Grand Chain (as, indeed, they might well be!). It was for me to learn, not to teach. I woke up crying, in an ecstasy of humility. (RSL, 341).

Many years later, Jane delighted in an outing to see "sixteen polar bears" performing in Paris. Although they were "not nearly so clever" as others she had seen, the experience proved to be "just like my dream come true for when the trainer-man tried to make them do their stunts they just shambled past him & went nosing about their own business."[20]

Jane spent the last decade of her life exploring the Russian soul through its language, although she denied being drawn to "the 'Slav soul' " (RSL, 341). After twenty-five years in the tumult of the emotional life, Jane drew back to observe that life from a distance. Language, which expressed the soul of a people and conveyed its perceptions of emotion without entangling one in it, became another means of comprehending the inner essence of a group. At the end of her life, Jane wished she had devoted herself to language: "Life itself may hit one hard, but always, always one can take sanctuary in language. . . . It reflects and interprets and makes bearable life; only it is a wider, because more subconscious, life" (RSL, 341).

The revolution of March 1917 made Jane "so happy" and she believed it to be "the best & biggest thing the war has brought," although her Russian friends remained more circumspect.[21] In 1918, she resented having to prepare that fall's Moncure Conway lecture in religion "lest it should interfere with my real bear-work in term time" and added, "oh those bears I should have been dead long ago but for them, bless them." She idealized the "Czecho-Slovaks" and invoked the image of "John Huss leading those pathetic simple peasants," with whom her sympathies lay; she hoped they would not be "exploited" by the victorious Bolsheviks after the November revolution.[22] Before Gilbert Murray came to Newnham to speak on the League of Nations, which he vigorously supported, Jane warned him to "be pleasant about the Bears (God Bless them) & point out all their spiritualities—or from the Chair I will denounce you."[23]

Although Jane felt an instinctive kinship with Russia, she often took on causes simply to be a thorn in the side of the typical Cambridge intellectual. Her visit with a "real live Bolshevik bear" in 1920 caused a stir in Cambridge, and she enjoyed the controversy as much as the opportunity to speak Russian with a native. She described the encounter to Gilbert Murray.

> I loved him so, & to my great joy I understood every word he said (except about two) tho, as soon as he found out I was sympathetic, he poured it all out in a torrent & his accent (as I proudly detected) was not the purest Moscow. . . . I was afraid he might be some scoundrel of a Baltic Junker—playing on their simplicity [he had married the daughter of a College nurse]—so I asked him to tea to spy out the land—& lo! there was a creature who might have been Dostoevsky—pure Slav type—sunken cheeks fanatical dreamy eyes & talking only Russian & Persian. . . . People here say I ought to have turned him out of the College instantly. As if I was likely when I had just caught a real Bolshevik & a Bear at that—Russians do go to my head & make me feel how common we all are—but I wish they didn't have such confusing names. . . . My bear was courteous about England but he couldn't quite hide a certain contempt for our Government. He said very quietly "England does not understand; she believes what the papers say; she did hinder . . . & interfere before she can do no harm now, we are strong now."
>
> Oh dear what is the use of a League of Nations without Russia—

> without Germany—I get disheartened—don't you? & civilized women say they "wouldn't sit down to tea with a Bolshevik"—well thank goodness I never asked them.
>
> I asked him, when I said goodbye, how long it would be before one could safely (& economically) go to Russia, adding that I was old & wanted to see both old & new Russia before I died—& he looked me over meditatively & said "Yes you are an old woman, you could not travel privately in Russia now—you might starve, for money is no use—but perhaps you will come as our guest—you will be safe." A frog would have answered "You Mademoiselle are always young and a young woman can travel unprotected in Russia."

Both her disillusionment with the aftermath of World War I and her enchantment with Russia showed in this letter, and clearly Newnham disapproved of the latter. After leaving Cambridge for France, Jane met one of her closest Russian friends during a visit to Pontigny, gathering place for French intellectuals during the 1920s. D. S. Mirsky was a Russian artistocrat who fled after the revolution, and Jane wrote Gilbert from Pontigny that she had lost her "aged heart to a Bear-Prince—why did I not meet him 50 years ago when I could have clamoured to be his Princess."[24]

As much as Jane loved Russia, however, it could not dispel the effects of age and the changed environment of postwar Cambridge. Most of her closest acquaintances had died by 1920. The death in 1916 of Margaret Merrifield Verrall, her closest remaining friend outside the Ritualist circle, left Jane feeling desolate and forced her to consider what to do with her future. Just before Margaret's death, Jane mourned the fact that her "friends seem moving away fast & I begin to feel I ought to be moving on to—but it makes me also feel that one must see the friends left while one can." Shortly before Margaret died in July, Jane wrote to Gilbert Murray and noted "what an empty place Cambridge will seem with that house closed."[25]

Other changes followed the end of the war. Frances Darwin Cornford, who had been so happy in her marriage, nevertheless suffered another breakdown in 1917. Virginia Woolf wrote to her sister, Vanessa Bell, in 1919 that Frances had "a delusion that she must never be tired, and has now spent 2 years in going from rest cure to rest cure," refusing "to see either her husband or children." Frances returned in 1919 on her doctors' advice, but they feared "she may be incurable. . . . All Darwins incline that way." Jane probably sympathized more with Frances's breakdown than with her sudden conversion to Catholicism after the war. Even in 1914, Jane had described her as "very funny now-adays—full of reactions—excited over the empire—& the importance of people being simple & rather stupid & doing their duty at home & having a religion."

She had not then joined the church, and Jane hoped she would reconsider as "it would worry Frank [Darwin]—tho he would stand aside & yawn heavily." She hoped in vain, however, for Frances did ultimately join the Catholic church.[26]

Virginia Woolf described Jane's consternation over the wave of conversions sweeping Cambridge in the postwar years. In 1923, she visited Jane in Paris and wrote to Jacques Raverat, husband of Frances's cousin, Gwen, about their visit. She described Jane as a "gallant old lady, very white, hoary, and sublime in a lace mantilla." Jane praised Woolf, Vanessa Bell, and "perhaps Lytton Strachey" as "the only ones of the younger generation" she could "respect." When Woolf baited her by invoking the name of the Darwins, Jane accused them of being " 'the blackest traitors of them all! With that name!' she cried, 'that inheritance! That magnificent record in the past!' " Woolf's appeal that " 'surely . . . our Gwen is secure?' " elicited the complaint that "Gwen . . . goes to Church (if not mass, still Church) every Sunday of her life." Jane guessed that Gwen's "marriage . . . may have weakened her brain," as her husband was "unfortunately French." Woolf promised to break off her longstanding friendship if this proved true, but reneged when she learned that Gwen was "a militant atheist." On hearing this news later from Woolf, Jane "replied, a little inconsistently, 'Thank God.' "[27]

In 1923, in a letter to Gilbert, Jane praised Francis's *Origin of Comedy,* although she "couldn't help laughing at first" over his "Freudian dramatic hero." She grudgingly admitted that his marriage had not deterred him from his work as much as she had expected (or perhaps hoped), and was "specially glad" that the *Origin of Comedy* was "so fine because it would clearly never have been written but for Frances & her psychoanalysis complex." She commented further on the nature of his marriage.

> I have always been worried about her reactionary influence on him—(as is natural enough in the supplanted one!) and I still would rather he had not repentently taken his four children to the font, but I see now that he owes a fine bit of work to her & I am relieved—if only he does not get sodden with domestic bliss! he is a born father as well as husband & that sometimes makes me anxious—the downward path well worn by tribal feet is so easy—but as long as she gives him ideas & she is full of them—all is well.

With Frances's periodic breakdowns, however, her husband was unlikely to become "sodden with domestic bliss." Jane probably felt he had gotten what he deserved. The betrayal rankled still, but anger had given way to a resigned bemusement.[28]

The high point of Jane's last decade at Newnham was her relationship with Hope Mirrlees, which grew stronger during the last few years of

Jane's tenure there. Hope seemed the natural choice of companion when Jane went to Paris in 1922. Some of Jane's close friends blamed Hope for deliberately driving a wedge between them, but Jane herself seemed eager to relinquish the tight grip of those relationships. Gilbert Murray admitted to Jessie Stewart that he "never understood what happened at the end of [Jane's] life" and asked, "did Newnham refuse to continue her Fellowship, and was she greatly hurt? Or did she, for other reasons, determine to leave Cambridge and Greek and her old associations? And what part did Hope play in it?" With the Frances-Francis disaster finally behind her and now facing old age, Jane may merely have wanted to escape Cambridge and its painful associations. But she must have cringed at the gradual change within Cambridge, both in the university as a whole and in Newnham itself. The university, trying to return to normalcy after the war, settled into a renewed intellectual and political conservatism. It still refused to grant women degrees, and the violent protests over this issue occurred just before Jane's departure. The women's colleges, now filled with modern young women who placed more value on a spirited game of field hockey than on intellectual achievement, must have seemed alien to her. She became "depressed because of the queer atmosphere of Truth not mattering which some of the young seem to live in" and felt alienated from the place that had been her spiritual and intellectual home for twenty-five years. She told Gilbert Murray that she wanted to retire gracefully rather than remain at Newnham and be "booted out" at the end of another year. In her letter of thanks for Newnham's parting gift, she said that she was sorry to leave but that "a voice from within said 'Go' " for "a College to my mind is best ruled and taught by the young."[29]

In her "Reminiscences," Jane stated that she left Cambridge with "measureless regret," feeling she had "lived too long the strait Academic life with my mind intently focussed on the solution of a few problems" (RSL, 346). She "wanted before the end came to see things more freely and more widely, and, above all, to get the new focus of another civilization" (RSL, 346). In reality, she needed to get her personal past in order. Every aspect of her life had been challenged in the preceding decade, and she needed to distance herself from her past before she could discern its pattern. At the war's end, she mourned the destruction of the quiet atmosphere that encouraged lively discussion of her beloved archaic age. She wrote poignantly to Gilbert Murray, "shall we ever wrangle again over the horns of Poseidon or the hoofs of Cheiron—I fear not—these lie slain by the war."[30]

Her last significant work of the Cambridge years appeared in 1921. The *Epilegomena to the Study of Greek Religion* briefly recapitulated, without the heated emotion or grand view, the ideas expressed so passionately in *Themis* and the *Prolegomena.* It distilled her views in forty pages, and Gilbert Murray praised its brevity and clarity—qualities never before associated with Jane's work. She reaffirmed the primacy of the group but jettisoned all appeals to the superiority of emotion, calling instead for asceticism. Gilbert Murray called it "a wonderful achievement" that unified all her previous work and made it more intelligible and cohesive. He appreciated her invocation of asceticism, and said it was "almost the most important practical piece of teaching that the world needs nowadays." In this letter, one of only a handful from Gilbert to Jane that survive, he displayed a lack of understanding that helps explain the unbridgeable distance that ultimately lay between them. Jane's conversion to asceticism stemmed from defeat. It represented a graceful but saddening end to a love affair with the irrational. The *Epilegomena* is concise and straightforward but less recognizable as Jane's work precisely because it lacks the passion of her earlier studies. It stands as a monument, however, to how far she had traveled in a quarter-century. For all its disappointing slimness, it still retains a kernel of Ritualist theory and reiterates a belief, albeit a qualified and subdued one, in the power of the group. The *Epilegomena* also represents Jane's closing of the door on her life's work. Having paid final tribute to her theories, she could leave behind that aspect of her life and turn her attention to more intense personal issues.[31]

The *Epilegomena*'s greatest attraction lies in its incorporation of Freudian theory. It bears the imprint of *Totem and Taboo* as much as of Ritualist theory. Jane accepted Freud's description of the killing of the father by the band of brothers, although she attributed their motives to social rather than individual psychological origins. Somewhere between *Themis* and the *Epilegomena,* Jane read Freud and recognized in him a kindred spirit. Indeed, she considered *Totem and Taboo* one of the greatest literary influences on her work. More to the point, however, she intuitively appreciated his work and used it to strengthen her belief in her own theories. Although she was "at first . . . sickened" by "the ugliness of" Freudian theory, she "struggled on, feeling somehow that behind and below all this sexual mud was something big and real" (RSL, 342). *Totem and Taboo* gave her a "sense of release" because Freud seemed to her to understand the "mysteries of sin, of sanctity, of sacrament." She appreciated his contribution to the study of religion but shied away from consciously accepting his emphasis on sexuality. That she unconsciously accepted it, though, becomes clear in the *Epilegomena.*[32]

In spite of her formal denial of the sexual element that Freud placed at the heart of totemic thought, sexual themes run like an undercurrent through much of her work. Noting the obsession with names common to both primitives and neurotics, Freud pointed out that names are preceived as "an essential part of a man's personality" and that knowing or even uttering a name could give one person power over another. The overriding theme in *Totem and Taboo,* however, is the divisiveness of sex, which lies at the heart of all religious impulse, and the uneasiness of modern society in general. "Sexual desires do not unite men but divide them"—Jane expressed that belief almost verbatim. Although the Oedipal conflict that Freud placed at the center of humanity's relation to God is based on a male model, Jane's experience of her father's abandonment made her sympathetic to the inadequacy of the distant, rational projections that replaced group projections and left an emotional void that could never be filled. Although Jane did not read Freud until late in her life and rarely referred to his work, his gloomy vision of a life spent controlling dangerous and ever-threatening forces loomed behind her philosophy and struck a responsive chord. She recognized both the power of his vision and its intimate relation to how she perceived the world around her. His influence affected her on a personal level much more than on an intellectual one.[33]

Writing the *Epilegomena,* however, could not help her totally to reconcile herself to the past. This reconciliation proved much more difficult than she had dreamed. In fact, she fled to Paris in an effort to break resolutely from it. To make the job easier, she burned all of her correspondence before leaving Cambridge. Her friends and colleagues collected three hundred pounds to aid her retirement, and most of Cambridge's classical dons, with the notable exception of William Ridgeway, signed the subscription to demonstrate their gratitude and respect.[34] With nothing remaining to tie her to Newnham and Cambridge, she traveled to Paris with Hope Mirrlees and a few personal possessions to widen her focus in her last years. The past nevertheless went with her, and she used her years in Paris to help heal some of the wounds she had suffered over the course of her long life.

Hope proceeded to Paris first to find them a place to live. In April 1922, Jane wrote from Cambridge with reminders of things to do in preparation for the move. The steadily declining exchange rate meant that lodging would be very expensive and Jane favored "the new furnished flats" as the best bargain. She urged Hope to pay attention to the rate she had to pay for her "excess luggage" on the return trip and also to remember to "reserve [her] seat *well* beforehand as just after Easter is a full time." Recognizing the magnitude of Hope's responsibilities, Jane added, "you poor beast—what a lot of things you have to think of. I wish I was by your side holding your small cold fur-paw & I wish there wasn't such a thing as money!" Nevertheless, in October 1922, they both left for Paris and stayed for several weeks in hotels. Just when Jane despaired of finding a suitable, more permanent home, Alys Russell persuaded the American University Women's Club to take them in.[35]

Jane described their new abode to Mary Murray in December 1922.

> This club is an interesting place & has made me revise many anti-American prejudices—I was really at wits' end how to live as our possession of three cases of books made the ordinary hotel keeper look on us almost as criminals. . . . I was afraid at one point we should have to come back to spacious England—space to move and an occasional wash are the only luxuries I ask for—Then—thanks to Alys Russell's kindness this hospitable place took us in—& we are in veritable clover—not to say almost sinful luxury—breakfast in your room . . . hot baths all day long if you like, kind (touched by America) & more than that a personal care & kindness that goes to one's heart. Best of all they have given me—*free—as a present* a big studio sitting room—where I can breathe & work & even think if the delights of Paris would leave me a free moment.

Her exposure to Americans did more than make her revise her prejudices. She wrote to Gilbert Murray that because of her stay among American women, she had come to see that her "manners to servants (which I always thought admirable!) are those of the superior slave driver." She liked "their horribly disgustingly opulent student type . . . the clothes these young women wear . . . the number & splendour of them simply abash me." Overall, she judged the American students "the handsomest, best-grown, best-groomed greediest most empty headed crew I ever beheld," and vowed to "try to get at what they think of us." In 1925, Jessie Stewart asked Jane's advice on sending her daughter, Jean, to Paris to study. Jane did not favor the plan, especially if Jean had to stay at the American club, because although "the people are kindness itself," they were "intellectually just no-where."[36]

Despite Jane's sharp criticism of her American benefactors and complaints about "the cold & damp that almost rivals Cambridge," these years proved happy ones. A very subdued courtship with D. S. Mirsky, the exiled Russian aristocrat, amused her in a way unthinkable twenty years earlier. Her "faithful and princely flirt" visited her in the Paris years, and they sometimes traveled together to Pontigny for the "entretiens" hosted by Charles Desjardins. These gatherings, held in August, were devoted to intellectual consideration of various questions. Jane assured Prince Mirsky he would receive a cordial welcome at Pontigny, as "M. Desjardins . . . is very anxious to get intellectual Russians." She did not immediately take to Desjardins but revised her opinion after several meetings.[37] In 1923, she wrote to Jessie Stewart that "the more I see of him the better I like him & I understand now that what put me off at first was a mere trick of manner." She felt especially attracted by his eyes, which were "like a good child's."[38] By the time of her visit to Pontigny in August 1924, however, the discussions had become "horribly metaphysical," and she attended chiefly for the "study they present of French mentality."[39] It is difficult to imagine Jane in this setting. Mealtimes seem to have resembled High Table at Newnham, but now Jane found herself surrounded by eminent figures in literature and philosophy rather than by adoring students focusing their attention on her. Furthermore, discussion of abstract issues outside of her field seem never to have appealed to Jane, which would account for her impatience with the group's "metaphysical" conversation.

In May 1925, Jane wrote to Prince Mirsky that "our delightful Club at last 'boots us out' & we go back to London in September to hunt for a flat." She felt "sad to leave Paris but my roots are deep in England." Before leaving Paris, however, Jane wrote her autobiography and revealed how far she had traveled in these few years, beginning her reconciliation with the painful events of the past.[40]

Like most autobiographies, Jane designed hers to conceal as much as she told, but some of her remarks shed new light on questions that plagued her throughout her life. This is not to say that Jane was happy. At best she reached a resigned peace with the past, which under the circumstances could be reckoned a triumphant achievement. She never forgave her father, Francis Cornford, or the world in general for betraying her love and faith, but she did ultimately embrace her Yorkshire roots and accept the possibility that one could fall in love again even after great disappointment. Moreover, she was able to balance the life of the individual against the life of the race. In so doing, she displayed what Hope called "an Olympian calm which seemed almost cold in its detachment," but which in reality represented reflective acceptance of her past.[41] Jane would have found this description ironic but fitting: reaching maturity, whether in the individual or in the group, meant replacing the tumultuous chaos of the emotional life with the more distant and less threatening order of the intellectual life.

Although Jane struggled always against provincialism, she confessed in her "Reminiscences" that despite her dislike of "the Empire" and "nearly all forms of patriotism," she was "intensely proud of being a Yorkshire woman" (RSL, 313). After a lifetime spent striving to assimilate into London and Cambridge culture, she recognized that her carefully designed persona hid a conservative and conventional core. She likened herself, "with all reverence," to George Eliot's Aunt Glegg: "I wear before the world a mask of bland cosmopolitan courtesy and culture, I am advanced in my views, eager to be in touch with all modern movements, but beneath all that lies Aunt Glegg, rigidly, irrationally conservative, fibrous with prejudice, deep-rooted in her native soil" (RSL, 313). She excused Yorkshire tendencies to be "gruff in manner, harsh and unsympathetic in soul" by examples from her own experience. Yorkshire people might be accused of exclusivity, but Jane had "heard a Yorkshire lady say 'there are some quite decent people in Scotland" (RSL, 313). She invoked the memory of a Yorkshire landlady who once gave her special treatment on the basis of an old acquaintance with Charles Harrison. During a visit to a Yorkshire inn, Jane's unnamed companion had left her alone for a day or two, and

> the landlady looked in on me in the morning, bearing a huge dead duck. "Yer'll maybe be lawnly wi'out Missie, happen yer'd fancy a duck fer yer dinner." I did, and I ate two huge slices of its fat breast with unlimited savoury trimmings. She looked in to mark my progress. "Aye, yer eat but poorly, yer've been living maybe wi' them Southerners." (RSL, 313)

At the end of her life she could tell this story lovingly, for she had learned to understand, if not share, the Yorkshire suspicion of "Southerners" and to appreciate northern virtues.

Jane's special consideration for her closest friends and her intense attachments to people had their roots in Yorkshire culture. As a result of its antithetical relationship to the South, Yorkshire was in a sense a closed circle and Yorkshire folk protected those within it. Rather than judging by appearance or individual actions, the typical Yorkshire person took in the whole picture before liking or disliking anyone. "Your particular deeds are of as little significance to him as your particular words: it is you, the whole of you, you 'in a loomp,' as he would say, that the Yorkshireman wisely reckons with" (RSL, 314). That meant judging outsiders on the basis of a purely intuitive perception, a feat at which Jane was particularly adept. Moreover, Yorkshire people shared with Jane's Russians a loathing of pretentiousness.

> I have heard one Russian charge another with pretentiousness; if it existed at all it was so infinitesimal as to be invisible to the naked English eye. Just so with the Yorkshireman. You may break every commandment of the Decalogue—he is easy enough, as long as you are a fairly good fellow he will pardon you—but try to show off, to impress him in any way, and you are done. (RSL, 314)

Despite her lifelong attempts to assimilate into bourgeois culture, then, she remained impatient with its trappings. The Yorkshire ethos seemed closer to the emotional, intuitive life she still valued.

Jane recognized the contradiction between her personal views and her work, although it never seemed to bother her. "By nature, I am sure, I am not an archaeologist—still less an anthropologist," she wrote, for "the 'beastly devices of the heathen' weary and disgust me" (RSL, 343). But her search for ritual had led her to study the very people whose actions disturbed her. She carried her prejudices over into her personal life, as her account of a visit with Victoria de Bunsen's family in 1902 illustrates. She was absorbed in the *Prolegomena* then, and the family invited her to meet some African visitors. Jane wrote to Gilbert Murray that "the principal guests (after ME) are two converted Blacks . . . from Uganda."

I believe I have read somewhere that you don't allow any crude statements about colour—but they really *are* blacker than any hat & I simply adore them. The blackest is called *Apolo* Kagwa & my hostess fearing I might suffer slipped a tract into my hand on my arrival which informs me that he took this name at his baptism "not after the heathen deity but from the Scripture name Apollos." They have lovely manners; they think it indelicate to talk at dinner & one of them when (not unreasonably) bored by the converse of his host curled himself up on the drawing room sofa & went softly to sleep.

She confessed later to Hope Mirrlees that she "had never met a foreigner who seemed to her like a real person." Intellectually Jane roamed far and wide, but her inner self remained conservative.[42]

In addition to coming to terms with her provincial heritage, Jane addressed the question of romantic disappointments and admitted the undeniable power of love in the emotional life. One could "go on loving, only your love, instead of a burning, fiery furnace, is the mellow glow of an autumn sun" (RSL, 346). She could even envisage "falling in love, and for the same foolish reasons—the tone of a voice, the glint of a strangely set eye—only you fall so gently." (RSL, 346). Best of all, "in old age you may even show a man that you like to be with him without his wanting to marry you or thinking you want to marry him" (RSL, 346). Once she had banished the specter of sexuality, Jane could finally relate more freely and openly to her close male friends.

Perhaps her sense of control triumphed at the end and enabled her to internalize her own explanation of the failures so completely that she came to believe it herself. It may also be that she simply defended herself extraordinarily well against overwhelming and painful memories. Jane, however, also seems to have reached a tentative understanding of her past that, despite its fragility, allowed her to begin to reconcile herself to these events. The betrayals still hurt, but as she grew older she stepped back from them and examined their pattern. She had begun this process earlier, in the essay "Crabbed Age and Youth" (1914), where she commented on youth's tendency to see itself at the center of the universe.

Humbled by life it learns that it is no centre of life at all; at most it is one of the myriads of spokes in the great wheel. In Old Age the speck, the individual life, passes out on the other side, no longer burning and yet not quite consumed. In Old Age we look back on the great wheel; we can see it a little because, at least partially, we are outside of it. . . . Occasionally nowadays I get glimpses of what that vision might be. I

> get my head for a moment out of the blazing, blinding, torturing wheel; the vision of the thing behind me and without me obscurely breaks. It looks strange, almost portentous, yet comforting; but that vision is incommunicable.[43]

Through the years Jane drifted further away from the center of the wheel, as she drifted away from the circles surrounding her, and she obtained a clearer vision of what lay beyond. She had been defeated, it is true, but accepted the defeat so gracefully she turned it into a reconciliation.

Finally, at the end of her life Jane perceived that neither individualism nor collectivism alone could be the best way to live in the world. As she grew older she internalized Bergson's concept of life as change and no longer felt threatened by the gap between youth and age. She began to see the relationship of the individual to the group, and of the young to the old. Youth's casual attitude toward her generation made her "sometimes sigh for a little 'deportment,' " but she admitted that "we of a past generation have no more right to impose our manners than we do our morals" (RSL, 318). Each generation contributes to the general fund of knowledge, and "as Mr. Sheppard observed: 'When the fathers think the Age of Reason is achieved, the sons may be trusted, if they are of good stock, to see that it is still far off' " (RSL, 319). She could finally relinquish her place in the circle's center to a new generation and make a quiet and dignified exit from a lively stage.

Jane described the evolution of her attitudes toward death and old age in her closing pages. In youth, "personal immortality seemed . . . axiomatic" and the "mere thought of Death" made her "furious" (RSL, 344). In old age, however, death became merely "a negation of life, a closing, a last and necessary chord" (RSL, 344). Although contemporary philosophy implied that the individual survived only through the race and that therefore "the unmarried and the childless cut themselves loose from racial immortality," Jane refused to subscribe to this belief which denied the importance of her own life (RSL, 344). Her communally lived life, a life spent surrounded by colleagues with similar interests, constituted a contribution of its own. Her scholarly works served as her children and her insurance of a place in the life of the race. Jane justified her lifelong journey and then could face the return to London with equanimity.

In March 1926, she and Hope came back to London to look for a flat, finally settling into Mecklenburgh Street in April. Her last two years were marked by periods of illness that may have blinded her to the resentment many of her old friends felt over Hope's protectiveness. Jane gradually lost interest in the Orphic studies to which she had returned late in her life through an attempt to find a connection between Orphic mysticism and Dante's *Divine Comedy.* Hope claimed that Jane "relaxed her hold on life when the Dante-Orphic scheme proved a *cul-de-*

sac. . . . She was very tired, she had a deep misgiving that her vital power was not equal to the understanding." She also abandoned her study of language. Hope asserted that she gave it up because "language was not to her, never could be Life. . . . it was either a means to the mysterious end she never reached; or else . . . a form of art, as she understood the function of art, i.e., and escape from Life." Hope failed to perceive that Jane let go of her intellectual work because she saw at the end that life's most fundamental impulses were incomprehensible mysteries best left unsolved. Rather than trying to escape from life, she glimpsed its deepest depths. It seems as if she gave up not out of frustration but rather out of comprehension of the sheer inexplicability of things.[44]

Jane's "Reminiscences" reveal her surrender to life's incomprehensibility and her acceptance of the world's tenuous grip on civilization. Reflecting on her brush with Chemistry at Cheltenham, she asserted that she was more grateful for the opportunity to study it than for anything else she learned there.

> You watch an experiment, someone pours some hydrosulphuric acid . . . on some loaf sugar, and in a moment the quiet white sugar is a seething black volcano. Things are never the same to you again. You know they *are* not what they seem; you picture hidden terrific forces, you can even imagine that the whole solid earth is only such forces held in momentous check. (RSL, 324)

At the end of her life, she envisioned a world delicately balanced between reason and emotion, between order and chaos. She finally understood that this balance was incomprehensible and stopped trying to make sense of it.

Gilbert Murray complained to Jessie Stewart that Hope "made a point of weaning Jane from her old friends" and blamed her influence for Jane's destruction of her letters when she left Cambridge. Victoria de Bunsen painted an even more sinister picture of Hope's control. Victoria visited the flat in Mecklenburgh Street where "Hope was of course *most* ungracious" and refused to allow Victoria to see Jane because of her illness. Hope immediately told Jane that Victoria had called, and Jane "said she *must* see me, so Hope had to run after me into the street." Despite having both Hope and a nurse to care for her, Jane looked unwashed and told Victoria " '*all* the life's gone out of me.' " Victoria suspected Hope wanted "to keep everybody away & said she could *not* write to Jane's friends or even answer the phone." Even Victoria admitted, however, that Hope was "very anxious & *very* devoted." Although Jane's friends considered Hope disagreeable, they may have overestimated her power. Jane's flight from Cambridge had eased an intensely personal need to sort out her complex life, and she could do so only by extricating herself from the bonds that had tied her so intimately to her friends for decades. After she returned to London, she fell ill and probably felt less inclined to encourage visitors.[45]

Jane's final letter to Gilbert Murray three months before her death revealed a spirit similar to that of the old days. They had not corresponded so regularly in the last few years, but she described a bout of sickness with some of the old fire. She had been gravely ill and remained terribly weak.

> Since I last saw you I have been through many strange & terrible things. Down by the sea at Camber I was smitten with phlebitis, they got me back to London in an ambulance. Think of a Ker in an ambulance! Wasn't it grand! Then at the end of August your Ker went right down to the gates of Hades & there she stayed fluttering to & fro, & it seemed that the gates must clang behind her. But after many long weary weeks with the help of two doctors, two nurses & a lusty masseur of Herculean build, the Younger Erinys [Hope] dragged her reluctant back to the upper air. And here I am now in bed, just able to put two feet to the ground if heraldically supported, but to think of standing alone or walking is like some wild dream.
>
> And here comes your birthday book to tell me there are pleasant things in the world. I shall not be able to read it for a long time properly, but I cut a page here & there & catch sight of Ther-like things which fill my inner spirit with laughter & delight.[46]

Three months later, on April 15, 1928, Jane died of leukemia.

Lytton Strachey wrote to Roger Fry just after Jane's death and offered his insights into her character. "She was such a charming rare person," he wrote, "very affectionate and appreciative, very grand, and very amusing. Her humour was unique. . . . What a wretched waste it seems that all that richness of experience and personality should be completely abolished!" He concluded by asking, "why, one wonders, shouldn't it have gone on and on?—Well! there will never be anyone at all like her again."[47]

Virginia Woolf encountered Hope Mirrlees just after Jane's death and visited the flat immediately. Her description of Jane in death is brief but deeply moving, and perhaps warrants the last word as it captures the spirit of her tumultuous life. "She lay dead outside the graveyard," Woolf recorded in her diary, "in that back room where we saw her lately raised on her pillows, like a very old person, whom life has tossed up, & left; exalted, satisfied, exhausted."[48] Looking back on the course of her seventy-eight years, Jane, I suspect, would have been content with that judgment.

APPENDIX

RECONSTRUCTING A LIFE: HOPE MIRRLEES, JESSIE STEWART, AND THE PROBLEM OF BIOGRAPHY

It is useless anyone writing about Jane unless (1) they know what she was like, & (2) as Cromwell said, "love what they know."
—*Gilbert Murray to Jessie Stewart, 1932*

Never say you know the last word about any human heart.
—*Henry James, "Louisa Tallant"*

THIRTY YEARS passed between Jane Harrison's death and the first attempt at a biographical study of her. Her most intimate friends discussed the format such a study should take and argued over who should write it. Ultimately, the battle pitted Jane's two spiritual daughters, Hope Mirrlees and Jessie Stewart, against each other. Their correspondence during this period, especially concerning Jessie's *Portrait,* reveals a great deal about their relationship to Jane and to each other, as well as about the nature of biography.

Jane's life had a ripple effect on Hope and Jessie. Her influence flowed in concentric circles through their lives, barely creating a stir on the surface but profoundly affecting them both. Jessie herself attributed "any smoothness or unity" in her *Portrait* to "30 years brooding over JEH." She and Hope unconsciously fought over Jane's affections in a battle that, in retrospect, suspiciously resembles sibling rivalry. Hope protected Jane's memory so fiercely that, in the end, she could not bear the thought of examining her inner life. An odd scrap of paper in Hope's notes contains an enigmatic message.

Private—*to be burnt*
One episode the key—JEH's
life—indiscreet to mention—
wd cripple her work—She should
have hated it published.

The message probably referred to the Francis-Frances affair. When pressed on the biography issue by Jessie, Hope admitted that "indeed, the problem of what to say & what to leave out is a very difficult one. And my inability to solve it is one of my principal reasons for wishing to abdicate." She sensed the enormous risk in confronting the past: "Jane was extremely reserved about her own past. She had weathered a great many storms, & I think wanted them to be forgotten—in fact, I feel almost certain that she did. And yet, if one omits them, the life looses [*sic*] what she would have called its 'pattern.' " Although, to her credit, Hope recognized the significance of many events in Jane's life, she also lacked the courage to face them.[1]

Gilbert Murray, as well as Hope, advised against revealing too much about Jane's life, and Hope suggested possible alternatives. She thought that the Woolfs' Hogarth Press might publish Jane's "Reminiscences" with Gilbert Murray's brief Newnham College memorial lecture as a preface. She also favored a study of Jane's work over a biography. She thought no one "more suited" to write such an appraisal than A. B. Cook and suggested that the *Journal of Hellenic Studies* might publish it along with a bibliography. Gilbert Murray's disapproval of a biography rested on the grounds that "there are too many biographies" and that "they imply a sort of attempt to make eternal a thing that is really transient, like turning Jane's 'Year Demon' into an Olympian."[2]

While Jessie Stewart toyed with the idea of writing the biography herself, she and Hope talked with others interested in writing about Jane. Hope consistently rejected all prospective biographers as not sufficiently reverential. She feared that a Mr. Wilkins "may only be vaguely interested in that circle of scholars of which [Jane] was the center & may have neither time nor inclination for writing about her." She showed even less enthusiasm for a certain Lady Trudy Bliss, stating, "I should have to know a great deal about her before allowing her to have a finger in the pie." Moreover, she expected Lady Bliss to live up to exacting standards. "Even though she may be quite a clever writer (I know nothing about her), she would have to be many other things as well (e.g., a model of refinement and discretion) to be working on collaborating in this most delicate task."[3]

While the three-cornered debate continued, Jessie Stewart sat quietly in Cambridge pondering the best way to approach Jane's life. She eventually decided on publishing some of Jane's letters to Gilbert Murray, filling in the gaps with her own commentary. That meant ignoring large chunks of Jane's life and focusing on her career at Newnham and her collaboration with Gilbert. Meanwhile, Hope vacillated between wanting to write Jane's biography and deriding any such attempt. She collected information from many of Jane's friends by writing to them, but when it came time to write the book, she dissociated herself from biographers and refused to try her own hand. Many of Jane's friends cooperated with Jessie on her *Portrait,* but Hope did not.

When the *Portrait* finally appeared in 1959, though, Hope's protectiveness reached its zenith. She had abdicated all responsibility for evaluating Jane's life and work, but she reacted bitterly to what she perceived as Jessie's desecration of Jane's memory. She began her letter on receipt of the *Portrait* innocuously enough, but her criticisms quickly grew heated.

> In two of the extracts that you cite there are touches that mar the portrait physically i.e. Bunny Garnett's description of her manner as *rough* & Virginia Woolf's delusion that she *stooped.* Her manners were noted for their gravity & her straight back was her pride. . . .
>
> And surely you have got the rhythm wrong of Virginia's sentence. I am quoting from memory but I think it runs like this: "And there by the grave of Cromwell's daughter, where Shelley used to walk, we kissed for Jane's death. . . ."
>
> But Oh Jessie how *could* you have put in some of the parts of the "Francis

& Frances" chapter? They were *certainly* not in the version that you showed me. I am *horribly* distressed that this has been published. Jane would simply have *loathed* it. She was almost morbidly reserved about her past. Moreover it gives an utterly wrong impression of her. She was obviously *not* her real self at that time, but on the verge of a nervous breakdown. She was normally so beautifully just & reasonable & had such splendid self-control. After all I ought to know, seeing that I lived with her off & on for 15 years. It was strictly from her that I learned the importance of justice & reason in the conduct of life, & she despised & detested as the worst form of selfishness any lack of self-control in human relationships. Oh if *only* it could be deleted![4]

Hope's remarkable outburst conveyed much more than despair at Jessie's revelations. She was taunting Jessie with her mention of the years she had lived with Jane, clearly, although perhaps unconsciously, implying that she had been the favored daughter.

Jessie responded reasonably to Hope's accusations. She reminded Hope that the Francis-Frances affair had indeed appeared in the earlier manuscript version. Jessie defended her decision to discuss it by pointing out that Frances Cornford and Gilbert Murray agreed it should be included, and asserted that "it was very important, for understanding Jane's mystic letters & much of 'Alpha-Omega.' " She and Hope both understood that life and work were intricately interwoven, but unlike Hope, Jessie possessed sufficient distance to examine the connections. Later, she wrote to Hope that "I shan't know till I stand before the Judgment Seat whether I did right or wrong!" But even Jessie remained reticent despite her distance, admitting that "there are many things in the letters & in my own experience which a biographer might relish, but which I would not like put in."[5]

Jane's destruction of her letters hampers a full understanding of her life. Jessie faced this problem in her *Portrait.* Gilbert Murray accused Hope of having "a good deal to do" with Jane's decision to destroy her letters and of "weaning Jane from her old friends." Jane's destruction of his letters obviously hurt him, and he asked Jessie to alter her explanation of their destruction in her manuscript. He felt her statement "that Jane burnt my letters" made it look "as if there had been some quarrel between us, which there never was." He asked her to say merely that "they 'were burnt.' " Possibly Hope did encourage Jane to destroy the letters, but I think it more likely that Jane chose that course herself. She was seventy-two when she left Cambridge, bitter and disillusioned. Rather than covering her tracks, she wanted, I think, merely to escape from a painful past. Scraps of paper with familiar handwriting, invoking bittersweet memories, probably seemed better consigned to the fire. The very fact of her reconciliation with her past, played out in Paris in Hope's company, indicated that Jane controlled her own emotions. If Hope had wielded such enormous power, she could have persuaded Jane to live out her life abroad. But having come to grips with her past, Jane insisted on returning home.[6]

Even with the richest resources, however, the full story ultimately remains a mystery. Biographers, like all historians, display selective vision when collecting evidence. Identification and sympathy are difficult to conceal but to some degree essential. Above all one must avoid the temptation of thinking that all can be explained. There is something magical about inexplicable things, as Jane well knew, and this magical quality makes them intriguing and powerful. The fragility and complexity of the individual life can never be fully understood. Perhaps that is for the best.

NOTES

PREFACE

1 Recent works analyze this trend. See Susan N. G. Geiger, "Women's Life Histories: Method and Content," *Signs* 11, no. 2 (Winter 1986): 334–51; Elizabeth Kamarck Minnich, "Friendship between Women: The Act of Feminist Biography," *Feminist Studies* 11, no. 2 (Summer 1985): 287–306; and Carol Ascher, Louise DeSalvo, and Sara Ruddick, eds., *Between Women* (Boston: Beacon Press, 1984).

2 Jessie Stewart, *Jane Ellen Harrison: A Portrait from Letters* (London: Merlin Press, 1959), pp. 200–01.

3 Robert Allen Ackerman, *The Cambridge Group and the Origins of Myth Criticism* (Ann Arbor, Mich.: University Microfilms International, 1969); idem, "Some Letters of the Cambridge Ritualists," *Greek, Roman and Byzantine Studies* 12 (Spring 1971): 113–36; idem, "Jane Ellen Harrison: The Early Work," ibid. 13 (Summer 1972): 209–30.

4 Harry Payne, "Modernizing the Ancients: The Reconstruction of Ritual Drama 1870–1920," *Proceedings of the American Philosophical Society* 122, no. 3 (June 9, 1978): 182–92. For a look at the larger implications of the ritual theory, see his "The Ritual Question and Modernizing Society, 1800–1945—A Schema for a History," *Historical Reflections* 11, no. 3 (Fall 1984): 403–32.

5 Walter Burkert, *Structure and History in Greek Mythology and Ritual* (Berkeley and Los Angeles: University of California Press, 1979); idem, *Homo Necans*, trans. Peter Bing (Berkeley and Los Angeles: University of California Press, 1983); idem, *Greek Religion*, trans. John Raffan (Cambridge: Harvard University Press, 1985; originally published Stuttgart: Verlag W. Kohlhammer, 1977).

6 Martha Vicinus, *Independent Women* (Chicago: University of Chicago Press, 1985), chap. 4.

7 JH to GM, 1908, Box 6, JEH.

8 Recently, Carl Degler has urged historians to pay more attention to psychological factors in their study of the past. See Carl N. Degler, "Should Historians Be Skeptical about Using Psychological Methods?" *Chronicle of Higher Education* 33, no. 37 (May 27, 1987): 80. Peter Loewenberg, in *Decoding the Past: The Psychological Approach* (Berkeley and Los Angeles: University of California Press, 1969), gives a lengthy and eloquent defense of the psychohistorical method.

9 J. H. Plumb, Introduction to *Studies in Social History: A Tribute to G. M. Trevelyan*, ed. J. H. Plumb (London: Longmans, Green & Co., 1955), p. xiii.

10 E. M. Butler, *The Tyranny of Greece over Germany* (Cambridge: Cambridge University Press, 1935), p. 8.

PROLOGUE

1 Virginia Woolf, *A Room of One's Own* (New York: Harcourt, Brace & World, 1929), p. 17.
2 H. Stuart Hughes, *Consciousness and Society: The Reorientation of European Social Thought 1890–1930* (New York: Knopf, 1961).
3 Robert Ackerman, "Frazer on Myth and Ritual," *Journal of the History of Ideas* 36 (1975): 115–34.
4 JH to GM, undated, Box 6, JEH.
5 Perhaps Jane Harrison and James Frazer did not agree on many things, but Stanley Edgar Hyman places them together in a Hebrew class in Cambridge (Stanley Edgar Hyman, *The Tangled Bank: Darwin, Marx, Frazer and Freud as Imaginative Thinkers* [New York: Atheneum, 1962], p. 190).
6 Frank Turner, *The Greek Heritage in Victorian Britain* (New Haven: Yale University Press, 1981) gives a fine analysis of Victorian classicists' perceptions of the ancient world.
7 Ibid., p. 8.

CHAPTER 1

1 *Dictionary of National Biography*, s.v. "Harrison, Jane Ellen," by Francis M. Cornford.
2 Hope Mirrlees, Notebook, "Marion Harrison," Box 15, JEH. Unless otherwise noted, Mirrlees's material is housed in this collection.
3 Ibid.
4 Stewart, *Portrait*, p. 5.
5 Mirrlees, Notebook, "Marion Harrison."
6 Ibid., "Various Tid-bits from My Own Memories."
7 Ibid., "Marion Harrison."
8 JH to D. S. Mirsky, May 6, 1926, Box 8, JEH. Unless otherwise noted, all of Jane's correspondence is housed in this collection. For an excellent analysis of the loss of the mother, see Nancy Anderson, "No Angel in the House: The Psychological Effects of Maternal Death," *Psychohistory Review* 11, no. 1:20–46.
9 Mirrlees, Notebook, "Lucy (Booty)."
10 Ibid. See also RSL, pp. 317–20.
11 Mirrlees, Notebook, "Lucy (Booty)."
12 Jane Ellen Harrison, "Crabbed Age and Youth," in *Alpha and Omega* (London: Sidgwick & Jackson, 1915; reprint. New York: AMS Press, 1973), pp. 11–12; hereafter cited as *A&O*.
13 Mirrlees, Notebook, "Mrs. Charles Mitchell."
14 Ibid., "Marion Harrison."
15 Deborah Gorham, *The Victorian Girl and the Feminine Ideal* (Bloomington: Indiana University Press, 1982), p. 201. See also M. Jeanne Peterson, "The Victorian Governess: Status Incongruity in Family and Society," in *Suffer*

and Be Still: Women in the Victorian Age, ed. Martha Vicinus (Bloomington: Indiana University Press, 1972), pp. 3–19.

16 Mirrlees, Notebook, "Marion Harrison"; Ibid., "Various Tid-bits"; Hilda Lane to Mirrlees, undated, Box 9.

17 Mirrlees, Notebook, "Lucy (Booty)."

18 Ibid., "Marion Harrison."

19 Hope Mirrlees, "Fragments of a Draft Biography," Box 15.

20 Mirrlees, Notebook, "Lucy (Booty)."

21 Ibid. Nevertheless, Charles Harrison managed to leave an estate of more than thirty thousand pounds, largely in property and railroad stock. Most of it went to his widow and his son, Herbert. The three daughters of the first marriage inherited a mere hundred pounds each, as they were already "provided for." The remaining daughters each received a percentage of Charles's railroad stock.

22 Ibid.

23 Ibid., "Marion Harrison."

24 Mirrlees, "Draft Biography."

25 Charles Harrison objected to a substitute clergyman in his Yorkshire parish because "he brought with him leaflets and new hymn-books and new hassocks. . . . He even put a little cross on the Communion Table, but this my father with his own hands swiftly and silently removed" (RSL, 314).

26 Mirrlees, Notebook, "Lucy (Booty)."

27 For a discussion of the rise of Evangelicalism in nineteenth-century Britain, see Ian Bradley, *The Call to Seriousness: The Evangelical Impact on the Victorians* (New York: Macmillan Publishing Co., 1976); and Richard Carwardine, *Transatlantic Revivalism: Popular Evangelicalism in Britain and America, 1790–1865* (Westport, Conn.: Greenwood Press, 1978), especially pp. 85–94. On Evangelical attitudes toward the family, see Elizabeth Jay, *The Religion of the Heart: Anglican Evangelicalism and the Nineteenth-Century Novel* (Oxford: Oxford University Press, 1979). John Clive, in *Macaulay: The Shaping of the Historian* (New York: Alfred A. Knopf, 1973), presents a fascinating study of the Evangelical influence on the formation of intellect. Edmund Gosse, in *Father and Son* (New York: C. Scribner's Sons, 1907), gives an autobiographical account of the same phenomenon. Samuel Butler, in *The Way of All Flesh*, treats it in novel form.

28 Helene Deutsch, *The Psychology of Women: A Psychoanalytic Interpretation* (New York: Greene & Stratton, 1945), p. 439; hereafter cited in the text. I rely on Deutsch partly because she is the only neo-Freudian to draw attention to stepmothers. Her work, however, also conveys a sense of hopelessness about family and interpersonal relationships that more fully illuminates them. Karen Horney, Anna Freud, and the older Melanie Klein emphasized the possibilities of breaking out of old molds. More than any of her colleagues, Deutsch remained Freud's "good daughter" by retaining his gloomy vision of the world. Deutsch also recognized female anger, which constitutes one of her most important contributions to the psychoanalytic interpretation of female personality. Despite her misogyny, or perhaps because of it, Deutsch's work remains critical to an understanding of female psychology. See also Karen Horney, *Feminine Psychology*, ed. Harold Kelmar (New York:

W. W. Norton & Co., 1967); Anna Freud, *The Ego and the Mechanisms of Defense* (London: Hogarth Press, 1937); and Janine Chassaguet-Smirgel, "Feminine Guilt and the Oedipus Complex," in *Female Sexuality: New Psychoanalytic Views,* ed. Janine Chassaguet-Smirgel (Ann Arbor: University of Michigan Press, 1970). Bruno Bettelheim explores the image of the wicked stepmother in *The Uses of Enchantment* (New York: Alfred A. Knopf, 1977), pp. 66–73. For a brief discussion of the emotional state of widowers in the nineteenth century, see Peter Gay, *Education of the Senses,* vol. 1, *The Bourgeois Experience* (New York and Oxford: Oxford University Press, 1984), pp. 236–37.

29 Jane Ellen Harrison, "Homo Sum," in *A&O,* pp. 95–97.

30 JH to MM, August 28, 1909, #395, Box 6.

31 Ibid.; JH to MM, September 17, 1912, #33, Box 8.

32 Cf. Gay, *Education of the Senses,* pp. 71–225. See also the lively debate in many of the reviews of his first volume: David Cannadine in the *New York Review of Books* 31, no. 19 (February 2, 1984), and Neil McKendrick in the *New York Times Book Review,* January 8, 1984, p. 1. Paul Robinson reviewed volume 2, *The Tender Passion* (New York and Oxford: Oxford University Press, 1986), in the *New York Times Book Review,* March 16, 1986, p. 6. Reviewers generally agreed that although Gay's work revealed the experience of a select group, it is difficult to extrapolate from that experience to make judgments about an entire culture.

33 Gorham, *The Victorian Girl,* p. 67. Jonathan Gathorne-Hardy explores the issue of self-control in *The Rise and Fall of the British Nanny* (New York: Dial Press, 1973). He attributes the efficiency of British civil servants in India to their nannies, who instilled in them an almost pathological need for order. He claims that nannies vented their frustrations on their charges as a means of maintaining their sense of self-worth in what was often a demeaning line of work. For a more sinister interpretation of the emphasis on self-control, especially in women, see Peter Cominos, "Innocent Femina Sensualis in Unconscious Conflict," in *Suffer and Be Still,* ed. Vicinus, pp. 155–72.

34 HM to JS, June 26, 1959, Box 14, JEH.

35 Mirrlees, Notebook, Commentary with no heading.

36 Ibid., "Various Tid-bits."

37 Ibid., "Lucy (Booty)."

38 "Fortunately [Charles Harrison] showed appreciation of his exceptional daughter and indulged her passion for education" (Stewart, *Portrait,* p. 5). Robert Ackerman claims that "after some struggle on [Jane's] part, her exceptional gifts caused her to be sent to school" (Ackerman, "The Early Work," p. 210). Both authors ignore the curate episode and, more important, Charles Harrison's promise to his first wife that he would not send her daughters away to school.

39 Mary Paley Marshall, *What I Remember* (Cambridge: Cambridge University Press, 1947), pp. 6–7. Many late Victorian and Edwardian women experienced various degrees of frustration with their early education. They suffered from the relentless boredom that useless lessons inspired. Many also shared Jane's tendency toward psychosomatically induced illness. A few, such as Florence Nightingale, verged on nervous breakdown because of their

stultifying lives. For comparisons, see Beatrice Webb, *The Diary of Beatrice Webb*, ed. Norman MacKenzie and Jeanne MacKenzie (Cambridge: Harvard University Press, 1982), especially vol. 1; Beatrice Webb, *My Apprenticeship* (London: Longmans, Green & Co., n.d.), especially chaps. 1 and 2; Dora Russell, *The Tamarisk Tree: My Quest for Liberty and Love* (New York: G. P. Putnam's Sons, 1975); and Allen F. Davis, *American Heroine: The Life and Legend of Jane Addams* (New York: Oxford University Press, 1973).

40 Cf. Joan Burstyn, *Victorian Education and the Ideal of Womanhood* (Totowa, N.J.: Barnes & Noble Books, 1980); Carol Dyhouse, *Girls Growing Up in Late Victorian and Edwardian England* (London: Routledge & Kegan Paul, 1981); and Gorham, *The Victorian Girl.* Burstyn sees education as a bona fide attempt to challenge traditional views of womanhood, whereas Dyhouse argues that even educational reform was essentially a conservative movement. Gorham focuses on general child-rearing practices designed to inculcate the feminine ideal in young girls.

41 Elizabeth Sewell, *Principles of Education* (London: Longman, Green, Longman, Roberts, & Green, 1865), 1:219; [Montagu Burrows], "Female Education," *Quarterly Review* 126 (April 1869): 238.

42 For a comparison of these two fascinating figures in early educational reform, see Josephine Kamm, *How Different From Us: A Biography of Miss Buss and Miss Beale* (London: Bodley Head, 1958).

43 Many works describe the debate over women's education in the nineteenth century, which seems to have attracted scholarly attention in two waves. One began around the turn of the century and lasted for twenty-five years or so. The other is more recent, having started in the last ten years. Some scholars focus on the political changes, and others on the psychological and social implications of educating women. The works by Burstyn, Dyhouse, and Gorham cited above are recent; there are many other useful and interesting recent works as well. Edward Ellsworth's *Liberators of the Female Mind: The Shirreff Sisters, Educational Reform, and the Women's Movement* (Westport, Conn: Greenwood Press, 1979), is an interesting biography of Emily and Maria Shirreff. He focuses on their efforts to open up educational doors for women. Sheila Fletcher's *Feminists and Bureaucrats* (Cambridge: Cambridge University Press, 1980); Margaret Bryant's *The Unexpected Revolution: A Study in the History of Education of Women and Girls in the Nineteenth Century* (London: University of London, Institute of Education, 1979); and Josephine Kamm, *Hope Deferred: Girls' Education in English History* (London: Methuen, 1965) chronicle the political struggles for women's education. Ann Phillips, eds., *A Newnham Anthology* (Cambridge: Cambridge University Press, 1979), is a collection of students' reminiscences. Rita McWilliams-Tullberg, in *Women at Cambridge: A Men's University—Though of a Mixed Type* (London: Victor Gollancz, 1975), discusses the struggle for the granting of degrees to women at Cambridge. Vera Brittain, *The Women at Oxford* (New York: Macmillan Co., 1960) and Annie M. A. H. Rogers, *Degree by Degrees* (Oxford: Oxford University Press, 1938), study the situation at Oxford. Among the older accounts, Sara A. Burstall, *English High Schools for Girls* (London: Longmans, Green, & Co., 1907), explores secondary education for women. Alicia Percival, *The*

English Miss To-day and Yesterday (London: George G. Harrap & Co., 1939), although not a terribly scholarly work, offers some perceptive insights into the influence of the father-daughter bond on a girl's desire for education; see especially pp. 49–50. Alice Zimmern, in *The Renaissance of Girls' Education in England: Fifty Years of Progress* (London: A. D. Innes & Co., 1898), celebrates the efforts of early reformers.

44 Amy Key Clarke, *A History of the Cheltenham Ladies' College 1853–1953* (London: Faber & Faber, 1953), p. 43.

45 Kamm, *How Different From Us,* p. 23.

46 Ibid., pp. 24–28.

47 Clarke, *Cheltenham Ladies' College,* p. 49.

48 R. L. Archer, *Secondary Education in the Nineteenth Century* (London: Frank Cass & Co., 1966), p. 242.

49 Kamm, *How Different From Us,* p. 82.

50 Clarke, *Cheltenham Ladies' College,* pp. 22, 27, 38.

51 Cheltenham: Kamm, *How Different From Us,* pp. 60–62, and Jonathan Gathorne-Hardy, *The Old School Tie: The Phenomenon of the English Public School* (New York: Viking Press, 1978), p. 244; North London Collegiate School: Zimmern, *Renaissance,* p. 65. The silence rule at Cheltenham into the 1970s.

52 Clarke, *Cheltenham Ladies' College,* pp. 49, 89.

53 Kamm, *How Different From Us,* p. 39.

54 Mirrlees, Notebook, "Lucy (Booty)."

55 Ibid. Jane was fortunate that this condition did not lead her family to take her away from school. Many critics of women's education considered amenorrhea a typical side effect of too much intellectual strain. As Deborah Gorham states, "the usual cure recommended by Victorian practitioners for amenorrhea itself . . . was adherence to wholesome living suited to the feminine temperament. . . . An unfeminine lifestyle could . . . be one in which the girl was involved in serious study, or where she sought to escape from the confines of family life. In short, the best safeguard against abnormal menstruation, and the ills that might accompany it, was vigorous conformity to the Victorian ideal of femininity" (Gorham, *The Victorian Girl,* p. 89).

56 Mirrlees, Notebook, Commentary with no heading.

57 Ibid., "Lucy (Booty)."

58 F. Cecily Steadman, *In the Days of Miss Beale: A Study of Her Work and Influence* (London: Ed. J. Burrow & Co., n.d,), p. 18.

59 Mirrlees, Notebook, "Mrs. Charles Mitchell."

60 Ibid.

61 Kamm, *How Different From Us,* pp. 24–25.

62 Mirrlees, Notebook, "Mrs. Charles Mitchell."

63 Hilda Lane to Mirrlees, undated, Box 9.

64 Mirrlees, Notebook, "Lucy (Booty)."

65 Mirrlees, Miscellaneous notes, Box 19.

66 David Friedrich Strauss, *The Life of Jesus Critically Examined,* 2 vols., trans. Marian Evans (New York: Calvin Blanchard, 1860).

67 Mirrlees, Miscellaneous notes, Box 15.

68 Steadman, *Miss Beale,* p. 18.

69 Mirrlees, Notebook, "Lucy (Booty)."
70 Mirrlees, "Outline of Life," Box. 15.

CHAPTER 2

1 [Burrows], "Female Education," p. 242; J. G. Fitch, "Women and the Universities," *Contemporary Review* 58 (August 1890), p. 243. For a sampling of other contemporary views, see "Feminine Wranglers," *Saturday Review* 18 (1864): 111–13; "Women at the Universities," *Saturday Review* 43 (1877): 660–61; Percy Gardner, "Women at Oxford and Cambridge," *Quarterly Review* 186 (1897): 529–51; and W. H. Davenport Adams, *Woman's Work and Worth in Girlhood, Maidenhood, and Wifehood* (London, 1880).
2 Burrows, "Female Education," pp. 243–48.
3 See, for example, Burstyn, *Victorian Education;* Dyhouse, *Girls Growing Up;* and Fletcher, *Feminists and Bureaucrats,* for more detailed discussion.
4 This chapter focuses, of necessity, on Newnham's founding. Barbara Stephen, *Emily Davies and Girton College* (London: Constable & Co., 1927; reprint. Westport, Conn.: Hyperion Press, 1976); M. C. Bradbrook, *That Infidel Place* (London: Chatto & Windus, 1969); and B. Megson and J. Lindsay, *Girton College, 1869–1959: An Informal History* (Cambridge: Heffers, 1960), give historical accounts of Girton College. Olive Jocelyn Dunlop, *Leaves from a Cambridge Notebook* (Cambridge: Heffer, 1907), and Louisa Lumsden, *Yellow Leaves* (London: Blackwood & Sons, 1933), provide student perspectives on Girton life. Annie Edwards, in *A Girton Girl* (London: R. Bentley, 1885), reveals the fantasy of those who hoped college women would come to their senses after kicking up their heels. Its Newnham counterpart is Alice Stronach, *A Newnham Friendship* (London: Blackie & Son, 1901).
5 Blanche Athena Clough, *A Memoir of Anne Jemima Clough* (London: Edward Arnold, 1897), p. 175. See also Stephen, *Emily Davies,* chap. 2.
6 Clough, *Memoir,* pp. 172–73. McWilliams-Tullberg, in *Women at Cambridge,* provides a thorough account of the battle for degrees.
7 Quoted in Barbara Stephen, *Girton College 1869–1932* (Cambridge: Cambridge University Press, 1933), p. 37; Ibid., p. 64.
8 Ibid., p. 28.
9 Ibid., pp. 145–46.
10 Clough, *Memoir,* pp. 147–49.
11 Henry Sidgwick, "The Theory of Classical Education," in *Miscellaneous Essays and Addresses* (London: Macmillan & Co., 1904), pp. 272–75; Clough, *Memoir,* p. 175; Henry Sidgwick, "Classical Education," pp. 272–75. For more on Sidgwick's life, see Arthur Sidgwick and Eleanor Sidgwick, *Henry Sidgwick: A Memoir* (London and New York: Macmillan, 1906). Many works have addressed the question of university reform in the Victorian era. See Sheldon Rothblatt, *The Revolution of the Dons: Cambridge and Society in Victorian England* (London: Faber & Faber, 1968); idem, *Tradition and Change in Liberal Education* (London: Faber & Faber, 1976); Alfred I. Tillyard, *History of University Reform from 1800 to the Present Time* (Cambridge: W. Heffer & Sons, 1913); F. M. Cornford, *The Cambridge*

Classical Course: An Essay in Anticipation of Further Reform (Cambridge: W. Heffer & Sons, 1903); and F. W. Farrar, ed., *Essays in a Liberal Education*, 2d ed. (London: Macmillan & Co., 1869).

12 Clough, *Memoir*, pp. 172, 174–75, 53.

13 Ibid., pp. 181, 169–70.

14 Ibid., p. 155.

15 Ibid., chaps. 1 and 2; p. 182.

16 Percival, *The English Miss*, p. 166.

17 Clough, *Memoir*, p. 153.

18 Ibid., p. 195.

19 Phillips, *Anthology*, p. 1.

20 Quoted in Marshall, *What I Remember*, p. 11; Clough, *Memoir*, p. 232.

21 Stephen, *Girton College*, p. 40; Phillips, *Anthology*, p. 2; Marshall, *What I Remember*, p. 10. Evangelicalism grew up separate from the universities, but "even so, Cambridge became closely associated with Evangelical teaching in the early nineteenth-century and, under the guidance of Charles Simeon, became a forcing-house for Evangelicals lay and clerical. The connection was important, if only because it gave some of the leading Evangelicals a concern for and an interest in scholarship which in general the movement lacked. Although many were unusually successful in business enterprise, they often revealed a deep, and perhaps just, suspicion that secular learning threatened the integrity of the Gospel" (V. H. H. Green, *Religion at Oxford and Cambridge* [London: SCM Press, 1964], p. 222).

22 See Ellen Condliffe Lagemann, *A Generation of Women: Education in the Lives of Progressive Reformers* (Cambridge: Harvard University Press, 1979), for a good discussion of fathers' importance to ambitious daughters. I myself can attest to the validity of this evidence through one small example. In 1977, I took a graduate seminar in Feminist Theory and Method at Sarah Lawrence College. Professor Virginia Yans-McLaughlin, who taught the course that semester, asked us to write brief autobiographies. When she returned them to us, she asked incredulously, "Where are your mothers?" It seems that all of us—in a class of about a dozen women—had written about the influence of our fathers and ignored our mothers.

23 Paley: Quoted in Clough, *Memoir*, pp. 197–98; Anne Clough: quoted in ibid., pp. 200–01.

24 Ibid., p. 205. For other descriptions of women's college life, see Eleanor Field, "Women at an English University," *Century Magazine* 42, n.s. 20 (1890); and Phillips, *Anthology*. Nicholas Pevsner, in *Cambridgeshire* (Harmondsworth, England: Penguin Books, 1970), pp. 194–97, describes Newnham's architecture. For an analysis of the architecture of women's colleges in America, see Helen Lefkowitz Horowitz, *Alma Mater: Design and Experience in the Women's Colleges from Their Nineteenth-Century Beginnings to the 1930s* (New York: Knopf, 1984).

25 Mirrlees, Notebook, "Mary Paley," JEH. Unless otherwise noted, Mirrlees's material is housed in this collection. Marshall, *What I Remember*, p. 22.

26 Ritchie: Mirrlees, Notebook, "Mrs. Herbert Paul (Elinor Ritchie)"; Dew-Smith: Mirrlees, "Draft Biography"; "fickle in her passions": Mirrlees, Notebook, "Mrs. Charles Mitchell."

27 Mirrlees, Notebook, Commentary with no heading; quoted in Stewart, *Portrait*, p. 8; Mirrlees, Notebook, "Alice Dew."
28 Vicinus, *Independent Women*,, p. 140.
29 "An Old Newnham Student," "The Social Life of an Undergraduate," *Girls' Realm* 5 (1902–03): 411, cited in Ibid.
30 Mary Agnes Hamilton, *Remembering My Good Friends* (London: Jonathan Cape, 1944), p. 37–38.
31 Marshall, *What I Remember*, pp. 17, 17–18, 21; Mirrlees, Notebook, "The Greek Play."
32 Marshall, *What I Remember*, pp. 15–21.
33 Ibid., p. 15; Mirrlees, "Fragmentary Notes on Early Newnham Days," Box 14.
34 Mirrlees, "Fragmentary Notes."
35 Ethel Sidgwick, *Mrs. Henry Sidgwick: A Memoir* (London: Sidgwick & Jackson, 1938), p. 37.
36 Phillips, *Anthology*, p. 53.
37 Mirrlees, "Fragmentary Notes."
38 Ibid.
39 Mirrlees, Notebook, Commentary with no heading; Clough, *Memoir*, pp. 194, 196.
40 Mirrlees, Notebook, "Mrs. Herbert Paul."
41 Ibid.
42 Ibid., "Alice Dew."
43 Ibid., "Mrs. Herbert Paul."
44 Ibid.
45 Marshall, *What I Remember*, pp. 8–9, 10–13; Janet E. Courtney, *Recollected in Tranquillity* (London: William Heinemann, 1926), p. 93.
46 Dyhouse, *Girls Growing Up*, pp. 33–35.
47 Jonathan Gathorne-Hardy briefly addresses the surrogate family issue in *The Old School Tie*. He studied secondary schools, but his comments apply to women's colleges as well. In his research, he "found a number of teachers (particularly at girls' schools) saying that in the boarding house the public schools had created the ideal substitute-family unit." He labels this assertion "rubbish," asking "who ever heard of a family unit with sixty children and one parent?" He claims that the "house system . . . like boarding itself . . . was an accident" (pp. 29–30). It seems to me that Gathorne-Hardy misses the point. The boarding system may indeed have been an accident. If it evolved into a surrogate family, however, it must be examined as such. Whether or not the founders wanted to establish a surrogate family is immaterial. It seems likely that they did not. But Gathorne-Hardy fails to see that although the family structure found in women's schools does not replicate the nuclear family they came from, women students restructured it to suit their needs. They needed the emotional sustenance associated with parents, but not parental authority and control. Thus, the students provided each other with support and validation of their experience while escaping parental control.
48 Woolf, *A Room of One's Own*; Dorothy Sayers, *Gaudy Night* (London: Victor Gollancz, 1935). Woolf's classic plea for female intellectual autonomy voiced

the desires of a specific group of women. She addressed the desires that concerned a small group of highly educated, upper-middle-class female intellectuals, but her work nevertheless captures an important concept: the individual's right to independent thought and creative expression. Dorothy Sayers infused her mystery story with an underlying theme. In essence, she portrayed a female community as fundamentally healthy. The academic women turn out not to have committed the crime—a solution that challenged public perceptions of their nature. Whether academic women could be assimilated into the larger culture remained debatable. Lily Briscoe in Virginia Woolf's *To the Lighthouse* (New York: Harcourt, Brace & World, 1927) represents the female intellectual as perennial outsider. For a look at the significance of women's education and the female intelligentsia in other European settings, see Karen M. Offen, "The Second Sex and the Baccalaureat in Republican France, 1800–1924," *French Historical Studies* 13, no. 2 (Fall 1983): 252–86; Samia Spencer, "Women and Education," in *French Women and the Age of Light,* ed. Samia Spencer (Bloomington: Indiana University Press, 1984); and Barbara Alpern Engel, *Mothers and Daughters: Women of the Intelligentsia in Nineteenth-Century Russia* (Cambridge: Cambridge University Press, 1983). In Jane's case, and I would argue generally, the female intelligentsia served a specific purpose: it provided emotional sustenance for women's forays into the world of male scholarship. Despite Jane's reliance on female support, she never lost sight of her complex and conflicted connection to male intellectual culture. I thank Elizabeth Fox-Genovese for an enlightening discussion on the issue of the female intelligentsia and intellect as power. See Elizabeth Fox-Genovese, "Culture and Consciousness in the Intellectual History of European Women," *Signs* 12, no. 3 (Spring 1987): 529–47.

49 Christine de Pisan, *The Book of the City of Ladies,* trans. Earl Jeffrey Richards (New York: Persea Books, 1982); Mary Astell, *A Serious Proposal for the Ladies* (1701; reprint. New York: Source Book Press, 1970). Both of these authors stressed women's need to free themselves of obligations to family, especially to men, in order to learn. Much of the recent debate over female culture centers on the nature of women's relationships. Young women frequently shared intense friendships in the nineteenth century. In the educational setting, I am inclined to attribute them to women's emulation of patterns set by their brothers, the rigidly enforced sex segregation that formed the basis of women's admission to universities, and the need for companionship less troubled by disagreements over social roles and expectations. Cf. Martha Vicinus, " 'One Life to Stand Beside Me': Emotional Conflicts of First-Generation College Women in England," *Feminist Studies* 8 (Fall 1982): 603–28; Nancy Sahle, "Smashing: Women's Relationships before the Fall," *Chrysalis* 8 (1979): 17–27: Leila Rupp, " 'Imagine My Surprise': Women's Relationships in Historical Perspective," *Frontiers* 5, no. 3 (1980): 61–70; and Lillian Faderman, *Surpassing the Love of Men: Romantic Friendship and Love between Women from the Renaissance to the Present* (New York: William Morrow & Co., 1981).

50 Unfortunately, not all women were able to break from their families and survive the alienation education caused. Jane broke successfully from her background, but many of her contemporaries stopped short of total rejection

and settled for redefining their roles as women. The most tragic case of the failure to form a surrogate family and its consequences is found in Victoria Glendinning, *A Suppressed Cry: The Life and Death of a Quaker Daughter* (London: Routledge & Kegan Paul, 1969). This wrenching true account tells the story of a young woman, Winnie Seebohm, whose family's opposition to her desire to be educated literally suffocated her.

51 Mirrlees, Notebook, "The Half-Sister, Jessie."

52 Ibid., "Mrs. Charles Mitchell"; Mirrlees, "Outline of Life," Box 15; *Dictionary of National Biography*, s.v. "Butcher, Samuel Henry."

53 Mirrlees, Notebook, "Mrs. Paul's Answers"; Elinor Ritchie Paul to HM, June 13, 1934, Box 14; Mirrlees, Notebook, "Outline of Life."

54 Mirrlees, Notebook, "Jessie."

55 Ibid., "Helen Salter (Helen Verrall)."

56 Mirrlees, "Draft Biography"; JH to JS, June 1900, Box 10.

57 Mirrlees, "Draft Biography."

58 Mirrlees, Notebook, "Outline of Life."

CHAPTER 3

1 Jane Ellen Harrison, *Introductory Studies in Greek Art* (New York: Macmillan and Co., 1882), p. vii; hereafter cited as *ISGA*.

2 Mirrlees, Notebook, "Helen Salter," JEH. Unless otherwise noted, Mirrlees's material is housed in this collection.

3 Alice Dew-Smith, *Newnham College Roll Letter*, January 1929, pp. 64–65.

4 Mirrlees, Notebook, "Hope Malleson." See Claire Richter Sherman and Adele M. Holcomb, eds., *Women as Interpreters of the Visual Arts* (Westport, Conn., and London: Greenwood Press, 1981), p. 35, for a brief discussion of Jane as a model for Eugenie Sellers at the beginning of Sellers's career.

5 Mirrlees, Notebook, "Mrs. Paul on the Homeric Theatricals"; ibid., Commentary with no heading; ibid., "Alice Dew."

6 Ibid., "Alice Dew"; JH to Hope Malleson, December 7, 1881, Box 8, JEH. Unless otherwise noted, all of Jane's correspondence is housed in this collection.

7 JH to Hope Malleson, October 20, 1881, Box 8, JEH. For a more detailed discussion of the association between classical study and male identity, see chap. 4.

8 *Pall Mall Gazette*, 1891, p. 2; undated clipping in the Newnham College Archive, Cambridge. Only the year it appeared in print has been marked.

9 Ibid.

10 Mirrlees, Notebook, "Lucy (Booty)."

11 Dew-Smith, *Roll Letter*, pp. 64–65; Mirrlees, Notebook, "Alice Dew-Smith."

12 Mirrlees, Notebook, "Professor Myres."

13 Dew-Smith, *Roll Letter*, p. 64.

14 Mirrlees, Notebook, "Homeric Theatricals."

15 Mirrlees, "Draft Biography."

16 Elinor Ritchie Paul to Mirrlees, June 13, 1934, Box 14.

17 Mirrlees, Notebook, "DSM."

18 Mirrlees, Notebook, "Hope Malleson." Hope Mirrlees wrote to Jessie Stew-

art that, on reflection, she thought Jane had grown "bored with sharing a house with Miss Get Wilson," who "had become a complete invalid, and couldn't do her share of the housekeeping, and often had to be nursed. And though Jane was quite fond of her she was not one of her *dear* friends" (HM to JS, March 4, 1951, Box 14).

19 Vicinus, *Independent Women*, pp. 1–9. See also Lee Holcombe, *Victorian Ladies at Work: Middle-Class Working Women in England and Wales, 1850–1914* (Hamden, Conn.: Archon Books, 1973).

20 For Jane's description of the Sesame Club, see Stewart, *Portrait*, pp. 39–40. Jane may have felt comfortable in a mixed club like the Sesame, which allowed both male and female members, because of her academic career. The club's "list of members . . . includes much that is best in the literary and educational world" (Eve Anstruther, "Ladies' Clubs," *Nineteenth Century* 45 [1899]: 601).

21 Dora Greenwall, "Our Single Women," *North British Review* 36 (1862): 35.

22 Alice Zimmern, "Ladies' Dwellings," *Contemporary Review* 77 (1900): 96–104.

23 Evelyn March-Phillips, "The Working Lady in London," *Fortnightly Review* 58 (1892): 193–203.

24 Anstruther, "Ladies' Clubs," pp. 598–611.

25 Harrison mentions Joanna's years of service in a letter to Gilbert Murray, December 31, 1914, Box 6; also quoted in Stewart, *Portrait*, pp. 158–59.

26 JH to Hope Malleson, April 30, 1882, Box 8.

27 Mirrlees, "Draft Biography."

28 Mirrlees, Notebook, "Notes on Jane's Early Life."

29 *Dictionary of National Biography*, s.v. "MacColl, Dugald Sutherland."

30 Augustus John, *Chiaroscuro* (London: Jonathan Cape, 1952), p. 49.

31 In her *Portrait*, Stewart discreetly refused to address the possibility of a love affair, and Ackerman dismissed Jane's attraction to Sutherland in a brief footnote (see Ackerman, "The Early Work," p. 213*n*14). Both acknowledged his influence on her work, and Stewart quoted some fairly revealing passages from Jane's letters to him during this period, but neither devoted much attention to his role in her life. The unpublished letters and notes tell a much more interesting story than has yet come to light.

32 Mirrlees, Notebook, "DSM."

33 Mirrlees, Notebook, "Alice Dew." Hope Mirrlees admitted late in her life that Jane "was frightfully shattered by Sutherland's marriage, tho' she had refused to marry him herself" (HM to JS, March 4, 1951, Box 14).

34 See Stewart, *Portrait*, pp. 121–22; Ackerman, "The Early Work," p. 213.

35 JH to DSM, February 6, 1887, Box 8. These letters are typescript copies of the originals, apparently done at Jessie Stewart's request.

36 Ackerman, "The Early Work," p. 223.

37 JH to DSM, undated; undated; January 13, 1887, Box 8.

38 JH to DSM, February 6, 1887, Box 8.

39 Mirrlees, "Notes for a Draft Biography"; Mirrlees, Notebook, "The Letters."

40 JH to DSM, undated, Box 8.

41 JH to DSM, undated; undated, Box 8.

42 JH to DSM, November 13, 1887, Box 8; Mirrlees, Notebook, "DSM's List of Dates"; Ibid., "DSM."

43 Jane Ellen Harrison and D. S. MacColl, *Greek Vase Paintings* (London: T. Fisher Unwin, 1894), p. 5.

44 Ackerman states that "*Mythology and Monuments of Ancient Athens* (1890) might be called the first book of the Cambridge Ritualists, even though Miss Harrison had at this time not even met Murray, Cornford, or Cook, because it indicated the general direction to be taken by the group later" (*The Cambridge Group*, p. 142). I believe the roots can be traced back even further, to *Myths of the Odyssey* (1882). Jane was a Ritualist long before she knew it.

45 Jane Ellen Harrison, *Myths of the Odyssey in Art and Literature* (London: Rivingtons, 1882), p. ix; cited hereafter in the text.

46 Harrison, *ISGA*, pp. v–vi; cited hereafter in the text.

47 JH to DSM, undated, Box 8.

48 Stewart, *Portrait*, pp. 107, 5.

49 "Extracts from DSM's letters from Greece," Box 8.

50 D. S. MacColl, "Diary of Greek Journey, 1888," Box 8.

51 Ibid.

52 Ibid.

53 Ibid.

54 Some women, of course, were forced by circumstance to travel alone or went off as wives to wild and unfamiliar territory. See Joanna Trollope, *Britannia's Daughters* (London: Hutchinson, 1983), and A. James Hammerton, *Emigrant Gentlewomen: Genteel Poverty and Female Emigration, 1830–1914* (London: Croom Helm, 1979). Studies of women who traveled for more personal reasons are Catherine Stevenson, "Female Anger and African Politics: The Case of Two Victorian 'Lady Travellers,' " *Turn-of-the-Century Women* 2, no. 1 (Summer 1985): 7–17; Katherine Frank, *A Voyager Out: The Life of Mary Kingsley* (Boston: Houghton Mifflin Co., 1986); and Susan Goodman, *Gertrude Bell* (Leamington Spa, England, and Dover, N.H.: Berg Publishers, 1985).

55 JH to Hope Malleson, June 6, 1888, Box 8.

56 JH to DSM, undated. There is no heading or date on this letter, but clearly it was meant for MacColl.

57 Mirrlees, Notebook, "DSM."

58 The travel information in this paragraph comes from Hope Mirrlees' Notebook, either "DSM" or "DSM's List of Dates." The papers also include a notice of D. S. MacColl's lecture series. According to Ethel Sykes, she and Sutherland taught Jane "dance-steps" during those years (Mirrlees, Notebook, "Ethel Sykes"). In addition, "Jane was one of the first people to encourage Isadore Duncan. I. D. began by dancing in Sargent's and other painters' studios, to Greek poetry read aloud" (Mirrlees, Notebook, "Margaret Marshall").

59 Mirrlees, "Outline of Life."

60 DSM to JS, November 1, 1943, Box 10.

61 Mirrlees, Notebook, "DSM."

62 JH to MM, March 15, 1902, #42, Box 6.

63 JH to DSM, August 15, 1909; January 27, 1903, and July 3, 1914; dated 1905; May 30, 1909, Box 8.

64 Even Hope Mirrlees admitted that "not getting the Chair at London University (Ernest Gardner was the successful candidate, a man whom she personally disliked, and whose approach to archaeology she detested) was a very bitter disappointment" (HM to JS, March 4, 1951, Box 14). But during her lifetime Jane kept her bitterness to herself. She may well not even have recognized until very late in her life how angry Ernest Gardner's appointment made her.

65 JH to Edmund Gosse, October 24, 1888, Edmund Gosse Papers, Brotherton Library, University of Leeds.

66 Stewart records Jane's memory of Margaret Merrifield's appointment as classical lecturer. Margaret flew into a "generous rage when she was preferred before her friend," and Jane recalled that she "came immediately to London to see me and blindly stamped about the room thereby healing her friend's hurt vanity." That was the only time Jane ever saw her "thoroughly irrational" (Stewart, *Portrait*, p. 10).

CHAPTER 4

1 "Note on the Award and Tenure of the Fellowship and on the Work Done by Fellows," JEH.

2 JH to GM, September 27, 1903, #151, Box 6, JEH. Unless otherwise noted, all of Jane's correspondence is housed in this collection.

3 Several biographies fill out the picture of early twentieth-century Cambridge. See, for example, Paul Levy, *Moore: G. E. Moore and the Cambridge Apostles* (New York: Holt, Rinehart & Winston, 1979); Victor Lowe, *Alfred North Whitehead: The Man and His Work*, vol. 1 (Baltimore and London: Johns Hopkins University Press, 1985); and Ronald Clark, *The Life of Bertrand Russell* (New York: Alfred A. Knopf, 1976).

4 Noel Annan, "The Intellectual Aristocracy," in *Studies in Social History*, ed. Plumb, pp. 241–87.

5 Raverat: Gwen Raverat, *Period Piece: A Cambridge Childhood* (London: Readers Union, Faber & Faber, 1954), pp. 30, 2; Jebb: Mary Reed Bobbitt, *With Dearest Love to All: The Life and Letters of Lady Jebb* (Chicago: Henry Regnery Co., 1960), p. 173; Glover: T. R. Glover, *Cambridge Retrospect* (Cambridge: Cambridge University Press, 1943), pp. 105–07. Countless Cantabridgians wrote their memoirs, but Raverat's is the most engaging. It is also one of the few that gives a female perspective on Cambridge culture. For others, see Marshall, *What I Remember*; Hamilton, *Remembering My Good Friends*; Dunlop, *Cambridge Notebook*; and Lumsden, *Yellow Leaves*. For a faculty wife's perspective, see Mrs. Ernest C. Roberts, *Sherburne, Oxford and Cambridge* (London: Martin Hopkinson, 1934). The women's memoirs contrast sharply with the men's. Cf. Charles B. L. Tennyson, *Cambridge from Within* (Philadelphia: George W. Jacobs & Co., n.d.); T. G. Bonney, *Memories of a Long Life* (Cambridge: Metcalfe & Co., 1921); T. Thornely, *Cambridge Memories* (London: Hamish Hamilton, 1936); and Glover, *Cambridge Retrospect*.

6 Mirrlees: Notebook, "V. de Bunsen," JEH; Malleson: Mirrlees, Notebook, "Hope Malleson." Unless otherwise noted, Mirrlees's material is housed in the JEH collection. In 1951, Hope Mirrlees wrote to Jessie Stewart that Jane's "return to Cambridge was a rather battered ship's return to port. She always talked about Newnham and communal life as something wonderfully peaceful. And I think coming back to Cambridge was what they call now an 'escape.' " Nevertheless, Hope also remembered "her telling me she was terrified in case she should loose [*sic*] touch with things, and from a sort of superstitious feeling she kept some rooms in London for the first few years she was at Cambridge" (HM to JS, March 4, 1951, Box 14).

7 Mirrlees, Notebook, "V. de Bunsen."

8 Virginia Woolf to Violet Dickinson, October 22, 1904, *Letters of Virginia Woolf*, ed. Nicholson and Trautmann, vol. 1, *1888–1912*, p. 145. Jane reciprocated Mrs. Maitland's lukewarm feelings. When the widowed Florence Maitland became Sir Francis Darwin's third wife, Jane wrote that she "couldn't marry Mrs. Maitland myself she is too fly away" (JH to GM, February 2, 1913, #599, Box 6).

9 V. H. H. Green, *The Universities* (Harmondsworth, England: Penguin Books, 1969), pp. 291–94.

10 Cf. Ackerman, *The Cambridge Group*, p. 150. He adheres to the view that when Jane returned to Newnham, she "rejoined the academic world, in which she felt at ease." I contend that she found the adjustment far more difficult than that.

11 Rothblatt, *Revolution of the Dons*, pp. 88, 21. For further discussion of class and status, see Charles Anderson and Miriam Schnaper, *School and Society in England: Social Backgrounds of Oxford and Cambridge Students* (Washington, D.C.: Public Affairs Press, 1952); Hester Jenkins and D. C. Jones, "Social Class of Cambridge University Alumni of the Eighteenth and Nineteenth Centuries," *British Journal of Sociology* 1, no. 2 (June 1950): 93–116; J. P. C. Roach, "Victorian Universities and the National Intelligentsia," *Victorian Studies* 3 (December 1959): 131–50; and Peter Musgrave, *Society and Education in England since 1800* (London: Methuen, 1968).

12 Rothblatt, *Revolution of the Dons*, p. 148. For discussion of the influence of the classical curriculum, see also Rothblatt, *Tradition and Change:* Q. D. Lewis, "Henry Sidgwick's Cambridge," *Scrutiny* 15 (December 1947); Martin L. Clark, *Classical Education in Britain 1500–1900* (Cambridge: Cambridge University Press, 1959); and Green, *The Universities.*

13 The question of classical education as indicator of social status is discussed in many comparatively recent works. In addition to those cited above, see also Turner, *The Greek Heritage*, chap. 1; Jenkins, *Victorians and Ancient Greece*, chap. 4; and Paul Bloomfield, *Uncommon People: A Study of England's Elite* (London: Hamish Hamilton, 1955).

14 A. H. Halsey and Martin Trow, *The British Academics* (Cambridge: Cambridge University Press, 1971), p. 40. See also Rothblatt, *Revolution of the Dons.*

15 Raverat, *Period Piece*, p. 163; JH to MM, December, 8, 1912, MM #34, Box 8.

16 Dyhouse, *Girls Growing Up*, p. 76; Burstyn, *Victorian Education*, p. 27.

17 Dyhouse, *Girls Growing Up,* p. 77; Mirrlees, Notebook, "V. de Bunsen." Robert Ackerman offers an explanation of Jane's attraction for both students and colleagues. "One of the keys to understanding Miss Harrison's life and achievement is perfectly obvious, but bears naming nevertheless—she was a woman. That is, if we may deal in generalizations, as a female she had not been brought up to stifle feeling or the expression of emotion, as had the majority of her male colleagues. . . . likewise she was not constrained as were her fellows by existing models of proper scholarly behavior. . . . Because she was a woman I am sure (without being able to prove it) that to some extent at least her world found her behavior charming where the same behavior in a man would have been thought childish or bizarre" (Ackerman, *The Cambridge Group,* p. 125). Jane's experience at Newnham proves this statement false. Newnham's administration particularly feared Jane's uniqueness and allowed her to return, much against its better judgment, only because of her reputation. She was undoubtedly more constrained than men by "models of proper scholarly behavior," but her unconscious decision to challenge those models enabled her to conduct herself the way she did.

18 "Our most brilliant resident don": Hamilton, *My Good Friends,* p. 60; Brown and Wilson: Phillips, *Anthology,* pp. 50, 67.

19 Phillips, *Anthology,* p. 45; Ethel Sidgwick, *Mrs. Henry Sidgwick,* p. 33; Ethel Sidgwick to JS, January 8, 1958; Hilda Lane to MM, undated, Box 9; Clark, *Bertrand Russell,* p. 144. Jane set herself a "daily allowance" of 30 cigarettes (JH to GM, July 21, 1902, #79, Box 6). Russell may have had reason to hold a grudge against Jane, who was a good friend of his first wife, Alys. Russell says that when he and Alys separated, few people knew the reason for the split. But "if there was a gap in the story it was soon filled in by rumour, at least in Cambridge, where it was borne along by Jane Harrison." He recorded that she professed to have " 'heard, on very reliable authority, that the real cause of his leaving Alys was a married woman in Cambridge, name unknown' " (Clark, *Bertrand Russell,* p. 144). In his biography of Alfred North Whitehead, Victor Lowe names Whitehead's wife, Evelyn, as the woman with whom Russell was in love, although it appears that they never actually had a sexual relationship (Lowe, *Alfred North Whitehead,* 1:246). Jane probably knew as much as Alys did. Like everyone else, despite his bravado, Russell hated to admit that other people might have suspected the truth.

20 Phillips, *Anthology,* pp. 47, 68.

21 Stewart, *Portrait,* p. 187.

22 Phillips, *Anthology,* p. 97.

23 Hilda Lane to HM, undated, Box 9.

24 Victoria de Bunsen in the *Newnham College Roll Letter,* January 1929, p. 66; Phillip, *Anthology,* p. 86; Mirrlees, Notebook, "V. de Bunsen"; Francis Cornford in the *Newnham College Roll Letter,* 1929, p. 72, quoted in Stewart, *Portrait,* p. 20.

25 de Bunsen, *Roll Letter,* p. 66; Mirrlees, Notebook, "V. de Bunsen"; JH to GM, undated, #32A, Box 6; JS to Mrs. Crum, undated, Box 10 ; JH to JS, JGS #22, July 1901, Box 10.

26 JH to MM, June 22, 1902, #70, Box 6; Mirrlees, Notebook, "Helen Salter"; JH to D. S. Mirsky, February 27, 1925, Box 8.

27 Dora Russell, *The Tamarisk Tree,* p. 40; Vera Brittain, *Testament of Youth* (New York: Macmillan Co., 1933); Josephine Kellet, *That Friend of Mine: A Memoir of Marguerite McArthur* (London: Swarthmore Press, 1920).

28 JH to JS, 1909, JGS #45, Box 10.

29 de Bunsen, *Roll Letter,* p. 67; JH to MM, April 19, 1902, #46, Box 6.

30 Stewart, *Portrait,* pp. 14, 12; JH to MM, June 15, 1900, #14A, Box 6.

31 JH to JS, June, 1900, JGS #14, Box 10.

32 JH to MM, June 15, 1900, #14A, Box 6.

33 JH to JS, September 28, 1900, JGS #3, Box 10. As with most of Jane's letters, Stewart has added the date in her own writing. She dated the letter 1899, but since the Greek trip occurred in 1901, it is more likely that the letter actually dated from 1900.

34 JS to Mr. Crum, March 27, 1901, Box 10.

35 JS to Mr. and Mrs. Crum, April 2, 1901, Box 10. For a similar encounter between Jane and classicist Andrew Lang, see chap. 5. English scholars, enamored of the alleged serenity of the classical age, considered Jane's work outrageous. Continental scholars, however, especially the German archaeologists, shared some of her feelings. See Butler, *The Tyranny of Greece;* Turner, *The Greek Heritage;* and Jenkins, *Victorians and Ancient Greece.*

36 JH to JS, 1901, JGS #27, Box 10; JH to Edith Crum, undated, Box 10; JH to JS, January 1, 1905, JGS #52, Box 10; JH to GM, 1902, #69, Box 6.

37 JH to JS, May 5, 1908, JGS #62, Box 10.

38 JH to JS, undated, JGS #45, Box 10; JH to JS, September 16, 1904, JGS #43, Box 10; December 1902, JGS #33, Box 10.

39 Mirrlees, Notebook, "Margaret Marshall"; JH to JS, April 12, 1904, Box 10.

40 JH to MM, September 3, 1904, #223, Box 6; JH to JS, Box 10. In *All Creatures Great and Small,* Yorkshire veterinarian James Herriot tells of his visit to a lorry driver who "kept a pig at the bottom of his garden for family consumption," but couldn't bear to see it slaughtered. Harriot stopped by on "one of these occasions" and the man "seized my hand in his and sobbed at me 'I can't bear it, Mr. Herriot. He was like a Christian was that pig, just like a Christian' " (James Herriot, *All Creatures Great and Small* [New York: St. Martin's Press, 1972], p. 277). In her "Reminiscences," Jane described Yorkshire as "a Paradise for dogs. . . . I have seen them crowding the platform at York station about the Twelfth of August, waited on assiduously by eager porters while their masters went neglected" (RSL, 326–27). Only in the north of England can sheepdog trials become one of the most popular televised sporting events. Jane came by her love of animals naturally.

41 JH to JS, September 5, 1905, JGS #55, Box 10.

42 Stewart, *Portrait,* p. 69.

43 Jane Ellen Harrison, "Scientiae Sacra Fames," in *A&O,* p. 18.

44 Stewart, *Portrait,* p. 18; JH to JS, November 1901, JGS #26, Box 10; Mirrlees, Notebook, "Outline of Life"; JH to JS, 1901, JGS #26, Box 10. Cf. Ackerman, "The Early Work," p. 211*n*5; idem, *The Cambridge Group,* p. 120.

45 Mirrlees, Notebook, "V. de Bunsen"; JH to JS, October 20, 1924, JGS #13, Box 10.

46 Mirrlees, Notebook, "Margaret Marshall."
47 Mirrlees, Notebook, "Outline of Life."
48 Vicinus, *Independent Women,* p. 331n100. Cf. Faderman, *Surpassing the Love of Men;* Carroll Smith-Rosenberg, "The Female World of Love and Ritual," *Signs* 1, no. 1 (Autumn 1975): 1–29; Nancy Cott, *The Bonds of Womanhood* (New Haven, Conn.: Yale University Press, 1977).
49 Mirrlees, Notebook, "Hope Malleson"; Virginia Woolf to Clive Bell, September 24, 1919, in *Letters of Virginia Woolf,* ed. Nicolson and Trautmann, vol. 2, *1912–1922,* p. 391.
50 JH to HM, July 3, 1910, Box 9; undated, Box 9; JH to Lina Mirrless, undated, Box 9; JH to HM, undated, Box 9.
51 JH to HM, undated, Box 9; undated, Box 9.
52 JH to HM, undated; undated; August 4, 1914, Box 9.
53 JH to HM, April 2, 1912; undated; December 25, 1914, Box 9.
54 JH to HM, November 10, 1913; September 2, 1913; undated, Box 9.
55 JH to HM, undated, Box 9; Mirrlees, Notebook, "The Letters."
56 In the Harrison family, "post-cards were an innovation and all innovations anathema" (RSL, 321).
57 JH to HM, May, 1914; July 13, 1915; July 15, 1915, Box 9.
58 JH to HM, March 26, 1918, Box 9.
59 JH to Lina Mirrlees, undated, Box 9.
60 JH to MM, August 28, 1904, #220, Box 6; JH to JS, September 30, 1901, JGS #23, Box 10.
61 Harrison, "Scientiae Sacra Fames," p. 117; hereafter cited in the text.
62 Zimmern, *Renaissance,* provides a contemporary account of the struggle for both women's colleges and degrees up to 1898 while glorifying the pioneer reformers. Bryant, *The Unexpected Revolution,* is a social history of the same movement that touches on universities throughout Great Britain. For the story of the Cambridge experience, see McWilliams-Tullberg, *Women at Cambridge;* Mary Agnes Hamilton, *Newnham: An Informal Biography* (London: Faber & Faber, 1936); and Stephen, *Girton College.* For Oxford's struggle, see Rogers, *Degree by Degrees;* and Brittain, *The Women at Oxford.*
63 See McWilliams-Tullberg, *Women at Cambridge.*
64 JH to GM, Spring, 1907, #295, Box 6.
65 JH to GM, October 30, 1912, #590, Box 6; JH to GM, March 19, 1922, #830, Box 6. The first underlined phrase occurs in a clipping from the London *Times,* October 30, 1912, p. 11, which Jane enclosed in her letter.
66 JH to GM, undated, #242, Box 6; March, 1919, #802, Box 6.
67 JH to GM, October 23, 1920, #815, Box 6; JH to GM, December, 1920, #816, Box 6.
68 JH to GM, December 25, 1920, #822, Box 6.
69 JH to GM, October 1921, #829A, Box 6; also quoted in Stewart, *Portrait,* p. 186. In a postscript, Jane added that "FMC [Cornford] says he feels it is his obvious duty to strangle his newborn son as belonging to a sex unfit for civilized life!" One can appreciate the sentiment yet cringe at its expression in such terms.

70 Rothblatt, *Revolution of the Dons*, p. 133; JH to GM, October 1921, #829A, Box 6.

CHAPTER 5

1 In his recent biography of Gilbert Murray, Francis West emphasizes Gilbert's criticism of Jane and the differences in their work, citing Murray's comment that her *Prolegomena* sounded " 'like Aunt Fanny trying to be naughty,' although 'in many ways she is so clever' " (p. 133). West relied on Murray's personal correspondence, housed at Oxford, for his evidence, and I fully believe that Murray made that comment. Since West does not include footnotes and neither cites the recipient of the letter nor explains the context in which it was written, however, I hesitate to devote much attention to the conflicts between them. All friendships that span nearly thirty years contain elements of tension and disagreement, especially when the friends are as passionate about and absorbed in their work as Jane and Gilbert were. Certainly Gilbert was not the saint that Jane imagined him, but the fact that she created this image is more interesting than a concrete understanding of his character. The overall serenity of their long friendship attests to their genuine respect and admiration for each other, regardless of specific instances of conflict. See Francis West, *Gilbert Murray: A Life* (London and Canberra: Croom Helm, 1984), especially pp. 132–38. His analysis of Murray's marriage (chap. 3, "A Whig Marriage"), while not directly applicable here, makes interesting reading.

2 Woolf: *The Diaries of Virginia Woolf*, ed. Anne Olivier Bell (New York: Harcourt Brace Jovanovich, 1977), vol. 1, *1915–1919*, p. 210; Dodds: Jean Smith and Arnold Toynbee, eds., *Gilbert Murray: An Unfinished Autobiography, with Contributions by His Friends* (London: George Allen & Unwin, 1960), pp. 18, 17; Berenson: Bernard Berenson to Bertrand Russell, March 22, 1903, *The Autobiography of Bertrand Russell* (Boston: Little, Brown & Co., 1951), 1:291; Thomson: J. A. K. Thomson to JS, December 6, 1957, Box 11, JEH.

3 Smith and Toynbee, *Murray*, pp. 13–14, 33–34, 25.

4 Ibid., pp. 87–88.

5 Dodds: Ibid., p. 16; Ridgeway: Glover, *Cambridge Retrospect*, p. 79.

6 See *Dictionary of National Biography*, s.v. "Cornford, Francis Macdonald; Ibid., s.v. "Cook, Arthur Bernard."

7 Ackerman, *The Cambridge Group*, pp. 122–23, 120–21, 121.

8 Ibid., p. 120. Ackerman later states emphatically that "we must deemphasize sentiment" as a factor in Jane's central position in the group (Ackerman, "The Early Work," p. 211). He ultimately attributes Jane's closeness to her male colleagues to her belief that "she was never as competent in her philological scholarship as she would have wished," and adds that "she suffered (or claimed she did) throughout her life from having begun the study of Greek relatively late" (Ibid., p. 210). Although it is true that Jane occasionally deprecated her philological skills, this self-deprecation should be seen as false modesty more than as a serious evalua-

tion of her shortcomings. For one thing, long before the "impostor syndrome" received its sociological name, women of keen intelligence played down their abilities in order to facilitate personal relations in a male world. Jane remained insecure throughout most of her academic life not so much because of real intellectual inadequacies as because of her sense of not belonging to the scholarly fraternity. Second, Jane's greatest work of scholarship depended more on her interpretation of ritual ceremonies than on strict philological studies. Relying on other scholars for assistance in translations would not necessarily invalidate her theories or indicate great weakness on her part. Finally, in her heart Jane believed her view of the ancient world was right and cared little, if at all, about other scholars' opinions.

9 Harrison, "Scientiae Sacra Fames," p. 139; hereafter cited in the text.

10 Harrison, "Homo Sum," in *A&O*, p. 111.

11 GM to JS, April 23, 1952, Box 17; October 26, 1953, Box 17.

12 Jacquetta Hawkes, Review of Jessie Stewart, *Jane Ellen Harrison: A Portrait from Letters, New Statesman,* June 20, 1959, p. 871; Patricia Meyer Spacks, *The Female Imagination* (New York: Avon Books, 1972), p. 6.

13 JH to GM, May 24, 1902, #65, Box 6.

14 JH to GM, August 24, 1900, #1, Box 6; December 1900, #2, Box 6; Mirrlees, Notebook, "V. de Bunsen"; JH to GM, December 24, 1900, #7, Box 6. Not everyone agreed with Jane's assessment of Gilbert's *History.* See Herbert Paul, "The New Learning," *Nineteenth Century* 42 (December 1897): 928–39. In this scathing review, Paul reproaches Gilbert for his lack of reverence toward classical authors. A round of what Jane would have called "langwidge" ensued: see Gilbert's response and Paul's defense in "Letters to the Editor," *Nineteenth Century* 42 (January 1898): 165–68. Unless otherwise noted, Mirrlees's material is housed in the JEH collection.

15 JH to GM, December 1900, #6, Box 6; JH to MM, February 1901, #11, Box 6.

16 JH to MM, July 8, 1903, #144, Box 6. For more on Mary's jealousy of Gilbert's many female friends, see West, *Gilbert Murray,* chap. 3.

17 JH to MM, March 28, 1903, #135, Box 6. For more on the Murrays' health, see West, *Gilbert Murray,* chap. 3.

18 JH to GM, January 1902, #25, Box 6; JH to MM, January 1902, Box 6.

19 JH to GM, September 1904, #227, Box 6; September 1911, #485, Box 6.

20 JH to MM, March 23, 1904, #197, Box 6.

21 JH to MM, September 17, 1911, MM #23, Box 8.

22 JH to GM, February 1, 1902, #31A, Box 6.

23 JH to GM, January 1902, #28, Box 6; February, 1902, #33A, Box 6.

24 JH to GM, May 15, 1902, #139, Box 6; November 20, 1902, #111, Box 6.

25 JH to MM, February 27, 1903, #132, Box 6.

26 JH to GM, November 30, 1909, #408, Box 6.

27 JH to GM, May, 1909, #385, Box 6.

28 JH to MM, March 15, 1902, #42, Box 6; February 27, 1912, MM #25A, Box 8.

29 JH to GM, July 1906, #290, Box 6; JH to MM, July 8, 1903, #144, Box 6.

30 JH to JS, June, 1909, JGS #70, Box 10; JH to Ruth Darwin, undated, Box 8.

31 JH to GM, 1906, #288, Box 6.

32 JH to GM, April 1906, #284, Box 6. Like Jane, Gilbert Murray frequented rest homes and clinics for the "cure" of real and fancied ailments.

33 JH to GM, 1915, #725, Box 6.

34 JH to MM, January 30, 1902, #30, Box 6; JH to GM, March 19, 1902, #43, Box 6.

35 Mirrlees, Notebook, "DSM."

36 JH to GM, October 11, 1903, #157, Box 6. As Jane noted in the *Prolegomena,* Keres "were, if not exactly evil spirits, certainly spirits that brought evil" (*PSGR,* 165). That she took her nickname from this malevolent creature seems interesting, if only because it highlights a darker side of her personality, which she hid so successfully otherwise.

37 Mary Murray: JH to MM, October 15, 1903, #158, Box 6; Eleanor Butcher: Mirrlees, "Draft Biography."

38 JH to GM, November 8, 1903, #161, Box 6.

39 JH to MM, April 19, 1904, #199, Box 6; JH to GM, February 1906, #282, Box 6; September 26, 1911, #489, Box 6; January 30, 1910, #418, Box 6.

40 JH to MM, December 10, 1901, #21, Box 6.

41 JH to GM, June 16, 1902, #68, Box 6; Ibid.; JH to MM, January 2, 1903, #121, Box 6; September 9, 1903, #147, Box 6; JH to GM, March 15, 1908, #330, Box 6; JH to MM, July 19, 1911, MM #22, Box 8; January 25, 1913, MM #35, Box 8.

42 JH to GM, 1913, #616A, Box 6; undated, #560, Box 6.

43 JH to GM, September 3, 1914, #686, Box 6; JH to MM, October 1914, MM #45, Box 8.

44 JH to GM, December 28, 1903, #174, Box 6; December 29, 1910, #465, Box 6.

45 JH to GM, Spring, 1912, #549, Box 6; JH to Frances Darwin, November 14, 1908, quoted in Ackerman, "Letters," p. 121.

46 JH to GM, 1905, #275, Box 6; 1908, #347, Box 6.

47 JH to GM, November 24, 1901, #18, Box 6; April 22, 1902, #49, Box 6; August 18, 1910, #445, Box 6.

48 JH to GM, November 24, 1901, #18, Box 6; GM to JH, September 30, 1906, Box 9; JH to GM, January 26, 1911, #472, Box 6.

49 JH to GM, May 18, 1909, #384, Box 6.

50 JH to GM, 1908, #351, Box 6.

51 JH to GM, February 1907, Box 6.

52 JH to GM, October 29, 1902, #102, Box 6.

53 JH to GM, September 17, 1909, #398, Box 6; December 22, 1902, #117, Box 6; September 17, 1909, #398, Box 6. For Jane's discussion of the Skiraphoria, see *PSGR,* pp. 134–35. Walter Burkert, who has reopened the debate over the meaning of *skira,* favors the translation of "white earth" that Jane used. He admits, however, that modern scholars have not made any more strides toward understanding the term than did ancient commentators, who expressed confusion themselves. See Burkert, *Homo Necans,* pp. 143–49.

54 JH to GM, April 27, 1902, #52, Box 6; May 2, 1902, #58, Box 6.

55 JH to GM, September 7, 1902, #86, Box 6.

56 JH to GM, September 9, 1902, #87, Box 6.

57 JH to GM, September 10, 1902, #88, Box 6.

58 JH to GM, October 11, 1902, #98, Box 6.
59 Harold Nicolson, Review of Jessie Stewart, *Jane Ellen Harrison: A Portrait from Letters, Observer* (London), June 21, 1959; GM to JS, September 16, 1928, Box 17.

CHAPTER 6

1 Gilbert Murray, "Francis Macdonald Cornford," *Proceedings of the British Academy* 29 (1943): 421–32.
2 Frances Darwin, quoted in Stewart, *Portrait,* p. 20; Mirrlees, Notebook, "Helen Salter," JEH. Unless otherwise noted, Mirrlees's material is housed in this collection.
3 JH to JS, July 10, 1904, JGS #42, Box 10; JH to GM, September 2, 1905, #263, Box 6; April 1, 1905, #239, Box 6, JEH. Unless otherwise noted, Jane's letters are all in this collection.
4 JH to GM, July 1906, #290, Box 6.
5 Margaret Verrall to MM, February 14, 1907, Box 6.
6 JH to GM, May 14, 1907, #301, Box, 6; Cornford, *Newnham Roll Letter,* p. 76.
7 JH to GM, May 14, 1907, #301, Box 6; June 1907, #305, Box 6; FMC to GM, June 18, 1907, quoted in Ackerman, "Letters," p. 120.
8 FMC to JS, June 8, 1907, Box 10.
9 Raverat, *Period Piece,* p. 191.
10 Ibid., p. 193; JH to Frances Darwin, December 1908 or early 1909, quoted in Ackerman, "Letters," p. 123.
11 Frances Darwin, quoted in Stewart, *Portrait,* p. 105; Mirrlees, Notebook, "The Letters."
12 Stewart, *Portrait,* p. 105; Raverat, *Period Piece,* p. 164; Stewart, *Portrait,* p. 105; JH to Frances Darwin, undated, CDP.
13 Frances Darwin: Stewart, *Portrait,* pp. 107, 106, 107; Francis Cornford: Cornford, *Newnham Roll Letter,* p. 75. Paul Delany, in *The Neo-Pagans: Rupert Brooke and the Ordeal of Youth* (New York: Free Press, 1987), calls Jane the "éminence grise of the Cornford-Darwin courtship." He states that the "match between Frances and Francis was of her making, and proved a credit to her insight" (p. 51). Evidence from Jane's private papers suggests otherwise.
14 The letters to follow are found in Hope Mirrlees's Notebook. They are copied in her handwriting and undated, but it seems reasonable to assume that because of her close relationship with Jane she had access to the originals at one time. The extracts are accompanied in the Notebook by Hope's own commentary.
15 The figure that prompted this drawing, a young woman sacrificing a pig, can be seen in *PSGR,* p. 126, fig. 10. For discussions of the meaning of the *khoiros* as vulva, see Jeffrey Henderson, *The Maculate Muse* (New Haven: Yale University Press, 1975), p. 131, par. 110 (cf. 111); Froma I. Zeitlin, "Cultic Models of the Female," *Arethusa* 15, nos. 1–2 (1982): 129–57, with a remark on "piglets, a well-known gloss for the vulva," on p. 144; and Walter Burkert, *Homo Necans,* trans. Peter Bing (Berkeley and Los Angeles:

University of California Press, 1983), pp. 258–59. I thank Thomas Africa for drawing my attention to the symbolic significance of this drawing.

16 John, *Chiaroscuro,* p. 64; JH to DSM May 30, 1909, Box 8.

17 JH to DSM, August 15, 1909, Box 8.

18 Stewart, *Portrait,* p. 107; JH to Frances Darwin, late 1908 or early 1909, quoted in Ackerman, "Letters," pp. 121–22.

19 JH to Frances Darwin, quoted in Ackerman, "Letters," p. 122; Stewart, *Portrait,* p. 107.

20 Scholars writing on Jane Harrison's life have ignored the full effect of her personal relationships on her life and work, especially in the case of her relationship with Francis Cornford. Jessie Stewart and Robert Ackerman scarcely comment on Francis, although for different reasons. Stewart knew something of the true story but discreetly withheld direct discussion of all its implications, instead relying heavily on Francis's and Frances's memories of Jane's ill health to excuse her behavior and emphasizing their genuine affection for her. She also avoided making connections between Jane's personal unhappiness and her poor health, choosing rather to laud Jane's scholarly achievements in the face of such physical sufferings. In fact, perhaps out of a desire to protect Jane and throw future historical hounds off the scent, Stewart blamed Jane herself, stating that "Jane felt resentment that she was no longer getting the same poetic inspiration from his mind" (*Portrait,* p. 112). Stewart thus implied, as might have been the case if there were not another side to the story, that this demand for inspiration constituted an unreasonable expectation. As one of Jane's closest friends, Stewart's refusal to discuss the situation in detail is understandable. Ackerman devotes even less attention to Jane's passionate attachment to Francis, his only reference to him being that Jane "seems to have been in love" with both him and, earlier, Sutherland MacColl. Furthermore, he claims that "in a sense . . . the Cambridge group may be seen biographically speaking, as a particularly happy time in Jane Harrison's life, when her emotional energies were most closely bound up with those of its three other members" (*The Cambridge Group,* p. 120). Cf. Stewart, *Portrait,* chap. 9; and Ackerman, *The Cambridge Group,* chap. 3.

21 JH to GM, 1908, #322, Box 6.

22 JH to GM, 1908, #335, Box 6; 1908; #332, Box 6; March 15, 1908, #330, Box 6.

23 JH to GM, 1908, #344, Box 6.

24 JH to GM, May 1908, #341, Box 6; JH to MM, May 14, 1908, MM #4, Box 6.

25 JH to GM, Spring, 1908, #327, Box 6; June 1908, #345, Box 6.

26 JH to GM, July 1908, #353A, Box 6.

27 JH to GM, August 2, 1908, #354, Box 6.

28 JH to JS, August 2, 1908, JGS #63, Box 10.

29 JH to Frances Darwin, August 2, 1908, CDP; GM to JS, September 3, 1908, Box 10.

30 JH to GM, 1908, #315, Box 6.

31 Frances Darwin to MM, October 4, 1908, CDP; JH to GM, September 30, 1908, #357, Box 6.

32 JH to Ruth Darwin, October 4, 1908, Box 8.
33 JH to GM, October 1908, #358, Box 6.
34 JH to MM, October 11, 1908, MM #6, Box 8; November 1908, MM #7, Box 6.
35 JH to GM, November 8, 1908, #364, Box 6.
36 JH to MM, December 1, 1908, #364A, Box 6.
37 Stewart, *Portrait*, p. 115.
38 JH to GM, December 16, 1908, #365, Box 6.
39 JH to DSM, May 30, 1909, Box 8.
40 JH to GM, December 26, 1908, #366, Box 6.
41 JH to GM, December 29, 1908, #368, Box 6.
42 JH to Frances Darwin, December 1908 or early 1909, quoted in Ackerman, "Letters," p. 123.
43 JH to MM, January 30, 1909, MM #11, Box 8.
44 JH to GM, January 8, 1908; February 26, 1909; April 1909; 1909; July 19, 1909, Box 6.
45 JH to MM, October 24, 1909, Box 6.
46 JH to GM, November 1909, Box 6.
47 Jane Ellen Harrison, "Heresy and Humanity," in *A&O*, p. 36.
48 Murray: JH to GM, April 4, 1910, #427, Box 6; August 12, 1910, #444, Box 6. Strachey: Quoted in Michael Holroyd, *Lytton Strachey: A Critical Biography* (New York: Holt, Rinehart & Winston, 1967), 1:457.
49 JH to GM, October 8, 1910, #450A, Box 6; October 27, 1910, #457, Box 6.
50 JH to GM, December 29, 1910, #465, Box 6.
51 JH to GM, January 4, 1911, #466A, Box 6; January 1911, #493, Box 6.
52 JH to GM, January 1911, #493, Box 6.
53 JH to GM, April 18, 1911, #480, Box 6; September 1911, #487, Box 6; JH to MM, December 25, 1911, MM #25, Box 8.
54 JH to GM, January 1912, #504A, Box 6; JH to MM, March 12, 1912, MM #26, Box 8.

CHAPTER 7

1 See Hughes, *Consciousness and Society.*
2 Friedrich Nietzsche, *The Birth of Tragedy from the Spirit of Music,* trans. Francis Golffing (New York: Doubleday, 1956), hereafter cited in the text as *BT;* J. J. Bachofen, "Mother Right," in *Myth, Religion and Mother-Right: Selected Writings of J. J. Bachofen,* trans. Ralph Manheim (Princeton: Princeton University Press, 1967); Harrison, *TH,* 125*n*2, and S. C. Humphreys, *Anthropology and the Classics* (London: Routledge & Kegan Paul, 1978), p. 96; *TH,* p. xxii*n*1. "The discovery [of the social origin of religion] was first formulated by the genius of Emil [*sic*] Durkheim in his brief paper, 'De la définition des phénomènes religieux,' in *L'Année sociologique* of 1898 [2 (1897–98): 1–28]. His theory has been since expanded in his *The Elementary Forms of the Religious Life . . .*"; Henri Hubert and Marcel Mauss, "Essai sur la nature et la function du sacrifice" appeared in *L'Année sociologique* 2 (1897–98): 29–138, and is cited on p. 137*n*1; Durkheim's "Prohibition de l'inceste et ses origines" appeared in *L'Année sociologique* 1 (1896–97): 1–

70, and is cited on p. 139*n*1; Henri Bergson, *Creative Evolution* (*L'Evolution créatrice*), trans. Arthur Mitchell (New York: Henry Holt & Co., 1911).

3 Jane owed a considerable debt to these scholars, for she drew heavily on their work for supporting evidence in both the *Prolegomena* and *Themis.* Frazer's *The Golden Bough* (1880s) and *Totemism* (1887), Robertson Smith's *Religion of the Semites* (1889) and E. B. Tylor's *Primitive Culture* (1878) and *The Early History of Mankind* (1873) appear frequently in her notes. For an analysis of Frazer's influence on the Ritualists, see Ackerman, "Frazer on Myth and Ritual," and Hyman, *The Tangled Bank*, pp. 187–291.

4 GM to JS, February 6, 1945, Box 17, JEH.

5 Jane Ellen Harrison, *Ancient Art and Ritual* (New York: Henry Holt & Co., 1913), p. v; hereafter cited in the text.

6 Turner, *The Greek Heritage,* examines Victorian British scholars' interpretations of the ancient world. See especially chap. 3, which discusses George Grote's *History of Ancient Greece.* See also Jenkyns, *Victorians and Ancient Greece,* chap. 8.

7 Harrison, *ISGA*, pp. 178, 263–64.

8 Ibid., pp. 178–80.

9 A useful recent survey of the origins and impact of *The Birth of Tragedy* is M. S. Silk and J. P. Stern, *Nietzsche on Tragedy* (Cambridge: Cambridge University Press, 1981). Euripides foreshadowed modern consciousness by facing at least the possibility that there are no gods. In his *Iphigenia in Aulis,* for instance, Clytemnestra, speaking of Achilles, says, "If gods exist, you, being an upright man, will taste / Their kindness; if not, nothing further's to be done" (Philip Vellacott translation, 11:1034–35). His sense of hopelessness and loss even touched Gilbert Murray and must certainly have appealed to Jane. In all fairness to Nietzsche, his precarious mental state probably heightened his awareness of the need for reason to balance emotion. Had Jane ever come so close to the abyss, she might have changed her tune as well. Her disillusionment with society at large after World War I is as close as she ever came to applauding reason (see chap. 8).

10 Harrison, *PSGR*, p. 262*n*1; Bachofen, "Mother Right," p. 79. Claude Levi-Strauss, in *The Raw and the Cooked,* trans. John Weightman and Doreen Weightman (New York: Harper & Row, 1969), offers an analysis of primitive connections between women and nature. Sherry Ortner, in "Is Female to Male as Nature Is to Culture?" in *Woman, Culture and Society,* ed. Michelle Rosaldo and Louise Lamphere (Stanford, Calif.: Stanford University Press, 1974), offers another view. Jane's interest in matriarchy connected her to theorists as diverse as Engels, who adapted Lewis Henry Morgan's work on the Iroquois in North America, and mainstream anthropologists such as E. B. Tylor, whose "The Matriarchal Family System" appeared in the *Nineteenth Century,* July 1896. See also Joseph Campbell's introduction to the collection of Bachofen's writings. Jane responded to the general climate of opinion on the question of matriarchy, but infused it with her own spirit.

11 Bachofen, "Mother Right," pp. 91, 75. See Jane Ellen Harrison, "The Influence of Darwinism on the Study of Religion," in *A&O*, pp. 143–78.

12 Harrison, *PSGR*, p. viii; hereafter cited in the text.

13 JH to GM, September 1905, #270, Box 6.

14 "Review of *Prolegomena to the Study of Greek Religion,*" *Cambridge Review,* March 10, 1904, p. 245. For another reaction, see Lewis Farnell, "Review of the *Prolegomena to the Study of Greek Religion* by Jane Ellen Harrison," *Hibbert Journal* 2, no. 8 (1903–04): 821–27.

15 Gilbert Murray, *Five Stages of Greek Religion* (Oxford: Clarendon Press, 1925), pp. 48–49.

16 Harrison, "The Influence of Darwinism," pp. 144, 152, 161.

17 Cornford, *Newnham College Roll Letter,* p. 75. Other writers have produced their works in similar fashion. For an interesting study of this process in a little-known but highly talented British woman novelist, see Gladys Mary Coles, *The Flower of Light: A Biography of Mary Webb* (London: Gerald Duckworth & Co., 1978), especially pp. 139–42. Mary Webb resembled Jane in many ways, not the least of which were her provincial background and her attempt to assimilate into London literary circles.

18 Harrison, *TH;* hereafter cited in the text.

19 JH to GM, 1908, #347A, Box 6; June 1908, #345, Box 6; Easter Eve, 1914, #671, Box 6; October 1911, #495, Box 6; JH to DSM, May 30, 1909, Box 22.

20 See Payne, "Modernizing the Ancients."

21 Mirrlees, Notebook, "Mrs. Charles Mitchell," JEH. Unless otherwise noted, Mirrlees's material is housed in this collection. Paul Delany is mistaken about Jane Harrison's attitude on nude bathing. He quotes Rupert Brooke's statement regarding "bathing naked by moonlight," in which Brooke asserted that he was "with Jane [Harrison] in these matters" (Delany, *Neo-Pagans,* p. 93). Brooke was probably invoking the authority of Jane's philhellenism, which included approval of Greek athletics but not necessarily nude bathing at Cambridge.

22 Arnold van Gennep paid homage to Jane's research in his 1909 *Rites de Passage* but criticized her for not recognizing the importance of the order in which the initiation ceremonies occur. See Arnold van Gennep, *The Rites of Passage,* trans. Monika B. Vizedom and Gabrielle L. Caffee (Chicago: University of Chicago Press, 1960), pp. 88–89.

23 See also her article s.v. "Mountain Mother," in *Hastings' Dictionary of Religion and Ethics.*

24 I thank Thomas Africa for identifying Lewis Farnell as the likely author of this review. Farnell did not review *Themis* any more kindly in the *Hibbert Journal.* See Farnell, "Review of *Themis: A Study of the Social Origins of Greek Religion,*" *Hibbert Journal* 11, no. 42 (1912–13): 453–59.

25 JH to GM, May 5, 1904, #203, Box 6.

26 Gilbert Murray, *Four Stages in Greek Religion* (New York: Columbia University Press, 1912), p. 7.

27 JH to GM, October 1903, #155, Box 6; February 1908, #323, Box 6.

28 JH to MM, February 24, 1901, Box 8.

29 JH to GM, April 1907, #300, Box 6; 1908, #350, Box 6; 1921, #821, Box 6; 1913, #607, Box 6.

30 JH to GM, April 3, 1912, #548, Box 6.

31 JH to GM, January 28, 1911, #474, Box 6; Charles Seltman to JS, October 15, 1943, Box 14.

32 JH to JS, September 1901, JGS #24, Box 10; September 12, 1902, JGS #30, Box 10.
33 Review: JH to GM, January 28, 1911, #474, Box 6; Lecture: JH to GM, February 16, 1911, #479, Box 6. Ackerman briefly touches on a central factor in Jane's aversion to her critics. He relates the Cambridge group's view of the world at large to its view of its critics, likening it to the Eniautos-Daimon always threatened with extinction by its enemies. In his words, "[Jane] and her friends must have thought of themselves as incarnations of the Eniautos-Daimon engaged in the recurrent and necessary battle with the force of the past, the forces of death." He adds that "admittedly such thoughts must have been felt to be as fanciful as they in fact are, but it is impossible for persons as imaginative as Miss Harrison and Murray not to have seen their lives in these mythic terms" (Ackerman, *The Cambridge Group,* p. 214). The fact that the group did indeed view itself in these terms helps account for the appeal of its work.
34 JH to GM, Summer, 1907, #303, Box 6; 1908; #328, Box 6; February 1910, #422, Box 6.
35 JH to GM, May 30, 1901, #13, Box 6.
36 JH to GM, December 1912, #583A, Box 6.
37 JH to GM, 1912, #555, Box 6.
38 Jane Ellen Harrison, "Crabbed Age and Youth," in *A&O,* p. 21 For an updated psychoanalytic interpretation of this relationship, see Peter Lowenberg, "Emotional Problems of Graduate Students," in his *Decoding the Past,* pp. 48–58.
39 Stewart, *Portrait,* pp. 109, 112.
40 JH to Frances Darwin, April 29, 1912; CDP; JH to GM, Easter Day, 1912, #551, Box 6.
41 JH to GM, April 16, 1913, #604, Box 6; JH to MM, July 10, 1913, MM #36, Box 8; JH to GM, Summer, 1913, #614, Box 6.
42 JH to GM, December 27, 1913, #634, Box 6; JH to MM, June 3, 1914, MM #42, Box 8.
43 Cornford, *Newnham College Roll Letter,* p. 75.
44 Ibid., pp. 77–78.

CHAPTER 8

1 Jane Ellen Harrison, "Unanism and Conversion," in *A&O,* pp. 71–73.
2 Harrison, "Heresy and Humanity"; hereafter cited in the text.
3 Harrison, "Crabbed Age and Youth"; hereafter cited in the text.
4 JH to GM, August 1914, #684, Box 6, JEH. Unless otherwise noted, all Jane's letters are housed in this collection.
5 Jane Ellen Harrison, "Epilogue on the War," in *A&O,* pp. 221–59; hereafter cited in the text.
6 JH to GM, September 17, 1914, #687, Box 6.
7 JH To GM, September 1914, #688, Box 6.
8 JH to GM, November 1914, #693, Box 6.
9 JH to GM, November 1914, #694, Box 6.
10 JH to GM, November 17, 1914, #697, Box 6.

11 JH to DSM, December 14, 1914, Box 8. See Sandra Gilbert, "Soldier's Heart: Literary Men, Literary Women, and the Great War," *Signs* 8, no. 3 (Spring 1983): 422–50; Roland Stromberg, *Redemption by War: The Intellectuals and 1914* (Lawrence: Regents Press of Kansas, 1982); and Paul Fussell, *The Great War and Modern Memory* (Oxford: Oxford University Press, 1975), for discussion of the effects of World War I on high culture.
12 JH to GM, December 19, 1914, #704, Box 6.
13 JH to MM, December 31, 1914, MM #47, Box 8.
14 JH to GM, January 1, 1915, #709, Box 6; 1915, #711, Box 6; April 1915, #718, Box 6; Spring, 1915, #719, Box 6.
15 JH to GM, 1915, #726, Box 6.
16 JH to GM, 1915, #726A, Box 6.
17 JH to GM, August 22, 1917, #764, Box 6.
18 JH to GM, October 1914, #688, Box 6.
19 Mirrlees, Notebook, "Outline of Life." Unless otherwise noted, all Mirrlees's material is housed in this collection. See also RSL, 341.
20 JH to D. S. Mirsky, February 27, 1925, Box 8.
21 JH to GM, March 18, 1917, #763, Box 6.
22 JH to GM, August 2, 1918, #775, Box 6.
23 JH to GM, November 3, 1918, #771, Box 6.
24 JH to GM, December 1920, #816, Box 6; August 1923, #849, Box 6.
25 JH to MM, May 31, 1916, MM #54, Box 8; JH to GM, June 28, 1916, #749, Box 6.
26 *Letters of Virginia Woolf*, ed. Nicolson and Trautmann, vol. 2, *1912–1922*, p. 377; JH to GM, August 27, 1919, #685, Box 6.
27 *Letters of Virginia Woolf*, ed. Nicolson and Trautmann, vol. 3, *1923–1928*, pp. 58–59.
28 JH to GM, January 1, 1923, #838, Box 6.
29 GM to JS, April 23, 1952, Box 11; JH to GM, August 1, 1921, #803, Box 6; 1921, MC; JH to Agnes Conway, January 1923, Box 17.
30 JH to GM, March 25, 1919, #803, Box 6.
31 GM to JH, July 30, 1921, #827, Box 6.
32 Jane Ellen Harrison, *Epilegomena to the Study of Greek Religion*, 1st Amer. ed. (New Hyde Park, N.Y.: University Books, 1962; originally published Cambridge: Cambridge University Press, 1921). See pp. xxiii–xxx.
33 Sigmund Freud, *Totem and Taboo*, trans. James Strachey (New York: W. W. Norton & Co., 1950), pp. 56, 144. In the preface to the second edition of *Themis*, Jane attributed her change of heart in the *Epilegomena* to Freud, whose work had taught her "that the full-blown god, the Olympian, has a biological function which could never be adequately fulfilled by the *daimon*."
34 JS to GM, September 28, 1922, Box 17.
35 JH to HM, 1922, Box 9.
36 JH to MM, December 25, 1922, Box 8; JH to GM, January 1, 1923, Box 6; JH to JS, May 12, 1925, Box 10.
37 JH to JS, January 24, 1923, JGS #103, Box 10; JH to HM, undated, Box 9; JH to D. S. Mirsky, undated, Box 8.
38 JH to JS, March 1923, JGS #104, Box 10.

39 JH to D. S. Mirsky, August 23, 1924, Box 8.
40 JH to Mirsky, May 9, 1925, Box 8.
41 Mirrlees, "Draft Biography."
42 JS to GM, June 1902, #68, Box 6; Mirrlees, Notebook, "D. S. MacColl."
43 Harrison, "Crabbed Age and Youth," p. 16.
44 Mirrlees, Notebook, Commentary with no heading.
45 GM to JS, October 26, 1953, Box 17; Victoria de Bunsen to JS, undated, Box 10.
46 JH to GM, January 8, 1928, #863, Box 6.
47 Holroyd, *Lytton Strachey*, p. 673.
48 *Diaries of Virginia Woolf*, ed. Bell, vol. 3, *1925–1930*, entry for April 17, 1928, p. 180.

APPENDIX

1 JS to HM, August 16, 1959, Box 14; Scrap, Box 14; HM to JS, March 29, 1943, Box 14, JEH. Unless otherwise noted, all their correspondence is housed in this collection.
2 HM to JS, June 11, 1950, Box 14; GM to JS, June 28, 1944, Box 16.
3 HM to JS, May 1946, Box 14; July 18, 1954, Box 14.
4 HM to JS, June 26, 1959, Box 14. Stewart quoted Virginia Woolf verbatim. Cf. Stewart, p. 200, and *Diaries of Virginia Woolf*, ed. Bell, vol. 3, *1925–1930*, p. 180.
5 JS to HM, June 28, 1959, Box 14; August 16, 1959, Box 14.
6 GM to JS, October 26, 1953, Box 16.

INDEX

Ackerman, Robert A., xi, 2; on Harrison's education, 22, 272*n*38; on D. S. MacColl, 71, 260*n*31; on Harrison's return to Newnham, 128, 263*n*10, 264*n*17; on Harrison's work, 261*n*44, 267*n*8, 275*n*33; on F. M. Cornford, 271*n*20
Aestheticism, 1, 55, 69; influence on Harrison, 76, 78, 83
Albemarle Club, 57, 70
Aldeburgh, 139, 171–72, 174
Alpha and Omega, 224, 247
Ancient Art and Ritual, 176, 220; discussed, 182–85
Annan, Noel, 92
Archaic period (Greece), 75–81, 179–211 passim
Art, Greek. *See* Greek art

Bachofen, J. J., 181, 207; on matriarchy, 186–87
Beale, Dorothea, 51; headmistress of Cheltenham College, 24–29
Berenson, Bernard, 126
Bergson, Henri, 181–82, 212, 242; influence on Harrison, 195–96, 198
Best, Theodore, 75
Bindorf, Otto, 90
Bosanquet, Bernard, 68
Brittain, Vera, 101
Browning, Robert, 62
Brunn, Heinrich, 58
Buddhism, xi, 108, 143
Burkert, Walter, xi, 269*n*53
Burne-Jones, Edward, 63
Burrows, Montagu, 32
Burstyn, Joan, 97, 253*n*40
Bury, J. B., 155
Bury, Jane, 155
Buss, Frances Mary, 24–25
Butcher, Augusta, 52, 63
Butcher, Eleanor, 52, 87, 142
Butcher, Rose Trench, 52–54, 58
Butcher, Samuel Henry, 58, 90; relationship with Harrison, 52–54; death, 176–77
Butler, Eliza Marian, xii

Cambridge Ritualists, 2–3, 124–222 passim; theory, 179–211 passim, 236. *See also* Cornford, Francis; Murray, Gilbert
Cambridge Universtiy, 34–35, 40–41, 92–96, 119–23. *See also* Newnham College
Cheltenham College, 13, 23–24, 243; Harrison at, 22, 26–27; background of, 25. *See also* Beale, Dorothea
Chtonic cults, 15, 179–211 passim. *See also* Greek religion
Clough, Anne, 33; Principal of Newnham College, 36–41, 45, 47–48
Clough, Blanche, 97; on Anne Clough, 36–38, 47
Colvin, Sidney, Sir, 54
Cook, Arthur Bernard, 127, 168, 215, 246; opposed university membership for women, 121–22; biographical information, 128; and the Ritualists, 130
Cornford, Francis Macdonald, 2, 63, 106, 123, 206, 239; on Harrison's work, 99, 194–95; as Ritualist, 124–30 passim, 215, 234; relationship with Harrison, 150–78 pas-

Cornford, Francis (*continued*)
sim, 189, 218–21, 224; marriage to Frances Darwin, 245–47
Courtney, Janet Hogarth, 50
"Crabbed Age and Youth," 9, 10; discussed, 218–19, 225–26, 241–42
Crofts, Ellen (Darwin), 92, 108, 218; at Newnham College, 45, 50; friendship with Harrison, 43, 96, 155–57
Cults, chtonic. *See* Chtonic cults
Curtius, Ernst, 90

Darwin, Frances (Cornford), 4, 178, 224, 233, 247; relationship with Harrison, 151, 156–57, 172, 217–19; marriage to F. M. Cornford, 158–69, 234; health, 233
Darwin, Francis (Frank), 50, 92, 108, 139, 150, 160; friendship with Harrison, 155–57, 164
Darwin, Ruth, 145, 169
Davies, Emily, 36, 37; on women's education, 32–35, 38
de Bunsen, Victoria, 99, 240; on Harrison, 100–02, 243
Desjardins, Charles, 239
Deutsch, Helen, 15–17, 251*n*28
Dew-Smith, Alice, 46, 114, 220; Harrison at Newnham, 41–42, 48; Harrison in London, 58, 62, 69
Dionysos worship, 179–211 passim
Dodds, E. R.: on Gilbert Murray, 126–27
Dorpfeld, Wilhelm, 84, 90, 104
Durkheim, Emile, 182, 212; influence on Harrison, 181, 189, 195–98
Dyhouse, Carol, 50, 97, 253*n*40

Eliot, George (Marian Evans), 47, 239
Epilegomena to the Study of Greek Religion, 235–37
"Epilogue on the War," 226–27
Euripides, 62; Victorian ideas on, 45; Harrison's view of, 46, 186; Murray's translations, 127, 147
Evangelicalism, 25, 71, 89; influence on Harrison, 10, 14–15

Farnell, Lewis, 216; review of *Themis*, 211–12; Harrison on, 213–14
Fawcett, Millicent Garrett, 35
Fitch, Joshua, 32
Frazer, James George, 3, 92, 213; Harrison on, 2, 182
Freud, Sigmund, xii; influence on Harrison, 182, 203, 236–37, 276*n*33
Fry, Roger, 62, 87–88, 244

Galsworthy, John, 175
Gardner, Ernest, 120, 212, 262*n*64
Gardner, Percy, 120; Harrison on, 215–16
Gathorne-Hardy, Jonathan, 252*n*33, 257*n*47
Gay, Peter, 19
Girton College, 1, 137; founding, 32–37
Gladstone, Helen, 46–47
Gladstone, William, 63; visits Newnham, 46
Glover, T. R., 93
Gorham, Deborah, 12, 19–20, 254*n*55
Gosse, Edmund, 90
Greek art, 59–60, 75–83
Greek religion, 83, 179–211 passim. *See also* Chtonic cults
Greek Vase Paintings, 55, 75

Hamilton, Mary Agnes, 44
Harrison, Charles (father), 30, 240; relationship with Harrison, 6–14, 22, 26; second marriage, 10; on religion, 14, 251*n*25
Harrison, Elizabeth (mother), 11–13, 20, 22; death, 6; influence on Harrison, 8–9
Harrison, Elizabeth (sister), 21, 169
Harrison, Gemimi Meredith (stepmother): relationship with Harrison, 10–19 passim, 30; religion, 14–15
Harrison, Harriet (aunt), 9–10, 12
Harrison, Jane Ellen: on Buddhism, xi, 108, 143; death of mother, 6;

family background, 6–9; relationship with father, 7–27 passim; relationship with stepmother, 10, 13–22 passim, 30; on Russia, 11, 230–33, 240; and sexuality, 19, 206–11 passim, 234, 236; early education, 23; at Cheltenham, 23–30 passim; illnesses, 26–27, 72–73, 138–43, 159–60, 166–76 passim; at Newnham, 30–52; and bears, 84, 109–15, 164, 231, 241; attitude toward chldren, 101, 104–05, 143–44; on the intellect: 105–07, 116–18, 128–31, 147–50; degrees for women, 116–22; relationship with Mary Murray, 138–39; on war, 226–30, 235; in Paris, 237–39. *See also* Butcher, Samuel Henry; Cornford, Francis; Mirrlees, Hope; Murray, Gilbert; Stewart, Jessie
Harrison, Jessie (aunt), 6–7, 52–53
Harrison, Lucy (sister), 14, 53; on mother's death, 8; on Harrison's early life, 9, 21–22, 26, 30
Harrison, Marion (cousin), 6
"Heresy and Humanity," 175, 224–25
"Homo Sum," 17–19, 129
Hughes, H. Stuart, 2, 181
Humphreys, S. C., 196
Hunt, Alfred, 87
Hunt, Violet, 48, 87

Introductory Studies in Greek Art, 1, 55; aestheticism in, 75, 31–83

Jackson, Henry, 90
James, Henry, 63
James, William, 196–97
Jebb, R. C., 90
John, Augustus, 68, 89; Harrison's portrait, 162–63, 174

Kennedy, Mary, 39
Keres: as spirits, 91, 141, 149, 154, 269*n*38; Harrison's nickname, 141, 143, 175, 177
Klein, Wilhelm, 90

Lane, Hilda, 12, 28, 98–99
Lane, William, 21, 28, 98
Leaf, Walter, 90
Lumsden, Louisa, 41; on college life, 34, 38–39

MacColl, D. S.: 4, 146, 148, 164, 196; relationship with Harrison, 27, 67–75, 87–89, 158, 162–63; Greek trip, 83–87
MacColl, Elizabeth, 87–88
McTaggart, J. M., 62
Maitland, Florence, 93, 263*n*8
Maitland, Frederick, 93
Malleson, Hope, 58–59, 64, 66–67, 86
Malleson, Mabel, 54, 57–58, 64
Mannhardt, Wilhelm, 75
Marriage, 17–19, 72, 106–08, 207–09
Marshall, Alfred, 45–46, 50, 107
Matriarchy, 179–211 passim; Bachofen on, 186–87
Merrifield, Margaret (Verrall), 50, 90, 92, 100, 124, 216; at Newnham, 41–45; friendship with Harrison, 57, 68–69, 153–54, 167, 262*n*66; collaboration with Harrison, 106; death, 233
Middleton, F. H., 90
Mirrlees, Hope, x, 41–47 passim, 87–88, 133; on Harrison's early life, 4–21 passim; on Henry Butcher, 52–54; on Harrison's London years, 57, 62, 67–68, 73, 75, 259–60; relationship with Harrison, 99–102, 109–15, 123; on Harrison's reaction to Cornford's marriage, 156–59 passim, 164–65; at Newnham, 234–35; in Paris, 237; return to London, 241–44; on biography, 245–48
Mirrlees, Lina, 109, 115
Mirski, Dimitri, 8, 233, 238–39
Mitchell, Caroline Dutton, 10, 26, 27
Moore, George E., 3, 92, 196
Murray, Basil, 144
Murray, Denis, 102

Murray, Gilbert, 2, 91, 100, 102, 162; relationship with Harrison, 124–54; as a Ritualist, 182, 193, 211–20, 236; on Harrison's later life, 243–44; on biography, 246–47
Murray, Mary: relationship with Harrison, 134–44 passim; on "Homo Sum," 18–19
Murray, Rosalind, 126, 171; marriage to Arnold Toynbee, 144–45
Murray, Stephen, 144
Myres, Frederick, 62
Mythology and Monuments of Ancient Athens, 1, 106
Myths of the Odyssey in Art and Literature, 1, 57–59; early Ritualist theory in, 75–81

Neil, Robert A., 141, 153, 155, 158, 189; to marry Harrison, 107–08; death, 108
Nettleship, Lewis, 87
Newnham College, 1–2, 14, 213; Harrison as student, 30–52 passim; Harrison as teacher, 90–123 passim, 232; Murray visits, 132, 137–38; Harrison leaves, 223. *See also* Cambridge University; Clough, Anne; Sidgwick, Eleanor Balfour; Sidgwick, Henry
Newton, Charles, Sir, 1, 64, 90; Harrison in London, 54–59
Nietzsche, Friedrich, 181, 186

Origins of religion, 179–211 passim

Paley (Marshall), Mary: education, 23; on Newnham life, 39–41, 45–46, 49–50; Newnham teacher, 106
Pater, Walter, 63
Pickard-Cambridge, Arthur, 219–20
Plumb, J. H., xii
Pontigny, 233, 238–39
Poole, Reginald, 90
Prolegomena to the Study of Greek Religion, 2, 92, 124, 154, 212; appears in print, 142–43; writing of, 148–49; Ritualist theory in, 178–95 passim, 198

Raleigh, Katherine, 63
Raleigh, Walter, 63
Raverat, Gwen, 156–57, 234; on Cambridge, 92; on Harrison, 96
Raverat, Jacques, 234
Religion. *See* Chtonic cults; Evangelicalism; Greek religion
Ridgeway, William, 212, 237; opposition to Ritualists, 127, 213–15; opposition to university membership for women, 121–22
Ritchie, Elinor (Paul), 108; Newnham life, 41, 46, 48, 53; on Harrison's London years, 58, 63
Rothblatt, Sheldon, 94–95, 122–23
Ruskin, John, 46
Russell, Alys, 19, 171–72, 178, 230; friendship with Harrison, 92; in Paris, 237–38
Russell, Bertrand, 3, 19, 92, 138, 196, 212; on Harrison, 98, 264*n*19; Harrison supports his stand on war, 230

"Scientiae Sacra Fames," 113, 116–18, 128–30
Seltman, Charles, 214–15
Sesame Club, 65, 93, 260*n*20
Sewell, Elizabeth, 23–24
Sexuality. *See* Harrison, Jane Ellen: and sexuality; Marriage
Shaw, George Bernard, 63, 126
Sidgwick, Arthur, 90, 98
Sidgwick, Eleanor Balfour, 106, 143; founding of Newnham, 33, 35; psychic research, 46; and smoking, 98
Sidgwick, Henry, 90; founding of Newnham, 33, 35–38, 45–46
Smith, William Robertson, 2, 182
Spacks, Patricia Meyer, 131
Stein, Mark Aurel, 143
Stewart, H. F., 102, 104
Stewart, Jessie, x, 4, 54, 238; *Portrait,* 7, 131; on Harrison, 22, 71, 260*n*31; relationship with Harri-

son, 99, 101–03, 109, 115; trip to Greece, 104–06; on biography, 245–47; on F. M. Cornford, 271*n*20
Strachey, Lytton, 3, 234; trip to Sweden, 175–76; on Harrison's death, 244
Strachey, Pernel, 3, 136; trip to Sweden, 175–76
Strauss, D. F.: influence of *Life of Jesus*, 28, 30

Tatton, R. G., 68
Tennyson, Alfred, Lord, 62–63
Tennyson, Lionel, 63
Themis, 2, 92, 124, 185, 235–36; writing of, 165, 174–78 passim; themes, 179–81; Ritualist theory in, 193–219 passim
Thomson, Edward Maunde, 90
Thomson, J. A. K., 126
Toynbee, Arnold, 126, 144–45
Turnbull, Arthur, 83–84
Turnbull, Peveril, 29, 69
Turner, Frank, 4
Tylor, Edward Burnett, 2, 182

"Unanimism and Conversion," 224

van Gennep, Arnold, 274*n*22
Verrall, A. W.: 46, 90, 92, 143, 215; marries Margaret Merrifield, 50; friendship with Harrison, 107–08, 132, 216–17; introduces Harrison and Gilbert Murray, 124; on Harrison's work, 149
Verrall Helen (Salter), 68, 100, 109
Vicinus, Martha, xi, 43–44, 111
Vurkano, 85–86

West, Francis, 133, 267*n*1
Whitehead, Alfred North, 3, 92
Wilson, "Get," 64, 66–67, 259*n*18
Women: secondary education, 3, 23–26; higher education, 31–37, 48–52; single women, 56–57, 64–66; degrees for women at Cambridge, 116–22. *See also* Matriarchy
Woolf, Virginia, 4, 246; on the Murrays, 124–25; on Harrison, 1, 93, 244; on Hope Mirrlees, 111; on Frances Darwin, 233–34

Zabé, Andrée, 69, 87–89